Rethinking Secularism

Rethinking Secularism

Edited by Craig Calhoun
Mark Juergensmeyer
Jonathan VanAntwerpen

OXFORD

UNIVERSITY PRESS

Oxford University Press, Inc., publishes works that further
Oxford University's objective of excellence
in research, scholarship, and education.

Oxford New York
Auckland   Cape Town   Dar es Salaam   Hong Kong   Karachi
Kuala Lumpur   Madrid   Melbourne   Mexico City   Nairobi
New Delhi   Shanghai   Taipei   Toronto

With offices in
Argentina   Austria   Brazil   Chile Czech   Republic France   Greece
Guatemala   Hungary   Italy   Japan   Poland   Portugal   Singapore
South Korea   Switzerland   Thailand   Turkey   Ukraine   Vietnam

Published by Oxford University Press, Inc.
198 Madison Avenue, New York, New York 10016

www.oup.com

Oxford is a registered trademark of Oxford University Press.

Library of Congress Cataloging-in-Publication Data
Rethinking secularism / edited by Craig Calhoun, Mark Juergensmeyer,
and Jonathan VanAntwerpen.
p. cm.
ISBN 978-0-19-979667-0; 978-0-19-979668-7 (pbk.)
1. Secularism.   2. Religion and politics.   I. Calhoun, Craig J., 1952–
II. Juergensmeyer, Mark.   III. VanAntwerpen, Jonathan, 1970–
BL2747.8.R47 2011   211'.6—dc22 2010052003

{ CONTENTS }

{ CONTRIBUTORS }

R. Scott Appleby is Professor of History at the University of Notre Dame, where he also serves as the John M. Regan, Jr. Director of the Joan B. Kroc Institute for International Peace Studies. Appleby is most recently the coauthor of *Strong Religion: The Rise of Fundamentalisms Around the World* (2003). He is also the editor of *Spokesmen for the Despised: Fundamentalist Leaders of the Middle East* (1997) and the coeditor, with Martin E. Marty, of the University of Chicago Press series on global fundamentalisms, which won the American Academy of Religion's Award for Excellence in the Study of Religion.

Talal Asad is Distinguished Professor of Anthropology at the Graduate Center of the City University of New York. He was born in Saudi Arabia and educated in Britain and has taught in various universities in the Middle East, as well as in Britain. His latest book is *On Suicide Bombing* (2007). Other publications include *Formations of the Secular* (2003) and *Genealogies of Religion* (1993).

Rajeev Bhargava is Senior Fellow and Director of the Centre for the Study of Developing Societies. He has held positions at universities in both India and the United States. His publications include the edited Secularism and Its Critics (1998) and The Promise of India's Secular Democracy (2010).

Craig Calhoun is President of the Social Science Research Council and Director of New York University's Institute for Public Knowledge. He is also University Professor of the Social Sciences at NYU. His most recent books include *Nations Matter: Culture, History, and the Cosmopolitan Dream* (2007), *The Roots of Radicalism* (2011), and *Cosmopolitanism and Belonging: From European Integration to Global Hopes and Fears* (2012). He is also coeditor of *Varieties of Secularism in a Secular Age* (2010).

José Casanova is Professor of Sociology at Georgetown University and a Senior Fellow at Georgetown's Berkley Center for Religion, Peace, and World Affairs. Casanova is the author of *Public Religions in the Modern World* (1994). His most recent research has focused primarily on globalization and religion and on the dynamics of transnational religion, migration, and increasing ethnoreligious and cultural diversity.

Elizabeth Shakman Hurd is an international political theorist and Assistant Professor of Political Science at Northwestern University. She is the author of

The Politics of Secularism in International Relations (2008), co-editor of *Comparative Secularisms in a Global Age* (2010), and co-PI of the research project "The Politics of Religious Freedom: Contested Norms and Local Practices." She is currently writing a book on the intersection of law and religion in global politics.

Mark Juergensmeyer is Director of the Orfalea Center for Global and International Studies, Professor of Sociology, and Affiliate Professor of Religious Studies at the University of California, Santa Barbara. His recent publications include *Global Rebellion: Religious Challenges to the Secular State, from Christian Militia to al Qaeda* (2008). His widely read *Terror in the Mind of God: The Global Rise of Religious Violence* (2000) is based on interviews with religious activists around the world and was listed by the *Washington Post* and the *Los Angeles Times* as one of the best nonfiction books of the year.

Peter J. Katzenstein is the Walter S. Carpenter, Jr. Professor of International Studies at Cornell University. He is the author, coauthor, editor, and coeditor of more than thirty books or monographs and more than one hundred articles or book chapters. His most recent books include the coauthored *Beyond Paradigms: Analytic Eclecticism in World Politics* (2010) and the edited *Civilizations in World Politics: Plural and Pluralist Perspectives* (2010).

Cecelia Lynch coeditor of On Rules, Politics, and Knowledge (2010), and Law and Moral Action in World Politics (2000), and author of Beyond Appeasement: Interpreting Interwar Peace Movements in World Politics (1999), which won the Edgar J. Furniss Prize for best book on international security and was a cowinner of the Byrna Bernath Prize of the Society for Historians of American Foreign Relations is Professor of Political Science at the University of California, Irvine. She is the coauthor of *Strategies for Research in Constructivist International Relations* (2007), coeditor of On Rules, Politics, and Knowledge (2010) and *Law and Moral Action in World Politics* (2000), and author of *Beyond Appeasement: Interpreting Interwar Peace Movements in World Politics* (1999), which won the Edgar J. Furniss Prize for best book on international security and was a cowinner of the Myrna Bernath Prize of the Society of Historians of American Foreign Relations.

Richard Madsen is Distinguished Professor of Sociology at the University of California, San Diego. His best-known works on American culture are those written with Robert Bellah, William Sullivan, Ann Swidler, and Steven Tipton: *Habits of the Heart* (1995) and *The Good Society* (1991). His latest book is *Democracy's Dharma: Religious Renaissance and Political Development in Taiwan* (2007).

Alfred Stepan is the Wallace Sayre Professor of Government and Director of the Luce-funded Center for the Study of Democracy, Toleration, and Religion at the School of International and Public Affairs, Columbia University. Stepan has published widely, and some of his publications include the coauthored *Crafting State-Nations: India and Other Multinational Democracies* (2011), the edited *Democracies in Danger* (2009), and *Problems of Democratic Transition and Consolidation* (1996).

Charles Taylor is Professor Emeritus of Philosophy at McGill University. His most recent books are *A Secular Age* (2007) and Dilemmas and Connections (2011). Among his other publications are *Hegel* (1975), *Philosophical Papers* (1985), *Sources of the Self* (1989), and *Modern Social Imaginaries* (2004). He is currently working on topics in social and political theory having to do with multiculturalism, secularization, and alternative modernities.

Jonathan VanAntwerpen is Program Director at the Social Science Research Council and Visiting Scholar at New York University's Institute for Public Knowledge. He is coeditor of *Varieties of Secularism in a Secular Age* (2010) and *The Power of Religion in the Public Sphere* (2011) and editor in chief of *The Immanent Frame,* a Social Science Research Council blog on secularism, religion, and the public sphere.

Peter van der Veer is Director of the Max Planck Institute for the Study of Religious and Ethnic Diversity and University Professor (Professor-at-Large) at Utrecht University. His major publications include *Gods on Earth* (1988), *Religious Nationalism: Hindus and Muslims in India* (1994), and *Imperial Encounters: Religion and Modernity in India and Britain* (2001). Currently, his work focuses on the interface among culture, society, and religion in India and China.

Rethinking Secularism

Introduction
Craig Calhoun, Mark Juergensmeyer,
Jonathan VanAntwerpen

Until quite recently, it was commonly assumed that public life was basically secular. On one hand, scholars could write with authority about politics, economics, and social behavior as though religion did not exist at all. Secularism, on the other hand, appeared to have no ideological significance of its own, other than the taken-for-granted absence or obsolescence of religion. In recent years, however, a host of political activists—some with avowedly religious agendas and others with stridently antireligious programs—have appeared on the global scene, challenging established understandings of how the terms "secularism" and "religion" function in public life and calling into question a supposedly clear division between the religious and the secular.

At the same time, there has been rising academic interest both in an ostensible "religious resurgence" and in the very features of secularism itself. This has come with increasing recognition of the fact that the uncritical deployment of the categories of the religious and the secular severely limits the analysis of international politics and social change throughout the world. Reigning theories of secularization have seen mounting critical attention, even as scholars in various fields have sought to deal in more detailed and concrete ways with the processes of "secularization," the practices of "the secular," and the political ethic of "secularism." Sociologists of religion have revisited long-standing general theories of secularization, and contemporary political theorists and anthropologists have brought greater attention to the "conceits of secularism" and "formations of the secular."[1]

Long the product of a relatively unexamined set of assumptions within the social sciences, dominant "modes of secularism" have also recently come under intensified scrutiny, laying the basis for a reconsideration of the relationship between religious movements and secular politics, for more nuanced analyses of secularization and religious expansion, for more sophisticated treatments of the complex patterns of religion's growth and decline in the contemporary world, and for a thoroughgoing rethinking of contemporary understandings of secularism.[2] Against this backdrop, the present volume seeks to take stock of the ongoing research on, and debates over, multiple forms of secularism. Our aim is to reframe discussions of religion in the social sciences by drawing attention to the central issue of how "the secular" is constituted and understood and to how new understandings of both religion and secularism shape analytic perspectives in the social sciences and various practical projects in politics and international affairs.

Issues of religion and secularism have, in fact, shaped the social sciences since their inception. Reference to the Peace of Westphalia gave the field of international relations not only a starting point for analyzing relations among sovereign nation-states but also a presumption of the adequacy of "secular" understanding. That this was rooted in a mythic understanding, rather than a clear historical appreciation of the relationship of states to religion in and after 1648, didn't reduce its power. But it did leave religion something to be "rediscovered" more recently. As Robert Keohane puts it, "the attacks of September 11 reveal that all mainstream theories of world politics are relentlessly secular with respect to motivation. They ignore the impact of religion, despite the fact that world-shaking political movements have so often been fueled by religious fervor."[3] The situation is not completely different in other social sciences. The basic notion of a differentiation of social institutions—or, in Weber's language, "value spheres"—informed the distinction among social-science disciplines such as political science, economics, and sociology, as well as ideas about the relative autonomy of state, economy, and civil society. But it also encouraged treating each of these—and especially state and economy—as separate from the proper domain of religion. This informs notions such as the idea that power and money organize state and economy as "non-linguistic steering media"— Talcott Parsons's formulation taken up by both Niklas Luhman and Jürgen Habermas. And it informed the late-nineteenth-century separation of social-science faculties from humanities faculties—and thus from religion and moral philosophy—in the universities of many countries, not least the United States.[4] This was in part a matter of insistence on the secular orientation reflected in the rhetoric of "value-freedom" and "objectivity." At the same time, social-science disciplines that were initially peopled in part by current former clergymen at first participated alongside religious organizations in social movements and then increasingly distanced themselves as secular and ostensibly neutral.

More generally, in their very pursuit of scientific objectivity (and status), the social sciences (some more than others) have tended to take account of religion less than one might expect based on its prominence in social life and often only in ostensibly value-free, external terms, leaving more hermeneutic inquiries to other fields. They also subscribed to the secularization narrative longer than dispassionate weighing of the evidence might have suggested.

When activists in new political movements around the world have challenged the supposed universality of Western secularism, their opposition has often been perceived in the West as the sign of a clash between secular and religious worldviews—that is, as an indication that they want to trump secular laws with religious ones, to employ religion to buttress political platforms, or to use religious values to provide the ideological basis and social identity for national or transnational political entities. But in bemoaning the reciprocal transgression of the realms of religion and secularism, the champions of each maintain and uphold what is now an increasingly challenged bifurcation. The common complaint heard in other parts of the world—that the Western distinction between "politics" and "religion" should not be uncritically exported to other regions— also raises the issue of how the two relate in the modern West. Indeed, social-scientific discussion of secularism centers largely on the role of religion in politics. What role should it play, if any? How autonomous should the state be with respect to religion? How autonomous should religion be with respect to the state?

At the same time, the discussion about morality in modern public life increasingly challenges accepted notions of "religion," and raises questions of whether religion can be thought of as a "thing" at all—that is, as an entity that can be reliably expected to command social responses and to provide a coherent alternative to secular ideologies and institutions.

These questions challenge our understanding of public life, even if we have no particular interest in religion—however it is defined—and think that public activities are largely a secular affair. The very use of the term "secular" signifies that we are buying into a secular/religious distinction that in some way defines not only the secular sphere itself but also the realm of the religious. However one defines secularity and secularism—a matter that we will get to below—it involves religion. It is either the absence of it, the control over it, the equal treatment of its various forms, or its replacement by the social values common to a secular way of life.

For although secularism is often defined negatively—as what is left after religion fades—it is not in itself neutral. Secularism should be seen as a presence. It is *something*, and it is therefore in need of elaboration and understanding. Whether it is seen as an ideology, a worldview, a stance toward religion, a constitutional framework, or simply an aspect of some other project—of science or a particular philosophical system—secularism is, rather than merely the absence of religion, something we need to think through.

Secularism, moreover, is only one of a cluster of related terms. Reference to the secular, secularity, secularism, and secularization can mean different things in confusing ways. There is no simple way to standardize usage now by trying to ensure an association of each term with only one clearly defined concept. But the fact that the different terms have a common linguistic root should not obscure the fact that they operate in different conceptual frameworks with

distinct histories. Although they sometimes inform one another, we should try
to keep distinct such different usages as reference to temporal existence, to
worldliness, to constitutions that separate religion from politics, or to a possible
decline of religion writ large.

Since so much of contemporary social conflict is linked to religion—or,
rather, to the notion that religion and secularism are in opposition—it is not
only appropriate but also urgent that we rethink the categories that make such
conflict possible. Through a multiyear project sponsored by the Social Science
Research Council, scholars have collaborated in a reconsideration of secularism and secularity in the context of contemporary global politics and transnational social change. The scholars participating in this project represent a
variety of fields that traverse the boundary between the humanities and the
social sciences. They come from sociology, political science, anthropology, and
international affairs, as well as from history, philosophy, literature, and religious studies. Moreover, they raise a number of fundamental and unavoidable
questions about secularism: To what degree is the concept shaped by the
European historical experience? Does it carry the baggage of Western, specifically Christian, notions of moral order? To what extent are religion and secularism twin concepts that speak to similar moral sensibilities? Is there currently
a decline in secularism, or is there, rather, a reformulation of the secular/reli-
gious distinction? Can this distinction be transcended through new ways of
thinking about civil society and the public sphere, political order and social
transformation, global politics and international affairs?

Secularism and Religion

In all cases, secularism is defined in tandem with its twin concept, religion, and
how we think about one of these paired concepts affects the way we think about
the other. The rise of politically active religion not only encroaches on the supposed relationship between religion and secularism, thus challenging our
thinking about the public role of religion, but it also queries our operative
notions of secularism. The rise of politically active religious movements com-
plicates our ideas about modern life—in particular, what many of us had
regarded as its essentially secular character.

Many of us are unconsciously affected by what Charles Taylor has described
as a grand narrative involving secularism in the spread of modernization and in
the historical path of Euro-American progress. It was this model of secular
modernization that many newly emerging non-Western nations attempted to
emulate in the latter half of the nineteenth century. Jawaharlal Nehru, the first
prime minister of independent India, put the matter succinctly when he
described secularism as one of the "pillars of modernity." In his mind, it was
unthinkable that India could progress into the modern world laden with what

he regarded as the prejudices and superstitions of its religious past. For someone like Nehru, secularism meant at least two different things: social attitudes that were free of intolerance and ideas undergirding the state's just laws and egalitarian political processes that were untainted with preferences for one group over another. Nehru had a clear image of the kind of religion he was against, and it was not a good thing.

Much the same can be said about the image of religion in the minds of the European reformers at the time of the Enlightenment. To some extent, the eighteenth-century antagonism against religion was, at bottom, a profound disdain for the power of the church and its clergy, which had held vast tracts of land and wielded enormous influence over the affairs of the state. With some justification, many Enlightenment thinkers saw the church as protecting an arrogant social hierarchy intent on keeping the masses enslaved to superstition and thus ignorant of justice and reason. But the concerns of many Enlightenment thinkers were about the preceding century's Wars of Religion and the need to find a new moral basis for social order in the absence of a specifically religious justification. In their minds, social progress could not be imagined without liberation from previous social and political institutions and the religious ties that had justified them. Although religion was integral to the thinking of many Enlightenment figures, they also extended the old idea of a differentiation of religion from the state to argue for a new and stronger separation. Many also preferred a "reasonable" religion, as John Locke put it, opposing excessive "enthusiasm".[5] They sensed a need to think of religion as a social construct that was potentially limited and controllable—something, in brief, that could be dominated by a different way of thinking. This new way of thinking was characterized by reason and secular ideals.

On the one hand, the Enlightenment image of the triumph of the secular over religion required a clear notion of the "religion" that was being contained; on the other hand, it required a definition of the secular order that was assumed to be succeeding it. The term "religion" was not one that was frequently used, even by Christians, until the Enlightenment's deployment of the secular/religious distinction. As historian of religions Wilfred Cantwell Smith has pointed out, before the Enlightenment, the terms "faith" and "tradition" were more commonly used.[6] The origins of the term "religion" are debated. Some claim that it comes from the Latin *relego*, "to read again" or "repeat," as one might do with scripture or creeds; others argue that it comes from another Latin term, *religare*, "to bind anew," as in a contract or covenant; still others aver that it comes from the Latin *res-legere*, "with regard to a gathering," as with a religious festival or group. In its modern usage as an ideological construct of beliefs joined with an institutionalized community unrelated to public life, "religion" makes sense only in juxtaposition to secularism. It is used to demarcate the ideas, practices, beliefs, and institutions that are related to particular faiths and traditions—such as Christianity, at once labeling these as religion and limiting religion's scope. This usage grew more prominent with the administrative need and academic desire to make legal frameworks that applied equitably to multiple religions and to compare regions. But it relied implicitly on a word, "religion," that is not easily translated into non-European languages.

Moreover, the secular containment of religion excluded the traditional moral dimension of social order—that is, the universal basis of good behavior and the moral obligations of citizenship. To re-create this dimension of social order in a secular world required new ideas. The *idéologues*, a group of French revolutionaries under the leadership of Count Antoine Destutt de Tracy, coined the term "ideology" in an attempt to fashion a secular "science of ideas" that could replace religion as a foundation for public morality. At the same time, churches in France were reappropriated and transformed into "temples of reason." Behind the salience of reason in public life and the notion of ideology as a template of moral purpose was the concept of the secular as a kind of antireligion.

Although today we think of *secular* as something that is contrasted with *religion,* the root notion of the term is something juxtaposed not to religion but to eternity. It derives from the same Latin etymological root—*saeculum*—as the French word *siècle,* meaning "century" or "age." The word *saeculum* first appeared as a unit of time among the Etruscans and was adopted by the Romans after them. For example, the lives of children born in the first year of a city's existence were held to constitute its first *saeculum.* The succession of *saecula* was marked with ritual. While some ancient texts held that this should be celebrated every thirty years, making *saeculum* roughly equivalent to the notion of a generation, others said this was every 100 or 110 years, reflecting the longest normal duration of a human life. The latter usage became predominant as calendars were standardized, and the *saeculum* became roughly the equivalent of a century.

By extension, *secular* referred to the affairs of a worldly existence and was used in the Middle Ages specifically to distinguish members of the clergy, who were attached to religious orders, from those who served worldly, local parishes (and who were therefore secular). It is something of an irony that this distinction between two kinds of clerical roles would become the basis for thinking of two kinds of social order, religious and secular, in which the life of the church and its clergy would be confined strictly to the former.

In the two centuries in which the Enlightenment's secular/religious distinction has been prevalent in European and American thought, it has come to be accepted as a commonplace dichotomy. It is still not clear, however, exactly what the distinction demarcates. One way of thinking about it is in strictly legal and political terms, that public institutions should be unfettered by influences that privilege particular moral creeds and associations. This notion of the secular order is not particularly antireligious, but rather continues a tradition of differentiating church and state that has existed for centuries in Christianity and is replicated in different ways in other traditions. In another view, secularism implies a framework of nonreligious ideas that is explicitly contrasted with religion. To be a secularist, in this sense, is to adopt a stance toward life that clearly separates religious from nonreligious ways of being. It is this view that is linked to expectations of a continued secularization within society and diminishing of the importance of religion in social affairs. Many have regarded such a pattern as a prerequisite of modernization, but Charles Taylor has described it as a misleading "subtraction story". His point is not just that religion has not declined as much as expected, but that it is impossible simply to remove such a central dimension of culture and leave the rest in tact.

Hence, it is commonly thought that secularism—the ideological underpinning of secular society and politics—goes hand-in-hand with modern progress. In the way that Nehru had imagined it, secularism provides the moral and theoretical basis for an equal, just, and tolerant social order. In the contemporary social milieu, the rise of new forms of religious politics has worried many who cherish the equality and freedom of secular society and its political institutions. Thus, at the same time that Muslims in Denmark and around the world protested what they regarded as a vilification of the Prophet Muhammad in a series of cartoons published in a Copenhagen newspaper, a clamor of voices of concerned citizens throughout Europe defended what they regarded as the rightful exercise of freedom of speech. In Turkey in 2007, when Islamic parties gained substantial legislative and executive power, hundreds of thousands of Turks in Istanbul and throughout the country took to the streets to rally in defense of secularism. In the minds of many secular Turks, it was a matter of not abandoning those elements of modern life that they regarded as essential to their secular—and implicitly European—Turkish identities.

Secularism and Secularization

Secularism is clearly a contemporary public issue in its own right. France proclaims secularism (*laïcité*) as a constitutive element of its national identity. This is, in part, a response to Islam and immigration, but it is also informed by a history of anticlericalism and a nationalist ideology forged during the Enlightenment and the French Revolution. French *laïcité* was incorporated into the blueprint of Mustafa Kemal Ataturk's Turkey, although it was inevitably transformed by its implantation in a quite different context. Secularism is also a central part of the Indian constitution and the policy formations through which that country deals with religious diversity. It is attacked by parts of the American religious right in its polemics against "secular humanism." In each of these contexts, secularism takes on its own meanings, values, and associations; in no case is it simply a neutral antidote to religious conflicts.

Having an idea of the secular, however, does not presume a secularist stance toward politics and public life. The Catholic church, for example, still follows the medieval custom of distinguishing priests with "secular" vocations from those with "religious" ones—those in monasteries or other institutions devoted wholly to contemplation and worship of God. A secular vocation, it should be clear, does not entail promoting secularism. It involves, rather, a calling to ministry in this world, helping people to cope with temporal existence and to maintain a religious orientation to their lives in this secular realm.

The idea of secularization, by contrast, suggests a trend, a general tendency toward a world in which religion matters less and various forms of secular reason and secular institutions matter more. It is a trend that has been expected at least since early modernity and has been given quasi-scientific status in sociological studies advancing a secularization thesis. But while there is a reality of secularization, the term is often deployed in a confused and confusing theorization.

On the one hand, there has been an enormous expansion in the construction of institutions for this-worldly, nonecclesial purposes. These are often distinguished from spiritual engagements, sometimes with restrictions on explicitly religious practices. They not only pursue goals other than the promotion of religion, but they also operate outside the control of specifically religious actors. Much of social life is organized by systems or "steering mechanisms" that are held to operate independently of religious belief, ritual practice, or divine guidance. Markets are a preeminent example. Participants may have religious motivations; they may pray for success or form alliances with coreligionists. Nonetheless, economists, financiers, investors, and traders understand markets mainly as products of buying and selling. It may take a certain amount of faith to believe in all of the new financial instruments they create, but this is not, in any strict sense, religious faith. For most, it is not faith in divine intervention but, rather, faith in the honesty and competence of human actors, the accuracy of information, the wisdom of one's own investment decisions, and the efficacy of the legal and technological systems underpinning market exchange. In short, it is a secular faith. Or, to put it another way, people understand what markets are by means of a social imaginary in which the relevant explanations of their operations are all this-worldly.

Not only markets but also a variety of other institutions have been created to organize and advance projects in this world. Schools, welfare agencies, armies, and water-purification systems all operate within the terms of what might be called a secular imaginary. Of course, some people's actions may be shaped by religious motives, and religious bodies may organize worldly institutions in ways that serve their own purposes. But even for those who orient their lives in large part toward religious or spiritual purposes, activities that take place within and in relation to such institutions are widely structured by this secular imaginary. Cause-and-effect relationships are understood in this-worldly terms as matters of nature, technology, human intention, or even mere accident. This is part of what Charles Taylor means when he describes modernity as a "secular age."[7] It is an age in which most people in modern societies, including religious people, make sense of things entirely or mainly in terms of this-worldly causality. In Taylor's phrase, they think entirely within "the immanent frame." They see nonmetaphysical, nontranscendent knowledge as sufficient to grasp a world that works entirely of itself. One of the aims of *A Secular Age* is to work out how people come to see this immanent frame as the normal, natural, tacit context for much or all of their action and how this transforms both religious belief and religious engagement with the world.

As the secular imaginary has become more prominent, various public institutions have been grounded in it, and in this sense, one might say that secularization is a reality. But discussions of secularization are generally not limited to secular ideas and institutions; they present modernity as necessarily involving a progressive disappearance of religion and its replacement by secularism. Particularly outside Europe, this simply hasn't happened, and there is almost no evidence of its imminence. Even within Europe, the story is more complex, as José Casanova, among others, has shown. There is more explicit unbelief, and there is also more compartmentalization of religion. But demarcation is not disappearance. Declaring oneself an unbeliever is different from accepting an order of society in which religion matters prominently in some affairs and does not in others or on some days of the week and not others.

Many accounts of secularization take the form of what Taylor calls "subtraction stories," accounts that suggest that religion used to fill a lot of space, space that has gradually contracted while leaving everything around it untouched. This is another sense of seeing the secular as the absence of religion, rather than a positive formation of its own, a presence that can be studied and analyzed. The importance of secular institutions, however, is not simply a result of the excision of their religious counterparts. It has facilitated some purposes and impeded others. Likewise, it has taken forms that have empowered some people over and against others.

Many secularization narratives presented religion as an illusory solution to problems that could be met in modernity by more realistic and efficacious methods. But without taking a position on the truth of any particular religion, one can recognize that religious practice takes many forms other than advancing propositions which may be true or false. From marriages to mourning, from solidifying local communities to welcoming newcomers into large and foreboding cities, from administering charities to sanctifying wars, religion involves a range of actions and institutions. Thus, changes in religion, including diminishments of religious belief or organized religious participation, cannot be mere subtractions. They are elements of more complex transformations.

Roots

It is worth noting that already in the ancient usage of *saeculum*, there is reference to both the natural conditions of life and the civil institutions of ritual and calendar. Each of these dimensions informed the contrast drawn by early Christian thinkers between earthly existence and eternal life with God. For many, it should be recalled, this was something that would come not simply after death but with the return of Christ after a thousand years (a millennium, or ten *saecula*). Here, too, an older idea was adapted. The Etruscans thought that ten *saecula* was the life span allotted to their city. Romans celebrated the thousandth anniversary of the founding of Rome with great ritual in 248 CE. This marked the beginning of a *saeculum novum*, although Rome's situation in this new era quickly became troubled. Christians started a new calendar, of course, marking years as before or after the birth of Christ and investing metaphysical hopes (and fears) in the millennium expected in 1000 CE. Here the succession of *saecula* counted the time until Christ's return and the end of history. In a very important sense, this was not what later came to be called secular time. It was temporary, a period of waiting, not simply time stretching infinitely into the future.

Likewise, when Saint Augustine offered his famous and influential distinction of the City of God from the City of Man, he did not mean to banish religion from "secular" affairs. On the contrary, his image of the City of God is the church—the body of religious people living in secular reality—and it is contrasted with those who live in the same world but without the guidance of Christianity. Augustine wrote shortly after the sack of Rome in 410 CE, an event that (not unlike the attacks of September 11, 2001) underscored the vulnerability of even a strong state. Augustine not only insisted that Christian suppression of pagan religion was not to blame but also argued that Christian faith was all the more important amid worldly instability. He urged readers to look inward to find God, emphasizing the importance of this connection to the eternal for their ability to cope with the travails of the temporal world. Humans—even a Christian emperor—needed to resist the temptation to focus on material gains or worldly pleasures. That the pagans lacked the advantage of Christianity is one reason they were often corrupt. Thus, Augustine distinguished a spiritual orientation from an orientation to worldly things.

Augustine further criticized pagan religion for its expectation that gods can be mobilized to protect or advance the worldly projects of their mortal followers. Christians, by contrast, look to God for a connection to what lies beyond such "secular" affairs. God shapes human affairs according to a plan, but this includes human suffering, tests that challenge and deepen faith, and demands for sacrifice. Knowing this helps Christians escape from the tendency to desire worldly rather than spiritual gains. We need, Augustine said, to put this world in the perspective of a higher good.

Augustine's discussion, along with others of the early Christian era, was informed by fear of an entanglement in worldly, sensual affairs. This is a theme dating back at least to Plato, a reflection of the prominence of ascetic and hermetic traditions in early Christianity, and an anticipation of the prominence of monastic life in the Middle Ages. Caught up in the material world, we lose sight of the ideal and run the risk of corruption. This is an anxiety that comes to inform ideas of the secular. It is not merely the world of human temporality in which we all must live until the Second Coming; it is also the world of temptation and illusion.

The contrast of sensuous and corrupt with ideal and pure is mapped onto the distinction between secular and eternal. Throughout one thread of the ensuing conceptual history, the secular is associated more with the fallen than simply with the created. Asceticism, retreat from worldly engagements, and monastic disciplines are all attempts to minimize the pull of worldly ends and maximize the focus on ultimate ends. In this context, Christianity has long had a special concern for sexual and bodily pleasures. These run from early Christian debates about marriage and celibacy, reflected in Paul's instructions to the Christians of Corinth, through the tradition of priestly celibacy, to nineteenth-century utopian communities such as the Shakers. The issue remains powerful in the current context, where the fault lines of politically contested debates over religion and the secular turn impressively often on issues of sexuality and of bodies in general: abortion, homosexuality, sexual education, and promiscuity have all been presented as reflections of a corrupt secular society in need of religious improvement.

Yet the very idea of subjecting the secular world to religious intervention is different from simply keeping it at a distance. The two notions have subsisted side-by-side throughout church history. Both parish ministry and monastic discipline have been important. There are "religious" priests in orders that call for specific liturgical practices. There are "secular" priests who have not taken vows specific to any of these orders and who live "in the world." But religious priests may also serve parishes or go out into the world as missionaries. This isn't the place to try to untangle a complex and sometimes contested distinction. But we should note that its meaning has shifted with changing contexts and over time. For example, in some colonial settings, indigenous priests were more likely secular and resented what they saw as preferential treatment given to priests in religious orders (who were more likely to be European). More generally, secular priests were crucial to a growing sense of the positive value of engagement with the world. Overlapping with the era of the Protestant Reformation, this shift in emphasis included figures such as Bartholomew Holzhauser, whose communitarian—perhaps even communist—Apostolic Union of Secular Priests was formed in the aftermath of the Thirty Years War to lead a renewal of religious life among laypeople.

This development coincided with what Taylor has called a new value placed on "ordinary happiness." A variety of this-worldly virtue received new levels of praise; new moral value was attached, for example, to family life.[8] Priests were increasingly called on to minister to the affairs of this world and its moral conditions, that is, not only to the connections between the human and the transcendent. In no sense uniquely Catholic, this trend runs from the seventeenth century to the present, as with issues such as the extent to which many Evangelical mega-churches today are organized as service providers of a sort. That is, they may espouse biblically literalist or fundamentalist or enthusiastically celebrationist theologies and religious practices, but they are also organized, in very large part, to deliver secular services in the world: marriage counseling, psychotherapy, job placement, education, help in relocating immigrants. They are, in that sense, secular-while-religious.

There is also a long and overlapping history around humanism and, indeed, humanitarianism. This appears in theological debates over the significance of the humanity of Christ, in late-medieval and early-modern humanism, and in questions about the spiritual status of New World peoples. The Valladolid controversy famously pitted Las Casas against Sepúlveda and made clear that answers to religious questions had secular consequences: "Do the natives have souls?" "Should we think about them as needing to be saved?" "Are they somehow like animals and thus to be treated as mere labor?" Versions of these debates were intertwined with missionary activity throughout the era of European colonialism. They influenced also the idea of humanitarianism as a kind of value and a virtue linked to progress in this world. Informed by the idea of imitating Christ, by the nineteenth century, to be a good humanitarian was to be somebody who helps humanity in general and advances progress in society. This was ultimately a secular project, although it might have distinctly religious motivations. And this remains important in humanitarian action today: emergency relief in situations of natural disaster, or war and refugee displacement, is an important project for religious people and organizations (as well as others), but it is organized very much in terms of ministering to the needs of people in the secular world.

Some of the same ideas can inform ethics—and spiritual engagements—that do not privilege the human. Seeing environmentalism as stewardship of God's creation is a religiously organized engagement with the world (quite literally construed). The deep ecology movement even introduces new metaphysical ideas, new notions of immanence. Others approach environmental issues with equal dedication but entirely within the immanent frame.

The Differentiation of Religion from Politics

Throughout the Christian era, a key question was how the church—and, after the splits of the Reformation, the various churches—would relate to states and politics. It's an issue that goes back to the first century CE. It forms the context for the Book of Revelation, written in the aftermath of the Jewish Wars. It shapes centuries of struggle over papal and monarchical power and ultimately issues with Marsilius of Padua in the doctrine of the Two Swords. Of course, this notion of distinct powers in different spheres was honored more in doctrine than in reality. This is to say that the pope and the monarchs of Europe, who represented a kind of secular counterpart to church power, didn't live up to the notion of separate-but-equal for very long.

The Protestant Reformation intensified the relationship of religion to politics, ultimately issuing in considerable violence within states as religious minorities were persecuted, sometimes on a large scale, as in France's St. Bartholomew's Day Massacre of 1572. It also issued in 150 years of interstate war. The "religious wars" that wracked Europe through the sixteenth and early seventeenth centuries were also wars of state building. In other words, they expanded secular power even when fought in the name of religion. Indeed, the conclusion of these wars with the 1648 Peace of Westphalia is often cited as the beginning of a secular state system in Europe and thus of modern international relations, understood as a matter of secular relations among sovereign states.

This is, in fact, profoundly misleading. The Peace of Westphalia did not make states secular. It established the principle of *cuius regio eius religio* ("who rules, his religion"). What followed was a mixture of migration, forced conversion, and legal sanctions against religious minorities. European states after the Peace of Westphalia were primarily confessional states with established churches. Members of some minorities moved to European colonies abroad, including English settlers who fled religious persecution only to set up state churches of their own in the American colonies they dominated.

There is much more to this story, of course, including different formations and transformations of nationalism. Sometimes closely related to religion, nationalism was an ostensibly secular narrative that established the nation as the always already identified and proper people corresponding to a state and thus a secular basis for legitimacy. It became harder for monarchs to claim divine right and more important for them to claim to serve the interests of the people. Where the power of absolutist states was closely tied up with religious claims to authority (and the daily domination of religious authorities)—as in France—revolution took up the mantle of secularism.

The European path to a relatively strong secularism was not charted directly from the Peace of Westphalia. It was, rather, shaped by struggles against the enforced religious conformity that followed the 1648 treaties. The strong French doctrine of *laïcité* was the product of unchurching struggles—struggles against priestly authority—that continued through the nineteenth century and into the twentieth. These gave a more strident form to secularism and positioned it as a dimension of social struggle and liberation. More generally, such secularizing struggles did not confront ancient state churches but new church-state partnerships forged in the wake of 1648. This, as José Casanova has argued as clearly as anyone, is central to what has made Europe particularly secular.[9] It contrasts with the situation in places where there is more of an open marketplace for religion. This is one reason, perhaps ironically, that the American separation of church and state has been conducive to high levels of religious belief and participation.

The unchurching struggles produced a militant *laïcité*. We see echoes of this today in European panics over alleged "Islamicization." These often strike a chord among populists and intellectuals alike that is not well recognized. They are misleadingly discussed in terms of the contrast between Enlightenment reason and unenlightened modes of faith, but this obscures their specific history. This European historical trajectory and concept formation also informs the *laïcité* of other countries where anxiety over religious-political rule is strong (not least Turkey), although transposing it into a new context changes at least some of its meaning.

Secularism can also designate a framework for religious pluralism, but this is by no means always the case. In fact, postcolonial societies around the world have given rise to most of the world's religiously plural and tolerant regimes. These are much less directly products of the European Enlightenment than is sometimes thought. While Europe's trajectory passed from state churches to militant *laïcité*, the United States, India, and a number of other postcolonial states have produced much stronger practices of religious pluralism. These, in turn, are supported by very different models of state secularism. For instance, separation is the rule in the United States, whereas the Indian state subsidizes religion but seeks to do so without bias for or against any.[10]

Nondominant religions may actually be disadvantaged by apparently neutral regimes that in some ways mask tacit assumptions about what constitutes legitimate religious identity. In other words, the secular realm is sometimes constructed in a manner that implicitly privileges one type of religion, while more or less expressly delegitimizing other sorts of religious engagement. And this disequilibrium is important, because ideas of citizenship have been constructed in secular terms in most of the societies of the world. The assertion of secularism may often seem to be no more than an assertion of neutrality vis-à-vis religion or religions. But when it is written into a constitution, it typically reflects events that are not in any way neutral: the ascendency of a new political party, a revolution, or an interstate conflict. So there is always a kind of political context, and it needs to be asked of particular secular regimes what they express in that political context and how they shape distributions of power and recognition.

What the Peace of Westphalia most directly produced was the founding myth of modern international relations. This includes the notion that each state is sovereign, without reference to any encompassing doctrine such as divine right. Carl Schmitt sees this as the transfer of the idea of the absolute from theology proper to political theology, rendering each state in a sense exceptional and thus beyond the reach of any discourse of comparative legitimacy. In any case, diplomatic practice and eventually the academic discipline of international relations would come to treat states as externally secular. That is, they attempted to banish religion from relations between states. The Peace of Westphalia produced a division of the international from the domestic modeled on that between the public and the private, and it urged treating religion as a domestic matter. Accounts of secularization have sometimes implied that the domestic and international spheres followed parallel paths, but this isn't so. The field of international relations so thoroughly absorbed the idea of its essential secularity that it became all but blind to religious influences on international affairs. After all, it is not as though religion were not a force in international politics between 1648 and 2001 and somehow erupted out of the domestic sphere to shape international politics only in this era of al-Qaeda and other nonstate actors. And it is not only Muslims, of course, who bring religion into international politics, as though they were simply confused about their proper, modern separation. Consider, to the contrary, recent U.S. legislation mandating an international defense of religious freedom. As Saba Mahmood has indicated, the ostensible secularism, or at least neutrality, of the legislation obscures the fact that it is strongly informed by specific religious understandings.[11] Much the same goes for the demonization of Islam in the name of a "secular" national security regime.

In this context, structured by an overriding concern to allot to religion its proper place in—or outside of—politics, that secularism is commonly treated as an absence rather than a presence. But there is growing recognition that constructs of the secular and governmental arrangements that promote secularism both vary a good deal. Constitutional regimes approach the secular in very different ways, as a look at the United States, India, France, and Turkey quickly suggests. Questions of the freedom of religion, of the neutrality of the state toward religion, and of the extent to which religious laws should be acknowledged by a secular state all put the various structures of secularism on the research agenda. Likewise, it is increasingly accepted that secularism is not simply a universal constant in comparative research. On the contrary, secularism takes different shapes in relation to different religions and different political and cultural milieus. We have discussed mainly the development of European secularism in a history dominated by Christianity, but distinct issues arise around secularism among Jews (in Israel and in the Diaspora), among Muslims in different regions, among Buddhists, among Hindus, and in countries where more than one of these and other religions are important.

Ideas of the secular concern not only the separation of religion from politics but also the separation—or relation—between religion and other dimensions of culture and ethnicity. Reform and purification movements in Europe in the late-medieval and early-modern periods sought to separate proper Christian practice from pre-Christian inheritance—that is, from magic, from superstition. This new policing of the proper content of religion entrenched its boundary with the secular, as with other religions and spiritual practices. It may also have made explicit professions of unbelief more likely. Furthermore, attempts to enforce doctrinal orthodoxy raise issues about the extent to which "a" religion is unitary and the extent to which different national or other cultures shape divergent versions of such an ostensibly unified religion. Do all Catholics in the world believe the same things? North American Catholics are a little bit shaky about this. Or are there strong national differences but a limited capacity to recognize them? The Islamic *ummah*—the global community of Muslims—is thought to be united by its common beliefs, but it is divided not just between Shi'a and Sunni and various theological schools but also along national lines. What is distinctive in Indonesia or in Pakistan or in Yemen? Again, intellectual resources for thinking through the relationships among "secular" culture, varied religious practices, and proclamations of religious unity are important but often underdeveloped. Catholicism and Islam offer just two examples. We could add the upheavals of the Anglican Communion to this picture or tensions over who is recognized as a Jew in different contexts. In general, it is unclear how far can we differentiate religion from culture, ethnicity, national identity, or a variety of other concepts constructed in secular terms.

Conversely, for some people, religion functions as a quasi-ethnic secular identity. That is, being Muslim, being Christian, being Hindu, being Jewish are mobilized, like ethnic categories, as secular identities. Religious identities are claimed as secular markers by people who don't practice the religion in any active sense and sometimes by people who explicitly declare themselves to be unbelievers.

But even people who are serious about their religious commitments and practices can be unclear about the relationship between the use of a religious label to denote religion as such, on the one hand, and to denote a population, on the other. Muslim attitudes toward the relation of religion to politics, for example, are shaped not just by religious ideologies but also by resentment of foreign political domination. Such resentment is common among Muslims, but it is misleading to see it as an attribute of Islam per se.[12] Indeed, it is striking how much of what goes on among—or is ascribed to—Muslims is understood by ostensibly secular Westerners as integral to Islam. More room needs to be made for attention to the secular institutions of the "Islamic" world.

Questions are recurrently raised about whether Islam can be separated from politics. Debates about this, however, are shaped by previous debates over the question of the division of religion and politics in Christendom. Aspects of European history are now projected onto and reworked in Islam. This isn't only a question about alleged theocracy or about clerical rule of one kind or another. It is also a question that shapes the whole idea of modernity or what counts as modern. The separation of religion from politics has become all but definitive of the modern for some.

Ironically, there are also concerns that this very separation has gone too far. These are producing discussions of "postsecularism." The term is confusing because it often isn't clear whether those who use it intend to describe a change in the attitudes of a large population or only a shift away from their own, previously more doctrinaire secularism. At stake in such discussions is whether the democratic public sphere (a) loses its capacity to integrate public opinion into its decision-making structure if it can't include religious voices and (b) is deprived of possible creative resources, insights, and ethical orientations if it isn't informed by ideas with roots in religion.

Both John Rawls and Jürgen Habermas have reconsidered their previous arguments that the public sphere has to be completely secular in order to be neutrally accessible to all. Both have been advocates for a mainly processual, nonsubstantive treatment of public discourse. They argue that constitutional arrangements and normative presuppositions for democracy should focus on achieving just procedures, rather than pursuing a particular substantive definition of the good.[13] Rawls initially excluded religious reasons from public debates; late in his life, he reconsidered his prior position and argued that they should be included as long as they could be translated into secular terms.[14] Habermas has gone further, worrying that the demand for "translation" imposes an asymmetrical burden; he is also concerned not to lose religious insights that may still have liberatory potential.[15] Habermas seeks to defend a less narrow liberalism, one that admits religion more fully into public discourse but seeks to maintain a secular conception of the state. He understands this as requiring impartiality in state relations to religion, including to unbelief, but not as requiring the stronger *laïc* prohibition on state action affecting religion, even if impartially. Indeed, he goes so far as to suggest that the liberal state and its advocates are not merely enjoined to religious tolerance but also—at least potentially—cognizant of a functional interest in public expressions of religion. These may be key resources for the creation of meaning and identity; secular citizens can learn from religious contributions to public discourse (not least when these help clarify intuitions that the secular register has not made explicit). But, Habermas insists, it remains the case that a direct appeal to the absolute, a transcendent notion of ultimate truth, is a step outside the bounds of reasoned public discourse.

Habermas's argument presumes that such absolutes, or higher-order values, are absent from ordinary rational discourse and introduced only by religious beliefs (or close analogues such as the nationalist politics informed by Schmitt). But it is in this context that Taylor makes a helpful suggestion: that all normative orientations, even those that claim to be entirely rational, in fact depend on higher-order values.[16] Being completely rational can be one such value. Some higher values are very this-worldly, as, for example, in economic discourses in which either some indicator of utility or some hedonic principle of human happiness is clearly the utmost good by which the entire analytic framework is organized and which has a standing apart from any merely incremental values. So it is not clear that reference to higher values clearly demarcates religious from secular reason. The question of how "secular" the public sphere can and should be remains contested.

Distinctions between the religious and the secular are embedded in a range of other differentiations that are imposed by the sociopolitical configurations of the modern era. Many of these are closely linked to states and their administrative practices—indeed, in both colonial and domestic administration, states helped to create the very category "religion" as one that would subsume a whole class of supposedly analogous phenomena. But the differentiation of states from market economies, sometimes understood to be self-moving, is also powerful. Indeed, Max Weber famously argued that the differentiation of values spheres—religious, economic, political, social, aesthetic—was basic to modernity.

The notion of value spheres is informative, but it should also be clear that there are tensions among projects, not just values. Secular and religious projects of world-making contend over the nature of institutions. The advance of the secular stems in part from creating new domains of efficacy and action. Science is important in this way, not just as a value system or ideology that clashes with religion. Medicine is not just another domain of knowledge but now meddles with the very nature of life through genetic engineering. The economy, the state, and social movements all involve world-making projects. The demarcation between religion and the secular is made, not simply found.

But, finally, we should recognize the prominence of a secularist ideology that goes beyond affirming the virtues of the ostensibly neutral. The secular is claimed by many, not just as one way of organizing life, not just as useful in order to ensure peace and harmony among different religions, but as a kind of maturation. It is held to be a developmental achievement. Some people feel they are "better" because they have overcome illusion and attained the maturity identified with secularism. That ideological self-understanding is itself powerful in a variety of contexts. It even shapes the way in which many think of global cosmopolitanism, that is, as a kind of escape from culture, national and religious, into a realm of apparently pure reason, universal rights, and global interconnections. We might, by contrast, think of cosmopolitanism as something to be achieved through the connections among all of the people who come from, are rooted in, and belong to different traditions, different social structures, different countries, and different faiths. There is a profound difference between an ideology of escape and an ideology of *ecumenae*.

The Current State of Play

Secularism is not simply the project of some smart people reflecting on problems of religion. It is a phenomenon in its own right that demands reflexive scholarship and sometimes critique. The chapters in this book are intended to respond to that demand, taking stock of the current state of play in an ongoing and interdisciplinary discussion regarding the politics of religion and secularism in a global context. Because the chapters presented here are the products of a multiyear working group, they represent not just the thinking of individual authors but also the intellectual ferment of this group's sustained interaction and engagement. At the same time, there remain both significant differences of approach and substantial disagreements among the contributors to this book.

The book opens with a chapter by philosopher and political theorist Charles Taylor, whose massive and complex *A Secular Age* has singularly shaped current discussions of secularism and secularity. Reprising what he suggests are key historical transformations in "the Western march toward secularity," Taylor revisits central themes from *A Secular Age* as he charts the distinctive path that led from the axial religions through Latin Christendom to the contemporary conditions of modern secularity. While noting that the term "secular" is both complex and ambiguous and subject to alterations and distortions as it travels from one context to another, Taylor nonetheless argues that Western secularity should be understood as the result of a fundamental change in sensibility marked by "disenchantment," or the systematic repression of the "magical" elements of religion, as well as by a concomitant historical movement toward the association of personal commitment with "true" religion. The broader historical context for these shifts was a "great disembedding" of social and collective life and a movement toward reform within Christianity, which, along with other historical developments, led not only to the rise of modern individualism but also to the possibility of conceiving of the world in purely immanent terms, shorn of all reference to the transcendent. The separation of the immanent from the transcendent, worked from within Latin Christendom itself, thus laid the groundwork for the assertion of a self-sufficient secular order. And it was the development of this possibility that led, in Taylor's account, to the existential condition he most closely associates with modern secularity, namely, the contemporary reality that belief in God, or in any transcendent reality, is considered just one option among many and therefore represents a fragile—and in some cases even difficult and embattled—form of commitment. By Taylor's lights, it is this shared condition of belief and commitment—defined in terms of what he elsewhere refers to as "the immanent frame"—that makes the current age a "secular" one.

A critical rethinking of secularism in our secular age, argues sociologist José Casanova, requires keeping in mind basic analytical distinctions between "the secular" and its cognate terms. The secular, Casanova suggests, has become a central modern epistemic category, used to construct, codify, grasp, and experience a realm or reality differentiated from "the religious." There are multiple ways of experiencing the secular—and, indeed, of being secular—and the challenge of social science is to investigate and understand these different forms of secularity. While "the religious" and "the secular" are mutually constitutive, however, and while a good deal of social-scientific effort has been dedicated to the study of religion, the development of a reflexive anthropology and sociology of the secular remains in its relative infancy.

"Secularization," on the other hand, has long been a staple of the social sciences, particularly sociology, where it has been associated with a general theory of institutional differentiation, religious privatization, and religious decline. Building on the analysis proposed in his landmark book *Public Religions in the Modern World*, Casanova recommends that patterns of decline, privatization, and differentiation be analytically distinguished, in order to capture diverse

historical patterns and ongoing global processes of secularization, sacralization, and religious denominationalism. Any discussion of secularization as a
global process, he suggests, should start by reflexively observing that the globalization of the category of "religion"—along with the "religious/secular"
binary it assumes and entails—is itself an important global trend. Yet the
proper boundaries between the religious and the secular remain hotly disputed
throughout the world, and such disputes are closely related to the existence of
multiple and competing "secularisms"—modern worldviews and ideologies
either unflexively held or elaborated into doctrines of statecraft, political theories, philosophies of history, and diverse cultural programs. Although "the
secular" first emerged as a particular Western Christian theological category,
understanding multiple secularisms today requires examining the extent to
which secularist assumptions of various sorts permeate the experience of ordinary people and the workings of institutions throughout the world.

A chapter by Craig Calhoun shifts the discussion away from Taylor's vast
historical canvas and Casanova's wide analytical overview and toward contemporary questions of political secularism, citizenship, and the public sphere. For
reasons ranging from academic soundness to practical fairness, Calhoun argues,
it is necessary to rethink the secularism implicit in established conceptions of
citizenship. Drawing on a critical engagement with the recent work of Jürgen
Habermas, Calhoun considers the various ways in which an unreflective secularism distorts much of the liberal understanding of the world. His chapter
seeks in particular to specify the challenges and complexities associated with
recent attempts to reconfigure the place of religion and religious reason-giving
in theories of ethical citizenship, political discourse, and the public sphere. The
classification of religion as an essentially private matter, he suggests, is mis-
guided—and, indeed, religion has never been essentially private. But approaches
to religion within liberal theory are also hampered by an overly "epistemic" or
cognitive approach to religion, by the presumption that the religious and the
secular can be clearly and easily distinguished from each other, and by the
view—consonant with older and now discredited theories of secularization—
that contemporary religion is a holdover from an earlier historical period,
rather than a fundamentally modern phenomenon. Such tacit presuppositions
have increasingly been reconsidered in recent years, including important shifts
in the thinking of Habermas himself. Yet Habermas's own rethinking of his
earlier secularism remains limited, Calhoun suggests—both by a mistaken
assumption that secular orientations do not depend on what Taylor has called
"hypergoods" and by an overly simplified understanding of the pursuit of
mutual understanding between religious and secular citizens. Seeking to move
beyond Habermas's conception of "translation," Calhoun intimates a theoretical approach that would thematize both more transformative processes of
mutual engagement and the wider generation of social solidarities integrative
of political communities.

Political theorist Rajeev Bhargava opens his chapter with an acknowledgment of some of the compelling contemporary criticisms of the doctrine of political secularism. Despite such criticisms, he argues that political secularism must be rehabilitated rather than abandoned. An authority on secularism in India and the editor of *Secularism and Its Critics*—an earlier collection of essays that helped to set the terms of the expanding debates over the politics of secularism in India and beyond—Bhargava argues that while political secularism is doubtless problematic, there is currently no reasonable moral and ethical alternative. Secularism, he says, "remains our best bet to help us deal with ever-deepening religious diversity and the problems endemic to it." In response to the political and intellectual challenges posed to the secularity of states, Bhargava argues, we must look beyond mainstream and liberal conceptions of secularism and examine instead the best practices of actually existing secular states, deriving from these a refashioned conception of secularism. Drawing on the Indian example, he puts forth a contextual understanding of secularism in which religions are treated according to a notion of "principled distance," which requires a flexible approach both to questions of the public inclusion or exclusion of religion and to the extent to which the state engages with it or disengages from it. This context-sensitive approach, Bhargava suggests, promises an alternative conception of secularism in which critique of religion is consistent with respect, and the choice between hostility to and respectful distance from religion is seen to be a false dichotomy. Indeed, it is a situational approach that opens the possibility of multiple secularisms and suggests that secularism cannot simply be written off as an exclusively Christian and Western doctrine.

In the next chapter, political scientist and scholar of comparative politics Alfred Stepan calls attention to the great variations in state-religion-society relations that exist in modern democracies, discussing the distinct patterns of relation that constitute these "multiple secularisms." Secularism, Stepan suggests, is neither a sufficient condition for democracy nor a concept necessary for its analysis, and it is generally more productive to refer to the "twin tolerations"—the minimal degree of toleration that democratic institutions need to receive from religion and the minimal degree of toleration that religion needs to receive from the state for a polity to be democratic. Yet the notion of multiple secularisms—which is for Stepan not just a normative assertion but also an empirical claim—allows for the analysis of four distinct patterns, or models, of secularism: "separatist," "established religion," "positive accommodation," and "respect all, positive cooperation, and principled distance." This chapter focuses in particular detail on the fourth pattern, building on Bhargava's conception of "principled distance," while also attending to the respect given by the state in private and public spheres to all major religions in the polity and to the extent of positive cooperation between religions and the state. Attention to patterns of secularism in Indonesia, Senegal, and India, Stepan argues, both challenges the idea that Muslims are generically resistant to secularism and motivates a rethinking of the assumption that religion must always be taken off the agenda in public, political arguments. In Senegal, for example, mutual "rituals of respect" between the state and all religions have facilitated policy cooperation even in some sensitive areas concerning human-rights violations. Given that patterns of secularism are socially and politically constructed, rather than simply fixed normative models, he concludes that theorizing about secularism needs to be attentive to the emergence of new patterns of relation among state, society, and religion and to reconstruct models of secularism in light of them.

Like Bhargava and Stepan, international-relations theorist Peter Katzenstein seeks to move beyond the assumption that secularism should be conceived of in the singular. If states, capitalisms, and democracies—three of the core components of secular politics—are now duly recognized as variegated and complex formations, he asks, why should secularism be conceptualized any differently? Katzenstein accordingly criticizes both liberal and realist approaches to the study of international relations. While liberalism, he says, is "sweet common sense" for many scholars of international relations and remains an "article of faith," it envisions history as a teleological process and sees secularization as the dominant trend characteristic of modernization, overlooking the continued relevance of religion to world politics. Cultural realism is more open to acknowledging the importance of religion, yet its "truncated analysis" is insufficient to the complexity, diversity, and difference at the core of civilizations and the collective identities they foster. As an alternative to these two dominant approaches and as a means of adequately conceptualizing the intermingling of multiple secularisms and religions in contemporary world politics, Katzenstein proposes instead the concept of "civilizational states." Conceiving of civilizations as "zones of prestige," Katzenstein distinguishes between axial-age civilizations and the civilization of modernity, with its multiplicity of different cultural programs and institutions, drawn from and grounded in different religious traditions. In the midst of a civilization of globalization, he argues, lies the possibility for "cultural commensurabilities" in relations between civilizational states. As the forces of globalization and the enactment of different religiously grounded cultural programs give rise to both homogenization and differentiation, they generate the partial yet consequential overlaps of multiple secular and religious traditions that mark all civilizational states. Such overlaps, Katzenstein suggests, create space for a "polymorphic globalism," in which intersections of secularisms and religions are created through constant processes of cooperation and adaptation, coordination and conflict.

Bridging work within political science and recent scholarship on secularism in a range of other disciplines, Elizabeth Shakman Hurd's chapter critically interrogates and seeks to destabilize the rigid and pervasive "secular/religious binary" within her own field of international relations. Prevailing distinctions between the religious and the secular, Hurd suggests, have embedded an assumption that religion has been effectively privatized and thus is no longer relevant in modern politics, leading scholars of international relations to miss or misunderstand some of the most important political developments of the contemporary period. While most scholars of this ilk remain committed to an unreflective secularism that blinds them to the importance of religious questions, actors, institutions, and processes, it is nonetheless not sufficient simply to augment attention to religion, since this "add and stir" approach leaves the basic categories of analysis untouched. A more robust rethinking of conventional approaches to international relations that suppose a rigid opposition between the secular and the religious, on the other hand, might loosen the hold of this binary on political and intellectual life, opening up new possibilities for thinking about and engaging in international politics. Such rethinking, Hurd suggests, requires a "suspension of disbelief" in the particularity of the secular—that is, it requires that an often taken-for-granted belief in the universalizing potential of secularization be reflexively reconsidered, so that the opposition between the secular and the religious is seen not as fixed and stable but, rather, as shifting, evolving, and elusive—a distinction that is constantly being negotiated and renegotiated via a range of different ontological presuppositions and epistemic commitments. Hurd illustrates her own approach through a discussion of relations between the United States and Iran and a consideration of the rise of the AK Parti (Justice and Development Party) in Turkey, two cases she discusses in greater depth in her own book, *The Politics of Secularism in International Relations*.

Sociologist Mark Juergensmeyer joins Hurd in critiquing the bifurcation of polities and politics into their secular and their religious aspects in a chapter on secular and religious treatments of violence. Why, Juergensmeyer asks, have religious language and identities become bound up in contemporary challenges to the prevailing social order? The answer, he suggests, derives from the way in which both secularism and religion have come to be conceived. Strident religious movements have erupted in response to what they perceive to be an aggressive secularism. Tracing out the origins of "secular nationalism" and the rise of the secular state, Juergensmeyer examines how secular politics sought to excise religion from public life and considers the manner in which secularism has recently been challenged and sometimes rejected outright by actors mobilizing religious language and ideologies as a form of political critique. Following Tocqueville, Juergensmeyer finds that secular nationalism is often perceived as a "strange religion" in its own right, spread throughout the world with "almost missionary zeal." The ideology of secular nationalism, he suggests, can be productively compared with religion, since both are "ideologies of order," or what Geertz referred to as "cultural systems." Both religion—understood in the broad sense—and secularism point to a moral sensibility toward social order, and in this way, they can be seen as "two ways of talking about the same thing." Yet in the modern period, religion has also come to take on a narrower definition, limited to particular doctrines and confessional communities and thereby contrasted with secular social values and political commitments. Thus have religion and secularism in their contemporary forms been not only inventions of modernity but also rival "expressions of faith." In this light, the mobilization of religious language in opposition to the power of the state can be seen as a comprehensible response to the new global reach of secular nationalism. The modern idea of religion, Juergensmeyer concludes, has become a potentially revolutionary construct, tied to movements that are frequently strident and violent.

Tracing out how the categories of the secular and the religious in international affairs work to produce assumptions about the nature of religious and secular beliefs and actions, political scientist Cecelia Lynch examines the activities of religious humanitarian workers in the context of the global politics of secularism. Drawing on in-depth interviews with NGO activists in Cameroon, Kenya, Jordan, the West Bank, New York, Geneva, and elsewhere, Lynch seeks to challenge the simplistic dichotomy between the religious and the secular that is prevalent in international relations and to focus instead on the multiple ways that the "constitutive constructs" of the religious and the secular shape the ethical imperatives articulated by humanitarian actors. She attends in particular to the construction of religious and secular identities and their concomitant modes of action in the context of results-oriented market discourses that prioritize efficiency while also valorizing liberal progress, demonstrable achievement, accountability, and "success"; to the effects on humanitarian actors of "war on terror" discourses that tie a contemporary fascination with religious actors to a recurrent concern with the root causes of political violence; and to the varied relations of traditional practices to the globalizing discourses of science and "world religions." In each of these cases, Lynch emphasizes the dynamic nature of the relationship between the secular and the religious and argues that the experiences of religious humanitarians suggest new places to look for the continued destabilization of the religious/secular binary. Whether focusing on the shift of humanitarian attention from HIV/AIDS to malaria, discussing the self-identifications of "secular" Muslims engaged in the promotion of networks of nonviolence, or exploring the fluid boundaries between "traditional" and "world" religions in postcolonial societies, Lynch shares with both Hurd and Juergensmeyer the concern to destabilize a rigid secular/religious binary and in the process to demonstrate some of the numerous ways in which that binary is disturbed by the contemporary political engagements of religious humanitarians.

The next two chapters engage with Charles Taylor's *A Secular Age* in order to map the contours of contemporary political and religious transformations within the context of the sweeping and large-scale historical shifts toward secularity that Taylor's work charts. Historian Scott Appleby revisits and reflects critically on the work of the Fundamentalism Project, the large-scale research initiative he codirected with Martin Marty. Is "fundamentalism," Appleby asks, merely a shibboleth, a construct of anxious or predatory opponents of politically engaged religious groups, or does the category have a more productive analytic utility? Acknowledging the widespread and persistent misuse to which the term has been put, Appleby nonetheless defends a revised conception of fundamentalism as a religious mode defined by both an intentional appropriation of constitutive elements of the secular and an antipathy to dominant forms of secularism. Thus, he argues, fundamentalists are best understood as trapped between increasing integration into the institutions, practices, and processes of secular modernity, on the one hand, and a militant, reactive, and absolutist reaction to "Westoxicated" secularism, on the other. Centrally "millennialist" in aspiration and outlook, fundamentalism denotes a specific religious logic that critically engages regnant secularisms, rejecting some forms and attempting to transform others. It is therefore an oversimplification to conceive of fundamentalist religion as simply "antisecular." Rather, it is a form of strong religion that admits of internal pluralism and complexity, an orientation toward both transcendence and practical politics that constantly negotiates and renegotiates the relationship between the secular and the religious. While fundamentalists share with other denizens of secular modernity the "immanent frame" that defines and shapes contemporary secularity, they spin that frame in the direction of openness to something beyond, simultaneously insisting on the radical otherness of the transcendent and seeking to bend the world to the will of the divine within the confines of secular time. As such, Appleby concludes, they represent an "extreme case" of what is and is not possible in contemporary religious encounters with secularity in our secular age.

Along with Appleby, sociologist Richard Madsen draws on a reading of *A Secular Age*, suggesting that Taylor's analytic framework for the understanding of modern secularity—explicitly limited to an analysis of the North Atlantic world—might nonetheless be productively mobilized in an examination of contemporary religious and secular developments in East and Southeast Asia. Focusing on political and religious transformations taking place in China, Indonesia, and Taiwan in the aftermath of the Cold War, Madsen seeks to show how the ostensibly secular façade of Asian political institutions has frequently masked an "interior spirit" of religiosity. Such religiosity, he argues, is often a matter not of personal belief but, rather, of collective ritual and socially "embedded" religion—a form of local practice increasingly tied to, and transformed by, global forms and forces. In the face of governmental attempts to suppress religious practices, co-opt religious leaders, or segregate religious communities, a plethora of new Asian religious practices have emerged, including a variety of hybrid cultural forms and religious identities. These practices have taken different shape in each of the three different contexts Madsen considers. In China, where the state sought to suppress religion, the reforms of Deng Xiaoping laid the basis for both modernized versions of an older polytheism and new openness to religious movements guided by visions that transcend the local, including, for instance, the proliferation of practices such as *qigong,* forms of which had been marked as "false" religion by the state. In Indonesia, where the state sought to co-opt religion and where religious commitments have been deeply intertwined with ethnic and regional attachments, new forms of religiosity have nonetheless emerged as the result of the influence of wider global movements, including both competitive, universalizing, and mission-oriented forms of Christianity and Islam, as well as more ecumenical and hybrid approaches seeking to produce religious "citizens of the world." And in Taiwan, where the state pursued a mix of suppression and co-optation and later moved toward a liberal model of toleration, new and modernizing religious movements have also emerged, including "socially engaged" strands of Buddhism.

Anthropologist Peter van der Veer also takes up the case of China, comparing the history of Chinese secularism with its Indian counterpart. He suggests that attention to secularization as a historical process must be supplemented by attention to secularisms as historical projects. Seeking to delineate the problems such projects have attempted to address in both China and India, van der Veer highlights the ideological and even religious elements of the secular projects in each location, emphasizing the violence entailed by their interventions. Chinese and Indian secularisms, he argues, have been emancipatory projects and by their very nature violent. While a millenarian and magical Chinese secular utopianism sought to violently eradicate certain forms of religion, in India, secularism sought to stem violence between religious communities, promoting the peaceful coexistence of equal religions by forwarding the idea of a neutral state. At the same time, van der Veer stresses the centrality of imperialism in shaping secularisms in both China and India. The imperial encounter, he suggests, was crucial in both contexts, yet the shape of its influence was fundamentally different in each. In India, where religion became the basis of resistance to the colonial state, the state sought to take a secular neutrality toward religion, and discussion centered around the reform of Indian traditions, rather than their attempted destruction. In China, on the other hand, reformers adopted a more aggressive antireligious stance, calling, for example, for the destruction of temples. Yet in neither location is secularism simply an antireligious project, although there are antireligious elements in each case. Secular projects in both China and India seek rather to transform religions into moral sources of citizenship and national belonging and thus demand not the eradication of religion but its attempted modernization.

In the final chapter of the book, renowned scholar of the secular Talal Asad takes up questions of blasphemy and freedom of speech. Approaching blasphemy claims through a range of moral, political, and aesthetic problems that have crystallized in the form of the idea of free speech, Asad reflects on what contemporary debates over Islamic blasphemy claims suggest about the shape of liberal secularity and its ideal of the free human. Secular liberal freedom, he suggests, is conceived as a form of self-ownership, an inalienable and individualized form of corporeal property, rooted in the living body. In theory, the self-owning secular subject has the ability to choose freely what to do and to publicly claim such freedom. Yet modern secular societies do place legal constraints on public speech. The strong secular resistance to charges of blasphemy, Asad argues, must therefore derive not simply from constraint but from the theological language in which such constraint is articulated, since theology invokes dependence on transcendental power, while secularism has rejected such power in the name of its own particular—and ideological—conception of human freedom. Central to this secular conception of freedom is not only the notion that speech is the personal property of the liberal subject but also a crucial distinction between coercion and seduction—with the former being positively valued as another sign of individual freedom. Yet seduction may also be counted as a form of coercion in its own right, interpreted, Asad writes, as "the dynamic between internal compulsion and external capture, between desire and power." After a consideration of the seductive aesthetics of modern violence, Asad concludes with a series of questions. "Why is it," he asks, "that aggression in the name of God shocks secular liberal sensibilities, whereas the art of killing in the name of the secular nation, of democracy, does not?"

Notes

1. Christian Smith, ed., *The Secular Revolution: Power, Interests, and Conflict in the Secularization of American Public Life* (Berkeley: University of California Press, 2003); William Connolly, *Why I Am Not a Secularist* (Minneapolis: University of Minnesota Press, 1999); Talal Asad, *Formations of the Secular: Christianity, Islam, Modernity* (Stanford, Calif.: Stanford University Press, 2003).

2. For "modes of secularism," see Charles Taylor, "Modes of Secularism," in Rajeev Bhargava, ed., *Secularism and Its Critics* (Oxford: Oxford University Press), 31–53.

3. Robert Keohane, "The Globalization of Informal Violence, Theories of World Politics, and 'The Liberalism of Fear,'" in C. Calhoun, P. Price, and A. Timmer, eds., *Understanding September 11* (New York: New Press, 2002), 72. See also Elizabeth Shakman Hurd, *The Politics of Secularism in International Relations* (Princeton, N.J.: Princeton University Press, 2007).

4. See Julie Reuben, *The Making of the Modern University* (Chicago: University of Chicago Press, 1996).

5. Jonathan Sheehan, "Enlightenment, Religion, and the Enigma of Secularization," *American Historical Review* 108, no. 4 (October 2003): 1061–1080; and David Sorkin, *The Religious Enlightenment: Protestants, Jews, and Catholics from London to Vienna* (Princeton, NJ: Princeton University Press, 2009).

6. Wilfred Cantwell Smith, *The Meaning and End of Religion* (Philadelphia: Fortress Press, 1962).

7. Charles Taylor, *A Secular Age* (Cambridge, Mass.: Harvard University Press, 2007). See also Michael Warner, Jonathan VanAntwerpen, and Craig Calhoun, eds., *Varieties of Secularism in a Secular Age* (Cambridge, Mass.: Harvard University Press, 2010).

8. Charles Taylor, *Sources of the Self* (Cambridge, Mass.: Harvard University Press, 1989).

9. José Casanova, *Public Religions in the Modern World* (Chicago: University of Chicago Press, 1994). See also Asad, *Formations of the Secular*.

10. See Alfred Stepan's review, "Religion, Democracy, and the 'Twin Tolerations,'" *Journal of Democracy* 11, no. 4 (October 2000): 37–57; and various chapters in Rajeev Bhargava, ed., *Secularism and Its Critics* (Oxford, New Delhi, and New York: Oxford University Press, 1998).

11. Saba Mahmood, "The Politics of Religious Freedom and the Minority Question: A Middle Eastern Genealogy," unpublished paper.

12. See Tariq Ramadan, "Manifesto for a New 'We,'" http://www.tariqramadan.com/spip.php?article743 (accessed March 12, 2010).

13. See Alastair MacIntyre, *Whose Justice, Which Rationality* (South Bend, Ind.: University of Notre Dame Press, 1989), and *After Virtue*, 3rd ed. (South Bend, Ind.: University of Notre Dame Press, 2007).

14. John Rawls, "The Idea of Public Reason Revisited," *University of Chicago Law Review* 64, no. 3 (Summer 1997): 765–807.

15. See Jürgen Habermas, *Rationality and Religion: Essays on Reason, God, and Modernity* (Cambridge, Mass.: MIT Press, 2002), and "Religion in the Public Sphere," *European Journal of Philosophy* 14, no. 1 (2006): 1–25.

16. See the discussion of "hypergoods" in Taylor, *Sources of the Self*, 63–73 et passim.

1

Western Secularity

Charles Taylor

I

We live in a world in which ideas, institutions, artistic styles, and formulas for production and living circulate among societies and civilizations that are very different in their historical roots and traditional forms. Parliamentary democracy spread outward from England, among other countries, to India; likewise, the practice of nonviolent civil disobedience spread from its origins in the struggle for Indian independence to many other places, including the United States with Martin Luther King Jr. and the civil rights movement, Manila in 1983, and the Velvet and Orange Revolutions of our time.

But these ideas and forms of practice don't just change place as solid blocks; they are modified, reinterpreted, given new meanings, in each transfer. This can lead to tremendous confusion when we try to follow these shifts and understand them. One such confusion comes from taking a word itself too seriously; the name may be the same, but the reality will often be different.

This is evident in the case of the word "secular." We think of "secularization" as a selfsame process that can occur anywhere (and, according to some people, *is* occurring everywhere). And we think of secularist regimes as an option for any country, whether or not they are actually adopted. And certainly, these *words* crop up everywhere. But do they really mean the same thing in each iteration? Are there not, rather, subtle differences, which can bedevil cross-cultural discussions of these matters?

I think that there are and that they do create problems for our understanding. Either we stumble through tangles of cross-purposes, or else a rather minimal awareness of significant differences can lead us to draw far-reaching conclusions that are very far from the realities we seek to describe. Such is the case, for instance, when people argue that since the "secular" is an old category of

Christian culture and since Islam doesn't seem to have a corresponding category, *therefore* Islamic societies cannot adopt secular regimes. Obviously, they would not be just like those in Christendom, but maybe the idea, rather than being locally restricted, can travel across borders in an inventive and imaginative way.

Let's look at some of the features of the "secular" as a category that developed within Latin Christendom. First, it was one term of a dyad. The secular had to do with the "century"—that is, with profane time—and it was contrasted with what related to the eternal, or to sacred time.[1] Certain times, places, persons, institutions, and actions were seen as closely related to the sacred or higher time, and others were seen as pertaining to profane time alone. That's why the same distinction could often be made by use of the dyad "spiritual/temporal" (e.g., the state as the "temporal arm" of the church). Ordinary parish priests are thus "secular" because they operate out there in the "century," as against those in monastic institutions—"regular" priests—who live by the rules of their order.

So there is an obvious meaning of "secularization" that dates from the aftermath of the Reformation. It refers specifically, in this sense, to when certain functions, properties, and institutions were transferred from church control to that of laymen.

These moves were originally made within a system held in place by the overarching dyad; things were moved from one niche to another within a standing system of niches. This configuration of the "secular," where it still holds, can make secularization a relatively undramatic affair, a rearrangement of the furniture in a space whose basic features remain unchanged.

But from the seventeenth century on, a new possibility gradually arose: a conception of social life in which the "secular" was all there was. Since "secular" originally referred to profane or ordinary time, in contradistinction to higher times, what was necessary was to come to understand profane time without any reference to higher times. The word could go on being used, but its meaning was profoundly changed, because its counterpoint had been fundamentally altered. The contrast was no longer with another temporal dimension, in which "spiritual" institutions had their niche; rather, the secular was, in its new sense, opposed to any claim made in the name of something transcendent of this world and its interests. Needless to say, those who imagined a "secular" world in this sense saw such claims as ultimately unfounded and only to be tolerated to the extent that they did not challenge the interests of worldly powers and human well-being.

Because many people went on believing in the transcendent, however, it was necessary for churches to continue to have a place in the social order. They could be essential in their own way to the functioning of society, but this functioning was to be understood exclusively in terms of "this-worldly" goals and values (peace, prosperity, growth, flourishing, etc.).

This shift entailed two important changes: first, it brought a new conception of good social and political order, which was unconnected to either the traditional ethics of the good life or the specifically Christian notion of perfection (sainthood). This was the new post-Grotian idea of a society formed of and by individuals in order to meet their needs for security and the means to life. The criterion of a good society in this outlook, mutual benefit, was not only emphatically "this-worldly" but also unconcerned with "virtue" in the traditional sense.

The hiving off of a specifically "earthly" criterion figured within a broader distinction, that which divided "this world," or the immanent, from the transcendent. This very clear-cut distinction is itself a product of the development of Latin Christendom and has become part of our way of seeing things in the West. We tend to apply it universally, even though no distinction this hard and fast has existed in any other human culture in history. What does seem, indeed, to exist universally is some distinction between higher beings (spirits) and realms and the everyday world we see immediately around us. But these are not usually sorted out into two distinct domains, such that the lower one can be taken as a system understandable purely in its own terms. Rather, the levels usually interpenetrate, and the lower cannot be understood without reference to the higher. To take an example from the realm of philosophy, for Plato, the existence and development of the things around us can only be understood in terms of their corresponding Ideas, and these exist in a realm outside time. The clear separation of an immanent from a transcendent order is one of the inventions (for better or worse) of Latin Christendom.

The new understanding of the secular that I have been describing builds on this separation. It affirms, in effect, that the "lower," immanent or secular, order is all that there is and that the higher, or transcendent, is a human invention. Obviously, the prior invention of a clear-cut distinction between these levels prepared the ground for the "declaration of independence" of the immanent.

At first, the independence claimed on the part of the immanent was limited and partial. In the "Deist" version of this claim, widespread in the eighteenth century, God was seen as the artificer of the immanent order. Since he is the creator, the natural order stands as a proof of his existence; and since the proper human order of mutual benefit is one that he designs and recommends, we follow his will in building it. Furthermore, it is still affirmed that he backs up his law with the rewards and punishments of the next life.

Thus, some religion, or a certain piety, is a necessary condition of good order. Locke will thus exclude from toleration not only Catholics but also atheists. This is the positive relation of God to good order, but religion can also have negative effects. Religious authority can enter into competition with secular rulers; it can demand things of the faithful that go beyond, or even against, the demands of good order; it can make irrational claims. So it remains to purge society of "superstition," "fanaticism," and "enthusiasm."

The attempts of eighteenth-century "enlightened" rulers, such as Frederick the Great and Joseph II, to "rationalize" religious institutions—in effect, treating the church as a department of the state—belong to this earlier phase of secularization in the West. So, too, in a quite different fashion, does the founding of the American republic, with its separation of church and state. But the first unambiguous assertion of the self-sufficiency of the secular came with the radical phases of the French Revolution.

The polemical assertion of secularity returns in the Third Republic, whose *laïcité* is founded on the ideas of the self-sufficiency of the secular and the exclusion of religion. Marcel Gauchet shows how Renouvier laid the grounds for the outlook of the Third Republic radicals in their battle against the church. The state has to be "*moral et enseignant.*" It has "*charge d'âmes aussi bien que toute Église ou communauté, mais à titre plus universel.*" Morality is the key criterion. In order not to be subordinate to the church, the state must have "*une morale indépendante de toute religion*" and must enjoy a "*suprématie morale*" in relation to all religions. The basis of this morality is liberty, and in order to hold its own before religion, the morality legitimizing the state has to be based on more than just utility or feeling; it needs a "*théologie rationnelle,*" like that of Kant.[2]

Needless to say, this spirit goes marching on in contemporary France, as one can see in the ongoing debate over banning the Muslim head scarf. The insistence is still that the public spaces in which citizens meet must be purified of any religious reference.

And so the history of this term "secular" in the West is complex and ambiguous. It starts off as one term in a dyad that distinguishes two dimensions of existence, identifying them by the particular type of time that is essential to each. But from the foundation of this clear distinction between the immanent and the transcendent, there develops another dyad, in which "secular" refers to what pertains to a self-sufficient, immanent sphere and is contrasted with what relates to the transcendent realm (often identified as "religious"). This binary can then undergo a further mutation, via a denial of the transcendent level, into a dyad in which one term refers to the real ("secular"), and the other refers to what is merely invented ("religious"); or where "secular" refers to the institutions we really require to live in "this world," and "religious" or "ecclesial" refers to optional accessories, which often disturb the course of this-worldly life.

Through this double mutation, the dyad itself is profoundly transformed; in the first case, both sides are real and indispensable dimensions of life and society. The dyad is thus "internal," in the sense that each term is impossible without the other, like right and left or up and down. After the mutations, the dyad becomes "external"; secular and religious are opposed as true and false or necessary and superfluous. The goal of policy becomes, in many cases, to abolish one while conserving the other.

In some ways, the post-Deist modes of secularism transpose features of the Deist template described above. In the Jacobin outlook, the designer is now nature, and so the "piety" required is a humanist ideology based on the natural. What is unacceptable, in turn, is any form of "public" religion. Faith must be relegated to the private sphere. Following this view, there must be a coherent *morale indépendante*, a self-sufficient social morality without transcendent reference. This demand, in turn, encourages the idea that there is such a thing as "reason alone" (*die blosse Vernunft*), that is, reason unaided by any "extra" premises derived from Revelation or any other allegedly transcendent source. Variants of these claims resurface often in contemporary discussions of secularism in the West.[3]

The Deist template has helped to define "good," or "acceptable," religion for much of the Western discussion of the last few centuries. A good, or proper, religion is a set of beliefs in God or some other transcendent power, which entails an acceptable or, in some versions, a "rational" morality. It is devoid of any elements that do not contribute to this morality and thus of "superstition." It is also necessarily opposed to "fanaticism" and "enthusiasm," because these involve by definition a challenge by religious authority to what "reason alone" shows to be the proper order of society.[4]

Religion can thus be an aid to social order by inculcating the right principles, but it must avoid becoming a threat to this order by launching a challenge against it. Thus, Locke is ready to tolerate various religious views, but he excepts from this benign treatment atheists (whose nonbelief in an afterlife undermines their readiness to keep their promises and respect good order) and Catholics (who could not but challenge the established order).

In both of these ways, positive and negative, the essential impact of good religion takes place *in foro interno*: on one hand, it generates the right moral motivation; on the other, by remaining within the mind and soul of the subject, it refrains from challenging the external order. So public ritual can be an essential element of this "rational" religion only if it can help by celebrating public order or by stimulating inner moral motivation.

Eventually, this constellation of terms, including "secular" and "religious," with all of its baggage of ambiguity and deep assumptions concerning the clear division between immanent and transcendent on one hand and public and private on the other, begins to travel. It is no surprise, then, that it causes immense confusion. Westerners themselves are frequently confused about their own history. One way of understanding the development of Western secularism is to see the separation of church and state and the removal of religion into a "private" sphere where it cannot interfere with public life as a result of the earlier distinction between the secular (or temporal) and the sacred (or eternal). The former would thus be, in retrospect, the ultimately satisfactory solution, whereby religion is finally relegated to the margins of political life.

But these stages are not clearly distinguished.[5] Thus, American secularists often totally confuse the separation of church and state from that of religion and state (Rawls at one point wanted to ban all reference to the grounds of people's "comprehensive views"—these included religious views—from public discourse. Moreover, the whole constellation generates disastrously ethnocentric judgments. If the canonical background for a satisfactory secularist regime is the three-stage history described above—distinction of church and state, separation of church and state, and, finally, sidelining of religion from the state and from public life—then obviously, Islamic societies can never make it.

Similarly, one often hears the judgment that Chinese imperial society was already "secular," totally ignoring the tremendous role played by the immanent/transcendent split in the Western concept, which had no analogue in traditional China. Ashis Nandy, in discussing the problems that arise out of the multiple uses of the term "secular," shows the confusions that are often involved in analogous statements about the Indian case (e.g., that the emperor Asoka was "secular" or that the Mughal emperor Akbar established a "secular" form of rule).

But this kind of (mis-)statement can also reflect a certain wisdom. In fact, Nandy distinguishes two quite different notions that consciously or unconsciously inform the Indian discussion. There is, first, the "scientific–rational" sense of the term, in which secularism is closely identified with modernity, and, second, a variety of "accommodative" meanings, which are rooted in indigenous traditions. The first attempts to free public life from religion; the second seek rather to open spaces "for a continuous dialogue among religious traditions and between the religious and the secular."[6]

The invocation of Akbar's rule as "secular" can thus function as a creative and productive way of redefining the term. Such redefinitions, starting from the problems that contemporary societies have to solve, often conceive of secularity as an attempt to find fair and harmonious modes of coexistence between religious communities and leave the connotations of the word "secular" as they have evolved through Western history quietly to the side. This takes account of the fact that formulas for mutually beneficent living together have evolved in many different religious traditions and are not the monopoly of those whose outlook has been formed by the modern, Western dyad, in which the secular lays claim to exclusive reality.[7]

II

What to do? We might think of starting again with another term, one less identified with a particular civilizational trajectory. But that is probably utopian. The word "secular" is much too entrenched in all sorts of discussion, historical and normative, to be displaced.

Obviously, we need a great deal of close study of other, non-Western contexts in order to help here, and I find myself very ill equipped to offer further useful contributions. But there might be a point in trying to give a more fine-grained account of the Western trajectory, so fine-grained that one would both lose any remaining temptation to see it as the universal road on which humanity as a whole is embarked and gain some interesting points of contrast with other civilizational histories. This is the project on which I have been embarked in recent years,[8] and I turn in the rest of this chapter to offer a sketch of this Western path and, in particular, of the important role that the construct we often refer to as Deism has played in it.

One of the main vectors during the last six or seven centuries in this civilization has been a steadily increasing emphasis on a religion of personal commitment and devotion, as opposed to forms centered on collective ritual. We can see this in the growth of a more Christocentric religion in the High Middle Ages. It is further evident both in devotional movements and associations, such as the Brethren of the Common Life in the fifteenth century, and in the nature of the demands made by church hierarchies and leaders on their members. An early example of the latter is the decision of the Lateran Council in 1215 to require all of the faithful to confess to a priest and be shriven, so as to receive communion at least once a year.

From that point on, the pressure to adopt a more personal, committed, and inward form of religion continues—through the preaching of the mendicant friars and others, through the devotional movements mentioned above—eventually reaching a new stage with the Reformation. The point of declaring that salvation comes through faith was radically to devalue ritual and external practice in favor of inner acknowledgment of Christ as savior. It was not just that external ritual was of no effect, but relying on it was tantamount to a presumption that we could control God. The Reformation also tended to delegitimize the distinction between fully committed believers and other, less devoted ones. As against a view of the church in which people operated at many different "speeds," with religious "virtuosi," to use Max Weber's term on one end and ordinary intermittent practitioners on the other, all Christians were expected to be fully committed.

But this movement toward the personal, committed, and inward didn't exist only in the Protestant Churches. There is a parallel development in the Counter-Reformation, with the spread of different devotional movements and the attempts to regulate the lives of the laity according to increasingly stringent models of practice. The clergy were reformed, their training was upgraded, and they were expected, in turn, to reach out and demand a higher level of personal practice from their flocks. A striking figure illustrates this whole movement. In the history of Catholic France, the moment at which the level of practice, as measured by baptisms and Easter communions, reached its highest has been estimated to fall around 1880.[9] This is well after the anticlericalism of the Revolution and its attempts at dechristianization and after a definite movement toward unbelief had set in among the educated classes. In spite of this incipient loss, the apogee of practice came this late because it stood at the end of a long

process in which ordinary believers had been preached at, organized, and sometimes bullied into patterns of practice that reflected heightened personal
commitment.

They had been pressed, we might be tempted to say, into "taking their religion seriously." To take my religion seriously is to take it personally—that is,
more devotionally, inwardly, and committedly. Just taking part in external rituals—those that don't require the kind of personal engagement that, for example,
auricular confession, with its self-examination and promises of amendment,
entails—is devalued on this understanding. That is no longer what religion is
really about.

Now, a striking feature of the Western march toward secularity is that it has
been interwoven from the start with this drive toward a personal religion, as has
frequently been remarked.[10] The connections are multiple. It is not just that the
falling off of religious belief and practice has forced a greater degree of reflection and commitment on those who remain faithful (this has perhaps become
more evident in more recent times). It is much more that the drive to personal
religion has itself been part of the impetus toward different facets of secularization. It was this drive, for instance, that powerfully contributed to the disenchantment of the world of spirits and higher forces in which our ancestors
lived. The Reformation and the Counter-Reformation repressed magical practices and then those facets of traditional Christian sacramental ritual that they
began to deem magical (for Calvinists, this even included the mass). Later, at
the time of the early American republic, a separation of church and state was
brought about, mainly to make space for, and avoid the contamination of,
personal religion, which itself had been given further impetus through the
Great Awakening.

We might identify two closely connected vectors here: toward personal commitment and toward the repression of what came to be understood as the
"magical" elements in religion: practices that suppose and draw on various
intracosmic spirits, good or bad, and higher powers inhering in things (relics,
for instance). I want to use the word "disenchantment" for this movement of
repression; this is a narrower sense than the one the word often bears, for it is
frequently synonymous with the sidelining of religion as such, but my usage
has some warrant in the original Weberian term *Entzauberung*.

Everyone can agree that one of the big differences between us and our ancestors of 500 years ago is that they lived in an "enchanted" world and we do not.
We might think of this as our having "lost" a number of beliefs and the practices
they made possible. Essentially, we become modern by breaking out of "superstition" and becoming more scientific and technological in our stance toward
our world. But I want to accentuate something different. The "enchanted" world
was one in which spirits and forces defined by their meanings (the kind of forces
possessed by love potions or relics) played a big role. But more, the enchanted
world was one in which these forces could shape our lives, both psychical and

physical. One of the big differences between our forerunners and us is that we live with a much firmer sense of the boundary between self and other. We are "buffered" selves. *We* have changed. We sometimes find it hard to be frightened the way they were, and, indeed, we tend to invoke the uncanny things they feared with a pleasurable frisson, as if sitting through films about witches and sorcerers. They would have found this incomprehensible.

Here you see the difference between a subtraction story and one that considers not only loss but also remaking.[11] On the subtraction story, there can be no epistemic loss involved in the transition from enchantment to disenchantment; we have just shucked off some false beliefs, baseless fears, and imagined objects. Looked at my way, the process of disenchantment involves a change in sensibility; one is open to different things, yet one has lost one important way in which people used to experience the world.

It is this sense of loss that underlies many attempts in our day to "reenchant" the world. This goal is frequently invoked, but it ought to be clear that what would be regained here is not what we have "lost."[12] People are talking of quite other ways of recovering an analogue of the original sensibility, whether in the sense of the forces moving through nature in the poems of Hölderlin or Wordsworth or through contact with spirits of the dead.

Disenchantment in my use really translates Weber's term *Entzauberung*, the kernel concept of which is *Zauber*, or "magic." In a sense, moderns constructed their own concept of magic from and through the process of disenchantment. Carried out first under the auspices of Reformed Christianity, the condemned practices all involved using spiritual forces against, or at least independently of, our relation to God. The worst examples were things such as saying a black mass for the dead to kill off your enemy or using the communion host as a love charm. But in the more exigent modes of reform, the distinction between white and black magic tended to disappear, and all recourse to forces independent of God was seen as culpable. The category "magic" was constituted through this rejection, and this distinction was then handed on to post-Enlightenment anthropology, as with Frazer's distinction between "magic" and "religion."[13]

The process of disenchantment, which involved a change in us, can be seen as the loss of a certain sensibility, which is really an impoverishment (as opposed to the simple shedding of irrational feelings). And there have been frequent attempts to "reenchant" the world, or at least admonitions and invitations to do so. In a sense, the Romantic movement can be seen as engaged in such a project. Think of Novalis's "magic realism"; think of the depiction of the Newtonian universe as a dead one, shorn of the life it used to have (Schiller's "The Gods of Greece").

But it is clear that the poetry of Wordsworth, or of Novalis or Rilke, can't come close to the original experience of porous selfhood. The experience it evokes is more fragile, often evanescent, and subject to doubt. It also draws on an ontology that is highly undetermined and must remain so.[14]

Indeed, "enchantment" is something that we, the products of the first vector—toward the personal, the committed, and the inward—have special trouble understanding. In Latin Christendom, movement along this vector increasingly tended to privilege belief, as opposed to unthinking practice. "Secular" people have inherited this emphasis and often propound an "ethics of belief."[15] So we tend to think of our differences from our remote forebears in terms of different *beliefs*, whereas there is something much more puzzling involved here. It is clear that for our forebears, and for many people in the world today who live in a similar religious world, the presence of spirits and of different forms of possession is no more a matter of (optional, voluntarily embraced) belief than the presence of this computer and its keyboard at the tips of my fingers is for me. There is a great deal that I don't understand about the inner workings of this computer (almost everything, in fact) and about which I could be induced by experts to accept various theories; but the encounter with a computer is not a matter of "belief"—it's a basic feature of my experience.

So it must have been for an elderly woman named Celestine, interviewed by Birgit Meyer, who, as a young woman, "walked home from Aventile with her mother, accompanied by a stranger dressed in a white northern gown."[16] When asked afterward, her mother denied having seen the man. He turned out to be the Akan spirit Sowlui, and Celestine was pressed into his service. In Celestine's world, the identification of the man with this spirit might be called a "belief," in that it came after the experience in an attempt to explain what it was all about, but the man accompanying her was just something that happened to her, a fact of her world.

We have great trouble getting our minds around this, and we rapidly reach for intrapsychic explanations, in terms of delusions, projections, and the like. But one thing that seems clear is that the whole situation of the self in experience is subtly, but significantly, different in these worlds and in ours. We make a sharp distinction between inner and outer, between what is in the "mind" and what is out there in the world. Whatever has to do with thought, purpose, and human meanings has to be in the mind, rather than in the world. Some chemical can cause hormonal changes and thus alter the psyche. There can be an aphrodisiac but not a love potion, that is, a chemical that determines the human, or moral, meaning of the experience it enables. A vial of liquid can cure a specific disease, but there can't be such vials as those brought back from pilgrimage at Canterbury, which contained a minuscule drop of the blood of Thomas à Becket and which could cure anything and even make us better people; that is, the liquid was the locus not of certain specific chemical properties but of a generalized beneficence.

Modern Westerners have a clear and firm boundary between mind and world, even mind and body. Moral and other meanings are "in the mind"; they cannot reside outside. But it was not so formerly. Let us take a well-known example of influence inhering in an inanimate substance, as this was understood in earlier times. Consider melancholy: black bile was not the cause of melancholy; rather, it embodied, it *was,* melancholy. The emotional life was porous here; it didn't simply exist in an inner, mental space. Our vulnerability to the evil and the inwardly destructive extended to more than just malevolent spirits; it went beyond them to things that have no wills but are nevertheless redolent with evil meanings.

See the contrast. A modern is feeling depressed, melancholy. He is told it's just his body chemistry; he's hungry, or there is a hormone malfunction, or whatever. Straightaway, he feels relieved. He can take a distance from this feeling, which is declared ipso facto unjustified. Things don't really have such a meaning; it just feels that way, which is the result of a causal process utterly unrelated to the meanings of things. This disengagement depends on our modern mind/body distinction and the relegation of the physical to being "just" a contingent cause of the psychical.

But a premodern might not be helped by learning that his mood comes from black bile, because this doesn't permit any distancing. Black bile *is* melancholy; now he just knows that he's in the grip of the real thing.

Here is the contrast between the modern, bounded self—I want to say "buffered" self—and the "porous" self of the earlier, enchanted world. What difference does this make? It makes, in short, for a very different existential condition. The last example, about melancholy and its causes, illustrates this well. For the modern, buffered self, the possibility exists of taking a distance, disengaging, from everything outside the mind. My ultimate purposes are those that arise within me; the crucial meanings of things are those defined in my responses to them. These purposes and meanings may be vulnerable to manipulation in various ways, including the use of chemicals, but this can, in principle, be met with a countermanipulation: I avoid distressing or tempting experiences, I don't shoot up the wrong substances, and so on.

This is not to say that the buffered self-understanding requires that one take this stance, but it does allow it as a possibility, whereas the porous one does not. By definition, for the porous self, the source of its most powerful and important emotions are outside the "mind," or, better put, the very notion that there is a clear boundary, allowing us to define an inner base area, grounded in which we can disengage from everything else, has no sense.

As a bounded self, I see the boundary as a buffer, such that the things beyond don't need to "get to me," to use the contemporary expression. That's the sense of my use of the term "buffered" here. This self can see itself as invulnerable, as master of the meanings that things have for it.

These two descriptions get at the two important facets of this contrast. First, the porous self is vulnerable (to spirits, demons, cosmic forces, etc.), and along with this go certain fears, which can grip it in the right circumstances. The buffered self has been taken out of the world of this kind of fear—removed, for instance, from the sorts of terrors vividly portrayed in some of Bosch's paintings.

It is true that something analogous can take its place. These images can also be seen as coded manifestations of inner depths, of repressed thoughts and feelings. But the point is that in this quite transformed understanding of self and world, we define these as inner, and, naturally, we deal with them very differently. Indeed, an important part of this treatment of the self is designed to make disengagement possible.

Perhaps the clearest sign of this transformation in our world is that many people today look back to the world of the porous self with nostalgia, as though the creation of a thick emotional boundary between us and the cosmos were now lived as a loss. The aim is to try to recover some measure of this lost feeling. So people go to movies about the uncanny in order to experience a frisson. Our peasant ancestors would have thought us insane. You can't get a frisson from what is really terrifying you.

The second facet is that the buffered self can form the aspiration of disengaging from whatever is beyond the boundary and of giving its own autonomous order to its life. The absence of fear can be not just enjoyed but also seen as an opportunity for self-control or self-direction.

And so the boundary between agents and forces is fuzzy in the enchanted world, and the boundary between mind and world is porous, as we see in the way in which charged objects could influence us. I have been speaking about the moral influence of substances, such as black bile, but a similar point can be made about the relation to spirits. The porosity of the boundary emerges here in the various kinds of "possession," all the way from a full taking over of the person, as with a medium, to various kinds of domination by, or partial fusion with, a spirit or God.[17] Here, again, the boundary between self and other is fuzzy, or porous, and this has to be seen as a fact of *experience*, not a matter of "theory" or "belief."

III

I want now to place this double vector (commitment-disenchantment) in an even deeper and broader historical context, that of the rise and forward march of what Jaspers called "axial" religions and spiritualities. The whole sweep, as it continues up to and into Western modernity, can be seen as a great disembedding of the "merely human," even of the human individual.[18] The full scale of this millennial change becomes clearer if we focus first on some features of the religious life of earlier, smaller-scale societies, insofar as we can trace these. There must have been a phase in which all humans lived in such small-scale societies, even though much of the character of life in this epoch can only be guessed at.

But if we focus on what I will call early religion (which partly covers what Robert Bellah, for instance, calls "archaic religion"), we note how profoundly these forms of life "embed" the agent and that they do so in three crucial ways.[19]

The first way is socially. In Paleolithic and even certain Neolithic tribal societies, religious life was inseparably linked with social life. The primary agency for important religious action—invoking, praying to, sacrificing to, or propitiating gods or spirits; coming close to these powers; receiving healing and protection from them; divining under their guidance, and so on—was the social group as a whole or some more specialized agency recognized as acting for the group. In early religion, we primarily relate to God as a society.

We see both aspects of this in, for example, ritual sacrifices among the Dinka, as they were described a half-century ago by Godfrey Lienhardt. On one hand, the major agents of the sacrifice, the "masters of the fishing spear," were in a sense "functionaries," acting for the whole society; while on the other, the whole community became involved, repeating the invocations of the masters until everyone's attention was focused and concentrated on the single ritual action. It was at the climax that those attending the ceremony were "most palpably members of a single undifferentiated body." This participation often took the form of possession by the divinity being invoked.[20]

Nor is this just the way things happen to be in a certain community. This collective action is essential for the efficacy of the ritual. You can't mount a powerful invocation of the divinities this way on your own in the Dinka world. In Lienhardt's words, the "importance of corporate action by a community of which the individual is really and traditionally a member is the reason for the fear which individual Dinka feel when they suffer misfortune away from home and kin."[21]

This kind of collective ritual action, in which the principal agents act on behalf of a community, which also becomes involved in its own way in the action, seems to figure virtually everywhere in early religion and continues in some ways up to our day. It certainly goes on occupying an important place as long as people live in an "enchanted" world—the world of spirits and forces, which is prior to what I am calling "disenchantment." The medieval ceremony of "beating the bounds" of the agricultural village, for instance, involved the whole parish and could only be effective as a collective act of this whole.

This embedding in social ritual usually carries with it another feature. Just because the most important religious action was that of the collective, and because it often required that certain functionaries—priests, shamans, medicine men, diviners, chiefs, and so on—fill crucial roles in the action, the social order in which these roles were defined tended to be sacrosanct. This is, of course, the aspect of religious life that was most centrally identified and pilloried by the radical Enlightenment. The crime laid bare here was the entrenchment of forms of inequality, domination, and exploitation through their identification with the untouchable, sacred structure of things; hence the longing to see the day "when the last king had been strangled in the entrails of the last priest." But this identification is, in fact, very old and goes back to a time when many of the later, more egregious and vicious forms of inequality had not yet been developed, before there were kings and hierarchies of priests.[22]

Behind the issue of inequality and justice lies something deeper, which touches what we would call today the "identity" of the human beings in those earlier societies. Just because their most important actions were those of whole groups (tribe, clan, subtribe, lineage), articulated in a certain way (the actions were led by chiefs, shamans, masters of the fishing spear), they couldn't conceive of themselves as potentially disconnected from this social matrix. It would probably never even occur to them to try.

What I'm calling social embeddedness is thus partly a matter of identity. From the standpoint of the individual's sense of self, it means the inability to imagine oneself outside of a certain matrix. But it also can be understood as a social reality, and in this sense, it refers to the way we collectively imagine our social existence—for instance, that our most important actions are those of the whole society, which must be structured in a certain way so as to carry them out. And we can see that it is growing up in a world where this kind of social imaginary reigns that sets the limits to our sense of self.

Embedding thus pertains to society, but this also brings with it an embedding in the cosmos. For in early religion, the spirits and forces with which we are dealing are involved in the world in numerous ways. We can see examples of this if we refer back to the enchanted world of our medieval ancestors. For all that the God they worshipped transcended the world, they nevertheless also trafficked with intracosmic spirits and dealt with causal powers that were embedded in things: relics, sacred places, and the like. In early religion, even the high gods are often identified with certain features of the world; and where the phenomenon that has come to be called totemism exists, we can even say that some feature of the world—an animal or plant species, for instance—is central to the identity of a group.[23] It may even be that a particular geographical terrain is essential to religious life. Certain places are sacred. Or the layout of the land speaks to us of the original disposition of things in sacred time. We relate to the ancestors and to this higher time through this landscape.[24]

Besides this relation to society and the cosmos, there is a third form of embedding in existing reality, which we see in early religion. This is what makes for the most striking contrast with what we tend to think of as the "higher" religions. What the people ask for when they invoke or placate divinities and powers is prosperity, health, long life, and fertility; what they ask to be preserved from is disease, dearth, sterility, and premature death. There is a certain understanding of human flourishing here that we can immediately understand, and that, however much we might want to add to it, seems to us quite "natural." What there isn't, and what seems central to the later ("higher") religions, is the idea that we have to question radically this ordinary understanding, that we are called in some way to go beyond it.

This is not to say that human flourishing is the end sought by all things. The divine may also have other purposes, some of which have harmful impacts on us. There is a sense in which, for early religions, the divine is never simply well disposed toward us; the gods (or some of them) may also be in certain ways indifferent. or there may also be hostility, jealousy, or anger, which we have to deflect. Although benevolence, in principle, may have the upper hand, this process may have to be helped along by propitiation or even by the action of "trickster" figures. But through all of this, what remains true is that the divinity's benign purposes are defined in terms of ordinary human flourishing. Again, there may be capacities that some people can attain, which go way beyond the ordinary human ones, which, say, prophets or shamans have. But these, in the end, subserve human well-being as ordinarily understood.

By contrast, with Christianity or Buddhism, for instance, there is a notion of the good that goes beyond human flourishing, which we may gain even while failing utterly in terms of the latter and even *through* such a failing (such as dying young on a cross) or which involves leaving the field of flourishing altogether (ending the cycle of rebirth). The paradox of Christianity, in relation to early religion, is that on one hand, it seems to assert the unconditional benevolence of God toward humans—there is none of the ambivalence of early divinity in this respect—and yet, on the other, it redefines our ends so as to take us beyond flourishing.

In this respect, early religion has something in common with modern exclusive humanism, and this has been felt and expressed in the sympathy of many modern post-Enlightenment people for "paganism." "Pagan self-assertion," John Stuart Mill thought, was as valid as, if not more valid than, "Christian self-denial."[25] (This is related to, but not quite the same as, the sympathy felt for "polytheism.") What makes modern humanism unprecedented, of course, is the idea that this flourishing involves no relation to anything higher.[26]

Now, as earlier mentions suggest, I have been speaking of "early religion" in contrast with what many people have called "postaxial" religions.[27] The reference is to what Karl Jaspers called the "axial age,"[28] the extraordinary period in the last millennium BCE when various "higher" forms of religion appeared, seemingly independently in different civilizations, marked by such founding figures as Confucius, Gautama, Socrates, and the Hebrew prophets.

The surprising feature of the axial religions, compared with what went before—what, in other words, would have made them hard to predict beforehand—is that they initiate a break in all three dimensions of embeddedness: social order, cosmos, and human good. Yet this is not so in all cases and all at once; perhaps in some ways, Buddhism is the most far-reaching, because it radically undercuts the second dimension: the order of the world itself is called into question, because the wheel of rebirth means suffering. In Christianity, there is something analogous: the world is disordered and must be made anew.

But some postaxial outlooks keep the sense of relation to an ordered cosmos, as we see in very different ways with Confucius and Plato; however, they mark a distinction between this and the actual, highly imperfect social order, so that the close link to the cosmos through collective religious life is made problematic.

Perhaps most fundamental of all is the revisionary stance toward the human good in axial religions. More or less radically, they all call into question the received, seemingly unquestionable understandings of human flourishing and hence, inevitably, the structures of society and the features of the cosmos through which this flourishing was supposedly achieved.

We might try to put the contrast in this way: unlike postaxial religion, early religion involved an acceptance of the order of things, in the three dimensions I have been discussing. In a remarkable series of articles on Australian aboriginal religion, W. E. H. Stanner speaks of "the mood of assent" that is central to this spirituality. Aboriginals had not set up the "kind of quarrel with life" that springs from the various postaxial religious initiatives.[29] The contrast is in some ways easy to miss, because aboriginal mythology, in relating the way in which the order of things came to be in the Dream Time—the original time out of time, which is also "everywhen"—contains a number of stories of catastrophe, brought on by trickery, deceit, and violence, from which human life recouped and reemerged but in an impaired and divided fashion, so that there remains the intrinsic connection between life and suffering, and unity is inseparable from division. Now, this may seem reminiscent of other stories of a fall, including that related in Genesis; but in contrast with what Christianity has made of this last, for the Aboriginals, the imperative to "follow up" the dreaming, to recover through ritual and insight their contact with the order of the original time, relates to this riven and impaired dispensation, in which good and evil are interwoven. There is no question of reparation of the original rift or of a compensation for the original loss. Moreover, ritual and the wisdom that goes with it can even bring them to accept the inexorable and to "celebrate joyously what could not be changed."[30] The original catastrophe doesn't separate or alienate us from the sacred or higher, as in the Genesis story; rather, it contributes to shaping the sacred order we are trying to "follow up."[31]

Now, axial religion didn't do away with early religious life. In many ways, it modified features of the latter to define majority religious life for centuries. Modifications arose, of course, not just from the axial formulations but also from the growth of larger-scale, more differentiated, and often urban-centered societies, with more hierarchical forms of organization and embryonic state structures. Indeed, it has been argued that these, too, played a part in the process of disembedding, because the very existence of state power entails some attempt to control and shape religious life and the social structures it requires and thus undercuts the sense of intangibility surrounding this life and these structures.[32] I think that there is a lot to this thesis, and, indeed, I invoke something like it below, but for the moment, I want to focus on the significance of the axial period.

This doesn't totally change the religious life of whole societies all at once, but it does open new possibilities of disembedded religion: seeking a relation to the divine or the higher, which severely revises the going notions of flourishing, or even goes beyond them, and can be carried through by individuals on their own and/or through new forms of sociality, unlinked to the established sacred order. So monks, *bhikhus*, *sanyassi*, or devotees of some avatar or God strike out on their own, and from this springs unprecedented modes of sociality: initiation groups, sects of devotees, the *sangha*, monastic orders, and so on.

In all of these cases, there is some kind of hiatus, difference, or even break in relation to the religious life of the whole society. This itself may be to some extent differentiated, with different strata or castes or classes, and a new religious outlook may lodge itself in one of them. But very often, a new devotion may cut across all of these, particularly where there is a break in the third dimension, with a "higher" idea of the human good emerging.

There is inevitably a tension here, but there often is also an attempt to secure the unity of the whole, to recover some sense of complementarity among the different religious forms, so that those who are fully dedicated to the "higher" forms can be seen at once as a standing reproach to those who remain in the earlier forms, supplicating the powers for human flourishing, and nonetheless as in a relationship of mutual help with them. The laity feed the monks, and by this they earn "merit," which can be understood as taking them a little farther along the "higher" road, but it also serves to protect them against the dangers of life and increases their health, prosperity, and fertility.

So strong is the pull toward complementarity that even in those cases in which a "higher" religion took over the whole society—as we see with Buddhism, Christianity, and Islam—and there is nothing supposedly left to contrast with, the difference between dedicated minorities of religious "virtuosi" and the mass religion of the social sacred, still largely oriented toward flourishing, survived or reconstituted itself, with the same combination of tension on one hand and hierarchical complementarity on the other.

One can argue that all of the "higher" civilizations experienced similar tensions between axial spiritualities and earlier religious forms but that these took on a particular nature, and frequently a greater intensity, in ancient Judaism and the religions that sprang from it, including Christianity and Islam. The ban on idolatry (or *shirk*, in Islam) can generate a drive to reform, even to abolish, earlier cults as modes of forbidden, or "false," religion, generating (in Christendom) the category of illicit "magic" that I alluded to above. We don't seem to find an analogous animus against popular cults in India or China until relatively recently, and then as part of a response to real or threatened invasion by Western imperial powers.[33] This important difference may be seen as a challenge to the whole category of "axial revolutions" as a class of similar transformations occurring in quite different societies, but we can't go into this question here.

In any case, from our modern perspective, with 20/20 hindsight, it might appear as though the axial spiritualities were prevented from producing their full disembedding effect because they were, so to speak, hemmed in by the force of the majority religious life, which remained firmly in the old mold. They did bring about a certain form of religious individualism, but this was what Louis Dumont called the charter for "*l'individu hors du monde*"—that is, it was the way of life of elite minorities, and it was in some ways marginal to, or in some tension with, the "world," where this means not just the cosmos, which is ordered in relation to the higher or the sacred, but also society, which is ordered in relation to both the cosmos and the sacred.[34] This "world" was still a matrix of embeddedness, and it still provided the inescapable framework for social life, including that of the individuals who tried to turn their backs on it, insofar as they remained, in some sense, within its reach.

What had yet to happen was for this matrix to be transformed, to be made over according to some of the principles of axial spirituality, so that the "world" itself would come to be seen as constituted by individuals. This would be the charter for *l'individu dans le monde*, in Dumont's terms, the agent who in his ordinary "worldly" life sees himself as primordially an individual, that is, the human agent of Western modernity.

This project of transformation is the one that I believe has been carried out in Latin Christendom. The vectors of commitment and disenchantment came about through a series of attempts at reform. The goal was to make over the lives of Christians, and also their social order, in a thoroughgoing way, so as to make them conform to the demands of the Gospel. I am talking not of a particular revolutionary moment but of a long, ascending series of attempts to establish a Christian order, of which the Reformation is a key phase. These attempts show a progressive impatience with older modes of postaxial religion in which certain collective, ritualistic forms of earlier religions coexisted uneasily with the demands of individual devotion and ethical reform that came from the "higher" revelations. In Latin Christendom, the attempt was to recover and impose on everyone a more individually committed and Christocentric religion of devotion and action and to repress or even abolish older, supposedly "magical" or "superstitious" forms of collective ritual practice. Social life was to be purged of its connection to an enchanted cosmos and all vestiges removed of the old complementarities between spiritual and temporal, between a life devoted to God and life in the "world," between order and the chaos on which it draws.

This project was thoroughly disembedding just by virtue of its mode of operation, which took the form of a disciplined remaking of behavior and social forms through objectification and an instrumental stance toward human action. But its ends were also intrinsically inclined to disembed. This is clear with the drive to disenchantment, which destroys the second dimension of embeddedness. We can also see it in the specifically Christian context. In one way, Christianity here operates like any axial spirituality—indeed, it operates in conjunction with another, namely, Stoicism—but there also were specifically Christian modes. The New Testament is full of calls to leave or at least to relativize the solidarities of family, clan, and society and to become part of the Kingdom. We see this reflected in the way of operating common to certain Protestant churches, in which one was not simply a member in virtue of birth but which one had to join by answering a personal call. This understanding in turn helped to give force to a conception of society as founded on covenant and hence as ultimately constituted by the decision of free individuals.

This is a relatively obvious filiation, but my thesis is that the effect of the Christian, or Christian-Stoic, attempt to remake society in bringing about the modern "individual in the world" was much more pervasive and multitracked. It helped to nudge first the moral, then the social imaginary in the direction of modern individualism. I believe that this is what we see emerging in the new conception of moral order of seventeenth-century Natural Law theory. This was heavily indebted to Stoicism, and its originators were arguably the Netherlands neo-Stoics Justus Lipsius and Hugo Grotius. But this was a Christianized Stoicism, and a modern one, in the sense that it gave a crucial place to a willed remaking of human society.

We could say that both the buffered identity and the project of reform contributed to the great disembedding. Embeddedness, as I said above, is both a matter of identity—the contextual limits to the imagination of the self—and of the social imaginary, or the ways in which we are able to think or imagine the whole of society. But the new buffered identity, with its insistence on personal devotion and discipline, increased the distance, the disidentification, and even the hostility to the older forms of collective ritual and belonging, while the drive to reform came to envisage their abolition. In both their sense of self and their project for society, the disciplined elites moved toward a conception of the social world as constituted by individuals.

So, to the two linked vectors of personal commitment and disenchantment we can add two more, also closely related: those of the movements of reform and disembedding, or the rise of modern individualism. And these are connected to a fifth, which I think is one of the basic features, if not *the* basic feature, of modern secularity.

What do we mean when we speak of Western modernity as "secular"? There are all sorts of ways of describing it: the separation of religion from public life, the decline of religious belief and practice. But while one cannot avoid touching on these, my main interest here lies in another facet of our age: belief in God, or in the transcendent in any form, is contested; it is an option among many; it is therefore fragile; for some people in some milieus, it is very difficult, even "weird." Five hundred years ago in Western civilization, this wasn't so.

Unbelief was off the map, close to inconceivable, for most people. But that description also applies to the whole of human history outside the modern West.

What had to happen for this kind of secular climate to come about? First, there had to develop a culture that marks a clear division between the "natural" and the "supernatural," and second, it had to come to seem possible to live entirely within the natural. The first condition was something striven for, but the second came about at first quite inadvertently.

Very briefly, I believe that it came about as the by-product of the series of actions in the vector that I have called reform. Its attempt was to make individuals and their society over so as to conform to the demands of the Gospel. Allied with a neo-Stoical outlook, this became the charter for a series of attempts to establish new forms of social order, drawing on new disciplines (Foucault enters the story here), which helped to reduce violence and disorder and to create populations of relatively pacific and productive artisans and peasants, who were increasingly induced, or forced, into the new forms of devotional practice and moral behavior, whether this was in Protestant England, Holland, Counter-Reformation France, or, later, the American colonies and the Germany of the *Polizeistaat*.

My hypothesis is that this new creation of a civilized, "polite" order succeeded beyond what its originators could have hoped for and that this, in turn, led to a new reading of what a Christian order might be, one that was seen increasingly in "immanent" terms (e.g., the polite, civilized order *is* the Christian order). This version of Christianity was shorn of much of its "transcendent" content and was thus open to a new departure, in which the understanding of good order (what I call the "modern moral order") could be embraced outside of its original theological, Providential framework and in certain cases even against it (as with Voltaire, Gibbon, and, in another way, Hume).

Disbelief in God arises in close symbiosis with this belief in a moral order of rights-bearing individuals who are destined (by God or nature) to act for one another's mutual benefit, an order that thus rejects the earlier honor ethic, which exalted the warrior, as it also tends to occlude any transcendent horizon. (We see one good formulation of this notion of order in Locke's *Second Treatise*.) This understanding of order has profoundly shaped the forms of social imaginary that dominate in the modern West: the market economy, the public sphere, the sovereign "people."[35]

In other words, the crucial change here could be described as the possibility of living within a purely immanent order; that is, the possibility of really conceiving of, or imagining, ourselves within such an order, one that could be accounted for on its own terms, which thus leaves belief in the transcendent as a kind of "optional extra"—something it had never been before in any human society. This presupposed the clear separation of natural and supernatural as a necessary condition, but it needed more than that. There had to develop a social order, sustained by a social imaginary that had a purely immanent character, which we see arising, for instance, in the modern forms of public sphere, market economy, and citizen state.

IV

So the vectors of personal religion and disenchantment work to marginalize collective ritual. I am speaking, of course, of ritual in the strong sense, in which prayer, sacrifice, exorcism, or anything else transforms us, our world, or our relation to God and some higher realm. Ritual *effects* something in the higher realm or in our relation to it. Of course, we go on having rituals—we salute the flag, we sing the national anthem, we solemnly rededicate ourselves to the cause—but the efficacy here is inner: we are, in the best case, "transformed" psychologically; we come out feeling more dedicated.

All ritual consists of bodily action, which has some "symbolic" meaning; that is, it invokes or makes palpable something that has an important life meaning: our cause or God's mercy, and so on. But the upshot of these two vectors is to reconceive of the efficacy of our action as its inward effect on our thoughts, emotions, and dispositions. The "symbol" now invokes in the sense that it awakens the thought of the meaning in us. We are no longer dealing with a real presence. We can now speak of an act as "only symbolic."

The movement fits well with a slide toward dualism, as the bodily is merely external, and what is important happens inwardly.

The two vectors generate a new understanding of "religion," which has affinities to what we often call Deism. One facet of this lies in the development of the modern moral order. The second facet makes impersonal orders paramount.

True religion in this view consists in a doctrine that is rationally defensible and that generates a morality that is endorsed by reason. It envisions a creator God, who gave us a universe in which we can read natural law, and then, as an optional extra, threw in an extra incentive to obey the law, in that he distributes rewards and punishments in an afterlife, based on how well we have fulfilled its demands. Everything else is superfluous and based on falsehood, like ritual, which is supposed to effect something real, and, indeed, forms of collective life that stifle the individual conscience, where the moral law has to reside.

This creates a template of true religion, which I described as Deist at the beginning of this chapter. People in other cultures can then take it up, or can find it taken up on their behalf, to show that they, too, have true religion or, indeed, even better examples of it than (orthodox) Christianity. Hence the reform proposals of Ram Mohan Roy in early–nineteenth-century Bengal and also Peng Guanyu, presenting at the 1893 Parliament of Religions in Chicago the orthodox view of Qing Dynasty scholars that Confucianism is not a religion (*zongjiao*) but, rather, a law and teaching (*jiao*) of proper human relations.

The same status was claimed for Buddhism and Daoism and had been for some centuries. What has to be shorn off "religion" in order to have the pure stuff is *wu*, or shamanism, which includes magic, witchcraft, sorcery, and the like.[36] Perhaps we have a case here of parallel development, which influences and is influenced by the Western move to Deism.

Notes

1. See the discussion of profane and sacred times in Charles Taylor, *A Secular Age* (Cambridge, Mass.: Harvard University Press, 2007), 54–61.

2. Marcel Gauchet, *La religion dans la démocratie* (Paris: Gallimard, 1998), 47–50.

3. I have discussed this at greater length in Charles Taylor, "Die blosse Vernunft," in Dilemmas and Connections (Cambridge, Mass.: Harvard University Press), pp. 326–346.

4. For a fuller discussion of the modern idea of moral order, see Charles Taylor, *Modern Social Imaginaries* (Durham, N.C.: Duke University Press, 2004).

5. Thus, American secularists often totally confuse the separation of church and state from that of religion and state. For instance, Rawls at one point wanted to ban all reference to the grounds of people's "comprehensive views" (these, of course, included religious views) from public discourse.

6. Ashis Nandy, *Time Warps* (Piscataway, N.J.: Rutgers University Press, 2002), chap. 3, esp. pp. 68–69, 80.

7. Ibid., 85. Amartya Sen also makes use of a similar point about Akbar's rule to establish the roots of certain modes of secularism in Indian history. See Amartya Sen, *The Argumentative Indian: Writings on Indian History, Culture, and Identity* (New York: Farrar, Straus and Giroux, 2005). For an excellent example of such a creative redefinition, see Rajeev Bhargava, "What Is Secularism For?" in R. Bhargava, ed., *Secularism and its Critics* (Delhi: Oxford University Press, 1998), 486–522 (see especially 493–494 and 520 for "principled distance"); and Rajeev Bhargava, "The Distinctiveness of Indian Secularism," in T. N. Srinavasan, ed., *The Future of Secularism* (Delhi: Oxford University Press, 2007), 20–58, especially 39–41.

8. See Taylor, *A Secular Age*.

9. See Robert Tombs, *France: 1814–1914* (London: Longman, 1996), 135.

10. See John McManners, "Enlightenment: Secular and Christian (1600–1800)," in John McManners, ed., *The Oxford History of Christianity* (Oxford: Oxford University Press, 1993), 277–278.

11. "Subtraction story" refers to the thesis of religion's ineluctable excision in the modern world, as people liberate themselves from prescientific, or prerational, systems of belief. See Taylor, *A Secular Age*, 26–29 et passim.

12. See, for instance, Akeel Bilgrami, "When Was Disenchantment?" in Craig Calhoun, Jonathan VanAntwerpen, and Michael Warner, eds., *Varieties of Secularism in a Secular Age* (Cambridge, Mass.: Harvard University Press, 2010).

13. Peter van der Veer shows how a not-dissimilar category—*wu*, which can be translated as either "shamanism" or "magic" and which emerged out of a parallel process of supposedly rational reform—was developed in modern China as a category for what was rejected as inferior, as not really religion. See Peter van der Veer, *The Spirit of Asia: Comparing Indian and Chinese Spirituality* (Princeton, N.J.: Princeton University Press, forthcoming).

14. See Taylor, *A Secular Age*, chap. 10.

15. See W. K. Clifford, *The Ethics of Belief and Other Essays* (Amherst, Mass.: Prometheus, 1999).

16. Birgit Meyer, *Translating the Devil* (Trenton, N.J.: Africa World Press, 1999), 181.

17. See the discussion of possession in ibid., 205–206.

18. See Taylor, *A Secular Age*, 146–158.

19. See Robert Bellah, *Beyond Belief* (New York: Harper & Row, 1970), chap. 2.

20. Godfrey Lienhardt, *Divinity and Experience* (Oxford: Oxford University Press, 1961), 233–235.

21. Ibid., 292.

22. As a matter of fact, it has been argued that the earliest forms of this religion were highly egalitarian in relation to later developments, just because the pervasive sense of a sacred order left little room for personal decision on the part of those charged with special functions. They couldn't yet parlay these into personal power. See, for instance, Pierre Clastres, *Les sociétés sans état* (Paris: Minuit, 1974).

23. See, for instance, Lienhardt, *Divinity and Experience,* chap. 3; Roger Caillois, *L'homme et le sacré* (Paris: Gallimard, 1963), chap. 3.

24. This is a much-commented-on feature of aboriginal religion in Australia; see Lucien Lévy-Bruhl, *L'expérience mystique et les symboles chez les primitifs* (Paris: Alcan, 1937), 180 and ff.; Caillois, *L'homme et le sacré,* 143–145; W. E. H. Stanner, "On Aboriginal Religion," a series of six articles in *Oceania* 30–33 (1959–63). The same connection to the land has been noted with the Okanagan in British Columbia; see Jerry Mander and Edward Goldsmith, *The Case against the Global Economy: And for a Turn toward the Local* (San Francisco, Calif.: Sierra Club Books, 1996), chap. 39.

25. John Stuart Mill, *On Liberty*, in John Stuart Mill, *Three Essays* (Oxford: Oxford University Press, 1975), 77.

26. In Taylor, *A Secular Age,* I define exclusive humanism as "accepting no final goals beyond human flourishing, nor any allegiance to anything else beyond this flourishing" (18).

27. See, for instance, S. N. Eisenstadt, ed., *The Origins and Diversity of Axial Age Civilizations* (Albany: State University of New York Press, 1986); see also Bellah, *Beyond Belief,* chap. 2.

28. Karl Jaspers, *Vom Ursprung und Ziel der Geschichte* (Zurich: Artemis, 1949).

29. W. E. H. Stanner, "On Aboriginal Religion" *Oceania* 30, no. 4 (June 1960): 276. See also W. E. H. Stanner, "The Dreaming," in W. Lessa and E. Z. Vogt, eds., *Reader in Comparative Religion* (Evanston, Ill.: Row, Peterson, 1958), 158–167.

30. W. E. H. Stanner, "On Aboriginal Religion," *Oceania* 33, no. 4 (June 1963): 269.

31. I have been greatly helped here by the much richer account of religious development in Bellah, *Beyond Belief.* My contrast is much simpler than the series of stages that Bellah identifies; the "primitive" and the "archaic" are fused in my category of "early" religion. My point is to bring into sharp relief the disembedding thrust of the axial formulations.

32. See Marcel Gauchet, *Le désenchantement du monde* (Paris: Gallimard, 1985), chap. 2.

33. See Peter van der Veer, "Smash Temples, Burn Books," 270–281, chap. 12 below.

34. Louis Dumont, *Essais sur l'individualisme* (Paris: Seuil, 1983), chap. 1.

35. I have developed this at greater length in Taylor, *Modern Social Imaginaries*.

36. Van der Veer, "Smash Temples, Burn Books: Comparing Secularist Projects in India and China."

2

The Secular, Secularizations, Secularisms
José Casanova

Rethinking secularism requires that we keep in mind the basic analytical distinction between "the secular" as a central modern epistemic category, "secularization" as an analytical conceptualization of modern world-historical processes, and "secularism" as a worldview and ideology. All three concepts are obviously related but are used very differently in various academic-disciplinary and sociopolitical and cultural contexts. I propose to differentiate the three concepts simply as a way of distinguishing analytically in an exploratory manner among three different phenomena, without any attempt to reify them as separate realities.[1]

The secular has become a central modern category—theological-philosophical, legal-political, and cultural-anthropological—to construct, codify, grasp, and experience a realm or reality differentiated from "the religious." Phenomenologically, one can explore the different types of "secularities" as they are codified, institutionalized, and experienced in various modern contexts and the parallel and correlated transformations of modern "religiosities" and "spiritualities." It should be obvious that "the religious" and "the secular" are always and everywhere mutually constituted. Yet while the social sciences have dedicated much effort to the scientific study of religion, the task of developing a reflexive anthropology and sociology of the secular is only now beginning.

Secularization, by contrast, usually refers to actual or alleged empirical-historical patterns of transformation and differentiation of "the religious" (ecclesiastical institutions and churches) and "the secular" (state, economy, science, art, entertainment, health and welfare, etc.) institutional spheres from early-modern to contemporary societies. Within the social sciences, particularly within sociology, a general theory of secularization was developed that conceptualized these at first modern European and later increasingly globalized historical transformations as part and parcel of a general teleological and progressive human and societal development from the primitive "sacred" to the modern "secular." The thesis of the "decline" and the "privatization" of religion in the modern world became central components of the theory of secularization. Both the decline and the privatization theses have undergone numerous critiques and revisions in the last fifteen years. But the core of the theory—the understanding of secularization as a single process of differentiation of the various institutional spheres or subsystems of modern societies, understood as the paradigmatic and defining characteristic of processes of modernization—remains relatively uncontested in the social sciences, particularly within sociology.

Secularism refers more broadly to a whole range of modern secular worldviews and ideologies which may be consciously held and explicitly elaborated into philosophies of history and normative-ideological state projects, into projects of modernity and cultural programs, or, alternatively, it may be viewed as an epistemic knowledge regime that may be held unreflexively or be assumed phenomenologically as the taken-for-granted normal structure of modern reality, as a modern *doxa* or an "unthought." Moreover, modern secularism also comes in multiple historical forms, in terms of different normative models of legal-constitutional separation of the secular state and religion; or in terms of the different types of cognitive differentiation among science, philosophy, and theology; or in terms of the different models of practical differentiation among law, morality, and religion, and so on.

This chapter presents an analytical elaboration of each of these concepts and some of the phenomenological experiences, institutional arrangements, historical processes, constitutional frameworks, and normative-ideological projects to which they refer.

The Secular

The secular is often assumed to be simply the other of the religious, that which is nonreligious. In this respect, it functions simply as a residual category. But paradoxically, in our modern secular age and in our modern secular world, the secular has come to encompass increasingly the whole of reality, in a sense replacing the religious. Consequently, the secular has come to be increasingly perceived as a natural reality devoid of religion, as the natural social and anthropological substratum that remains when the religious is lifted or disappears. This is the conception or epistemic attitude that Charles Taylor has critically characterized as "subtraction theories."[2]

The paradox resides in the fact that rather than being a residual category, as was originally the case, the secular appears now as reality *tout court,* while the religious is increasingly perceived not only as the residual category, the other of the secular, but also as a superstructural and superfluous additive, which both humans and societies can do without.

Theories of secularization have emerged as explanatory conceptions of this process of differentiation and liberation of the secular from the religious, understood as a universal world-historical process, while secularist worldviews function as justificatory explanations of the paradoxical inversion in the dyadic relation of the religious and the secular, vindicating not only the primacy of the secular over the religious but also the superseding of the religious by the secular. Both function as uncritical and unreflexive ideologies insofar as they disregard, indeed mask, the particular and contingent historicity of the process, projecting it onto the level of universal human development. Moreover, by postulating the secular as the natural and universal substratum that emerges once the superstructural religious addition is lifted, theories of secularization, as well as secularist social science, have avoided the task of analyzing, studying, and explaining the secular, or the varieties of secular experience, as if it is only the religious, but not the secular, that is in need of interpretation and analytical explanation.

Any discussion of the secular has to begin with the recognition that it emerged first as a theological category of Western Christendom that has no equivalent in other religious traditions or even in Eastern Christianity. Originally, the Latin world *saeculum*, as in *per saecula saeculorum,* only meant an indefinite period of time. But eventually, it became one of the terms of a dyad, religious/secular, that served to structure the entire spatial and temporal reality of medieval Christendom into a binary system of classification separating two worlds, the religious-spiritual-sacred world of salvation and the secular-temporal-profane world. Hence the distinction between the "religious" or regular clergy, who withdrew from the world into the monasteries to lead a life of Christian perfection, and the "secular" clergy, who lived in the world along with the laity.

In its original theological meaning, to secularize meant to "make worldly," to convert religious persons or things into secular ones, as when a religious person abandoned the monastic rule to live in the *saeculum* or when monastic property was secularized following the Protestant Reformation. This is the original Christian theological meaning of the term "secularization" that may serve, however, as the basic metaphor of the historical process of Western secularization. In fact, the historical process of secularization needs to be understood as a particular reaction to the structuring dualism of medieval Christendom, as an attempt to bridge, eliminate, or transcend the dualism between the religious and the secular world. In this respect, the very existence of the binary system of classification served to determine the dynamics of the process of secularization. Even within the Christian West, however, this process of secularization follows two different dynamics.

One is the dynamic of internal Christian secularization that aims to spiritualize the temporal and to bring the religious life of perfection out of the monasteries into the secular world, so that everybody may become "a secular ascetic monk," a perfect Christian in the *saeculum.* Such a dynamic tends to transcend the dualism by blurring the boundaries between the religious and the secular, by making the religious secular and the secular religious through mutual reciprocal infusion. This was the path initiated by the various medieval move- ments of Christian reform of the *saeculum,* which was radicalized by the Protestant Reformation and has attained its paradigmatic expression in the Anglo-Saxon Calvinist cultural area, particularly in the United States.

The other different, indeed almost opposite, dynamic of secularization takes the form of laicization. It aims to emancipate all secular spheres from clerical- ecclesiastical control, and in this respect, it is marked by a laic/clerical antago- nism. Unlike in the Protestant path, however, here the boundaries between the religious and the secular are rigidly maintained, but those boundaries are pushed into the margins, aiming to contain, privatize, and marginalize every- thing religious, while excluding it from any visible presence in the secular public sphere. When the secularization of monasteries took place in Catholic coun- tries, first during the French Revolution and later in subsequent liberal revolu- tions, the explicit purpose of breaking the monastery walls was not to bring the religious life of perfection into the secular world, as had been the case with the Protestant Reformation, but rather to laicize those religious places, dissolving and emptying their religious content and making the religious persons, monks and nuns, civil and laic before forcing them into the world, now conceived as merely a secular place emptied of religious symbols and religious meanings. This is precisely the realm of *laïcité,* a sociopolitical sphere freed from religious symbols and clerical control. Such a path of laicization, which is paradigmatic of the French-Latin-Catholic cultural area, although it found diverse manifes- tations throughout continental Europe, could well serve as the basic metaphor of all subtraction narratives of secular modernity, which tend to understand the secular as merely the space left behind when this-worldly reality is freed from religion.

With many variations, these are the two main dynamics of secularization that culminate in our secular age. In different ways, both paths lead to an over- coming of the medieval Christian dualism through a positive affirmation and revaluation of the *saeculum,* that is, of the secular age and the secular world, imbuing the immanent secular world with a quasi-transcendent meaning as the place for human flourishing. In this broad sense of the term "secular," that of "living in the secular world and within the secular age," we are all secular, and all modern societies are secular and are likely to remain so for the foreseeable future, one could almost say *per saecula saeculorum.*

There is a second, narrower meaning of the term "secular," that of self- sufficient and exclusive secularity, when people are simply "irreligious," that is, devoid of religion and closed to any form of transcendence beyond the purely secular immanent frame. Here, secular is no longer one of the units of a dyadic pair but is constituted as a self-enclosed reality. To a certain extent, this consti- tutes one possible end result of the process of secularization, of the attempt to overcome the dualism between religious and secular, by freeing oneself of the religious component altogether.

In his recent work *A Secular Age*, Charles Taylor has reconstructed the process through which the phenomenological experience of what he calls "the immanent frame" becomes constituted as an interlocking constellation of the modern differentiated cosmic, social, and moral orders. All three orders— the cosmic, the social, and the moral—are understood as purely immanent secular orders, devoid of transcendence and thus functioning *etsi Deus non daretur*, "as if God would not exist." It is this phenomenological experience that, according to Taylor, constitutes our age paradigmatically as a secular one, irrespective of the extent to which people living in this age may still hold religious or theistic beliefs.[3]

The question is whether the phenomenological experience of living within such an immanent frame is such that people within it will also tend to function *etsi Deus non daretur*. Taylor is inclined to answer this question in the affirmative. Indeed, his phenomenological account of the secular "conditions" of belief is meant to explain the change from a Christian society around 1500 CE in which belief in God was unchallenged and unproblematic, indeed "naïve" and taken for granted, to a post-Christian society today in which belief in God not only is no longer axiomatic but also becomes increasingly problematic, so that even those who adopt an "engaged" standpoint as believers tend to experience reflexively their own belief as an option among many others, one moreover requiring an explicit justification. Secularity, being without religion, by contrast tends to become increasingly the default option, which can be naïvely experienced as natural and, thus, no longer in need of justification.

This naturalization of "unbelief" or "nonreligion" as the normal human condition in modern societies corresponds to the assumptions of the dominant theories of secularization, which have postulated a progressive decline of religious beliefs and practices with increasing modernization, so that the more modern a society is, the more secular, the less "religious," it is supposed to become. That the decline of religious beliefs and practices is a relatively recent meaning of the term "secularization" is indicated by the fact that it does not yet appear in the dictionaries of most modern European languages.

The fact that there are some modern non-European societies, such as the United States or South Korea, that are fully secular in the sense that they function within the same immanent frame and yet their populations are also at the same time conspicuously religious, or the fact that the modernization of so many non-Western societies is accompanied by processes of religious revival, should put into question the premise that the decline of religious beliefs and practices is a quasi-natural consequence of processes of modernization. If modernization per se does not produce necessarily the progressive decline of religious beliefs and practices, then we need a better explanation for the radical and widespread secularity one finds among the populations of most western

European societies. Secularization in this second meaning of the term "secular," that of being "devoid of religion," does not happen automatically as a result of processes of modernization or even as the result of the social construction of a self-enclosed immanent frame, but it needs to be mediated phenomenologically by some other particular historical experience.

Self-sufficient secularity, that is, the absence of religion, has a better chance of becoming the normal taken-for-granted position if it is experienced not as an unreflexively naïve condition, as just a fact, but actually as the meaningful result of a quasi-natural process of development. As Taylor has pointed out, modern unbelief is not simply a condition of absence of belief or merely indifference. It is a historical condition that requires the perfect tense, "a condition of 'having overcome' the irrationality of belief."[4] Intrinsic to this phenomenological experience is a modern "stadial consciousness," inherited from the Enlightenment, which understands this anthropocentric change in the conditions of belief as a process of maturation and growth, as a "coming of age," and as progressive emancipation. For Taylor, this stadial phenomenological experience serves, in turn, to ground the phenomenological experience of exclusive humanism as the positive self-sufficient and self-limiting affirmation of human flourishing and as the critical rejection of transcendence beyond human flourishing as self-denial and self-defeating.

In this respect, the historical self-understanding of secularism has the function of confirming the superiority of our present modern secular outlook over other supposedly earlier and therefore more primitive religious forms of understanding. To be secular means to be modern, and therefore, by implication, to be religious means to be somehow not yet fully modern. This is the ratchet effect of a modern historical stadial consciousness, which turns the very idea of going back to a surpassed condition into an unthinkable intellectual regression.

The function of secularism as a philosophy of history, and thus as ideology, is to turn the particular Western Christian historical process of secularization into a universal teleological process of human development from belief to unbelief, from primitive irrational or metaphysical religion to modern rational postmetaphysical secular consciousness. Even when the particular role of internal Christian developments in the general process of secularization is acknowledged, it is in order to stress the universal significance of the uniqueness of Christianity as, in Marcel Gauchet's expressive formulation, "the religion to exit from religion."[5]

I would like to propose that this secularist stadial consciousness is a crucial factor in the widespread secularization that has accompanied the modernization of western European societies. Europeans tend to experience their own secularization, that is, the widespread decline of religious beliefs and practices in their midst, as a natural consequence of their modernization. To be secular is experienced not as an existential choice that modern individuals or modern societies make but, rather, as a natural outcome of becoming modern. In this respect, the theory of secularization mediated through this historical stadial consciousness tends to function as a self-fulfilling prophecy. It is, in my view, the presence or absence of this secularist historical stadial consciousness that explains when and where processes of modernization are accompanied by radical secularization. In places where such secularist historical stadial consciousness is absent or less dominant, as in the United States or in most non-Western postcolonial societies, processes of modernization are unlikely to be accompanied by processes of religious decline. On the contrary, they may be accompanied by processes of religious revival.

Following this reconstruction one may distinguish three different ways of being secular: (a) that of *mere secularity,* that is, the phenomenological experience of living in a secular world and in a secular age, where being religious may be a normal viable option; (b) that of *self-sufficient and exclusive secularity,* that is, the phenomenological experience of living without religion as a normal, quasi-natural, taken-for-granted condition; and (c) that of *secularist secularity,* that is, the phenomenological experience not only of being passively free but also actually of having been liberated from "religion" as a condition for human autonomy and human flourishing.

Secularizations

In the book *Public Religions in the Modern World,* I proposed to disaggregate analytically what was usually taken to be one single theory of secularization into three disparate and not necessarily interrelated components or subtheses, namely, (a) the theory of the institutional differentiation of the so-called secular spheres, such as state, economy, and science, from religious institutions and norms; (b) the theory of the progressive decline of religious beliefs and practices as a concomitant of levels of modernization; and (c) the theory of privatization of religion as a precondition of modern secular and democratic politics.[6] Such an analytical distinction makes possible the testing of each of the three subtheses separately as different empirically falsifiable propositions.

Since in Europe the three processes of secular differentiation, privatization of religion, and religious decline have been historically interconnected, there has been the tendency to view all three processes as intrinsically interrelated components of a single general teleological process of secularization and modernization, rather than as particular and contingent developments. In the United States, by contrast, one finds a paradigmatic process of secular differentiation, which is not accompanied, however, either by a process of religious decline or by the confinement of religion to the private sphere. Processes of modernization and democratization in American society have often been accompanied by religious revivals, and the wall of separation between church and state, though much stricter than the one erected in most European societies, does not imply the rigid separation of religion and politics.

While the two minor subtheses of the theory of secularization, namely, "the decline of religion" and "the privatization of religion," have undergone numerous critiques and revisions in the last fifteen years, the core of the thesis, namely, the understanding of secularization as a single process of functional differentiation of the various secular institutional spheres of modern societies from religion, remains relatively uncontested.[7] Yet one should ask whether it is appropriate to subsume the multiple and very diverse historical patterns of differentiation and fusion of the various institutional spheres (that is, church and state, state and economy, economy and science) that one finds throughout the history of modern Western societies into a single teleological process of modern functional differentiation.[8]

Moreover, rather than viewing secularization as a general universal process of human and societal development culminating in secular modernity, one should begin with the recognition that the very term "secularization" derives from a unique Western Christian theological category, that of the *saeculum*. Talal Asad has called our attention to the fact that "the historical process of secularization effects a remarkable ideological inversion.... For at one time 'the secular' was a part of a theological discourse (*saeculum*)," while later, "the religious" is constituted by secular political and scientific discourses, so that "religion" itself as a historical category and as a universal globalized concept emerges as a construction of Western secular modernity.[9]

Thus, any thinking of secularization beyond the West has to begin with the recognition of this dual historical paradox. Namely, that "the secular" emerges first as a particular Western Christian theological category, while its modern antonym, "the religious," is a product of Western secular modernity. The contextualization of our categories, "religious" and "secular," should begin, therefore, with the recognition of the particular Christian historicity of western European developments, as well as of the multiple and diverse historical patterns of differentiation and fusion of the religious and the secular, as well as of their mutual constitution, within European and Western societies.

Such recognition, in turn, should allow a less Eurocentric comparative analysis of patterns of differentiation and secularization in other civilizations and world religions and, more important, the further recognition that with the world-historical process of globalization initiated by the European colonial expansion, all of these processes everywhere are dynamically interrelated and mutually constituted. Without questioning the actual historical processes of secular differentiation, such analysis contextualizes, pluralizes, and in a sense relativizes those processes by framing them as particular Christian-Western historical dynamics, which allows for a discourse of multiple modernities within the West and, of course, even more so for multiple non-Western modernities.

As Peter van der Veer has stressed, the very pattern of Western secularization cannot be fully comprehended if one ignores the crucial significance of the colonial encounter in European developments.[10] Indeed, the best of postcolonial analysis has shown how every master reform narrative and every genealogical account of Western secular modernity needs to take into account the colonial and intercivilizational encounters. Certainly, any comprehensive narrative of the modern civilizing process must take into account the western European encounter with other civilizations. The very category of civilization in the singular only emerges out of these intercivilizational encounters.[11]

This is even more clearly the case when one attempts a genealogical reconstruction of the unique modern secular category of "religion," which has now also become globalized.[12] Indeed, any discussion of secularization as a global process should start with the reflexive observation that one of the most important global trends is the globalization of the category of "religion" itself and of the binary classification of reality, "religious/secular," that it entails. While the social sciences still function with a relatively unreflexive general category of religion, within the newer discipline of "religious studies," the very category of religion has undergone numerous challenges, as well as all kinds of critical deconstructions. There has been much debate in the last two decades concerning the competing genealogies of the "modern" category of religion and its complex relation to the pluralization of Christian confessions and denominations in early modernity, to the Western colonial expansion and the encounter with the religious "other," to the Enlightenment critique of religion and the triumph of "secular reason," the hegemony of the secular state, and the disciplinary institutionalization of the scientific study of religion, and to the Western "invention of the world religions" and the classificatory taxonomies of religion which have now become globalized.[13]

It is therefore appropriate to begin a discussion of global religious and secular trends with the recognition of a paradox, namely, that scholars of religion are questioning the validity of the category of "religion" at the very same moment when the discursive reality of religion is more widespread than ever and has become for the first time global. I am not claiming that people today everywhere are either more or less religious than they may have been in the past. Here I am bracketing out altogether the question that has dominated most theories of secularization, namely, whether religious beliefs and practices are declining or growing as a general modern trend throughout the world. I am only claiming that "religion" as a discursive reality, indeed, as an abstract category and as a system of classification of reality, used by modern individuals as well as by modern societies across the world, by religious as well as by secular authorities, has become an undisputable global social fact.

It is obvious that when people around the world use the same category of religion, they actually mean very different things. The actual concrete meaning of whatever people denominate as "religion" can only be elucidated in the context of their particular discursive practices. But the very fact that the same category of religion is being used globally across cultures and civilizations testifies to the global expansion of the modern secular/religious system of classification of reality that first emerged in the modern Christian West. This implies the need to reflect more critically on this particular modern system of classification, without taking it for granted as a general universal system.[14]

Moreover, while the religious/secular system of classification of reality may have become globalized, what remains hotly disputed and debated almost everywhere in the world today is how, where, and by whom the proper boundaries between the religious and the secular ought to be drawn. There are in this respect multiple competing secularisms, as there are multiple and diverse forms of religious fundamentalist resistance to those secularisms. For example, American, French, Turkish, Indian, and Chinese secularism, to name only some paradigmatic and distinctive modes of drawing the boundaries between the religious and the secular, represent not only very different patterns of separation of the secular state and religion but also very different models of state regulation and management of religion and of religious pluralism in society.

Similarly, despite "family resemblances" observed among the diverse religious fundamentalisms, one should resist the temptation to view them all as diverse manifestations of a single process of religious fundamentalist reaction against a single general global process of progressive secularization.[15] Each of the so-called religious fundamentalist movements—American Protestant, Jewish, Muslim, Hindu, and so on—besides being internally plural and diverse, are particular responses to particular ways of drawing the boundaries between the religious and the secular. Moreover, those responses are not only reactive but also proactive attempts to seize the opportunity offered by processes of globalization to redraw the boundaries. Above all, always and everywhere, the religious and the secular are mutually constituted through sociopolitical struggles and cultural politics. Not surprisingly, everywhere one finds also diverse resistances to attempts to impose the European or any other particular pattern of secularization as a universal, teleological model.

Indeed, if one finds that European patterns of secularization are not simply replicated either in the "Christian" United States or in Catholic Latin America, much less should one expect that are they going to be simply reproduced in other non-Western civilizations. The very category of secularization becomes deeply problematic once it is conceptualized in a Eurocentric way as a universal process of progressive human societal development from "belief" to "unbelief" and from traditional "religion" to modern "secularity" and once it is then transferred to other world religions and other civilizational areas with very different dynamics of structuration of the relations and tensions between religion and world or between cosmological transcendence and worldly immanence. Moreover, in the same way as Western secular modernity is fundamentally and inevitably post-Christian, the emerging multiple modernities in the different postaxial civilizational areas are likely to be post-Hindu, or post-Confucian, or post-Muslim; that is, they will also be particular and contingent refashionings and transformations of existing civilizational patterns and social imaginaries mixed with modern secular ones.

We should think of processes of secularization, of religious transformations and revivals, and of processes of sacralization as ongoing mutually constituted global processes, rather than as mutually exclusive developments. Indeed, adopting a necessarily fictitious global point of view, one can observe three different, parallel, yet interrelated global processes that are in tension and often come in open conflict with one another. There is, first, a global process of secularization that can best be characterized as the global expansion of what Taylor has characterized as "the secular immanent frame." This frame is constituted by the structural interlocking constellation of the modern cosmic, social, and moral secular orders.[16] But as the ongoing debates between the European and American paradigms and the discourse of American and European "exceptionalisms" make clear, this process of secularization within the very same immanent frame may entail very different "religious" dynamics.[17]

Despite its many variations, the general European pattern is one of secularization (i.e., secular differentiation) and "religious" decline (i.e., decline of church religiosity and loss of ecclesiastical power and authority). But the American pattern is one of secularization combined with religious growth and recurrent religious revivals. Thus, the fundamental question for any theory of secularization is how one is to account sociologically for the radical bifurcation in the religious situation today between Western societies on both sides of the North Atlantic, that is, between the radical secularity of European societies, which, indeed, appear to match perfectly Taylor's phenomenological account of *A Secular Age* and the predominant condition of religious belief among the vast majority of the American population.[18]

I concur with Dipesh Chakrabarty in the need to "provincialize" Europe and to turn the European theories of American exceptionalism upside down.[19] Instead of being the norm, the historical process of secularization of European Latin Christendom is the one truly exceptional process, which is unlikely to be reproduced anywhere else in the world with a similar sequential arrangement and with the corresponding stadial consciousness. Moreover, non-Western and non-Christian societies, which did not undergo a similar process of historical development and always confronted Western secular modernity from its first encounter with European (Christian) colonialism as "the other," are more likely to recognize the European process of secularization for what it truly was, namely, a particular Christian and post-Christian historical process, and not, as Europeans like to think, a general or universal process of human or societal development.

Without such a stadial consciousness, it is unlikely that the immanent frame of the secular modern order will have similar phenomenological effects on the conditions of belief and unbelief in non-Western societies. It is an open empirical question which kind of "religious" dynamic will accompany secularization, that is, the expansion of the secular immanent frame and of secular differentiation in non-Western cultures. For instance, one can certainly view the process of desacralization of the traditional caste system in India, which must perforce accompany modern processes of democratization, as a particular form of Indian secularization. But such a secularization, even when legally imposed, is unlikely to have the same secularizing phenomenological effect on the conditions of belief and unbelief that ecclesiastical disestablishment may have had in the European confessional context. The very post-Reformation Christian categories of "belief" and "unbelief" might be totally unfitting in the context of India or "Hinduism."

If, as I have suggested, globalization entails a certain decentering, provincializing, and historicizing of Europe and of European secular modernity, even in relation to the different religious pattern of American modernity within the same immanent frame, then it is unlikely that what Taylor calls "our" secular age will simply become the common global secular age of all of humanity or that "our" secular age will become absolutely unaffected by this process of globalization and by the encounter with the emerging non-Western and in many respects nonsecular modernities.

Parallel to the general process of secularization, which started as a historical process of internal secularization within Western Christendom but was later globalized through the European colonial expansion, there is a process of constitution of a global system of "religions," which can best be understood as a process of global religious denominationalism, whereby all of the so-called world religions are redefined and transformed in contraposition to "the secular" through interrelated reciprocal processes of particularistic differentiation, universalistic claims, and mutual recognition.

But the modern "secular" is by no means synonymous with the "profane," nor is the "religious" synonymous with the modern "sacred." Only "the social as religious" is synonymous with the "sacred" in Durkheimian terms. In this respect, modern secularization entails a certain profanation of religion through its privatization and individualization and a certain sacralization of the secular spheres of politics (sacred nation, sacred citizenship, sacred constitution), science (temples of knowledge), and economics (through commodity fetishism). But the truly modern sacralization, which constitutes the global civil religion in Durkheim's terms, is the cult of the individual and the sacralization of humanity through the globalization of human rights.[20]

It is an open empirical question, which should be the central focus of a comparative-historical sociology of religion, how these three ongoing global processes of secularization, sacralization, and religious denominationalism are mutually interrelated in different civilizations, sometimes symbiotically, as in the fusions of religious nationalisms or in the religious defense of human rights, but often antagonistically, as in the violent conflicts between the sacred secular immanent norms (of individual life and freedom) and transcendent theistic norms. From the Salman Rushdie affair to the Danish cartoons, from the destruction of the Babri Masjid to suicide murders, from the assassination of Theo van Gogh to the confrontation between the German pope and the German chancellor over the papal absolution of the excommunication of Bishop Richard Williamsons, an unrepentant "integralist" who dared to commit publicly the sacrilegious crime of denying the Holocaust, what we are repeatedly observing in the "glocal" media of the global public sphere can best be understood not so much as clashes between "the religious" and "the secular" but, rather, as violent confrontations over "the sacred," over blasphemous and sacrilegious acts and speeches, and over the profanation of religious and secular taboos.

It is all part and parcel of ongoing global struggles over universal-particular mutual human recognition.

Secularisms

As indicated above, "secularism" can refer most broadly to a whole range of modern worldviews and ideologies concerning "religion," which may be consciously held and reflexively elaborated or, alternatively, which have taken hold of us and function as taken-for-granted assumptions that constitute the reigning epistemic *doxa* or "unthought." But secularism also refers to different normative-ideological state projects, as well as to different legal-constitutional frameworks of separation of state and religion and to different models of differentiation of religion, ethics, morality, and law.

It may be fruitful to begin by drawing an analytical distinction between secularism as statecraft doctrine and secularism as ideology. By secularism as statecraft principle, I understand simply some principle of separation between religious and political authority, either for the sake of the neutrality of the state vis-à-vis each and all religions, or for the sake of protecting the freedom of conscience of each individual, or for the sake of facilitating the equal access of all citizens, religious as well as nonreligious, to democratic participation. Such a statecraft doctrine neither presupposes nor needs to entail any substantive "theory," positive or negative, of "religion." Indeed, the moment the state holds explicitly a particular conception of "religion," one enters the realm of ideology. One could argue that secularism becomes an ideology the moment it entails a theory of what "religion" is or does. It is this assumption that "religion," in the abstract, is a thing that has an essence or that produces certain particular and predictable effects that is the defining characteristic of modern secularism.[21]

One can distinguish two basic types of secularist ideologies. The first type are secularist theories of religion grounded in some progressive stadial philosophies of history that relegate religion to a superseded stage. The second type are secularist political theories that presuppose that religion is either an irrational force or a nonrational form of discourse that should be banished from the democratic public sphere. They can be called, respectively, "philosophical-historical" and "political" secularisms.

My aim here is not to trace, from the perspective of a history of ideas, the origins of both forms of secularism in early-modern Europe and the ways in which they came together in Enlightenment critiques of religion and became separated again in the different trajectories of positivism, materialist atheism, atheist humanism, republican laicism, liberalism, and so on. I am also not interested here in examining the secularist "philosophical-historical" assumptions permeating most theories of secular modernity, such as Jürgen Habermas's theories of "rationalization of the life-world" and "linguistification of the sacred," or the "political" secularist assumptions permeating prominent liberal democratic political theories such as those of John Rawls or Habermas, although both began to revise their secularist premises in their later works.[22]

As a sociologist, more than on the high intellectual versions of both types of secularism, I am interested in examining the extent to which such secularist assumptions permeate the taken-for-granted assumptions and thus the phenomenological experience of ordinary people. Crucial is the moment when the phenomenological experience of being "secular" is not tied anymore to one of the units of a dyadic pair, "religious/secular," but is constituted as a self-enclosed reality. Secular then stands for self-sufficient and exclusive secularity, when people are not simply religiously "unmusical" but are actually closed to any form of transcendence beyond the purely secular immanent frame.

Earlier here, I argued that it is the presence or absence of what I have called a "secularist historical stadial consciousness" that explains to a large extent when and where processes of modernization are accompanied by radical secularization. In places where such secularist historical stadial consciousness is absent, as in the United States or in most non-Western postcolonial societies, processes of modernization are unlikely to be accompanied by processes of religious decline. On the contrary, they may be accompanied by processes of religious revival.

The different ways in which European and American publics respond to public-opinion polls trying to measure their religiosity—how strongly they believe in God, how frequently they pray, how frequently they go to church, how religious they are, and so on—may serve as a confirming illustration of my thesis. We know for a fact that both Americans and Europeans lie to the pollsters. But they tend to lie in opposite directions. Americans exaggerate their religiosity, claiming to go to church and to pray more frequently than they actually do. We know this for a fact because sociologists of religion, trying to prove that modern secularization is also at work in the United States, have shown that Americans are less religious than they claim to be and that one should not trust their self-reporting religiosity.[23] But the interesting sociological question is why Americans would tend to exaggerate their religiosity, claiming that they are more religious than they actually are, unless they somehow believe that to be modern and to be American, which for most Americans means exactly the same thing, also entails being religious.

Europeans, by contrast, if and when they lie to the pollsters, tend to do so in the opposite direction; they tend to undercut their own persistent religiosity. I cannot offer general evidence for all of Europe, but there is clear evidence for this tendency in the case of Spain. The 2008 Bertelsmann *Religion Monitor* offers overwhelming confirmation of the drastic secularization of Spanish society in the last forty years.[24] There is a persistent and consistent decline in self-reported religiosity across all categories of religious belief, church attendance, private prayer, and importance of religion in one's life. But I find most interesting the even lower figures in religious self-image. The proportion of Spaniards who view themselves as "quite religious" (21 percent) is much smaller than that of those who express a "strong" belief in God (51 percent), significantly smaller than that of those who attend religious services at least monthly (34 percent), and much smaller than that of those who claim to pray at least weekly (44 percent). I am inclined to interpret the discrepancy between self-reported religiosity and religious self-image as an indication that Spaniards would prefer to think of themselves as less religious than they actually are and that being religious is not considered a positive trait in a predominantly secular culture.

The natural response of Europeans to the question of whether they are "religious" would seem to be "Of course, I am not religious. What do you think? I am a modern, liberal, secular, enlightened European." It is this taken-for-granted identification of being modern and being secular that distinguishes most of western Europe from the United States. To be secular in this sense means to leave religion behind, to emancipate oneself from religion, over-coming the nonrational forms of being, thinking, and feeling associated with religion. It also means growing up, becoming mature, becoming autonomous, thinking and acting on one's own. It is precisely this assumption that secular people think and act on their own and are rational autonomous free agents, while religious people somehow are unfree, heteronomous, nonrational agents, that constitutes the foundational premise of secularist ideology. It entails in this respect both "subtraction" and "stadial" theories of secularity.

Taylor characterizes as "subtraction" theories those accounts of secular modernity that view the secular as the natural substratum that is left behind and revealed when this anthropologically superfluous and superstructural thing called religion is somehow taken away. The secular is precisely the basic anthro-pological substratum that remains when one gets rid of religion. Stadial the-ories add genealogical or functionalist accounts of how and why this superstructural thing, religion, emerged in the first place, usually in the primitive history of humanity, but has now become superfluous for modern secular individuals and for modern societies.

Political secularism per se does not need to share the same negative assumptions about religion or assume any progressive historical development that will make religion increasingly irrelevant. It is actually compatible with a positive view of religion as a moral good or as an ethical communitarian reservoir of human solidarity and republican virtue. But political secularism would like to contain religion within its own differentiated "religious" sphere and would like to maintain a secular public democratic sphere free from religion. This is the basic premise behind any form of secularism as statecraft doctrine, the need to maintain some kind of separation between "church" and "state," or between "religious" and "political" authorities, or between "the religious" and "the political." But the fundamental question is how the boundaries are drawn and by whom. Political secularism falls easily into secularist ideology when the political arrogates for itself absolute, sovereign, quasi-sacred, quasi-transcendent character or when the secular arrogates for itself the mantle of rationality and universality, while claiming that "religion" is essentially nonrational, particularistic, and intolerant (or illiberal) and, as such, dangerous and a threat to democratic politics once it enters the public sphere. It is the essentializing of "the religious" but also of "the secular" or "the political," based on problematic assumptions of what "religion" is or does, which is in my view the fundamental problem of secularism as ideology.

It is, indeed, astounding to observe how widespread is the view throughout Europe that religion is "intolerant" and "creates conflict." According to the 1998 ISSP public-opinion survey, the overwhelming majority of Europeans, more than two-thirds of the population in every western European country, held the view that religion was "intolerant."[25] This was a widespread view, moreover, already before September 11, 2001. Since people are unlikely expressly to recognize their own intolerance, one can assume that in expressing such an opinion, Europeans are thinking of somebody else's "religion" or, alternatively, present a selective retrospective memory of their own past religion, which they consider themselves fortunately to have outgrown. It is even more telling that a majority of the population in every western European country, with the significant exceptions of Norway and Sweden, shares the view that "religion creates conflict."

It should seem obvious that such a widespread negative view of "religion" as being "intolerant" and conducive to conflict can hardly be grounded empirically in the collective historical experience of European societies in the twentieth century or in the actual personal experience of most contemporary Europeans. It can plausibly be explained, however, as a secular construct that has the function of positively differentiating modern secular Europeans from "the religious other," either from premodern religious Europeans or from contemporary non-European religious people, particularly Muslims.

So when they think of religion as "intolerant," Europeans obviously are not thinking of themselves, even when many of them may still be religious, but, rather, they must be thinking either of the religion they have left behind or of the religion of "the other" within their midst, which happens to be Islam. Insofar as they identify religion with intolerance, they seem to imply that they have happily left their own intolerance behind by getting rid of religion. The argument for tolerance becomes in this sense a justification for secularity as the source of tolerance.

Most striking is the view of "religion" in the abstract as the source of violent conflict, given the actual historical experience of most European societies in the twentieth century. "The European short century," from 1914 to 1989, using Eric Hobsbawm's apt characterization, was, indeed, one of the most violent, bloody, and genocidal centuries in the history of humanity. But none of the horrible massacres—not the senseless slaughter of millions of young Europeans in the trenches of World War I; or the countless millions of victims of Bolshevik and Communist terror through revolution, civil war, collectivization campaigns, the great famine in Ukraine, the repeated cycles of Stalinist terror, and the gulag; or the most unfathomable of all, the Nazi Holocaust and the global conflagration of World War II, culminating in the nuclear bombing of Hiroshima and Nagasaki—can be said to have been caused by religious fanaticism and intolerance. All of them were, rather, products of modern secular ideologies.

Yet contemporary Europeans obviously prefer selectively to forget the more inconvenient recent memories of secular ideological conflict and retrieve instead the long-forgotten memories of the religious wars of early-modern Europe to make sense of the religious conflicts they see today proliferating around the world and increasingly threatening them. Rather than seeing the common structural contexts of modern state formation, interstate geopolitical conflicts, modern nationalism, and the political mobilization of ethnocultural and religious identities, processes central to modern European history that became globalized through the European colonial expansion, Europeans seemingly prefer to attribute those conflicts to "religion," that is, to religious fundamentalism and the fanaticism and intolerance that are supposedly intrinsic to "premodern" religion, an atavistic residue that modern secular enlightened Europeans have left behind.[26] One may suspect that the function of such a selective historical memory is to safeguard the perception of the progressive achievements of Western secular modernity, offering a self-validating justification of the secular separation of religion and politics as the condition for modern liberal democratic politics, for global peace, and for the protection of individual privatized religious freedom.

In fact, existing European democracies are not as secular as secularist theories of democracy seem to imply. European societies may be highly secular, but European states are far from being secular or neutral. One only needs to point out that every branch of Christianity, with the exception of the Catholic church, has privileged establishment, and not only a symbolic one, in some European democracy: the Anglican Church in England, the Presbyterian church in Scotland, the Lutheran church in all Nordic countries (Denmark, Norway, Iceland, Finland) except Sweden, and the Orthodox church in Greece. Even in laicist France, 80 percent of the budget of private Catholic schools is covered by state funds. Indeed, between the two extremes of French *laïcité* and Nordic Lutheran establishment, all across Europe is a whole range of very diverse patterns of church-state relations, in education, media, health and social services, and so on, which constitute very "unsecular" entanglements, such as the consociational formula of pillarization in the Netherlands or the corporatist official state recognition of the Protestant and Catholic churches in Germany (as well as of the Jewish community in some *Länder*).[27]

One should focus less on secularism as an allegedly prescriptive democratic norm or as a functionalist requirement of modern differentiated societies and more on the critical comparative historical analysis of the different types of secularism that have emerged in the process of modern state formation. As a statecraft doctrine, every form of secularism entails two principles, which are well captured by the dual clause of the First Amendment to the U.S. Constitution, namely, the principle of separation (i.e., "no establishment") and the principle of state regulation of religion in society (i.e., "free exercise"). It is the relationship between the two principles that determines the particular form of secularism and its affinity with democracy.

Concerning the first principle, there are all kinds of degrees of separation between the two extremes of "hostile" and "friendly" separation. Indeed, in places in which there was no ecclesiastical institution with monopolistic claims, such as the Catholic church before the Second Vatican Council, or compulsory confessional state churches, such as the ones that became institutionalized through the Westphalian system of European states under the principle *cuius regio eius religio,* one does not need, properly speaking, a process of disestablishment, and one may have a process of friendly separation, as was the case in the United States.

As Ahmet Kuru has shown, the type of separation at the formative period of the modern state will be very much determined by the particular configuration of relations between religious and political authorities during the ancient regime.[28] Postcolonial states are likely to have their own particular dynamics. In colonial America, for instance, there was no national church across the thirteen colonies from which the new federal state needed to separate itself. However, the separation was friendly, not only because there was no need to have a hostile separation from a nonexistent established church but, more important, because the separation was constituted in order to protect the free exercise of religion, that is, in order to construct the conditions of possibility for religious pluralism in society.

Ultimately, the question is whether secularism is an end in itself, an ultimate value, or a means to some other end, be it democracy and equal citizenship or religious (i.e., normative) pluralism. Indeed, if the secularist principle of separation is not an end in itself, then it ought to be constructed in such a way that it maximizes the equal participation of all citizens in democratic politics and the free exercise of religion in society. Taking the two clauses together, one can construct general gradual typologies of hostile/friendly separation, on the one hand, and models of free/unfree state regulation of religion in society, on the other.

One could advance the proposition that it is the "free exercise" of religion clause, rather than the "no establishment" clause, that appears to be a necessary condition for democracy. One cannot have democracy without freedom of religion. Indeed, "free exercise" stands out as a normative democratic principle in itself. Since, on the other hand, there are many historical examples of secular states that were nondemocratic, the Soviet-type regimes, Kemalist Turkey, or postrevolutionary Mexico being obvious cases, one can therefore conclude that the strict secular separation of church and state is neither a sufficient nor a necessary condition for democracy. The "no establishment" principle appears defensible and necessary primarily as a means to free exercise and to equal rights. Disestablishment becomes a necessary condition for democracy whenever an established religion claims monopoly over a state territory, impedes the free exercise of religion, and undermines equal rights or equal access to all citizens.

Understandably, most discussions of the secular and secularism are internal Western Christian secular debates about patterns of Christian Western secularization. As Noah Feldman has pointed out, this is basically a debate about how we got from Saint Augustine to where we are today.[29] We should be cautious in trying to elevate this particular and contingent historical process to some general universal historical model. Indeed, we should remind ourselves that "the secular" emerged first as a particular Western Christian theological category, a category that not only served to organize the particular social formation of Western Christendom but also very much structured thereafter the dynamics of how to transform or free oneself from such a system. Eventually, however, as a result of this particular historical process of secularization, "the secular" has become the dominant category that serves to structure and delimit, legally, philosophically, scientifically, and politically, the nature and the boundaries of "religion."

As it happened, this particular dynamic of secularization became globalized through the process of Western colonial expansion, entering into dynamic tension with the many different ways in which other civilizations had drawn boundaries between "sacred" and "profane," "transcendent" and "immanent," "religious" and "secular." We should not think of these dyadic pairs of terms as being synonymous. The sacred tends to be immanent in preaxial cultures.

The transcendent is not necessarily "religious" in some axial civilizations. The secular is by no means profane in our secular age. Indeed, we would need to enter into a much more open analysis of non-Western civilizational dynamics and be more critical of our Western Christian secular categories, in order to expand our understandings of the secular and secularisms.

Notes

1. This chapter builds on and expands the argument developed in José Casanova, "The Secular and Secularisms," *Social Research* 76, no. 4 (Winter 2009): 1049–1066.

2. Charles Taylor, *A Secular Age* (Cambridge, Mass.: Harvard University Press, 2007).

3. Ibid.

4. Ibid., 269.

5. Marcel Gauchet, *The Disenchantment of the World: A Political History of Religion* (Princeton, N.J.: Princeton University Press, 1997).

6. José Casanova, *Public Religions in the Modern World* (Chicago: University of Chicago Press, 1994). For a critical revision of the thesis, see José Casanova, "Public Religions Revisited," in Hent de Vries, ed., *Religion: Beyond a Concept* (New York: Fordham University Press, 2008), 101–119.

7. José Casanova, "Rethinking Secularization: A Global Comparative Perspective," *Hedgehog Review* 8, nos. 1–2 (Spring/Summer 2002): 7–22.

8. For a poignant critique of the thesis of differentiation, see Charles Tilly, *Big Structures, Large Processes, Huge Comparisons* (New York: Russell Sage, 1984), 43–60.

9. Talal Asad, *Formations of the Secular: Christianity, Islam, Modernity* (Stanford, Calif.: Stanford University Press, 2003), 192.

10. Peter van der Veer, *Imperial Encounters* (Princeton, N.J.: Princeton University Press, 2007).

11. Johann P. Arnason, *Civilizations in Dispute* (Leiden: Brill, 2003).

12. Talal Asad, *Genealogies of Religion* (Baltimore, Md.: Johns Hopkins University Press, 1993); Wilfred Cantwell Smith, *The Meaning and End of Religion* (New York: Macmillan, 1963).

13. Hans Kippenberg, *Discovering Religious History in the Modern Age* (Princeton, N.J.: Princeton University Press, 2002); Tomoko Mazusawa, *The Invention of World Religions* (Chicago: University of Chicago Press, 2005); Russell McCutcheon, *Manufacturing Religion* (New York: Oxford University Press, 1982); Jonathan Z. Smith, "Religion, Religions, Religious," in Mark C. Taylor, ed., *Critical Terms for Religious Studies* (Chicago: University of Chicago Press, 1998), 269–284; Hent de Vries, ed., *Religion: Beyond a Concept* (New York: Fordham University Press, 2008).

14. Peter Beyer, *Religions in Global Society* (London: Routledge, 2006).

15. Gabriel A. Almond, R. Scott Appleby, and Emmanuel Sivan, *Strong Religion: The Rise of Fundamentalisms around the World* (Chicago: University of Chicago Press, 2003).

16. Taylor, *A Secular Age*.

17. José Casanova, "Beyond European and American Exceptionalism," in Grace Davie, Paul Heelas, and Linda Woodhead, eds., *Predicting Religion* (Aldershot, U.K.: Ashgate, 2003), 17–29.

18. Peter Berger, Grace Davie, and Effie Fokas, *Religious America, Secular Europe? A Theme with Variations* (Aldershot, U.K.: Ashgate, 2008).

19. Dipesh Chakrabarty, *Provincializing Europe* (Princeton, N.J.: Princeton University Press, 2000).

20. Emile Durkheim, *The Elementary Forms of the Religious Life* (New York: Free Press, 1995); José Casanova, "The Sacralization of the *Humanum*: A Theology for a Global Age," *International Journal of Politics, Culture and Society* 13, no.1 (Fall 1999): 21–40.

21. Asad, *Genealogies of Religion* and *Formations of the Secular*.

22. Jürgen Habermas, *The Theory of Communicative Action* (Boston: Beacon Press, 1984 and 1987), *The Structural Transformation of the Public Sphere* (Cambridge, Mass.: MIT Press, 1989), *Religion and Rationality: Essays on Reason, God and Morality* (Cambridge, Mass.: MIT Press, 2002), and *Between Naturalism and Religion* (Cambridge, U.K.: Polity, 2008); John Rawls, *A Theory of Justice* (Cambridge, Mass.: Harvard University Press, 1971) and *A Brief Inquiry into the Meaning of Sin and Faith, with "On My Religion"* (Cambridge, Mass.: Harvard University Press, 2009).

23. Kirk Hadaway, Penny Long Marler, and Mark Chaves, "What the Polls Don't Show: A Close Look at US Church Attendance," *American Sociological Review* 58 (1993): 741–752.

24. José Casanova, "Spanish Religiosity: An Interpretative Reading of the Religion Monitor Results for Spain," in Bertelsmann Stiftung, ed., *What the World Believes* (Guetersloh: Verlag Bertelsmann Stiftung, 2009), 223–255.

25. Andrew Greeley, *Religion in Europe at the End of the Second Millennium* (New Brunswick, N.J.: Transaction, 2003), 78.

26. José Casanova, "The Problem of Religion and the Anxieties of European Secular Democracies," in Gabriel Motzkin and Yochi Fischer, eds., *Religion and Democracy in Contemporary Europe* (London: Alliance, 2008), 63–74; and *Europa's Angst vor der Religion* (Berlin: Berlin University Press, 2009).

27. John Madeley has developed a tripartite measure of church-state relation, which he calls the TAO of European management and regulation of religion-state relations by the use of Treasure (T, for financial and property connections), Authority (A, for the exercise of states' powers of command), and Organization (O, for the effective intervention of state bodies in the religious sphere). According to his measurement, all European states score positively on at least one of these scales, most states score positively on two of them, and more than one-third (sixteen out of forty-five states) score positively on all three. John T. S. Madeley, "Unequally Yoked: The Antinomies of Church-State Separation in Europe and the USA," paper presented at the Annual Meeting of the American Political Science Association, Chicago, August 30-September 2, 2007.

28. Ahmet Kuru, *Secularism and State Policies toward Religion* (New York: Cambridge University Press, 2009).

29. Noah Feldman, "Religion and the Earthly City," *Social Research* 76, no. 4 (Winter 2009): 989–1000.

3

Secularism, Citizenship, and the Public Sphere
Craig Calhoun

The tacit understanding of citizenship in the modern West has been secular. This is so despite the existence of state churches, presidents who pray, and a profound role for religious motivations in major public movements. The specifics of political secularism vary from case to case—separation of church and state in America, fairness in allocation of public support to different religious groups in India, *laïcité* and the exclusion of religious expression from even nonpolitical public life in France and Turkey.

In general, political secularism hinges on a distinction of public from private and the relegation of religion to the private side of that dichotomy. But of course, political secularism is also influenced by secularism more generally, which has numerous meanings, from belief that scientific materialism exhausts the explanation of existence, to the view that values inhere only in human orientations to the world and not in the world itself, to the notion that there is no world of transcendent meaning or eternal time that should orient people in relation to actions in the everyday world. Not least, the notion of secularization as an inevitable long-term cumulative decline in religion has also influenced thinking about religion and citizenship.

The main issue was once religious diversity. Faith was assumed, but conflicts of faith undermined political cohesion. Some governments sought national cohesion through religious conformity, others by accepting diversity but limiting the public role of religion. Today the issue is often faith itself. This arises not only with regard to public funding of religion but also with the question of whether religious arguments have a legitimate place in public debates. Participation in the political public sphere is a central dimension of citizenship, so restrictions on public debate are significant. Many liberals think restrictions on religious argumentation are unproblematic, however, not only because of long habit but also because they approach the public sphere with an ideal of rationality that seems to exclude religious arguments as irrational. The issue here is not simply whether any specific beliefs are true or false but whether they are subject to correction and improvement through rational arguments appealing to logic and evidence in principle shareable by all participants. Arguments based on faith or divine inspiration don't qualify.

Regardless of one's opinion about the truth of religious convictions, this is a big issue for democratic citizenship. It bears directly on the extent to which one of the most fundamental of all citizenship rights is open to all citizens. It shapes the astonishment of Europeans at American politics, with its public professions of faith and demonstrations of piety. Although American liberals are not astonished, many are embarrassed or anxious, indeed, alienated from large parts of American public life (and skewed in their understanding because they seldom participate in discussions where religion is taken seriously). In other words, secularists propose a limit on religion in the public sphere, which they take to be a basis for equal inclusion, but at the same time insulate themselves from understanding religious discourse, practicing an ironic exclusion.

At the same time, restrictive conceptions of legitimate participation in the public sphere also shape European difficulties in incorporating Muslim citizens. It is disturbing to many not simply that their religion is unfamiliar—although this is certainly a factor—or that it is associated at least in public understanding with terrorism but that many are so actively religious. Europeans also have been surprised by the enduring prominence of Catholicism and startled by Polish proposals to include recognition of God and Christianity in the European basic law and by the fact that these were not without resonance elsewhere. Sometimes the anxieties about religious expression in public and anxieties about specific religions become mutually reinforcing, as in opposition to allowing the creation of an Islamic cultural center near the former World Trade Center site (the so-called ground zero) in New York City.

Unreflective secularism distorts much liberal understanding of the world—encouraging, for example, thinking about global civil society that greatly underestimates the role of religious organizations or imagining cosmopolitanism as a sort of escape from culture into a realm of reason where religion has little influence. To get a handle on this, we need to look a bit further at how secularism has been understood—including how it has been tacitly incorporated into political theory, often as though it were simply the absence of religion rather than the presence of a particular way of looking at the world—or, indeed, ideology. To move forward, it is helpful to look at the recent and controversial effort of Jürgen Habermas to theorize a place for religion in the public sphere—after leaving it almost completely out of his famous study of the *Structural Transformation of the Public Sphere*. We will see not only a courageous effort but also some limits and problems that suggest that there is work still to be done. Seeing religion as a fully legitimate part of public life is a specific version of seeing culture and deep moral commitments as legitimate—and, indeed, necessary—features of even the most rational and critical public discourse. Too often, liberals understand these issues through a contrast between the local and the cosmopolitan in which culture is associated with the former, and the latter is understood as an escape from it. But of course, culture is not only that which separates and locates but also that which integrates and connects human beings. Public life at even the most cosmopolitan of scales is not an escape from ethnic, national, religious, or other culture but a form of culture-making in which these can be brought into new relationships.

Religion in the Public Sphere

Religion appears in liberal theory first and foremost as an occasion for tolerance and neutrality. This orientation is reinforced by (a) the classification of religion as essentially a private matter, (b) an "epistemic" approach to religion shaped by the attempt to assess true and false knowledge, (c) the notion that a clear and unbiased distinction is available between the religious and the secular, and (d) the view that religion is in some sense a "survival" from an earlier era—not a field of vital growth within modernity. Each of these reinforcements is problematic. So, while the virtues of tolerance are real, the notion that matters of religion can otherwise be excluded from the liberal public sphere is not sustainable.

The secularization story derives partly from an Enlightenment-rationalist view of religion as mere superstition and tradition inherited from the past without a proper ground in modernity. So, even while religion had not disappeared as rapidly as many expected, a declining role in the public sphere made sense to many thinkers, because they regarded religion as a personal belief that could not properly be made subject to public discourse. It might be a reason for people's political positions, but it was not the sort of reason that could be subjected to rational political debate. Therefore, liberal theorists have commonly suggested that religion should remain private or that religious arguments have a legitimate place in the public sphere only to the extent that they can be rendered in (ideally rational) terms that are not specifically religious. In short, much liberal theory conceptualizes citizenship as essentially secular, even where citizens happen to be religious. It is as though theorists reworked the famous medieval notion of the king's two bodies—imagining citizens to exist distinctly in private and public realms.[1]

This use of the public/private distinction to enforce a kind of secularism is embarrassingly reminiscent of the use of the same distinction to minimize not only women's political participation but also opportunities to put certain issues associated with the gendered private sphere on the ostensibly gender-neutral public agenda. Not surprisingly, whether there is an adequate place for religious argumentation and views in public life has increasingly been presented as an issue of inclusive citizenship. Given the prominence of religious people and voices in American politics, it is easy for secular academics to scoff at the notion that they are excluded, and in most material senses, they are not. But it is nonetheless striking how hard a time liberal political theory has had finding a place for religion—other than as simply the object of toleration.

Perhaps chafing at critiques from the right, some liberal theorists have been moved to recognize religious identities and practices as more legitimate in public life. After initially espousing a more straightforwardly secularist exclusion of religion from politics as an essentially private matter of taste, for example, John Rawls in his later work suggested that religiously motivated arguments should be accepted as publicly valid but only insofar as they were translatable into secular claims not requiring any specifically religious understanding.[2] In recent work that has surprised some of his followers, Habermas recognizes that this discriminates. He suggests, moreover, that religion is valuable as a source and resource for democratic politics.[3] It offers semantic potential, the potential for new meaning, not least to a political left that may have exhausted some other resources.

Habermas labels the present era, in which religion must be taken seriously, as "postsecular." The term is potentially confusing. When, we might ask, was the secular age that we are now "post"? In his book *A Secular Age*, Charles Taylor traces a set of transformations that gather speed from about 1500 and by the mid-nineteenth century issue in (a) an era in which may people find conscious unbelief (not merely low levels of participation in institutional religion) to be normal, (b) an era in which believers are challenged in compelling ways by both a plurality of beliefs and powerful achievements based on science and institutions not based on traditional religion, and (c) an era in which states and other institutions recurrently demand a distinction between religion and "the secular" (even though each may be hard to define). Taylor does not believe that we have entered a postsecular age. On the contrary, he thinks that believers and nonbelievers alike must live within a secular age. He seeks not a return to some imaginary presecular orientation but, rather, a recognition that everyone works with some evaluative commitments that are especially strong or deep and put their other values into perspective and that some of these legitimately transcend limits of scientific materialism.[4] None of us actually escapes cultural and other motivations and resources for our intellectual perspectives; none of us is perfectly articulate about all of our moral sources (although we may struggle to gain clarity). The import of this is that the line between secular and religious is not as sharp as many philosophical and other accounts suggest.[5] On the one hand, religious people cannot escape the prominence and power of the secular in the modern world, and on the other hand, while the norms of secular argumentation may obscure deep evaluative commitments, they do not eliminate them.

So the term "postsecularism" may be a bit of a red herring. I think we should not imagine that Habermas means simply a return of the dominance of religious ideas or an end to the importance of secular reason. Rather, I think he is better read as suggesting the emergence of deep difficulties in holding to (a) the assumption that progress (and freedom, emancipation, and liberation) could be conceptualized adequately in purely secular terms and (b) the notion that a clear differentiation could be maintained between discourses of faith and those of public reason. Loss of confidence on these dimensions is challenging for liberalism. And it leads Habermas to wonder whether exclusion of religious argumentation from the public sphere may be impoverishing.

The notion of religion as somehow private has informed the modern era in a host of ways, mostly misleading but also constitutive of social practices and understandings. Religion simply was never in every sense private, any more than it was always conservative. On the contrary, the United States has seen successive Great Awakenings and arguably is seeing another now. The Social Gospel informed major dimensions of public discourse and action in the early twentieth century. The civil rights movement is inconceivable without black churches. Contrast with Europe is not new, having informed both Tocqueville and Weber after their travels in the United States. But the Protestant Reformation was not the last time religion mattered in Europe. We should remember the antislavery movement and the influence of especially low-church Protestant religion on a range of other late-eighteenth-century and early-nineteenth-century social movements. We should note that many large-scale popular devotions, such as pilgrimages to Lourdes, have relatively modern origins. We should not neglect the mid-nineteenth-century renewal of spiritualism, even if much of it was outside religious orthodoxy, and we should not lose sight of its fluid relationships with Romanticism, utopian socialism, and humanitarianism. We should see religious internationalism both under the problematic structure of colonial and postcolonial missionary work and in the engagements shaped by Vatican II, the peace movement, and liberation theology.

Faith has thus figured frequently in modern public life, well before the current waves of Evangelicalism and Islam. Rather than a distinction of personal piety from more outward forms of religious practice, the "privacy" of religion has been bound up with (a) the notion that religious convictions were to be treated as matters of implicitly personal faith rather than publicly authoritative reason and (b) the idea of a separation from the state (which was as much a demand for states not to interfere as for particular religious views not to dominate states). In the former sense, religious freedom could be recognized as a right, but it was implicitly always a right to be wrong or to have a peculiar taste and thus not to have matters of faith arbitrated by the court of public opinion. In the latter sense, religion was private in something of the same sense in which property was private: it could be socially organized on a large scale but was still seen as a matter of individual right and in principle separate from affairs of state.

The Peace of Westphalia, for example, established a framework for seeing sovereignty as secular and religion as private (or essentially domestic) with regard to the relations among sovereigns. Bringing a series of partially religious wars to an end, it helped in 1648 to usher in an era of nationalism and building of modern states, as well as the very idea of international relations. The academic discipline of international relations, not least as it recast itself after World War II, incorporated this secularist assumption about states and their interests into its dominant intellectual paradigms. It requires a considerable effort today for international-relations specialists to think of secularism as a substantive position on states rather than virtually a defining feature of states, as a "something" rather than an "absence." This reflects a wider tendency to see religion as a presence and secularism as its absence. But of course, secularisms are themselves intellectual and ideological constructs.

What issued from the 1648 Peace of Westphalia was not a Europe without religion but a Europe of mostly confessional states, mandating an official religion with varying degrees of tolerance for others. The principle that reigned was still *cuius regio, eius religio* ("whose realm, his religion"). Religion has never been essentially private.[6] Rather, the Westphalian frame of discourse constructed a particular misrecognition of the way religion figured (or didn't) in public life. And if the Westphalian frame did this for international affairs, others did it domestically. Habermas's own account of the public sphere and its transformations, for example, pays almost no attention to religion. In this, it extends a European Enlightenment tradition of imagining religion to be properly outside the frame of the public sphere.[7] The Enlightenment theorists did not so much not report on social reality as seek to construct a new reality in which religion would be outside the frame of the public sphere. Kant's effort to reconstruct religion "within the limits of reason alone" was, of course, a challenge to the lived orientations of many religious people. If it respected a certain core of faith—"the *Eigensinn* of religion"—it did so only by excluding it from the realms of reason and the public sphere. Faith became available only on the basis of leaps beyond reason—as Kierkegaard recognized.

Religious Roots of Public Reason

As Habermas rightly notes, the very ideas of freedom, emancipation, and liberation developed in largely religious discourses in Europe, and this continues to inform their meaning. This genealogy is not simply a matter of dead ancestry; the living meaning of words and concepts draws both semantic content and inspiration from religious sources. The word "inspiration" is a good example and reminds us that what is at stake is broader than the narrowest meanings of politics and ethics and necessarily includes conceptions of the person that make meaningful different discourses of freedom, action, and possibility—and that shape motivation as well as meaning. What is at stake is also broader than measures of participation in formally organized religion, since a variety of "spiritual" engagements inform self-understanding and both ethical and moral reasoning.

Religion is part of the genealogy of public reason itself. To attempt to disengage the idea of public reason (or the reality of the public sphere) from religion is to disconnect it from a tradition that continues to give it life and content. Habermas stresses the importance of not depriving public reason of the resources of a tradition that has not exhausted the semantic contributions it can make. Equally, the attempt to make an overly sharp division between religion and public reason provides important impetus to the development of counter- or alternative publics, as well as less public and less reasoned forms of resistance to a political order that seeks to hold religion at arm's length. Moreover, to exclude religion is arguably to privilege a secular middle class in many countries, a secular "native" majority in Europe, and a relatively secular white elite in the United States in relation to more religious blacks, Latinos, and immigrant populations.

Not only is there valuable content for public reason to gain if it integrates religious contributions, but it is a requirement of political justice that public discourse recognize and tolerate but also fully integrate religious citizens. Official tolerance for diverse forms of religious practice and a constitutional separation of church and state are good, Habermas suggests, but not by themselves sufficient guarantees of religious freedom: "It is not enough to rely on the condescending benevolence of a secularized authority that comes to tolerate minorities hitherto discriminated against. The parties themselves must reach agreement on the always contested delimitations between a positive liberty to practice a religion of one's own and the negative liberty to remain spared of the religious practices of others."[8] This agreement cannot be achieved in private. Religion, thus, must enter the public sphere. There, deliberative, ideally democratic processes of collective will formation can help parties both to understand each other and to reach mutual accommodation if not always agreement.

Giving Reasons

Rawls's account of the public use of reason allows for religiously motivated arguments but not for the appeal to "comprehensive" religious doctrines for justification. Justification must rely solely on "proper political reasons" (which means mainly reasons that are available to everyone, regardless of the specific commitments they may have to religion or substantive conceptions of the good or their embeddedness in cultural traditions). This is, as Habermas indicates, an importantly restrictive account of the legitimate public use of reason—one that will strike many as not truly admitting religion into public discourse. It is in the nature of religion that serious belief is understood as informing—and rightly informing—all of a believer's life. This makes sorting out the "properly political" from other reasons both practically impossible in many cases and an illegitimate demand for secularists to impose. Attempting to enforce it would amount to discriminating against those for whom religion is not "something other than their social and political existence."[9]

While opening the rules of ordinary citizenship, Habermas seeks to maintain a strictly secular conception of the state. Legislators, thus, must restrict themselves to "properly political" justifications, independent of religion. Standing rules of parliamentary procedure "must empower the house leader to have religious statements or justifications expunged from the minutes."[10] Still, Habermas goes so far as to suggest that the liberal state and its advocates are not merely enjoined to religious tolerance but—at least potentially—cognizant of a functional interest in public expressions of religion. These may be key resources for the creation of meaning and identity; secular citizens can learn from religious contributions to public discourse (not least when these help clarify intuitions that the secular citizens have not made explicit).

In this "polyphonic complexity of public voices," the giving of reasons is still crucial. Public reason cannot proceed simply by expressive communication or demands for recognition, although the public sphere cannot be adequately inclusive if it tries to exclude these. The public sphere will necessarily include processes of culture-making that are not reducible to advances in reason and that nonetheless may be crucial to capacities for mutual understanding. But if collective will formation is to be based on reason, not merely participation in common culture, then public processes of clarifying arguments and giving reasons for positions must be central. Religious people, like all others, are reasonably to be called on to give a full account of their reasons for public claims. But articulating reasons clearly is not the same as offering only reasons that can be stated in terms fully "accessible" to the nonreligious.[11] Conversely, though the secular (or differently religious) may be called on to participate in the effort to understand the reasons given by adherents to any one religion, such understanding may include recognition and clarification of points where orientations to knowledge are such that understanding cannot be fully mutual. And the same goes in reverse. Since secular reasons are also embedded in culture and belief and not simply matters of fact or reason alone, those who speak from nonreligious orientations are reasonably called on to clarify to what extent their arguments demand such nonreligious orientations or may be reasonably accessible to those who do not share them.

In one sense, indeed, one could argue that a sharp division between secular and religious beliefs is available only to the nonreligious. While the religious person may accept many beliefs that others regard as adequately grounded in secular reasons alone—about the physical or biological world, for example—he or she may see these as inherently bound up with a belief in divine creation. This need not involve an alternative scientific view—such as creationists' claims that the world is much newer than most scientists think. It may rather involve embedding widely accepted scientific claims in a different interpretative frame, as revealing the way God works rather than absence of the divine. The religious person may also regard certain beliefs as inherently outside religion, but even if he or she uses the word "secular" to describe these, the meaning is at least in part "irreligious" (a reference to a different, nonreligious way of seeing things and not simply to things ostensibly "self-sufficient" outside religion or divine influence).

Indeed, many struggles over the secular take place inside religions. Think, for example, of Opus Dei, the "secular institution" formed in the Catholic Church not as part of but alongside its normal hierarchy, sometimes with strong papal patronage. Opus Dei has a strong engagement with business elites and thus a larger affirmative relation to contemporary capitalism. This is a secular position and one that puts Opus Dei at odds in many settings with more "progressive" priests. In Peru, for example, where Opus Dei has achieved an unusually strong position at the top of the ecclesiastical hierarchy—a majority of bishops—this occasions a struggle with parish priests, more of whom are informed by liberation theology and many of whom are engaged in practical social projects in tension with aspects of capitalism or ministering to (and perhaps bolstering the movements of) the poor who suffer in contemporary—secular—circumstances. Likewise, Evangelical Christians in the United States may debate whether to exploit or conserve what they regard as God's Creation—a question about religious engagement with both secular social activity (business, environmental movements) and material conditions in secular time (nature).

Translation and Transformation

For purposes of public discourse in a plural society, Habermas demands that the religious person consider his or her own faith reflexively, see it from the point of view of others, and relate it to secular views. Although this requires a cognitive capacity that not all religious people have, it is not intrinsically contrary to religion, and equivalent demands are placed on all citizens by the ethics of public discourse.[12] Interestingly, Habermas does not think the same demand will be equally challenging for the nonreligious. This seems to be because he does not believe that they have deep, orienting value commitments not readily articulated as moral reasons. That is, Habermas seems to believe that in addition to their judgments of the issues at hand, and perhaps on a different level, religious people make a prior and less rational prejudgment but that the nonreligious are at least potentially free of such prejudgments, making only a variety of judgments.[13] This seems a mistake. Both religious orientations to the world and secular, "Enlightened" orientations depend on strong epistemic and moral commitments made at least partly prerationally.

In any case, the liberal state must avoid transforming "the requisite *institutional* separation of religion and politics into an undue *mental* and *psychological* burden for those of its citizens who follow a faith."[14] And with this in mind, Habermas also suggests that the nonreligious bear a symmetrical burden to participate in the translation of religious contributions to the political public sphere into "properly political" secular terms; that is, they must seek to understand what is being said on religious terms and determine to what extent they can understand it (and potentially agree with it) on their own nonreligious terms. In this way, they will help to make ideas, norms, and insights deriving from religious sources accessible to all and to the more rigorously secular internal discursive processes of the state itself.

This line of argument pushes against a distinction that Habermas has long wanted to maintain between morality and ethics, between procedural commitments to justice and engagements with more particular conceptions of the good life.

We make a *moral* use of practical reason when we ask what is equally good for everyone; we make an *ethical* use when we ask what is respectively good for me or for us. Questions of justice permit under the moral viewpoint what all could will: answers that in principle are universally valid. Ethical questions, on the other hand, can be rationally clarified only in the context of a specific life history or a particular form of life. For these questions depend on the perspective of an individual or a specific collectivity with a desire to know who they are and, at the same time, who they want to be.[15]

Habermas does not abandon the pursuit of a context-independent approach to the norms of justice. But he does now recognize that demanding decontextualization—separation from substantive conceptions of the good life—as a condition for participation in the processes of public reason may itself be unjust.

Habermas wants to find a way to incorporate insights historically bound up with faith (and religious traditions) into the genealogy of public reason. He clearly sees faith as a source of hope, both in the sense of Kant's practical postulate that God must exist and in the sense that it can help to overcome the narrowness of a scientific rationalism always at risk of bias in favor of instrumental over communicative reason. He is prepared also to recognize that reason is not entirely self-founding, especially in the sense that it does not supply the contents of conceptions of the good on its own but also in the sense that the historical shaping of its capacity includes religious influences that cannot be accounted for "within the bounds of reason alone."

This line of thought also raises questions about whether the idea of an autonomous epistemic individual is really viable. Are knowers so discrete? Is knowledge a property of knowers in this classical Cartesian sense? Or do human beings participate in processes of (perhaps always partial) knowledge creation or epistemic gain that are necessarily larger than individuals? Habermas has already criticized the "philosophy of the subject" and argued for an inter-subjective view.[16] It is worth reemphasizing this in relation to secularism, though, since individualist epistemology undergirds many secularist arguments. Two further questions are also opened that may prove challenging for efforts to preserve a strong understanding of (and wide scope for) context independence and universality in moral reasoning. First, is a genealogical or language-theoretical reconstruction of reason adequate without an existential connection between social and cultural history on the one hand and individual biography on the other? Second, is "translation" an adequate conceptualization of what is involved in making religious insights accessible to nonreligious participants in public discourse (and vice versa)?

The two questions are closely related, for the issue is how communication is achieved across lines of deep difference. As helpful as translation may be, it is not the whole story. Rawls uses the notion of translation to describe the ways in which the rational arguments of religious people are rendered accessible to secular interlocutors. This would appear to involve a kind of expurgation as well, the removal of ostensibly untranslatable (because irrational) elements of faith. But translation is also a common metaphor for describing communication across lines of cultural difference; indeed, many anthropologists speak of their work as the "translation of culture." Translation implies that differences between languages can be overcome without interference from deeper differences between cultures or, indeed, from incommensurabilities of languages themselves. It implies a highly cognitive model of understanding, independent of inarticulate connections among meanings or the production of meaning in action rather than passive contemplation.

But the idea of translating religious arguments into terms accessible to secular fellow citizens is more complicated. To be sure, restricting attention to argumentative speech reduces the extent of problems, because arguments are already understood to be a restricted set of speech acts and are more likely to be commensurable than some others. But the meaning of arguments may be more or less embedded in broader cultural understandings, personal experiences, and practices of argumentation that themselves have somewhat different standing in different domains.

Bridging the kinds of hermeneutic distance suggested by the notion of having deeply religious and nonreligious arguments commingle in the public sphere cannot be accomplished by translation alone. Perhaps translation is meant not literally but only as a metaphor for the activity of becoming able to understand the arguments of another—but that is already an important distinction. We are, indeed, more able to understand the arguments of others when we understand more of their intellectual and personal commitments and cultural frames ("where they are coming from," in popular parlance). In this regard, Habermas sometimes signals a "mutual interrogation" or "complementary learning process" that is more than simply translation.[17] This is important and true to his earlier emphasis on intersubjectivity. But this is still a very cognitive conception and one that implies parties to a discussion—perhaps a Platonic symposium—who arrive at new understandings without themselves being changed.[18]

Where really basic issues are at stake, it is often the case that mutual understanding cannot be achieved without change in one or both of the parties. By participating in relationships with one another, including by pursuing rational mutual understanding, we open ourselves to becoming somewhat different people. The same is true at collective levels: mutual engagement across national or cultural or religious frontiers changes the preexisting nations, cultures, and religions, and future improvements in mutual understanding stem from this change, as well as from "translation." Sectarian differences among Protestants or between Protestants and Catholics are thus not merely resolved in rational argumentation. Sometimes they fade without resolution because they simply don't seem as important to either side.[19] A shifting context and changed projects of active engagement in understanding and forming intellectual and normative commitments change the significance of such arguments (as, for example, when committed Christians feel themselves more engaged in arguments with non-Christians and the irreligious—including arguments with those who believe that secular understandings are altogether sufficient—than they are in arguments with one another). But a process of transformation in culture, belief, and self is also often involved. We become people able to understand one another.[20] This may improve our capacity to reason together, but the process of transformation is not entirely rational. It involves particular histories that forge particular cultural connections and commonalities.

Cultures of Integration

National traditions are examples. The Peace of Westphalia did not immediately issue in a world of nation-states, and of course, the hyphen in "nation-state" masked a variety of failures to achieve effective fit between felt peoplehood and political power, legitimacy and sovereignty. Rather, national integration was achieved in processes of cultural integration—sometimes oppressive and sometimes creative—over the next 200 years. The Westphalian settlement informed a process of continuing history in which national projects wove together particular cultural commonalities and collective processes of mutual understanding. This was not entirely a matter of reason, and it is by no means entirely a happy history (the era marked by the Peace of Westphalia led, by way of both empire and nationalism, to world wars). But at least many of the national projects that flourished after 1648, especially in western Europe, produced histories and cultures that both integrated citizens across lines of religious difference and provided for "secular" discourse about the common good (where "secular" means not merely the absence of religion but the capacity for effective discourse across lines of religious difference). National integration was a product of popular demands, as well as elite domination. It is thus an interesting juxtaposition that Habermas's writings on a postsecular era should come on the heels of his considerations of a "postnational constellation."[21] One might suggest that he is calling attention to the contemporary inadequacy of older national identities, traditions, and discursive frameworks to incorporate new religious discourses—and the need to forge new cultures of integration.[22]

Such cultures of integration are historically produced bases for the solidarity of citizens. Whether they can be construed in evolutionary terms as "advances" in truth or only along some other dimension is uncertain. As Eduardo Mendieta suggests, questions of religion crystallize the tension "between reason as a universal standard and the inescapable fact that reason is embodied only historically and in contingent social practices."[23] This bears on the nature of collective commitments to processes of public reason and the decisions they produce. The Rawlsian liberal model itself depends on a "reasonable background consensus" that can establish the terms and conditions of the properly political discourse. Wolterstorff doubts whether this exists.[24] Habermas is more hopeful—and reason for hope seems strongest if what is required is only what Rawls called an "overlapping consensus," not a more universal agreement. Hope may be still greater if the overlapping consensus may be forged in multiple vernaculars and out of cultural mixing, not simply linguistic neutrality.[25] This suggests, however, that what is required is a practical orientation rather than an agreement regarding the truth. This is precisely Wolterstorff's (and Habermas's) concern: "that majority resolutions in an ideologically divided society can at best yield reluctant adaptations to a kind of *modus vivendi*."[26] A utilitarian compromise—based on the expectation of doing better in the next majority vote—is an inadequate basis for continuing solidarity where there is a disagreement not merely over shares of commonly recognized goods but over the very idea of the good: "Conflict on existential values between communities of faith cannot be solved by compromise."[27]

This is, of course, a crucial reason for Habermas to hold that we must separate substantive questions about the good life from procedural questions about just ways of ordering common life. I believe that he retains the conviction that this separation is important and possible.[28] It is intrinsic to his support for constitutional patriotism. But it is challenged by recognition that it may be unjustly difficult or even impossible for religious citizens to give reasons in terms "accessible" to secular citizens. And it is challenged further if one agrees that religious faith but also specificities of cultural traditions may make it difficult for citizens to render all that is publicly important to them in the form of criticizable validity claims.

Conflicts between worldviews and religious doctrines that lay claim to explaining man's position in the world as a whole cannot be laid to rest at the cognitive level. As soon as these cognitive dissonances penetrate as far as the foundations for a normative integration of citizens, the political community disintegrates into irreconcilable segments, so that it can only survive on the basis of an unsteady modus vivendi. In the absence of the uniting bond of a civic solidarity, which cannot be legally enforced, citizens do not perceive themselves as free and equal participants in the shared practices of democratic opinion and will formation wherein they *owe one another reasons* for their political statements and attitudes. This reciprocity of expectations among citizens is what distinguishes a community integrated by constitutional values from a community segmented along the dividing lines of competing worldviews.[29]

The basic question is whether or how much commonalities of belief are crucial to the integration of political communities. How important is it for citizens to believe in the truth of similar propositions "explaining man's position in the world"? At the very least, there are many other sources for the solidarity of citizens, from webs of social relations to institutions and shared culture. Moreover, religion figures in these processes in ways that transcend "beliefs."[30]

Conclusion

Rethinking the implicit secularism in conceptions of citizenship is important for a variety of reasons, from academic soundness to practical fairness. It is all the more important because continuing to articulate norms of citizen participation that seem biased against religious views will needlessly drive a wedge between religious and nonreligious citizens. This would be most unfortunate at a time when religious engagement in public life is particularly active and when globalization, migration, and economic stresses and insecurity all make strengthening commitments to citizenship and participation in shared public discourse vital.

Rethinking secularism need not mean abandoning norms of fairness or state neutrality among religions. It does mean working through the debates of the public sphere to find common ground for citizenship, rather than trying to mandate the common ground by limiting the kinds of reason citizens can bring to their public discussions with one another.

Notes

1. See Ernest H. Kantorowitz, *The King's Two Bodies: A Study in Medieval Political Theology* (Princeton, N.J.: Princeton University Press, 1957).

2. John Rawls, *The Law of Peoples* (Cambridge, Mass.: Harvard University Press, 2001).

3. Page numbers in the following remarks refer to one of several overlapping texts that Habermas published on "Religion in the Public Sphere," *Holberg Prize Symposium for*

2005: Jürgen Habermas, Religion, and the Public Sphere (Bergen: Holberg Prize, 2005). Habermas's thought has (as usual) continued to develop. See *Between Naturalism and Religion* (Cambridge: Polity, 2008) and his contributions to Eduardo Mendieta and Jonathan VanAntwerpen, eds., *The Power of Religion in the Public Sphere* (New York: Columbia University Press, 2011), and Craig Calhoun, Eduardo Mendieta, and Jonathan VanAntwerpen, eds., *Habermas and Religion* (Cambridge: Polity, forthcoming). The continued development hasn't stopped, and a new book is on the way.

4. See Charles Taylor, *Sources of the Self* (Cambridge, Mass.: Harvard University Press, 1989); Charles Taylor, *A Secular Age* (Cambridge, Mass.: Harvard University Press, 2007). Taylor sees frameworks of "strong evaluation" or orientations toward a "fullness" as basic not only for religious people but for everyone, including materialists and others who insist that they act only on interests, not values.

5. Taylor and Habermas explicitly disagree on this point (with some encouragement from me to clarify this) in their dialogue in Mendieta and VanAntwerpen, eds., *The Power of Religion*, 60–67. Taylor holds that many of the issues that Habermas ascribes specifically to religious difference apply to deep cultural differences in general.

6. See, perhaps most notably on this, José Casanova, *Public Religions in the Modern World* (Chicago: University of Chicago Press, 1994).

7. This is a tradition associated with the Enlightenment, which certainly had powerful secularizing dimensions, but it is not altogether true to the historical Enlightenment, which included a variety of religious reformers alongside the committedly antireligious. One has only to ask if Swedenborg and followers such as William Blake really shared nothing with the Enlightenment or to consider the extent to which the Scottish Enlightenment included not just Hume's famous atheism but also the effort of a number of churchgoers both to increase the role of reason and reflection and to minimize the purchase of "enthusiasm." This tradition of reading the Enlightenment as always already radically secular leads also to a misleading grasp of earlier history, as, for example, the vibrant public sphere of seventeenth-century England doesn't figure in Habermas's account of the genesis of the late-eighteenth-century golden age of the public sphere. See David Zaret, *Origins of Democratic Culture: Printing, Petitions, and the Public Sphere in Early Modern England* (Princeton, N.J.: Princeton University Press, 1999), and "Religion, Science, and Printing" in C. Calhoun, ed., *Habermas and the Public Sphere* (Cambridge, Mass.: MIT Press, 1992), 259–288. It is worth noting that the petitions and sermons that Zaret favors as examples reveal the extent to which it is not just religious ideas, matters of content, that figure in the genealogy of public reason but also religious practices and experiences. Reformation-era debates were part of the genesis of a rational-critical form of public reason, and throughout the time since, it has often been in religious contexts that people learned to speak in public and even to participate in reciprocal reason-giving (even if the reasons in question—such as Bible quotations—are not ones that secular rationalists find persuasive). Since the English translation of *Structural Transformation of the Public Sphere* appeared in 1989, identifying earlier and earlier public spheres or proto-public spheres has become a veritable cottage industry among English historians.

8. Jürgen Habermas, "Religion in the Public Sphere," *European Journal of Philosophy* 14, no. 1 (2006): 5.

9. Ibid., 9.

10. Ibid., 12. Habermas has partially but not completely relaxed this notion in subsequent discussions, speaking of explaining religious references in secular terms rather than expunging them. See Mendieta and VanAntwerpen, eds., *The Power of Religion*, 64.

11. See Thomas M. Schmidt's discussion of the role of philosophy of religion in "Religious Pluralism and Democratic Society: Political Liberalism and the Reasonableness of Religious Beliefs," Philosophy and Social Criticism 25, no. 4 (1999): 43–56, but note that expectations for philosophy of religion must be different from expectations for the everyday discourse of civil society, even the public sphere of civil society at its most articulate.

12. This is not to say that religious people will always like being called to such reflexivity. One might argue that the demands that Habermas urges are similar to those that Socrates posed in his questioning of Athenian youth, which did lead to charges of teaching impiety.

13. In *Sources of the Self* (Cambridge, Mass.: Harvard University Press, 1989), Charles Taylor described such strong moral commitments as involving "hypergoods," which set horizons that give perspective to other moral evaluations. While some people may regard themselves as viewing all potential goods equally—say, as merely so many costs or benefits, pleasures or pains in a hedonistic calculus—in fact, their reason typically does involve more or less unarticulated appeals to hypergoods, such as, in this case, the primacy and autonomy of the experiencing individual. See also Hans-Georg Gadamer, *Truth and Method* (New York: Continuum, 1974 [1960]), and Taylor's dialogue with Habermas in Mendieta and VanAntwerpen, eds., *The Power of Religion*, 60–67.

14. Habermas, "Religion in the Public Sphere," 10.

15. The distinction is developed in many works and examined in detail in Jürgen Habermas, *Between Facts and Norms* (Cambridge, Mass.: MIT Press, 1996).

16. Among a range of texts, see Jürgen Habermas, *The Philosophical Discourse of Modernity* (Cambridge, Mass.: MIT Press, 1987).

17. Jürgen Habermas, "Dialektik der Säkularisierung," *Blätter für Deutsche und Internationale Politik* 4 (2008): 33–46. See also Jürgen Habermas and Joseph Ratzinger, *The Dialectics of Secularization* (Fort Collins, Colo.: Ignatius, 2007).

18. This is coupled to a tendency to treat religion mainly as a matter of propositional contents rather than a mode of engagement with the world—prophetic, musical, poetic, prayerful—that exceeds any summarization in a set of truth claims. See Craig Calhoun, "Afterword: Religion's Many Powers," in Mendieta and VanAntwerpen, eds., *The Power of Religion*, 118–132.

19. See Thomas McCarthy, "Legitimacy and Diversity," in Andrew Arato, ed., *Habermas on Law and Democracy* (Berkeley: University of California Press, 1998).

20. See Craig Calhoun, *Critical Social Theory: Culture, History, and the Challenge of Difference* (Oxford: Blackwell, 1995), chap. 2. Such processes of historical transformation are not necessarily advances in reason, they are not necessarily symmetrical, and they are specific histories among multiple possible histories.

21. Jürgen Habermas, *The Postnational Constellation* (Cambridge, Mass.: MIT Press, 2000).

22. See Craig Calhoun, *Nations Matter* (London: Routledge, 2007), on the issue of cultures of integration, the reasons that older national solidarities continue to matter even while the production of new and potentially transcending patterns of integration is under way, and the reasons that transcending the older national solidarities is a matter of new but still historically specific solidarities, not simply cosmopolitan universalism.

23. Eduardo Mendieta, "Introduction," in Habermas, *Religion and Rationality*, 1.

24. Robert Audi and Nicholas Wolterstorff, *Religion in the Public Square* (Lanham, Md.: Rowman and Littlefield, 1997), 160.

25. See Sheldon Pollock, "Cosmopolitan and Vernacular in History," *Public Culture* 12, no. 3 (2000): 591–625; and Audi and Wolterstorff, *Religion in the Public Square*, chap. 4.

26. Audi and Wolterstorff, *Religion in the Public Square*, 13–14.

27. Ibid.

28. For a relatively recent, nuanced statement, see Jürgen Habermas, *Truth and Justification* (Cambridge, Mass.: MIT Press, 2003 [1999]), 213–235.

29. Ibid.

30. Taylor, somewhat surprisingly and for all of his other differences with Habermas, also approaches religion very largely in terms of belief; see Taylor, *A Secular Age*.

{ 4 }

Rehabilitating Secularism
Rajeev Bhargava

During the last three decades, secular states, virtually everywhere, have come under severe strain. It is hardly surprising, then, that political secularism, the doctrine that defends them, has also come under heavy criticism. Some scholars have concluded from this that the criticism is so profound and justified that it is time to abandon political secularism. In this chapter, I do not deny that the crisis of secularism is real, but I reject the conclusion that it should be rejected. There is a big gap between criticizing a practice or an idea and withdrawing support from it. I argue that the criticism of secularism looks indefeasible only because critics have focused on one or two doctrinal versions of Western secularism. I claim that it is time we shifted focus away from doctrines and toward the normative practices of a wide variety of states, including the best practices of non-Western states such as India.

Once we do this, we will begin to see secularism differently, as a critical perspective not against religion but against religious homogenization and institutionalized religious domination. This is why "really existing secularisms" are both more accommodating toward some aspects of religion *and* deeply critical of its other dimensions. Once these alternative conceptions implicit in the normative practices of states are dredged up, we might see that we still do not possess a reasonable, moral, and ethical alternative to secularism. Secularism remains our best bet to help us deal with ever-deepening religious diversity and the problems endemic to it. In short, I argue that we need to rehabilitate, not forsake, secularism.

I

The contemporary crisis of secularism started with the establishment of the first modern theocracy in Iran and spread to Egypt, Sudan, Algeria, Tunisia,

Ethiopia, Nigeria, Chad, Senegal, Turkey, Afghanistan, Pakistan, and Bangladesh.[1] Movements that challenged the seemingly undisputed reign of secular states were not restricted to Muslim societies. Singhalese Buddhist nationalism in Sri Lanka, Hindu nationalists in India, religious ultra-orthodoxy in Israel, and Sikh nationalists who demanded a separate state partly on the ground that Sikhism does not recognize the separation of religion and state all signaled a deep challenge to the secular character of states.[2]

Strong anti-Muslim and anti-Catholic movements of Protestants decrying secular states emerged in Kenya, Guatemala, and the Philippines. Religiously grounded political movements arose in Poland, and Protestant fundamentalism became a force in American politics. In western Europe too, where religion is largely a personal response to divinity still largely private, rather than an organized system of practices, the challenge to the secular character of states has come both from migrant workers of former colonies and from intensified globalization. This has thrown together a privatized Christianity with Islam, Sikhism, and pre-Christian, South Asian religions that do not draw a boundary between the private and the public in the same way. These strange bedfellows have created a deep religious diversity the like of which has never before been known in the West.[3] As the public spaces of Western societies are claimed by these other religions, the weak but distinct public monopoly of single religions is beginning to be challenged by the very norms that govern these societies. This is evident in Germany and Britain but was most dramatically highlighted by the head-scarf issue in France.[4] The suppressed religious past of these societies is now foregrounded, and robust secular character of their states has begun to be questioned.

Only someone with blinkered vision would deny the crisis of secularism. Party idéologues, public intellectuals, and academics, both its supporters and its opponents, share the view that it is endangered. However, an ambiguity lying at the very heart of this claim has not altogether been dispelled: Is the crisis caused primarily by external factors, as when a good thing is undermined by forces always inimical to it, when it falls into incapable or wrong hands, when it is practiced badly? Or is it, rather, that the blemished practice is itself an effect of a deeper conceptual flaw, a bad case of a wrong-footed ideal? Our strategy for how to deal with this crisis will vary depending on how we assess the relative strengths of external and internal threats to secularism. The crisis may be severe but may not go very deep if the problem is one of, say, public translation. For example, Indian critics have frequently argued that secularism has long been confined to an English-speaking, metropolitan elite and has never been properly disseminated to the wider public.[5] If this alone were the case, rehabilitating secularism would mean a reworking of public cultures without any change in the ideal itself. However, if the normative and conceptual structure of the doctrine is blemished, rehabilitation requires a substantial reworking of the ideal itself. I believe that secularism is internally threatened. I agree that the conceptual structure of secularism is not properly worked out and that as it stands, its normative structure is inadequate. At the same time, the conviction that an ideal can be rehabilitated presupposes another belief that it is not irretrievably malfunctional. It follows that the rehabilitation of secularism means seeking an alternative conception of secularism rather than an alternative to secularism.

Identifying an alternative conception is not always easy. In order to do so, we need to keep in mind the distinction between (a) those practices of the state that embody norms governing their relationship with religion; (b) the articulation of these norms in representations and reflections found in laws enacted by legislatures, executive decisions, judicial pronouncements, and constitutional articles; and finally, (c) normative ideals governing the relationship between state and religion and expressed in doctrines, ideologies, and political theories.

I believe that the doctrinal, ideological, and theoretical formulations of Western secularism are by now highly restricted and inadequate. The rehabilitation of secularism is virtually impossible unless we reduce our reliance on these formulations. These doctrines and theories have become part of the problem, hurdles to properly examining the issues at stake. Wittgenstein's warning that the hold of a particular picture is so strong that it prevents, even occludes, awareness of other conceptions of reality is apt here. We are so seized by one or two conceptions that we simply cannot notice other conceptions that have been pushed into the background. Once we have shifted away from currently dominant models and focused on the normative practices of a broader range of Western states beyond the more familiar ones, indeed also on non-Western states, we shall see that better forms of secular states and much more defensible versions of secularisms are available. And although in some contexts, minimally decent religion-centered states may be adequate, by and large, they will not do, because they, too, are as much a part of the problem as are some secular states.

So we need to move away from these doctrinal formulations of political secularism and unearth different versions found in the best practices of many states and in their judicial pronouncements and constitutional articles. Another reason to go to these practices and reflections is that norms implicit in practices keep shifting, but these shifts are largely hidden from public view. When practices that do not match doctrinal formulations come to light, two options are available: first, to withdraw the practice because it falls short of the ideal; second, to withdraw the doctrinal ideal and to rearticulate the norms and build another conception of secularism. When it comes to the crunch, many Western states take the first easy option. They withdraw ethically sensitive, democratically negotiated arrangements and practices and take refuge in the entrenched ideals. This is frequently a retrogressive step. Focusing on normative practices and constitutional articles and refashioning secularism will help us displace a worn-out ideal and shift the norm, bringing it closer to how people wish to lead their lives, rather than how they should lead their lives in accordance with a more or less redundant ideal.

II

Two assumptions must be made explicit before I proceed, one factual, the other normative. The factual component is that most societies today are characterized by religious diversity. The pressing question before us, then, is how we deal with this diversity and the problems that accompany it. The normative component involves a commitment to the view that the question of whether we should retain or abandon a commitment to a secular state—whether we should jettison or try to rehabilitate secularism—cannot be properly answered unless we raise it within a comparativist value-based framework.

What do I mean by religious diversity? To begin with it, I mean diversity *of* religion. Diversity of religion exists in a society when it has a populace professing faith in, say, Christian, Jewish, or Islamic ideals. A society has deep diversity of religion when its people adhere to faiths with very diverse ethoses, origins, and civilizational backgrounds. This happens, for example, when a society has Hindus and Muslims or Hindus and Jews or Buddhists and Muslims and so on. The second kind of diversity is *within* religion. This diversity may be of two kinds. The first might be called horizontal diversity, which exists when a religion is internally differentiated. For example, Christianity has different confessions, denominations, and sects. Muslims are divided into Shi'a, Sunni, Ismaili, Ahmedi, and so on. Likewise, Hindus could be seen to be differentiated into Vaishnavite and Shaivite and so on. Religions are characterized, however, by another kind of diversity, which may be called vertical diversity. Here, people of the same religion may engage in diverse practices that are hierarchically arranged. A religion might mandate that only some may engage in certain kind of practices and others are excluded from them. For example, caste-ridden Hinduism makes a distinction between pure and impure practices. Practices performed by certain castes are pure, and members of other castes are excluded from them. For instance, women or *dalits* may not be allowed entry into the inner sanctum of temples and in many cases even into the precincts of an upper-caste temple. This example already brings home a point that I ought to have made at the very outset of this discussion. Every form of diversity, including religious diversity, is enmeshed in power relations. If so, endemic to every religiously diverse society is an illegitimate use of power whereby the basic interests of one group are threatened by the actions of another. It further follows that inherent in religiously diverse societies is the possibility of both interreligious and intrareligious domination—a broad term that encompasses discrimination, marginalization, oppression, exclusions, and the reproduction of hierarchy.[6] (Two other forms of domination are also possible: the domination by the religious of the nonreligious and the domination of the religious by the nonreligious.)

My second point about answering this question within a comparative framework is grounded in the following conviction. All good ethical reasoning must be contextual and comparative. It must ask not just the question of whether our constitutions should be committed to secular states but, rather, the question of whether, given the context of different forms of religion-related dominations and given the existence of alternatives X, Y, and Z, our constitutions should be committed to secular states. More specifically, we should ask whether, given the existence of religion-related domination and given that the feasible alternatives to secular states are different kinds of religion-centered states, we should be committed to secular states. We should also ask what ethical or moral gains would ensue if we were to transit from religion-centered states to secular states and vice versa. Another way of asking the same question might be: given our commitment to counter the four types of religion-related dominations mentioned above, which of the several kinds of states, religion-centered or secular, will minimize one, some, or all of them? A positive answer in favor of some secular states considerably enhances the prospect of the rehabilitation of secularism.

III

I have spoken above of secular and religion-centered *states*. The use of the plural needs to be stressed, because the internal distinction *within* secular and religion-centered states is as important as the distinction *between* secular and religion-centered states. These two sets of distinctions are important because they help to show (a) why most religious-centered states are likely to encourage religious homogenization and therefore unlikely to reduce forms of domination mentioned above, (b) why, in order to serve the same purposes, some secular states may be even worse than some religion-centered states, and (c) why some forms of secular states may be best equipped to reduce forms of domination and deal sensibly with religious diversity.

RELIGION-CENTERED STATES

What are religion-centered states and secular states? To understand these distinctions, allow me to introduce another set of distinctions. States may be strongly connected to religion or disconnected from it. Such connection or disconnection may exist at three distinct levels: at the level of ends, at the level of institutions and personnel, and at the level of public policy and, even more relevantly, law. With the aid of these conceptual tools, let me first specify what I mean by religion-centered states. Such states are of at least two kinds. The first, theocracy, is connected to religion at all three levels. Here, a priestly class directly rules in accordance with what it believes are divine laws. Thus, there is no distinction between priestly and political orders (strong connection at the level of institutions and personnel). The principal values of religion *are* also the values of the political order (strong connection at the level of ends). Religious precepts themselves have a status of laws. The Islamic republic of Iran as Khomeini aspired to run it is an obvious example.

A theocratic state must be distinguished from a state that establishes religion. Here, religion is granted official, legal recognition by the state, and while both benefit from a formal alliance with each other, the sacerdotal order does not govern a state where religion is established. Because they do not identify or unify church and state but install only an alliance between them, states with an established church are in some ways disconnected from it. In these political orders, there is a sufficient degree of institutional differentiation between the two social entities. Distinct functions are performed in each by different personnel. Yet there is a more significant sense in which the state and the church are connected to each other: they share a common end largely defined by religion. By virtue of a more primary connection of ends, the two benefit from a special relationship with each other. There is, finally, another level of connection between church and state at the level of policy and law. Such policies and laws flow from and are justified in terms of the union or alliance that exists between the state and the church. The institutional *disconnection* of church and state—at the level of roles, functions, and powers—goes hand-in-hand with the first-level and third-level *connection* of ends and policies. It is the second-order disconnection of church and state that differentiates a state with established church/religion from a theocracy.

SECULAR STATES

Secular states are different from both of these religion-centered states. To understand this difference at a more abstract and general level, let me lean once again on the distinction made above and distinguish three orders of disconnection to correspond with the already-identified three orders of connection. A state may be disconnected from religion first at the level of ends, second at the level of institutions, and third at the level of law and public policy. A secular state is both nontheocratic and against the establishment of religions. It establishes neither one religion nor many. The second-order disconnection, church-state separation, demarcates it from a theocracy. The first-order disconnection from religion distinguishes secular states from both theocracies and states with established religion. A secular state has its own secular ends.

AMORAL SECULAR STATES

Secular ends are at the very least of two kinds. The first kind might be called amoral. Amoral secular states are so called because their entire purpose is to maximize power, wealth, or both. They may have moral pretensions but really no commitment to values such as peace, liberty, or equality. Usually, they are imperial and autocratic. A good example of such a predominantly secular state, despite the not-infrequent allegation of its biased, Christian character, is the British colonial state in India, which, motivated almost exclusively by power, wealth, and social order, had a policy of tolerance and neutrality toward different religious communities. This is not surprising, given that empires are interested in the labor or tribute of their subjects, not in their religion. Such self-aggrandizing, amoral states may or may not disconnect with religion at the third level, the level of law and policy. They may have a hands-off approach to all religions, purely for instrumental reasons. However, if it serves their instrumental purpose, they may also connect with religion.

VALUE-BASED SECULAR STATES AND MAINSTREAM, DOCTRINAL SECULARISMS

Distinct from amoral states are value-based secular states. These values include peace, toleration, religious liberty (including the freedom to criticize and revise dominant interpretations of one's own religion and at the very extreme to reject the religion into which one is born), and equality of citizenship in both its passive dimension (the right to receive benefits such as physical security and a minimum of material well-being regardless of one's religion) and its active dimension (the right to vote, to stand for public office, and to participate in public deliberation about matters of common concern).[7]

These value-based secular states differ from one another in their respective understandings of the relationship with religion at the third level. Some are committed to disconnection, by which they mean *mutual exclusion* of religion and state. Such states maintain a policy of strict or absolute separation. Here, religion is excluded from the affairs of the state, but the state, too, is excluded from the affairs of the religion. The state has neither a positive relationship with religion—for example, there is no policy of granting aid to religious institutions—nor a negative relationship with it. It is not within the scope of state activity to interfere in religious matters, even when the values professed by the state are violated. This noninterference is justified on the ground that religion is a private matter, and if something is amiss within the private domain, it can be mended only by those who have a right to do so within that sphere. This, according to proponents of this view, is what religious freedom means. Mutual exclusion is justified on grounds of negative liberty and is identical with the privatization of religion. Others reject complete disconnection and adopt instead a policy of *one-sided exclusion* of religion from state. Such states exclude religions in order to control or regulate them and sometimes even to destroy them. This control may be exercised by hindering religions or sometimes even by helping them, but the motive in both cases is to control them, largely because of the belief that religion is false consciousness or obscurantist or superstition or because they see religion as intrinsically oppressive and hierarchical. Thus, intervention in religion may be justified also on grounds of freedom and equality. Such secular states are decidedly antireligious. Finally, there are still other states that reject both one-sided exclusion and mutual exclusion and follow a policy of *principled distance*, a sophisticated relation with religion in which the state may connect or disconnect with religion depending entirely on whether the values to which it is committed are promoted or undermined by one or the other way of relating to religion.

There are at least three types of secular states and several versions of secularism. The first type includes amoral secular states, which are likely to fare poorly on an index of freedom and inequality. The second type includes states that have strongly perfectionist ends, a single, robust conception of the good life, which translates into deep skepticism about the truth claims and value of religions, about their public role, and about their capacity ever to prevent forms of oppression and domination. This is true in different degrees of some of the formerly Communist states, of the Republican conception that pervaded the public life in France, and of strongly perfectionist liberal conceptions that invoke rational autonomy to rebuke religions. These antireligious secular states have a poor record in promoting or even protecting religious freedom. Indeed, states that fail to protect religious freedom usually trample on other freedoms, too. Over time, they also develop a hierarchy between the secular and the religious and might perpetuate the domination by the nonreligious of the religious. Thus, such states are also likely to fare badly on the index of freedom and equality, because in order to promote more rigorous conceptions of positive freedoms and substantive equalities, they may cross minimal thresholds of morality and decency. If they are insensitive to interreligious inequalities because their brand of secularism blinds them to the religious content of their culture, they may even unwittingly perpetuate interreligious domination.

That leaves us with only one other type of secular state, one that erects a wall of separation between itself and religion to protect freedom and equality. Such a state is likely to fare well on an index of minimal conceptions of negative liberty and procedural equality. But such a conception has no room for positive freedom. It cannot get the state to act in ways that might facilitate freedom and equality. For it, any intervention is tantamount to control. The only way to respect religion is to leave it alone. Moreover, it might be indifferent to the lack of freedom and equality within religions. It is even more indifferent to inequalities between religions, between majority and minority religions. Deep down, it allows, sometimes in unnoticed and very subtle ways, both intra- and interreligious dominations.

Our public and political culture is dominated by these forms of secular states and these antireligious, republican, or libertarian conceptions, doctrines, and theories of secularism. Each of these conceptions disseminates images and representations either of the sidelining of religion altogether or of indifference to, if not exactly encouragement of, subtle forms of interreligious domination.

Add to this the widespread feeling among ordinary citizens everywhere—people who also happen to be engaged in everyday forms of religiosity—that secular states that run in accordance with these doctrinal secularisms are also amoral, if not inside their own countries, then at least with respect to the world outside. This makes the crisis of secularism even more severe.

All of this has not gone unnoticed in academic literature. Several critics have noted the problems of secularism (although they frequently fail to see, in fact, that they focus only on doctrinal and ideological formulations of secularism). First, secularism takes separation to mean exclusion of all religions on a non-preferential basis. It wishes by fiat to eliminate religion from public life and from politics more generally. For example, liberal secularism enjoins the citizen to support only those coercive laws for which there is public justification. Why? Because if others are expected to follow a law in terms that they do not understand and for reasons or justifications that they cannot endorse, then the principle of equal respect is violated.[8] If other reasonable and conscientious citizens have good reason to reject a particular rationale in support of a coercive law, then this rationale does not count as public justification. Because a religious rationale is a paradigmatic case of a reason that other citizens have good reasons to reject, it does not count as public justification, and because it does not count as public justification, a law grounded solely on a religious rationale must never be enacted. In short, purely religious convictions or commitments have no role to play in democratic and pluralist polities. This requirement that religious reasons be excluded from liberal democratic politics is offensive to religious persons who, like others, wish to support their favored political commitments on the basis of their conscience.[9] If people believe that their politics must be consistent with their morality and, since morality is derived from religion, with their religious connections, then why should they be discouraged or stigmatized for doing so? Besides, it is a mistake to assume that only religious people bring passion and sectarianism into politics or, as Richard Rorty believes, that only religion is a conversation stopper.[10] By asking a religious person to exercise restraint and exclude religious reasons in his or her justification for a coercive law, liberal secularism forces that person to act against his or her conscience, and in doing so, it fails not only to respect the moral agency of that person but also violates its own principle of equal respect. Indeed, the demand that restraint be exercised is counterproductive, because exclusion from the larger public sphere forces the religious to form their own narrow public where resentment and prejudice will flourish.[11] This would lead not only to the freezing of identities but also to the building of unbreachable walls between religious and nonreligious citizens. Therefore, "engagement with religious people is typically better than shunning them."[12]

Second, this secularism does not understand the believer's life as it is lived from the inside. It misses out on perhaps the most significant feature of most religions: that they encourage their members to choose to live a disciplined, restricted, rule-bound, and desire-abnegating life. A religious life is not just a life of personal and whimsical attachment to a personal God but one in which one submits to his commands and lives obediently by them. This may be a nightmare for a standard liberal but gets the constitutive features of most religions rather better than liberal secularism does.

Third, by interpreting separation as exclusion, it betrays its own sectarianism; it can live comfortably with liberal, Protestantized, individualized, and privatized religions but has no resources to cope with religions that mandate greater public or political presence or have a strong communal orientation. This group-insensitivity of secularism makes it virtually impossible for it to accommodate community-specific rights and therefore to protect the rights of religious minorities. In short, while this secularism copes with interreligious domination, it does not possess resources to deal with interreligious domination.

Fourth, Western secularism is a product of Protestant ethic and is shaped by it. Therefore, its universal pretensions are perhaps its greatest drawback. Moreover, it presupposes a Christian civilization that is easily forgotten because, over time, it has silently slid into the background. Christianity allows this self-limitation, and much of the world innocently mistakes this rather cunning self-denial for its disappearance.[13] But if this is so, this "inherently dogmatic" secularism cannot coexist innocently with other religions.[14] Given the enormous power of the state, it must try to shape and transform them—a clear instance of illegitimate influence, if not outright violence. Thus, with all of its claims of leaving religions alone, of granting religions liberty, this secularism is hostile to nonliberal, non-Protestant believers.[15] Overall, it would not be wrong to say, then, that this secularism forces upon us a choice between active hostility and benign indifference.

Fifth, liberal secularism relies excessively on a rationalist conception of reason that imposes unfair limits on the manner in which issues are to be brought into the public domain. Some issues are constitutively emotive; others become emotive because they are articulated by people who are not always trained to be rational in the way liberals mandate.[16] In short, the model of moral reasoning typical of secularism is context-insensitive, theoreticist, absolutist (noncomparative), enjoining us to think in terms of this or that, and too heavily reliant on monolithic ideas or values considered to be true or superior or wholly nonnegotiable.

These are powerful critiques, and I agree with some of them. But I also have serious disagreement with the conclusion that they rebut political secularism altogether. I agree that in our imagination of social and public life, greater space must be given to nonliberal religions; such ways of life have moral integrity that liberal secularism frequently fails to realize. Yet in our effort to accommodate such religions, we cannot ignore that these very religions also continue to be a source of severe oppression and exclusion. States that align with religions frequently condone these morally objectionable practices. In Pakistan, the religiously sanctioned law of evidence, Qanoon-e-Shahadat, holds on par the evidence of two women or two non-Muslims with that of a single male Muslim, thereby establishing the intrinsic superiority of Muslim men over women and minorities and contravening the fundamental principle of equality.[17] In Hinduism, religiously sanctioned customs related to purity and pollution continue to exclude women from the affairs of their own religion and perpetuate an institutionalized system of subordination of women.

Indeed, if we contrast these secular states with religion-centered states, and provided that we have a sustained commitment to the reduction of religion-related domination, we might rediscover our faith, if not exactly in existing secular states, at least in the prospect of rehabilitating secularism. Even a cursory evaluation of these states shows that they are all deeply troublesome. Take the first historical instances of states that established a single church—the unreformed established Protestant churches of England, Scotland, and Germany and the Catholic churches in Italy and Spain—in which the state recognized a particular version of the religion enunciated by that church as the official religion, compelled individuals to congregate for only one church, punished them for failing to profess a particular set of religious beliefs, levied taxes in support of one particular church, paid the salaries of its clergy, and made instruction of the favored interpretation of the religion mandatory in educational institutions or in the media.[18] In such cases, there was inequality not only among religions (Christians and Jews) but also among the churches of the same religion, and while members of the established church may have enjoyed a modicum of religious liberty, those belonging to other churches or religions did not enjoy any or the same degree of liberty.[19] States with substantive establishments have not changed color with time. Wherever one religion is not only formally but substantively established, the persecution of minorities and internal dissenters continues today.[20] One has to cite only the example of Saudi Arabia to prove this point.[21] In many states, political exclusion is built into the basic law of the land. By making adherence to a particular religion mandatory for anyone aspiring to the highest offices in the country, religion-centered constitutions ensure the exclusion of religious minorities from high political office. Pakistan is a good example.[22] What of states with multiple establishments of churches? Historically, New York or Massachusetts in the middle of the seventeenth century officially respected more than one denomination.[23] These states levied a religious tax on everyone and yet gave individuals the choice to remit the tax money to their preferred church. They financially aided schools run by religious institutions but on a nondiscriminatory basis. They may have punished people for disavowing or disrespecting the established religion but did not compel them to profess the beliefs of a particular denomination.

States with substantive establishment of multiple churches or religions are better in some ways than states with singular establishment. For example, such states are likely to be relatively peaceful. Members of different denominations are likely to tolerate one another. There may be general equality among all members of a religion (although, historically, this has not always been the case, women and blacks have been the usual victims in the United States). The state grants each denomination considerable autonomy in its own affairs. But states with establishment of multiple churches have their limitations. For a start, they may continue to persecute members of other religions and atheists. Second, they are indifferent to the liberty of individuals within each denomination or religious group. They do little to foster a more general climate of toleration that prevents the persecution of dissenters. Closed and oppressive communities can thrive in such contexts. Third, they may not have legal provisions that allow an individual to exit from his or her religious community and embrace another religion or to remain unattached to any religion whatsoever. Fourth, such states give recognition to particular religious identities but fail to recognize what may be called nonparticularized identities, those that simultaneously refer to several particular identities or transcend all of them. Fifth, such states are unconcerned with the *nonreligious* liberties of individuals or groups. Finally, such states are entirely indifferent to citizenship rights.

What lessons are to be learned from this discussion of secular and religion-centered states? What does all of this show? It demonstrates three things. First, we must be sensitive simultaneously to the moral integrity of liberal and non-liberal religious ways of living, as well as to religion-based oppression and exclusions. Second, states that are strongly aligned to religions may be sensitive to the moral integrity of nonliberal religions but not always to their oppressions. Third, a policy of noninterference (mutual exclusion) typical of liberal secularism is self-defeating. In short, a conception of secularism needs to be worked out that goes beyond liberal, libertarian, and republican theories and does justice to both of the dimensions referred to above. Moreover, we need to combat the doctrinal and theoretical version of secularism that appears aggressive, aims to install a fully secularized state, one that strictly separates itself from completely privatized religions, or has a project of taking away from religion any role in public life. The proper way to fight this is not to indulge in purely negative critiques but to offer constructive alternatives. In this context, a general failure to explore alternative versions of secularism that are able effectively to meet the challenge of some of these critiques and imaginatively open up new possibilities of expanding our horizons is deeply disappointing. But do such versions exist? I think that such a version that is not parochial, neither wholly Christian nor Western, does exist. This model meets the secularist objection to nonsecular states and the religious objection to some forms of secular states. Where do we look in order to identify this model? I believe that we have to go to the practices and less doctrinal statements— the normative practices of the French, British, even American states. Just one example is the public funding of faith-based schools. Officially, American secularism does not sanction public financing of religion. Yet public funding of religion exists, albeit without proper assessment of the dilemmas of recognition and cooperation. Likewise, in practice, the French state not only directly and indirectly funds Roman Catholic schools but also tries to accommodate even Muslim minorities.[24]

However, to illustrate my point, I shall go to the Indian example, because it is what I know best. When we examine its best practices and constitutional articles, we can identify seven features of Indian secularism that clearly mark it out from other variants. First is its multivalue character. Indian secularism more explicitly registers its ties with values forgotten by Western conceptions—for example, peace among communities—and interprets liberty and equality both individualistically and nonindividualistically. It has a place not only for the rights of individuals to profess their religious beliefs but also for the right of religious communities to establish and maintain educational institutions crucial for the survival and sustenance of their religious traditions. Second, because it was born in a deeply multireligious society, it is concerned as much with interreligious domination as with intrareligious domination. Thus, it recognizes community-specific sociocultural rights. Although community-specific political rights (special representation rights for religious minorities such as Muslims) were withheld in India for contextual reasons, the conceptual space for them is present within the model. Third, it is committed to the idea of principled distance, poles apart from one-sided exclusion, mutual exclusion, and strict neutrality or equidistance.

In addition to these features, there are others that further distinguish Indian secularism from the mainstream conception. Fourth, it admits a distinction between depublicization and depoliticization, as well as between different kinds of depoliticization. Because it is not hostile to the public presence of religion, it does not aim to depublicize it. It accepts the importance of one form of depoliticization of religion, namely, the first- and second-level disconnection of state from religion, but the third-level depoliticization of religion is permitted purely on contextual grounds. Fifth, it is marked by a unique combination of active hostility to some aspects of religion (a ban on unsociability and a commitment to make religiously grounded personal laws more gender-just) with active respect for its other dimensions (religious groups are officially recognized, state aid is available nonpreferentially to educational institutions run by religious communities, and there is no blanket exclusion of religion as mandated by Western liberalism). This is a direct consequence of its commitment to multiple values and principled distance. The Indian model accepts the view that critique is consistent with respect, that one does have to choose between hostility and respectful indifference. In this sense, it inherits the tradition of the great Indian religious reformers who tried to change their religions precisely because it meant so much to them. Sixth, it is committed to a different model of moral reasoning that is highly contextual and opens up the possibility of different societies working out their own secularisms. In short, it opens out the possibility of multiple secularisms. Seventh, it breaks out of the rigid interpretative grid that divides our social world into the Western modern and the traditional, indigenous non-Western. Indian secularism is modern but departs significantly from mainstream conceptions of Western secularism.

PRINCIPLED DISTANCE

Let me further elucidate two of these features: Indian secularism's contextual character and the idea of principled distance. As seen above, for mainstream Western secularism, separation means mutual exclusion. The idea of principled distance unpacks the metaphor of separation differently. It accepts a disconnection between state and religion at the level of ends and institutions but does not make a fetish of it at the third level of policy and law. (This distinguishes it from all other models of secularism, moral and amoral, that disconnect state and religion at this third level.) How else can it be in a society where religion frames some of its deepest interests? Recall that political secularism is an ethic whose concerns relating to religion are similar to theories that oppose unjust restrictions on freedom, morally indefensible inequalities, intercommunal domination, and exploitation. Yet a secularism based on principled distance is not committed to the mainstream Enlightenment idea of religion. It accepts that humans have an interest in relating to something beyond themselves, including God, and that this manifests itself as individual belief and feeling, as well as social practice in the public domain. It also accepts that religion is a cumulative tradition, as well as a source of people's identities.[25] But it insists that even if it turned out that God exists and that one religion is true and others are false, then this does not give the "true" doctrine or religion the right to force itself down the throats of others who do not believe it. Nor does it give a ground for discrimination in the equal distribution of liberties and other valuable resources.

Similarly, a secularism based on principled distance accepts that religion may not have special public significance antecedently written into and defining the very character of the state or the nation, but it does not follow from this that it has no public significance at all. Sometimes, in some versions of it, the wall-of-separation thesis assumes precisely that. As long as religion is publicly significant, a democratic state simply has to take it into account. Indeed, institutions of religion may influence individuals as long as they do so through the same process, by access to the same resources as anyone, and without undue advantage or unduly exploiting the fears and vulnerabilities that frequently accompany people in their experience of the religious.

But what precisely is principled distance? The policy of principled distance entails a flexible approach to the question of inclusion or exclusion of religion and the engagement or disengagement of the state, which at the third level of law and policy depends on the context, nature, or current state of relevant religions. This engagement must be governed by principles undergirding a secular state, that is, principles that flow from a commitment to the values mentioned above. This means that religion may intervene in the affairs of the state if such intervention promotes freedom, equality, or any other value integral to secularism. For example, citizens may support a coercive law of the state grounded purely in a religious rationale if this law is compatible with freedom or equality.[26] Equally, the state may engage with religion or disengage from it, engage positively or negatively, but it does so depending entirely on whether or not these values are promoted or undermined. A state that intervenes or refrains from interference on this basis keeps a principled distance from all religions. This is one constitutive idea of principled distance. This idea is different from strict neutrality, whereby the state may help or hinder all religions to an equal degree and in the same manner, and if it intervenes in one religion, it must also do so in others. Rather, it rests on a distinction between equal treatment and treating everyone as an equal.[27] The principle of equal treatment, in the relevant political sense, requires that the state treat all of its citizens equally in the relevant respect, for example, in the distribution of a resource of opportunity. On the other hand, the principle of treating people as equals entails that every person or group is treated with equal concern and respect. This second principle may sometimes require equal treatment, say, equal distribution of resources, but it may also occasionally dictate unequal treatment. Treating people or groups as equals is entirely consistent with differential treatment. This idea is the second ingredient in what I have called principled distance.

I said that principled distance allows for differential treatment. What kind of treatment do I have in mind? First, religious groups have sought exemptions from practices in which states intervene by promulgating a law to be applied neutrally to the rest of society. This demand for noninterference is made on the ground either that the law requires them to do things not permitted by their religion or that it prevents them from doing acts mandated by it. For example, Sikhs demand exemptions from mandatory helmet laws and from police dress codes to accommodate religiously required turbans. Muslim women and girls demand that the state not interfere in their religiously required *chador*. Jews and Muslims seek exemption from Sunday closing laws on the ground that this is not required by their religion. Principled distance allows, then, that a practice that is banned or regulated in one culture may be permitted in the minority culture because of the distinctive status and meaning that it has for its members. For the mainstream conception, this is a problem because of the simple, somewhat absolutist morality that gives overwhelming importance to one value, particularly to equal treatment, equal liberty, or equality of individual citizenship. Religious groups may demand that the state refrain from interference in their practices, but they may equally demand that the state interfere in such a way as to give them special assistance so that these groups are also able to secure what other groups are able to get routinely by virtue of their social dominance in the political community. It may grant authority to religious officials to perform legally binding marriages or to have their own rules or methods of obtaining a divorce. Principled distance allows the possibility of such policies on the grounds that to hold people accountable to an unfair law is to treat them as unequals.

However, principled distance is not just a recipe for differential treatment in the form of special exemptions. It may even require state intervention in some religions more than in others, considering the historical and social conditions of all relevant religions. For the promotion of a particular value constitutive of secularism, some religion, relative to other religions, may require more interference from the state. For example, if the value to be advanced is social equality and requires in part undermining caste hierarchies, then the state must interfere in caste-ridden Hinduism more than, say, in Islam or Christianity. However, if a diversity-driven religious liberty is the value to be advanced by the state, then it may have to intervene in Christianity and Islam more than in Hinduism. If this is so, the state can neither strictly exclude considerations emanating from religion nor keep strict neutrality with respect to religion. It cannot antecedently decide that it will always refrain from interfering in religions or that it will interfere in each equally. Indeed, it may not relate to every religion in society in exactly the same way or intervene in each religion to the same degree or in the same manner. To want to do so would be plainly absurd. All it must ensure is that the relationship between the state and religions is guided by nonsectarian motives consistent with some values and principles.

How is principled distance different from the very productive idea introduced into the discourse by Alfred Stepan? For Stepan, both democratic institutions and religion must tolerate each other.[28] This means (a) that religious institutions should not have "constitutionally privileged prerogatives" that allow them authoritatively to mandate public policy to democratically elected governments and (b) that individuals and religious communities must have complete freedom to worship privately, to advance their values in civil society publicly, to sponsor organizations and movements in political society and even to form political parties, as long as the liberties of other citizens, democratic institutions, and the law are not violated. These two minimal freedoms, for Stepan, are compatible with a broad range of patterns of religion-state relations in political systems. Thus, democracy requires neither strict separation of religion and the state nor hostility toward religion. Clearly, we both agree that idealized versions of American or French conceptions of secularism are not required for democracy. We are committed to the same values and reject mutual exclusion and one-sided exclusion of religion from state. What, then, is the difference between us? First, the idea of principled distance is less friendly to any kind of establishment of religion in religiously diverse societies. For the principled-distance variety of secularism, even formal establishment of religion violates minimal notions of equality of citizenship. Second, the notion of twin tolerations is far more ambiguous regarding whether or not the state may facilitate the exercise of religious freedom by communities, particularly minority communities. It also does not explicitly specify the conditions under which the state may intervene in religions to promote more substantive conceptions of equality, say, gender equality or intercaste equality within religion.

CONTEXTUAL SECULARISM

A context-sensitive secularism, based on the idea of principled distance, is what I call contextual secularism. Contextual secularism is contextual not only because it captures the idea that the precise form and content of secularism will vary from one to another context and from place to place but also because it embodies a certain model of contextual moral reasoning. It does because of its character as a multivalue doctrine. To accept that secularism is a multivalue doctrine is to acknowledge that its constitutive values do not always sit easily with one another. On the contrary, they are frequently in conflict. Some degree of internal discord and therefore a fair amount of instability are an integral part of contextual secularism. For this reason, it forever requires fresh interpretations, contextual judgments, and attempts at reconciliation and compromise. No general a priori rule of resolving these conflicts exists, no easy lexical order, no preexisting hierarchy among values or laws that enables us to decide that no matter what the context, a particular value must override everything else. Almost everything, then, is a matter of situational thinking and contextual reasoning. Whether one value overrides or is reconciled with another cannot be decided beforehand. Each time, the matter presents itself differently and will be differently resolved. If this is true, then the practice of secularism requires a different model of moral reasoning from the one that straitjackets our moral understanding in the form of well-delineated, explicitly stated rules.[29] This contextual secularism recognizes that the conflict between individual rights and group rights cannot always be adjudicated by a recourse to some general and abstract principle. Rather, these conflicts can only be settled case by case and may require a fine balancing of competing claims. The eventual outcome may not be wholly satisfactory to either but still be reasonably satisfactory to both. Multivalue doctrines such as secularism encourage accommodation—not giving up one value for the sake of another but, rather, their reconciliation and possible harmonization, to make each work without changing the basic content of apparently incompatible concepts and values.

This endeavor to make concepts, viewpoints, and values work simultaneously does not amount to a morally objectionable compromise. Rather, it captures a way of thinking characterized by the following dictum: "why look at things in terms of this or that, why not try to have both this and that"?[30] In this way of thinking, it is recognized that although we may currently be unable to secure the best of both values and therefore be forced to settle for a watered-down version of each, we must continue to have an abiding commitment to search for a transcendence of this second-best condition.[31] It is frequently argued against Indian secularism that it is contradictory because it tries to bring together individual and community rights and that articles in the Indian constitution that have a bearing on the secular nature of the Indian state are deeply conflictual and at best ambiguous.[32] This is to misrecognize a virtue as a vice. In my view, this attempt to bring together seemingly incompatible values is a great strength of Indian secularism. Indian secularism is an ethically sensitive negotiated settlement between diverse groups and divergent values. When it is not treated as such, it turns either into a dead formula or a façade for political maneuvers.

IS SECULARISM A CHRISTIAN AND WESTERN DOCTRINE?

What, then, of the claim that secularism is a Christian, Western doctrine and therefore is unable to adapt itself easily to the cultural conditions of, say, India, infused as they are by religions that grew in the soil of the subcontinent. As the Indian example shows, this necessary link between secularism and Christianity is exaggerated, if not entirely mistaken. It is true that the institutional separation of church and state is an internal feature of Christianity and an integral part of Western secularisms. But as we have seen, this church-state disconnection is a necessary but not a sufficient condition for the development of secularism even in societies with church-based religions. It is clearly not a necessary condition for the development of all forms of secularisms. Moreover, as I have argued, the mutual exclusion of religion and the state is not the defining feature of secularism. The idea of separation can be interpreted differently. Nor are religious integrity, peace, and toleration (interpreted broadly to mean "live and let live") uniquely Christian values. Most non-Christian civilizations have given significant space to each. Therefore, none of them is exclusively Christian. It follows that even though we find in Christian writings some of the clearest and most systematic articulation of this doctrine, even the Western conception of secularism is not exclusively Christian.

All right, one might say, secularism is not just a Christian doctrine, but is it not Western? The answer to this question is both yes and no. Up to a point, it is certainly a Western idea. More specifically, as a clearly articulated doctrine, it has distinct Western origins. Although elements that constitute secularism assume different cultural forms and are found in several civilizations, one cannot deny that the idea of the secular first achieved self-consciousness and was properly theorized in the West. One might then say that the early and middle history of secularism is almost entirely dominated by Western societies. However, the same cannot be said of its later history. Nationalism and democracy arrived in the West after the settlement of religious conflicts, in societies that had been made religiously homogeneous or had almost become so (with

the exception of the Jews, of course, who continued to face persistent persecution). The absence of deep religious diversity and conflict meant that issues of
citizenship could be addressed almost entirely disregarding religious context;
the important issue of community-specific rights to religious groups could be
wholly ignored. This had a decisive bearing on the Western conception of secularism. However, for non-Western societies, such as India, the case is different.
Both national and democratic agendas in countries such as India had to face
issues raised by deep religious difference and diversity. In India, nationalism
had to choose between the religious and the secular. Similarly, the distribution
of active citizenship rights could not be conceived or accomplished by ignoring
religion. It could be done either by actively disregarding religion (as in all
political rights) or by developing a complex attitude toward it, as in the case of
cultural rights, where it had to balance claims of individual autonomy with
those of community obligations and claims of the necessity of keeping religion
"private" with its inescapable, often valuable presence in the public. By doing
so, Indian secularism never completely annulled particular religious identities.

In addressing these complex issues, the idea of political secularism was taken
further than it had been evolved in the West. Mainstream theories or ideologies
in modern, Western societies have taken little notice of these features. Hence,
they are struggling to deal with the postcolonial religious diversity of their societies. The later history of secularism is more non-Western than Western.[33] In
the past, I have suggested that to discover its own rich and complex structure,
Western secularism can either look backward, to its own past, or else look side-
ways, at Indian secularism, which mirrors not only the past of secularism but,
in a way, also its future. Doing so will certainly benefit the secularisms of many
Western societies. For example, French secularism needs to look beyond its
own conceptions of *läicité* in order to take into account its own multicultural
and multireligious reality. It cannot continue to take refuge in claims of exceptionalism. A good, hard look at Indian secularism could also change the
self-understanding of other Western secularisms, including a very individualist
American liberal secularism. I would now add that these models can be altered
and reinvigorated, at least partly, also by unearthing their own best contemporary practices. An articulation of these practices would show that these models
are closer to the Indian variant and quite far removed from their theoretical
and doctrinal self-understandings.

Let me sum up. How can secularism be rehabilitated? For a start, we should
jettison seeing secularism as a mere strategy, even as an institutional strategy.
Second, secularism should sever its ties with amoral secular states. This means
coming to realize that, somewhat paradoxically, secularism is against some
secular states. Third, the discussion of secular states must be done with a model
of comparative moral and ethical reasoning. Fourth, we must rethink disconnection or separation and jettison the hold of two hitherto paradigmatic models
of exclusion and talk instead in terms of principled distance. Fifth, the ends in

question should be a mixture of the moral and the ethical. Put differently, the focus should be on ending religion-related domination. Sixth, political secularism must be viewed as part of critical social secularism, indeed, as a self-critical social perspective that is against four types of domination: interreligious, intrareligious, domination of religious by secular, and domination of secular by religious. We need to conceive it anew as not against religion but against institutionalized religious domination. Finally, we need to give up the binary opposition between the secular and the religious. A new, refashioned conception of secularism must not see a necessary opposition between the secular and the religious. On the contrary, it must encourage a way of conceiving a world inhabited by both religious and nonreligious people but where the four religion-related dominations, particularly intra- and interreligious dominations, are minimized, if not altogether eliminated.

Notes

1. David Westerlund, *Questioning the Secular State* (London: Hurst, 1996). Gilles Kepel, *The Revenge of God: The Resurgence of Islam, Christianity, and Judaism in the Modern World* (University Park, Pa.: Penn State University Press, 1994). I. Ahmed, *The Concept of an Islamic State: An Analysis of the Ideological Controversy in Pakistan* (London: Frances Pinter, 1987). Amena Mohsin, "National Security and the Minorities: The Bangladesh Case," in D. L. Sheth and Gurpreet Mahajan, eds., *Minority Identities and the Nation-State* (New Delhi: Oxford University Press, 1999).

2. Mark Juergensmeyer, *New Cold War? Religious Nationalism Confronts the Secular State* (Berkeley: University of California Press, 1994).

3. Bryan S. Turner, "Cosmopolitan Virtue: On Religion in a Global Age," *European Journal of Social Theory* 4, no. 2 (2001): 134.

4. Jane Freedman, "Secularism as a Barrier to Integration? The French Dilemma," *International Migration* 42, no. 3 (2004): 5–27.

5. Sudipta Kaviraj, "Religion, Politics and Modernity," in U. Baxi and B. Parekh, eds., *Crisis and Change in Contemporary India*, (Delhi: Sage, 1995), 295–316.

6. Of course, what is dominant is hard to identify; a practice that is freedom-enabling may itself have another aspect to it that is the carrier of domination. The same practice may be both freedom- and domination-enhancing. Furthermore, what is freedom to one might be domination to other. In a controversial example, veiling is a marker of inequality, of sexist oppression, but it may also be a marker of individual identity and of protest against interreligious domination.

7. For a fuller discussion, see Rajeev Bhargava, "The Distinctiveness of Indian Secularism," in T. N. Srinivasan, ed., *The Future of Secularism* (Oxford: Oxford University Press, 2007).

8. Robert Audi, "The Place of Religious Argument in a Free and Democratic Society," *San Diego Law Review* 30 (Fall 1993): 701. Lawrence Solum, "Faith and Justice," *DePaul Law Review* 39 (1990): 1095. Stephen Macedo, *Liberal Virtues: Citizenship, Virtue and Community in Liberal Constitutionalism* (Oxford: Clarendon, 1990), 249. John Rawls, *A Theory of Justice* (Cambridge, Mass.: Belknap, 1971), 337–338. Paul Weithman, *Religion*

and Contemporary Liberalism (Notre Dame, Ind.: University of Notre Dame Press, 1997), 6. Charles Larmore, *The Morals of Modernity* (Cambridge: Cambridge University Press, 1996), 137.

9. Michael J. Sandel, "Freedom of Conscience or Freedom of Choice," in Terry Eastland, ed., *Religious Liberty in the Supreme Court* (Washington, D.C.: Ethics and Public Policy Center, 1993), 483–496.

10. Richard Rorty, "Religion as a Conversation Stopper," Common Knowledge 3, no. 1 (1994): 2.Christopher J. Eberle, *Religious Conviction in Liberal Politics* (Cambridge: Cambridge University Press, 2002), 77.

11. Jeff Spinner-Halev, *Surviving Diversity: Religion and Democratic Citizenship* (Baltimore, Md.: Johns Hopkins University Press, 2000), 150–156.

12. Ibid., 155.

13. William E. Connolly, *Why I Am Not a Secularist* (Minneapolis: University of Minnesota Press, 1999), 24.

14. John Keane, "Secularism?" *Political Quarterly* 71, no. 1 (2000): 14. T. N. Madan, "Secularism in Its Place," in Rajeev Bhargava, ed., *Secularism and Its Critics* (New Delhi: Oxford University Press, 1998), 298.

15. Philip Hamburger, *Separation of Church and State* (Cambridge, Mass.: Harvard University Press, 2002), 193–251.

16. Connolly, *Why I Am Not a Secularist*, 27.

17. Perhaps the most outrageous instance of indirect internal exclusion is the Hudood ordinance, an antiwomen measure that punishes women who are unable to establish that they have been raped. Under the Hudood ordinance, rape convictions require four male witnesses. A failure to produce such witnesses results in the prosecution of the complainant, who is liable for punishment for fornication (*zina*). See Iftikhar H. Malik, *Religious Minorities in Pakistan* (London: Minority Rights Group International, 2002), 18.

18.Leonard W. Levy, *The Establishment Clause: Religion and the First Amendment* (Chapel Hill: University of North Carolina Press, 1994), 5.

19. One exception to this, however, was the Millet system of the Ottoman Empire, which had Islam as the established religion but in which three other religious communities—Greek Orthodox, Armenian Orthodox, and Jewish—were treated as equals and given a respectable degree of autonomy.

20. The distinction between formal and substantive establishment is important. In Saudi Arabia, Islam is both formally and substantively established. Britain has a formally established church (the Anglican Church). But apart from a few exceptions, only a secular state grants liberty and equality to all.

21. Malise Ruthven, *A Fury for God: The Islamist Attack on America* (London: Granta, 2002), 172–181.

22. Malik, *Religious Minorities*, 16.

23. Levy, *The Establishment Clause*, 12.

24. But such acts of accommodation coexist clumsily, sometimes with official denials in public.

25. Wilfred Cantwell Smith, *The Meaning and End of Religion* (Minneapolis, Minn.: First Fortress, 1991), 154–169.

26. Principled distance rejects the standard liberal idea that the principle of equal respect is best realized only when people come into the public domain by leaving their reli-

gious reasons behind. Principled distance does not discourage public justification. Indeed, it encourages people to pursue public justification. However, if the attempt at public justification fails, it enjoins religiously minded citizens to abandon restraint and support coercive laws that are consistent with freedom and equality based purely on religious reasons. See Christopher Eberle, *Religious Conviction in Liberal Politics* (Cambridge: Cambridge University Press, 2002).

27. Ronald Dworkin, "Liberalism," in Stuart Hampshire, ed., *Public and Private Morality* (Cambridge: Cambridge University Press, 1978), 125.

28. Alfred Stepan, *Arguing Comparative Politics* (Oxford: Oxford University Press, 2001), 213–253.

29. Charles Taylor, "Justice after Virtue," in John Horton and Susan Mendus, eds., *After MacIntyre: Critical Perspectives on the Work of Alasdair MacIntyre* (Cambridge: Polity, 1994), 16–43.

30. Granville Austin, *The Indian Constitution: Cornerstone of a Nation* (New Delhi: Oxford University Press, 1972), 318.

31. Such contextual reasoning was not atypical of the deliberations of the Constituent Assembly, in which great value was placed on arriving at decisions by consensus. Yet the procedure of majority vote was not given up altogether. On issues that everyone judged to be less significant, a majoritarian procedure was adopted.

32. Stanley J. Tambiah, "The Crisis of Secularism in India," in Bhargava, ed., *Secularism and Its Critics,* 445–453.

33. And by implication, the history of secularism must include the history of other non-Western societies that have sought to install and maintain secular states.

5

The Multiple Secularisms of Modern Democratic and Non-Democratic Regimes
Alfred Stepan

What is the variety of possible, and actual, democratic patterns of state-religion-society relations? I want to suggest seven responses, not all of which I have space to develop and defend fully but which I will weave through this chapter.

First, patterns of state-religion-society relations that happen to coexist with democracy at any given time are best seen as conjunctural, socially constructed, political arrangements, rather than as fixed, normative models.

Second, religions are transnational, and we are living in a time of global movement of populations that are able to stay in contact with the sources of their religion and influence the interpretation and practice of their religion, as well as being influenced by it, via the media, the Internet, and actual religious leaders from their countries resident in the diasporas. Thus, most conjuncturally settled patterns of state-society-religion relations are becoming conjuncturally unsettled and in need of some social, religious, and political reconstruction.

Third, the modern political analysis of democracy, while it absolutely requires use of such concepts as voting and relative freedom to organize, does not necessarily need the concept of secularism. But democratic institutions do need sufficient political space from religion to function, just as citizens need to be given sufficient space by democratic institutions to exercise their religious freedom. I call this mutual giving of space the "twin tolerations." A central point that I will develop in this chapter is that there are many varieties of secularism that can satisfy the twin tolerations and be democratic.[1] Fourth, if we want to use the concept of secularism, it should be conceptually reformulated as "multiple secularisms," for many of the same reasons that S. N. Eisenstadt and, later, Sudipta Kaviraj reformulated and used the concept of "multiple modernities."[2] Many analysts and advocates think that the "separatist pattern" found in France and the United States is the norm in modern Western democracies. It is not. I will demonstrate that western Europe has two other patterns that are not strictly separatist: the "established religion" pattern dominant in such twentieth-century democracies as Sweden, Denmark, and Norway and what I call the "positive accommodation" pattern quite prominent in such democracies as the Netherlands, Belgium, Switzerland, and Germany.

Fifth, if we examine closely the three countries in the world with large Muslim populations and whose political systems receive the highest ranking for the quality of their democracy—India, Senegal, and Indonesia—all of them have a fourth pattern that I call the "respect all, positive cooperation, principled distance" model.

Sixth, all four state-society-religion models I will discuss (and there are more) have at some time coexisted with democracies and respected the twin tolerations; hence the "multiple secularisms" of modern democracies.

Seventh, "separatist secularism," as well as the other patterns of secularism, can be and, as I will show, have been an integral part of regimes that are non-democratic. Secularism is thus not a sufficient condition of democracy and, as we shall now see, is not a necessary concept for the analysis of democracy.

Is the Concept of "Secularism" Necessary to Analyze Democracy?

Robert Dahl, Arend Lijphart, and Juan L. Linz (the first three winners of the Johan Skytte Prize, often called the Nobel Prize of Political Science) have not felt the need to include any discussion of secularism in their definitions of modern democracies, much less to include secularism as a "necessary condition" for a democracy. Dahl, in his elaboration of the "institutional guarantees" that must be created for the functioning of a democracy, or what he prefers to call a "polyarchy," nowhere mentions secularism.[3] Neither does Lijphart in his analysis of long-standing democracies in the modern world.[4] Linz and I, in our analysis of what we considered the five major regime types in the modern world in *Problems of Democratic Transition and Consolidation*, also decided not to use the concept of secularism in characterizing any of our regime types, because each type includes some regimes that call themselves secular.[5]

Linz and I are, of course, aware that many countries that are now democratic could not have become so without a variety of empirical and historical processes, often called "secularization," that facilitated the reduction of religious prerogatives in the polity, but it did not seem to us conceptually or empirically correct to use the normative concept of secularism as a defining or distinguishing characteristic of any regime type per se.

Despite my general reservation about the term "secularism," in my current research, I use the concept of "multiple secularisms" to get around some of the difficulties of a single meaning of "secular" and to help me identify and analyze the great variations in state-religion-society relations that can and do exist in modern democracies.

Many people view secularism through a narrow prism, defining it as the end result of the narrative of modernity. Some simplistic versions of modernization theory imply that there are at least four reinforcing and compounding dichotomies related to modernity and religion: traditional versus modern societies; high-religious-practicing societies versus low-religious-practicing societies; little separation of religion and state versus strict separation of church and state; and nondemocratic regimes versus democratic regimes. According to this view, properly modern polities are on the right-hand side of *all* four dimensions.

In a strict sense, however, perhaps only France between 1905 and 1959 is found on the right-hand side of all four dichotomous sets. Eisenstadt, in his important *Daedalus* article on "multiple modernities," draws attention to the United States as the first Western case of an exception to the modernity thesis, because the United States, though obviously a modern democracy, falls on the high-religious-practicing side in the dichotomous set listed above.[6] In the same issue of *Daedalus,* Sudipta Kaviraj correctly notes that India in some respects has been modernizing, while parts of Hinduism have been "re-traditionalizing."[7] In a later, magisterial work, Kaviraj develops a convincing argument about how and why different "modernities" were socially and politically crafted.[8]

In general, I find it more useful when discussing democracy and the world's religions to speak of what I have called the twin tolerations. By this I mean the minimal degree of toleration that democracy needs to receive or induce from religion and the minimal degree of toleration that religion (and civil society, more generally) needs to receive or induce from the state for the polity to be democratic. Religious institutions should not have constitutionally privileged prerogatives that allow them authoritatively to mandate public policy to democratically elected officials or effectively to deny critical freedoms to any citizens. The minimal degree of toleration that religion needs to receive from democracy, if a democracy respects Dahl's eight institutional guarantees, is not only the complete right to worship but the freedom of religious individuals and groups to advance their values in civil society publicly and to sponsor organizations and movements in political society, as long as their public advancement of these beliefs does not impinge negatively on the liberties of other citizens or violate democracy and the law by violence or other means.[9] After a period of self-secularization, the Christian Democratic political parties of Europe, as Stathis N. Kalyvas has shown, became autonomous democratic parties in contexts where neither of the twin tolerations was violated.[10]

Let us briefly examine three different models of secularism as they relate to state-religion-society relations in modern European and North American democracies, with the intention of reflecting on what these models mean, and do not mean, for religion, peaceful societal pluralism, and democracy in general and, specifically, for polities such as India, Indonesia, and Senegal, with sharply different histories and conditions.

Separatist Model: Varieties and Vicissitudes

The historical influence of the American and the French revolutions and the fact that both France and the United States are close to the "separatist" pole make many commentators assume that separatism is the normatively preferable and empirically predominant form of modern democracies.

But, for comparative purposes, particularly for readers in the United States, it is important to be aware of how many of the existing twenty-seven members of the European Union violate U.S. norms of a "wall of separation between the state and religion" but are nonetheless strong democracies. Indeed, any serious analysis of state policies toward religion in the twenty-seven European Union democracies documents that 100 percent of them fund religious education in some way: 89 percent have religious education in state schools as a standard offering (many, but not all, with the option not to attend), 44 percent fund the clergy, and 19 percent have established religions. (See Table 5.1.)

Table 5.1, by itself, should make it absolutely clear that complete separation of religion and the state is not a necessary condition for democracy to function and that complete separation of religion and the state is not the empirical norm in modern European democracies.

TABLE 5.1 Percentage of the 27 European Union Countries with State Policies of Support for Religion

Form of State Policies of Support (or Monitoring) of Religion	Percentage
Government funding of religious schools or education	100
Religious education standard (optional in schools)	89
Official government department for religious affairs	67
Government positions or funding for clergy	44
Government taxes collected for religious organizations	37
Government funding of religious charitable organizations	33
Some clerical positions made by government appointment	26
Established religion	19

Notes: In western Europe itself, the percentage of states with an established religion is significantly higher, because Iceland and Norway have established churches. Sweden also had an established church until 2000. Additionally, while Bulgaria does not have an official established religion, Article 13 of its constitution considers the Bulgarian Orthodox church to be the "traditional religion." The twenty-seven countries in the European Union are the following (italics denote countries with official established religions): Austria, Belgium, Bulgaria, Cyprus, Czech Republic, *Denmark*, Estonia, *Finland*, France, Germany, *Greece*, Hungary, Ireland, Italy, Latvia, Lithuania, Luxembourg, *Malta*, the Netherlands, Poland, Portugal, Romania, Slovakia, Slovenia, Spain, Sweden, and the *United Kingdom*. Sweden began a process of disestablishment in 2000. Finland and the United Kingdom have two established religions each.

Source: All data from Jonathan Fox, *A World Survey of Religion and the State* (Cambridge and New York: Cambridge University Press, 2008).

We should also be aware that "separatism" as a model, even in its democratic variants, can historically be established for completely different purposes, with sharply different results. France and the United States are the two long-standing democracies with the greatest legal separation between religion and state. However, the forms of separation of religion and state are polar opposites in their origins and consequences. In France, the Catholic church had been an intrinsic part of the prerevolutionary regime and continued to be a powerful part of the anti-Republican coalition in the Third Republic. *Laïcité* was thus created in France in 1905 as a clerically hostile form of "freedom of the state from religion." In sharp contrast, the First Amendment to the U.S. Constitution was passed as a clerically friendly form of "freedom of religion from the federal state."

But the U.S. story is more complicated than this implies. By and large, of course, American societies, and the American colonies, created a very supportive context for religion. However, the U.S. Constitution's First Amendment, which states that the "Congress shall make no law respecting an establishment of religion, or prohibiting the free exercise thereof," is misunderstood by many contemporary U.S. citizens. The amendment did not prohibit the thirteen original states from having *their own established* religions. The First Amendment was meant to ensure that the federal Congress could never establish one official religion for the United States as a *whole*. In fact, on the eve of the Revolution, only three of the thirteen colonies—Rhode Island, Pennsylvania, and Delaware—had no provision for an established church. Even after the Revolution, the South Carolina constitution of 1778 established the "Christian Protestant Religion." Four New England states continued for some time with state-subsidized, largely Congregational churches.[11]

Moreover, even if it exists, complete separatism may produce its own tensions and inflexibilities in democracies. The classic French and U.S models have not changed fundamentally since they were created, but their societies certainly have, in ways that challenge their models' capacity to sustain the twin tolerations. France, because of its model of republican representation of interests, finds it difficult to manage the ethnic and religious demands of some of its second- and third-generation Muslim citizens. Affirmative action is virtually illegal. The census cannot collect much information about religion. French citizens with Arabic- or Muslim-appearing names have been in a sharply disadvantageous position in job applications, despite all of the rhetoric of republican equality. Moreover, the French state has had more restrictive policies toward Muslims than almost any other western European state.[12] Such policies include the ban on students wearing head scarves in public primary and secondary schools, the bureaucratic barriers against mosque construction, and the lack of significant funding for Islamic instruction, although since 1959, France funds Catholic primary schools.[13]

The United States, because of its great toleration of almost all activities of religious groups, finds it politically and to some extent even constitutionally difficult to control some of the demands of rapidly growing and politically assertive fundamentalist religious groups from virtually all religions. For example, at least forty U.S.-based Christian Evangelical and Jewish religious groups violate the U.S. Tax Code, international law, and the formal goals of U.S. policy by funding the growth of illegal settlements in the West Bank. They also get a tax break for doing so. One of the many reasons the U.S. government does not prosecute offenders is that the religiously friendly U.S. tradition discourages detailed inquiry into sources and uses of religious funds. As a page one *New York Times* story noted, "tax breaks for the [illegal] donations remain largely unchallenged and unexamined by the American government."[14] In many cases, this violation of U.S. law is completely open. For example, the Web site of Christian Friends of Israeli Communities explicitly campaigns for donations that are *exclusively* for settlements in the West Bank, settlements that international and U.S. law say are illegal.

Separatist Secularism as Dichotomy (and as Democratic-Authoritarian Continuum)

There can be separatist secularisms with very low state controls on minority and majority religions and secularisms with such high controls on minority and majority religions that the label "separatist autocracy," "authoritarian secularism," or even "fundamentalist secularism" might be appropriate. Low-state-controlling separatist secularism is fully consistent with the twin tolerations in a democracy, while state controls at the high end of the continuum are not.

Turkey is seen by many scholars as following the 1905 French model of strict separation of church and state (*laïcité*) and thus democratic secularism. The fallacy of this approach is its exclusive focus on the separatist-versus-non-separatist dichotomy and its implicit modernist assumption that since Turkey is on the separatist side, this implies that its secularism is fundamentally democratic. With dichotomous lenses, France and Turkey are both classifiable as forms of *laïcité* separatism and are thus seen by many as politically similar. But from the perspective of a continuum, we can and should classify political systems by how much and how they control minority and majority religions.

Consider the following six sharp differences between Turkey and France. First, in Turkey, the Diyanet (the department of religious affairs under the prime minister), a state office, determines the weekly topics of Friday sermons (*Hutbe*) recited by the imam in mosques nationwide. Every word of the sermon text is written by the Diyanet. There is nothing comparable concerning control of the content of prayers for majority or minority religions in France. Second, in Turkey, all mosques that are allowed to have public ceremonies are controlled by the state, and clerics in these mosques must be authorized and approved state employees. No similar nationalization and control of religious establishments and of the clergy are found in France. Third, in Turkey, two large groups of citizens—Sufis, even though they are Sunni Muslims, and Alevis, who self-identify as nontraditional Sunni Muslims—are excluded from the financial support of the Diyanet. More important, from the perspective of the twin tolerations, neither Sufis nor Alevis are allowed to practice their religion in a public space. It is illegal for them to construct religious spaces. While it is somewhat difficult for some religions to build places of worship in France, no mainstream religion is prohibited from constructing such buildings.[15] Fourth, in Turkey, the graduates of public Islamic schools (*imam-hatip*) are not allowed to attend universities, except the departments of theology, whereas in France, the graduates of Catholic schools have no such exclusion. Fifth, it is banned in Turkey to teach the Qur'an to those younger than twelve, while in France, there is no prohibition on teaching the Qur'an or the Bible. Sixth, the Turkish state still does not fully recognize the rights of association and temple construction of non-Muslim minorities, despite the reforms the current AKP government has pursued in order to conform more closely to European Union norms.[16] Each of the above practices violates one of Dahl's eight institutional guarantees that he argues are necessary for a democracy.

Jonathan Fox, for more than a decade, has been working on a database that examines laws passed by states that control religion. The lowest score is zero if there are no controlling laws (but of course, there could still be controlling state behavior). When one examines the constitutions of Turkey, France, and Senegal (which was a French colony that from 1848 until independence in 1960 sent elected deputies to the French Assembly every year elections for this chamber were held in France), one notes that all three declare their commitment to separatist *laïcité*. However, Senegal has negotiated its relations between Islam and Catholicism, and among its four major Sufi orders, while passing only one religious controlling law and thus receives a score from Fox of 1. France, given its origins in a hostile separation of church and state and wanting to have "freedom of the state from religion," scores 6 on the Fox scale. Turkey, following a policy I would call "control all religions, but financially support (and control) the majority religion," scores 15 in Fox and in our continuum.[17]

I argued earlier that the degree of secularism is not always an indicator of the degree of democracy. Here, I simply note that when I combine Fox's 2008 scores for control over minority religions and majority religions, four Middle Eastern regimes normally classified as authoritarian are less controlling of religion than Turkey. For example, on the Fox religious-control index, authoritarian Algeria receives 9, and Tunisia, Morocco, and Egypt received scores of 11, 12 and 14, respectively, but Turkey received a score of 15, indicating that it has more control measures over religion than any of those authoritarian regimes.[18]

It goes without saying that many authoritarian regimes, such as contemporary Syria, call themselves secular. Separatist secularism is obviously neither a necessary nor a sufficient condition for social peace and democracy.

The "Established Religion" Model: Varieties and Problems

From the perspective of democratic theory, what can we say, and not say, about the established religion model? Many twentieth-century western European democracies, such as Sweden, Norway, Iceland, Denmark, Finland, and the United Kingdom, had established religions, so obviously, there can be democracies with established religions. However, we need to analyze the possible interrelationships and tensions among democracy, the twin tolerations, and established religions.

A polity with an established religion can respect the twin tolerations. For example, all of the Scandinavian states—Norway, Sweden, Denmark, Finland, and Iceland—have had constitutionally embedded Evangelical Lutheranism as their established religion.[19] Church officials in the social-democratic welfare-state era by and large did not enjoy prerogatives to block policies of democratically elected officials or to constrain the individual religious freedom of the members of the majority or minority religions. However, before the democratic period, the state, in almost all of these established religion polities, exercised such strong "erastian," or what Max Weber called "caesaropapist," control over religion that they violated this aspect of the twin tolerations. In fact, in many of the Scandinavian countries, any religion besides Evangelical Lutheranism was illegal until around the 1870s. The United Kingdom has established churches in England and Scotland, and Greece has established the Greek Orthodox church, all of which have more prerogatives than the Scandinavian official churches; and as their populations change, they also will have to change. Obviously, some established religions violate the twin tolerations, and some do not. Thus, if we want to assess the impact of established religions on individual religious freedom and democracy, it is best to analyze established religions not only as a dichotomous variable (established religion versus no established religion) but also as a *continuum* of the degree of state control *within* the polities that have established religions. For example, Jonathan Fox's valuable "Religion and State Dataset" allows us to construct a continuum of state control of majority religions. This continuum has a four-point scale for eleven variables concerning state control of majority religions. Composite scores on this continuum range from zero (Denmark and Norway) to 1 (Bangladesh) to 5 (Pakistan and Egypt). We can also construct a continuum for state control of minority religions based on scores for sixteen variables. The composite scores for control of minorities in polities with established religions range from 1 (Denmark) to 3 (Norway and Bangladesh) to 21 (Pakistan) to 38 and 46, respectively, for the two most controlling (Iran and Saudi Arabia). (See Table 5.2.)

So far, we have clearly documented that some countries have established religions but are nonetheless inclusive democracies in which the rights of religious minorities and majorities are respected. But can we make reasonable estimates about the societal and religious conditions in a society that would be relatively

TABLE 5.2 Some Established Religions in Democracies and Nondemocracies: Continuum of
Controls over Majority and Minority Religions

Country	Restrictions on Majority Religion	Restrictions on Minority Religions	Total Score
Denmark	0	1	1
United Kingdom	0	1	1
Norway	0	2	2
Finland	0	3	3
Bangladesh	1	2	3
Greece	1	5	6
Pakistan	8	13	21
Egypt	11	18	29
Iran	4	34	38
Saudi Arabia	8	38	46

Sources: All data are from the "Religion and State Dataset" gathered by Jonathan Fox. All values are calculated within the dataset for 2002. For purposes of this table, I could not use Fox's book *A World Survey of Religion and the State* (Cambridge and New York: Cambridge University Press, 2008), because while it contains a discussion of European democracies, no quantitative evaluation for them for these indicators is given; therefore, for comparative purposes, I use his somewhat older unpublished studies. For a discussion of these data, see also Jonathan Fox, "World Separation of Religion and State into the 21st Century," *Comparative Political Studies* 39, no. 5 (2006): 537–569.

supportive or relatively unsupportive of such outcomes? The following proposition seems plausible. The greater the degree of religious homogeneity in a polity and the less the intensity of religious practices, the easier it will be for an established religion and an inclusive democracy to coexist.

Let us compare Denmark and Northern Ireland. Denmark—the country with an established religion that used to (but no longer does) score best on tolerance toward minority and majority religions—has high religious and denominational homogeneity and low intensity of religious practice. For much of the 1980s, roughly 95 percent of Denmark's population was Lutheran, and 3 percent was other Protestants. From 1973 to 1999, the percentage of respondents in Denmark who said they went to church at least once a week, 3 percent to 7 percent, was the lowest in Europe.[20] Northern Ireland is near the opposite pole: 53 percent of the population is Protestant, and 44 percent is Catholic.[21] Also, from 1973 to1992, the percentage of all respondents in Northern Ireland who said they went to church at least once a week never fell below 54 percent.[22] Given this combination of religious heterogeneity, intensity of religious practice, and ethnoreligious conflict, the Anglican Church was disestablished in Northern Ireland in 1920.[23]

John Madeley has created invaluable maps and tables of the "Historic Mono-Cultural" zones in Europe. The only country in western Europe that has an established religion and that is not in one of Madeley's historic monoculture zones is the United Kingdom, which has witnessed historic conflicts over Catholic rights. It will be increasingly important to assess how the prerogatives of the established Anglican Church of England (its monopoly of religious representation in the House of Lords, its control over entrance to the state-financed but Anglican-run schools in England, and, indeed, its veto on some matters of the entire state-school curriculum) are increasingly coming into tension with new socioreligious migrant populations and thus have more contested issues concerning the status of the official religion than in the Scandinavian countries. Religious homogeneity in the United Kingdom was never as high as in the Scandinavian countries or religious practice as low. In the last few decades, migration into the United Kingdom of committed Muslims from Pakistan and Bangladesh, Hindus from India, Evangelical Protestants from Africa and the Caribbean, and a new wave of Catholics from Poland has reduced religious homogeneity and increased religious intensity. The state-society-religion formula has undergone great changes in its societal and religious components but not enough in its overall formula.

In 2000, Sweden started a process of disestablishment of the Evangelical Lutheran church and an opening up of numerous lines of contact with Muslim immigrants. Denmark did neither. Partly as a result of these openings, Sweden managed the cartoon crisis much better than Denmark did.[24]

The "Positive Accommodation" Model

The hypothesis that established religions in a democracy fare best in a context of high religious homogeneity and low religious intensity is borne out when we consider major European countries that have never had an established church in the democratic age. Since World War I, *none* of the historically most multiconfessional polities in western Europe—such as Germany, the Netherlands, or Switzerland—had or created established religions.[25] Also, given the important role that religion played in social life, the separatist model was not adopted in any of these multiconfessional polities. Rather, they are the home of intensely negotiated "consociational" power and "space-sharing" arrangements that I call the "positive accommodation" model of democratic secularism. "Positive" because, as one of Germany's leading analysts of state-religion relations in Germany, Gerhard Robbers, has written, "Neutrality...means *positive neutrality*. This concept obligates the state to actively support religion and to provide for the space religion needs to flourish in the polity. This makes possible and requires for example that the state include religious needs in planning law.... This concept of positive neutrality is predominant in the official discourses and not only in law. It is actively supported and implemented by the courts and state officials."[26] The word "accommodation" is also crucial because this model accommodates the major traditional Christian religions in numerous areas. Robbers estimates that there is near parity in numbers among Catholics and Protestants in Germany (26.1 million Catholics and 25.8 million Protestants).[27]

The state accommodates these two largest churches by helping them collect a church tax. According to Robbers, "the rate of the church tax is between eight and nine percent of the individual's wage and income liability.... Approximately 80 percent of the entire budget of the two major religious communities, the Catholic and the Protestant Churches...is covered by the church tax."[28] With this money, the social power of the two major churches is not only accommodated but also reinforced. "Hospitals run by religious communities, which in some parts of Germany make up the majority of the available hospital beds, are thus part of the public-run financing systems for hospitals."[29] However, Muslims, whom Robbers estimates as having a population in Germany of 3.2 million, had not yet legally won acceptance as a German public law corporation and thus did not have the benefits of this arrangement.[30]

The Netherlands is a particularly strong example of negotiated accommodation that resulted in constitutionally and socially embedded *positive* public policies and consociational practices. In 1917, there was a heated conflict among Catholics, Calvinists, and a secularizing liberal government over the role of the traditional churches in education, a conflict that at times threatened to create a deep crisis in democracy. In the constitution of 1917, a consociational formula was introduced by which local communities, if they were overwhelmingly of a specific religious community, could choose to have the local school be a private Calvinist or a private Catholic school *and* to receive state support. By 1975, almost 75 percent of Dutch children were in state-financed Calvinist or Catholic schools, and the programming on the two largest radio and television state-owned networks were run largely by dues-paying Calvinist members (NCRV) or dues-paying Catholic members (KRO).[31] As in Germany, such arrangements are part of a positive accommodation, or consociational, public philosophy. For example, in the judgment of one of the leading authorities on state-religion relations in the Netherlands, Sophie van Bijsterveld, "in the field of subsidies, public authorities may not exclude confessional organizations from subsidies just because they are confessional; their application for subsidy must be considered purely on the basis of whether they fulfill the objective criteria that are set."[32] Elsewhere, she has argued that the Dutch constitution entails that the "government should enable the free exercise of religion, not make it impossible. So [it means] the positive protection of religion," and that article 23 of the constitution, which provides for virtual full funding at all levels of privately given religious education, should be interpreted as a "neutrality clause which requires a *positive attitude* toward religion."[33]

The positive accommodation model in countries such as Germany, the Netherlands, Belgium, and Switzerland has proved quite flexible in facilitating mutual accommodations among the historic Christian religions in their countries with one another and with democratic state authorities, secular or not.

New immigrants, such as Muslims, in principle, could be included in such accommodation, but much of the positive accommodation has historically been developed by the European states' tradition of treating religions as hierarchical legal bodies that qualify as public corporations that can enter into legal agreements with state authorities. In Germany, the state raises the church tax for Catholics, Protestants, and, in some Länder, Jews but not for Muslims. This is so because from the German state's perspective, Muslims do not yet qualify as a public corporation, mainly for reasons of their internal diversity, which makes them difficult to fit into long-standing German law. In Belgium, all "faiths" concerning spirituality are recognized, and clerics and leaders of five religions, as well as "nonbelieving humanists," receive salary support, but Muslim imams do not receive such salary support, because the state, as in Germany, says that it does not know which body represents the imams. The state in the Netherlands often treats groups, even Muslim groups, not only as public corporations but as parts of civil society negotiating with the state and does give some funds to Muslims, but the literature nonetheless frequently analyzes the special difficulties of Muslim self-organization and political integration into existing state/society forms of cooperation.

A major feature of the positive accommodation model, therefore, is that it has historically emerged in Europe fundamentally as a way of managing conflict involving Christian religions. Non-Christian religions were not sociologically and politically present as constituent parts of these historically constructed and negotiated, often consociational, bargains of the eighteenth, nineteenth, and early twentieth centuries. To the extent that these legal formulas acquired a certain path-dependency—such as state money only flowing to religions as legal corporations—such requirements often made new non-Christian religions nonrecipients, not as a matter of principle but as a matter of practice, convenient or not.

Are Muslims "Secular-Resistant"? What State-Religion-Society Models Seem to Work?

In the spirit of this book's general concern with "rethinking secularism" and my specific concern with the "multiple secularisms" of contemporary democracies, I would like to offer a challenge to the idea that Muslims are generically "secular-resistant" to all types of secularism. I will do this through an analysis of two Muslim majority democracies, Indonesia and Senegal, and of India, whose democracy has the third-largest Muslim population of any country in the world.

I pick these three countries because for much of the last decade, Indonesia, Senegal, and India have been highly ranked democracies. For example, in the most recent ranking of all countries in the world on the democracy scale in Ted Gurr's *Polity IV*, of the forty-three Muslim-majority countries ranked, Senegal and Indonesia received the highest scores, and India has been ranked at that level for more than thirty years.

Polity uses a twenty-one-point scale, with +10 being the most democratic and -10 being the least; India, Senegal, and Indonesia all received +7 or +8 in *Polity IV*. With the exception of Lebanon, which had a +5, every other Arab majority country ranked at least ten points lower than India, Senegal, or Indonesia.

The other frequently cited survey is the "Freedom in the World Index" by Freedom House, which, despite its different panel of experts, methodology, and political orientation, arrives at virtually the same overall rankings as *Polity IV*. On the Freedom House's seven-point scale (1 is the best score, 7 the worst), Senegal, Indonesia, and India in 2007 (and Muslim-majority Albania and Mali) all received a score of 2. None of the sixteen Arab countries in the same survey received a score higher than 5 for that year.

From a quantitative perspective, the point is not so much that Muslims do not do well on these indicators but that Arab Muslims do not. In a study using 2004 data, I documented that 396 million Muslims—that is, 50 percent of the total population of Muslims who lived in non-Arab League Muslim-majority states—lived in "electorally competitive states" but that *none* of the 269 million Muslims living in Arab League Muslim-majority states did so.[34] The issue, therefore, is not that there are no Muslim-majority states classifiable as democracies but that there are no Arab countries that are. There are many issues raised by these data that must be researched in much greater detail, such as whether the "oil curse," the Arab-Israeli conflict, the presence of "tribes," and a widely shared common language weaken the territorial dimension of democratic claims in many Arab countries.

In this chapter, however, I explore another potentially important factor that may help us analyze our cases of relative democratic success—indeed, "democratic overperformance," if we just look at socioeconomic data—in Indonesia, Senegal, and India. Did the models of state-religion-society facilitate or hinder social peace and political pluralism in these countries?

What is theoretically interesting for our examination of varieties of democratic secularism is that none of these three democratically exemplar countries has either a U.S.- or French-style notion of secularism, meaning a strict separation of religion and the state or an established religion. All, however, have a strong degree of "positive accommodation," indeed, of what I will describe as "positive cooperation." Taken as a whole, Indonesia, Senegal, and India are variants of a fourth, quite distinctive model of secularism that is compatible with democracy and the twin tolerations.

The "Respect All, Positive Cooperation, Principled Distance" Model

The remainder of this chapter describes the "respect all, positive cooperation, principled distance" model.[35] I call attention to three features of this model or, better, ideal type to show how it contrasts or compares with the other three models discussed so far; state-given respect in the private *and* public spheres to all major majority and minority religions in the polity, positive cooperation, and principled distance.[36]

"RESPECT" IN THE PUBLIC SPHERE FOR MAJORITY AND MINORITY RELIGIONS

One indicator of the degree to which the state gives respect in the public sphere to majority and minority religions alike is whether the state mandates at least one obligatory paid public holiday for minority religions if it mandates such holidays for the majority religion. When we look at three key separatist polities (France, the United States, and Turkey), three of the most inclusive established religion polities (Denmark, Norway, and Sweden), and three of the most inclusionary of the positive accommodationist polities (Germany, the Netherlands, and Switzerland), we note that none of the countries offer holidays for the minority religion. In the case of the Christian countries, there is a combined number of seventy-nine paid obligatory Christian holidays but none for any minority religion. In sharp contrast, the three "respect all" polities (Senegal, Indonesia, and India) have eighteen obligatory paid holidays for the majority religion but *even more,* twenty-three, for the minority religions.[37] (See Table 5.3.)

Such recognition in the public sphere of minority and majority religions is a key part of the respect all model and puts it in sharp contrast with three dominant European and U.S. models that we have discussed so far. Table 5.3 also reveals a state attitude toward religion that is quite different from Muslim-majority Turkey and from most Arab Muslim-majority countries, many of whose leaders in the immediate postindependence period were not Islamists but, like Egypt's Gamal Abdel Nasser, Algeria's Ahmed Ben Bella, or Tunisia's Habib Bourguiba, were secular nationalists who (like Turkey's Atatürk) used authoritarian measures to control and repress many religious leaders in the name of modernity.

What approaches toward secularism were and were not used in India, Senegal, and Indonesia? Nehru privately was a secularist, and he admired Atatürk, but as a democratic political leader of a mass democratic movement for independence in a religiously heterogeneous society, he chose not to be an aggressive secularist; neither was Senghor in Senegal nor Sukarno in Indonesia.

The public respect accorded to majority and minority religions as indicated in Table 5.3 meant that none of these three countries, whether in the predemocratic independent periods or democratic periods, has, unlike Turkey, ever declared any major majority or minority religion illegal or ineligible for state aid.

Likewise, none of the founding leaders in this model, Nehru and Gandhi, Senghor, or Sukarno, unlike the founding leader of Turkey, Atatürk—or many of the Arab nationalist independent leaders—ever attempted, in the

TABLE 5.3 Comparison of Paid Religious Holidays in Four State-Religion-Society Models

Country	SEPARATIST			ESTABLISHED CHURCH				POSITIVE ACCOMMODATION		RESPECT ALL		
	France	Turkey	U.S.A.	Denmark	Norway	Sweden	Germany	Netherlands	Switzerland	India	Indonesia	Senegal
Majority Religion	Christian	Muslim	Christian	Christian	Christian	Christian	Christian	Christian	Christian	Hindu	Muslim	Muslim
Paid Religious Holidays for Majority Religion	6	2	1	11	10	10	8*	8	7*	5	6	7
Paid Religious Holidays for Minority Religion	0	0	0	0	0	0	0	0	0	10	7	6

*Notes: India currently has 17 compulsory public holidays, of which 3 are secular, 4 Muslim, 2 Christian, 1 Buddhist, 1 Jain, 1 Sikh, and 5 Hindu. 3 of the 5 Hindu holidays are chosen from a list by each state. Each individual is allowed to choose 2 additional paid holidays. For detailed information on India's holidays, see Government of India, Ministry of Personnel, Public Grievances and Pensions, F. No. 12/5/2009-JCA-2(2010). Available at india.gov.in./govt/pdf/govt_holiday_list-10.pdf. Individual Swiss cantons and German Lieder have additional paid religious holidays, decided on by local governments. In Switzerland, 8 additional holidays are celebrated by between one and fourteen Swiss Cantons (Corpus Christi, 14: All Saints' Day, 14; Saint Berchtold's Day, 13; Assumption Day, 13; Immaculate Conception, 10; Saint Joseph's Day, 6; Epiphany, 4; Saints Peter and Paul, 1). In Germany, 6 additional holidays are celebrated in between one and eight German Lieder (Corpus Christi, 8; Reformation Day, 5; All Saints' Day, 5; Epiphany, 3; Assumption Day, 2; Repentance Day, 1).

Source: http://www.qppstudio.net/publicholidays.htm

name of modernity and secularism, to drive groups such as the Sufis or the Alevis out of the public square or to stop them from building visible structures in which to worship.

Far from hostility to any religion, all three countries within this model embraced an *inclusive interreligious positive accommodation,* whereas Germany, the Netherlands, and Switzerland are, in fact, examples of *restricted intra-Christian positive accommodation.* In India, Indonesia, and Senegal, active policy cooperation between the state and all religions is more pronounced. In the widely disseminated version of the Senegalese constitution, the second president of independent Senegal, Abdou Diouf, is clear that Senegalese *laïcité* involves both accommodation and respect: "*Laïcité* in itself is a manifestation of respect of others. It acts in this way if it is not to be antireligious, but neither if it is a true *laïcité* can it become an established religion. I would say further that such a laic state cannot ignore religious institutions. From the fact that Citizens embrace religion flows the obligation for the state to facilitate the practice of that religion, as it does for all other vital activities of citizens.... Respect of religion does not only mean tolerance, it does not mean only to allow or to ignore, but to respect the beliefs and practices of the other. *Laïcité* is the consequence of this respect for the other, and the condition of our harmony."[38]

To rule Senegal effectively without costly military conflicts and to develop the interior of the country commercially with Sufi help, the French colonial state itself, in a fascinating accommodation illustrating the great contextuality of secularism, adopted a radically different form of *laïcité* from what it was then following in either French colonial Algeria or Third Republic France. In Senegal in the early twentieth century, the French dropped their form of religiously hostile secularism and aspired to be an "Islamic power." To further this goal, they supported pilgrimages of influential Sufis to Mecca, gave financial support for mosque construction, supported Arabic-language training for Islamic schools, increasingly attended major Sufi ceremonies, and were seen to give public respect to Sufi religious leaders known as marabouts.[39] All of these policies violated 1905 French-style *laïcité*, but none of them violated human rights, democratic values, or the twin tolerations.

Given the profoundly different normative and empirical implications of *laïcité* in 1905 France and in contemporary Senegal, it should be clear why I argue that democratic theorists should speak not of "secularism" as a singular democratic universal but, instead, of the "multiple secularisms of modern democracies."

Let us now look at the question of an established religion in Muslim-majority Indonesia and Senegal and Hindu-majority India. The first thing we must take cognizance of is that, unlike Scandinavia, India and Indonesia have high religious heterogeneity, coupled with high intensity of religious practice. It is thus a sign of respect, or at least accommodation, of this religious pluralism that neither India nor Indonesia nor somewhat more homogeneous Senegal has an established religion.[40]

Let us explore why and how Indonesia, the world's most populous Muslim-majority state, did not establish an Islamic state. The most influential actors and arguments were Indonesian, and as Rajeev Bhargava argued was the case for India, the secularism that has emerged is multivalued; a positive value is attached to a successful and peaceful nationalism, a positive value—or at least the positive recognition—of Indonesia's inherent diversity, and a positive interpretation of what Islam entailed, and did not entail, concerning religious and public life.

In Indonesia, Bali has a Hindu-majority population, many of the smaller outer islands have Catholic or Protestant majorities, Buddhist and Confucian Chinese businessmen are prominent in the major cities, and, of course, there are varieties of Islam and strong animist traditions. In this context, the demand by some Islamist groups in Indonesia for a shari'a state during the constitution-making moments of 1945 and 1955 and after the recent democratic transition began in 1998 was defeated. Shari'a as an obligatory state policy for all citizens in Indonesia was defeated because it was perceived by religious minorities, as well as by many Muslims, secular or not, as a policy that would create threats to Indonesia's territorial integrity, social peace, and way of life.

A key aspect of the 1945 Indonesian compromise version of state-society-religious relations was the doctrine of Pancasila (a Sanskrit word). The five principles of Pancasila that were included in the preamble to the Indonesian constitution of 1945 were: (1) belief in God, (2) a just and civilized humanitarianism, (3) national unity, (4) Indonesian democracy through consultation and consensus, and (5) social justice.

Despite numerous challenges from Islamists who wanted an Islamic state, Pancasila has endured. The five principles were developed by Sukarno, the nationalist leader of the independence movement and the first president of independent Indonesia. He developed the doctrine with the active collaboration of some military leaders—some secularist, some not—who were frightened by the threat of religious conflict and territorial fragmentation and some Islamic leaders, including the father of the three-times-elected president of Indonesia's largest Muslim organization, NU, Abdurrahman Wahid, who also wanted to avoid such conflicts.[41]

Pancasila has some political virtues in Indonesia's intensely religious and heterogeneous society. Pancasila facilitates the state recognition and granting of some financial and bureaucratic support to the five largest organized religions in addition to Islam: Buddhism, Hinduism, Catholicism, Protestantism, and, with the advent of democracy, Confucianism. Official state inclusion in the Pancasila system means that these five non-Islamic religions, with a total of 27 million adherents, all were accorded rights within Indonesia.[42] In my interviews with leaders of minority religions in Indonesia, it became clear that such official recognition is valued highly because it allows them to call upon, and demand as a right, protection by the state coercive apparatus if they are threatened and also to have some call on state financial resources.

Who articulates public arguments in Indonesia for or against a shari'a state in Indonesia? And why? And how? In my article on the twin tolerations, I argued that all religions are multivocal. What this means for Islam is that any officially implemented system of shari'a law must necessarily have a strong element of "state shari'a," because one side of the multivocality would be state-privileged and have the coercive powers of the state behind it. Given the deep differences between "traditionalist" democratic Muslims in Nahdatul Ulama (NU) and "modernist" democratic Muslims in Muhammadiyah—and their political and cultural sensitivity to the existence and rights of Hindus, Buddhists, Christians, and nonpracticing Muslims—leaders of both of these massive organizations, with members numbering more than 30 million each, are now opposed to an Islamic state, which they argue would lead to the nonconsensual imposition on a diverse polity of a single group's vision of "state shari'a."

Amien Rais, a former president of Muhammadiyah, speaker of the Consultative Assembly, and presidential candidate, again and again advanced variants of the following argument against Indonesia becoming a shari'a state: "First of all, the Qur'an does not say anything about the formation of an Islamic state, or about the necessity and obligations on the part of Muslims, to establish a shari'a or Islamic state. Secondly, the Qur'an is not a book of law but a source of law. If the Qur'an is considered a book of law, Muslims will become the most wretched people in the world.... We should not establish Islamic justice as it will create controversy and conflict. Indonesia should be built on the principles of Pancasila to be a modern state, and to allow every citizen of Indonesia to pursue his or her aspiration."[43]

Abdurrahman Wahid (who died in December 2009) of NU rejected, in particular, any Rawlsian idea of "keeping religion off the public agenda." Precisely because he knew that in multivocal Indonesia there are religious advocates of an exclusionary approach to religion and politics, he articulated alternative public discourses. He was a constant participant in public arguments making the case for why Indonesia, given its great social and religious diversity, which he saw as an *empirical fact,* should make the normative *political choice* for a pluralist polity—a tolerant inclusive Islam in a tolerant inclusive Indonesia.[44] He also worked to create religious schools and organizations that advance these religious and democratic goals not only inside religious spaces but also in civil society and in political society. He could not have carried out these public-sphere agendas in a context of Turkish secularism or, in the judgment of the leading specialist on Indonesian-French comparisons, John Bowen, even of French secularism.[45]

THE "POSITIVE COOPERATION" DIMENSION

The three polities in this model, normally within the twin tolerations, all have an explicit positive accommodation but also *policy cooperation* approach to state-religion-society relations. More than in Germany or Switzerland, they give state aid to help all religions carry out some of their activities. In Senegal, this started even under the French once they announced that they were a "Muslim power" in West Africa. This positive accommodation has been continued and broadened after independence. The Senegalese state now gives some support to Catholics to take pilgrimages to the Vatican.

In India, as D. E. Smith has stressed, "the idea that government should not extend financial aid and other forms of patronage to religion finds no support in Hindu, Buddhist, or Islamic traditions.... [Also] during certain periods in the eighteenth and nineteenth centuries, grants of money were given by the British government for the support of Hindu temples and Muslim mosques."[46] The constitution of independent and democratic India kept up the tradition of some financial support for all religions. Article 30 stipulates: "All minorities, whether based on religion or language, shall have the right to establish and administer educational institutions of their choice." To make this right financially possible, Article 30 further stipulates: "The state shall not, in granting aid to educational institutions, discriminate against any educational institution on the ground that it is under management of a minority, whether based on religion or language." Significantly, the positive norm of the state helping religious minorities fulfill their religious duties is so entrenched that even under Hindu nationalist BJP governments, the tradition of the state giving subsidies to help Muslims make pilgrimages to Mecca was maintained.

In Indonesia, Hindu, Buddhist, Confucian, Catholic, and Protestant organizations, as well as Muslim ones, as part of Pancasila, can apply for financial support to carry out their functions to the section in the Ministry of Religion dedicated to their religion.[47]

In Indonesia in particular, but also in Senegal, the combination of a very inclusive positive accommodation toward religions, with some financial aid to religious schools, has opened the way to forms of active, policy-making cooperation between the "respect all" secular state and religions. For example, in Indonesia, if a religious school wants official recognition, there has recently been a growing process of consensual co-design of books on the history of religion by state authorities from the Ministry of Education and religious leaders from major Muslim organizations. Robert W. Hefner and Muhammad Zaman have recently edited an invaluable book that reviews *madrasas* in eight different countries. One of the most inclusive and tolerant systems described in the volume, and the one that now works most cooperatively with a democratic state, is in Indonesia. The chapter on Indonesia shows how NU and Muhammadiyah, via negotiations facilitated by Pancasila, have made substantial contributions to this educationally high-quality and politically pluralist outcome.[48]

In Senegal, the constant mutual rituals of respect, between the state and all religions and between all religions and the state, have facilitated policy cooperation even in some sensitive areas of human-rights abuses. They have also facilitated an atmosphere in which religious leaders have felt free to make arguments *from within Islam* against practices and policies that violate human rights. When I argued in "The Twin Tolerations" that all religions are "multivocal," I also drew the conclusion that this necessarily implied, *contra* early John Rawls, that it would be a mistake to "take religion off the agenda."[49] I did so because proponents of some human-rights-violating policies often use religious arguments to support their positions. There thus must be the possibility of a religious counterresponse in defense of rights put on the agenda.

Ideally, this response is not only from abroad, in the name of "universal human rights." The most effective counterresponse is by a local authoritative figure, who, from within the core values of the religion and culture of the country, makes a powerful, religiously based argument against the specific practice that violates human rights. Let us look at an example of such Senegalese state-religion policy cooperation in the area of human rights, the campaign against female genital mutilation (FGM).

A variety of national and international feminist and human-rights movements wanted to ban the practice of FGM but had been countered by powerful religious-based attacks. In the end, secular movements in the government and some national and international NGOs were greatly helped by Senegalese religious leaders. The secretary general, N'Diaye, of the National Association of Imams of Senegal (ANIOS) publicly argued that there is nothing in the Qur'an commanding the practice and that there was no evidence in Haddiths that the Prophet had his own daughters circumcised.[50] A law banning female circumcision was passed in 1999. To avoid the law being a dead letter, ANIOS enlisted the help of government health authorities to train imams in how to speak authoritatively about the health problems that circumcision presents and to help with anti-FGM talks by imams on radio and television. Since patterns of female circumcision are closely related to perceptions of marriage eligibility, the government, ANIOS, and national and international women's rights organizations worked together with entire adjacent villages to develop policies of "coordinated abandonment" of female circumcision, so as to preclude jeopardizing marriage prospects within participating villages.[51]

Even with such a law banning FGM, the law can best start to become a growing social reality if the most authoritative religious bodies in the country continue to campaign against the practice so that it is increasingly delegitimized in the religious norms and social customs of the country. To help advance this crucial goal, Abdoul Aziz Kebe, coordinator for the Tivaouane-based largest Sufi order in Senegal, the Tijans, wrote a powerful forty-five-page attack on FGM. The report systematically argued that FGM is a violation of women's rights, bodies, and health, with absolutely no justification in the Qur'an or in approved Haddiths. Kebe argued that not only is there no Islamic justification for FGM, but given current medical knowledge and current Islamic scholarship, there is a moral obligation for communities and individuals to bring a halt to FGM. The report was distributed by Tijan networks, secular ministries, and the World Health Organization.[52]

THE "PRINCIPLED DISTANCE" DIMENSION

I can be quite brief about the question of "principled distance" because the concept has been brilliantly developed by my colleague, the Indian political theorist, Rajeev Bhargava.[53] India and also to a lesser extent Indonesia and Senegal all have versions of the secular state that can impose, if necessary, some normative and constitutional constraints on religious majoritarianism and/or on possible religious violations of human rights by following the norm of "principled distance." Along with Bhargava, I use the term "principled distance" *not* to mean "equidistance" between all religions. If religion A is violating citizens' rights and religion B is not, neither the principle of "equidistance" nor that of "neutrality" should be invoked to restrain the state from employing its legitimate democratic coercive powers against religion A and not against religion B.

Many of India's independence leaders were not strongly attracted to the U.S. "wall of separation" doctrine or to what I have labeled U.S. "freedom of religion from the state" secularism. Hinduism involves the public practice of religion as much as, or more than, private worship. Thus, the tradition of forbidding what were then called "untouchables" from entering Hindu temples was considered by many, especially by the chair of the Drafting Committee of the Constitution for the Constituent Assembly, ex-untouchable B. R. Ambedkar, as a violation by the majority religion of Hindu citizens' basic human and democratic rights. Therefore, the Indian constitution, in Article 17, directly declared illegal a fundamental aspect of Hinduism when it mandated that "'Untouchability' is abolished and its practice forbidden. The enforcement of any disability arising out of 'untouchability' shall be an offence punishable in accordance with law." Article 25, clause 1, opens with a declaration that "all persons are equally entitled to freedom of conscience and the right freely to profess, practice, and propagate religion." But clause 2 of Article 25 goes on to state a classic principle of "principled distance" thinking, and, I believe, of the twin tolerations: that nothing in clause 1 about religious freedom should prevent the state from "throwing open Hindu religious institutions of a public character to all classes and sections of Hindus." Armed with this constitutional principle, state after state in India's federal system passed highly debated temple entry laws.

To show how different such Indian "principled distance" actions by the state to reform religious institutions is from much U.S. jurisprudence concerning state-religion relations, I note that the standard account of Indian secularism by a U.S. scholar, Donald E. Smith, critically argues that Article 25 and the subsequent "temple entry laws...raise[s] important questions of religious freedom."[54]

In Senegal, Leopold Senghor used principled-distance-type reasoning to block strong demands by Muslim religious leaders to weaken the relatively progressive family code left by the French. In Indonesia, rule-of-law arguments and principled-distance-type arguments have had to be urged upon state authorities to try to make them less responsive to some majoritarian demands that might violate citizens' rights and, at times, safety.

HAS THE "RESPECT ALL, POSITIVE COOPERATION, PRINCIPLED DISTANCE" MODEL BEEN ASSOCIATED WITH RELATIVELY DEMOCRATIC OR RELATIVELY NONDEMOCRATIC ATTITUDES OF CITIZENS?

I opened the section on the respect all model with documentation showing that three of the most highly democratically ranked polities in the world with Muslim majority or large Muslim populations are Indonesia, India, and Senegal. All three polities follow variants of the respect all model.

But do we have any evidence that such a model is actually associated with democratic or nondemocratic attitudes among citizens at large in these polities, especially among those citizens, of whatever religion, who indicate in their self-reported responses to a battery of questions that they are in the most intensely religious practicing category of respondents?

I do not want to make the case that the Indian model of secularism, by itself, created the attitudinal and behavioral patterns I am about to present. In our book *Crafting "State Nations": India and Other Multinational Democracies*, Juan J. Linz, Yogendra Yadav, and I argue that many things in India's "state nation" acceptance of more than fifteen official languages, its asymmetrical federal system, and its coalition-requiring and coalition-sustaining parliamentary system have been crucial to the functioning of India's often troubled but long-standing democracy. But I believe that the "respect all, positive cooperation, principled distance" qualities of India's secular model helped Indians address their great religious heterogeneity and their great intensity of religious practice and might have been constitutive of the remarkable prodemocratic consensus among all religions concerning democracy that I will document.[55]

India has some of the highest levels of religious belief and practice in the world: 93 percent of the population describe themselves as believing in God, 87 percent as being "very" or "somewhat" religious, 53 percent as praying daily. Almost half (at least 400 million people) say they have gone on a pilgrimage or traveled to another place for religious purposes in the last ten years. Finally, against this very high base, 3.9 times as many respondents say that in the last ten years, their "family's engagement in religious activities" has *increased* as say they have *decreased*.[56]

The first point I would like to stress is that the percentage of members of *all* four of the major religions in India who self-identify as having a "preference for democracy as opposed to any other system" is very high by world standards: Muslims 71 percent, Hindus 71 percent, Sikhs 71 percent, and Christians

74 percent.[57] The Muslims, the largest and the least socioeconomically developed religious community in India, essentially have the same percentage as the national norm of all four of the categories concerning democracy. (See Table 5.4.)

Given the self-reported increase in religious practice in India, Linz, Yadav, and I constructed an index of religious intensity, from low to medium to high, to see if the trend toward growing intensity of religious practice correlates with growing undemocratic attitudes and practices, as some fear. From our data, the exact opposite is found. For *all* four major religions in India, for each increase in religious intensity, there is an increase in support for democracy. (See Figure 5.1.)

For the *State of Democracy in South Asia Survey: 2005*, Yadav, Linz, and I also constructed a battery of questions exploring the relationship between religion and democracy. Unfortunately, our sample size (5387 compared with the 27,189 for the *National Election Study, India: 2004*) permits us to do detailed comparative study of only the two largest religions in India: Hinduism and Islam. The sample size for other minority religions is too small for a robust analysis. A key question we wanted to explore was the relationship of increased levels of "the intensity of religious practice," our independent variable, to four critical components of democratic political society, which will be our dependent variables: "political efficacy," "overall trust in political institutions," "satisfaction with the way democracy works in this country," and "voting ratios." As Table 5.5 makes clear, again counterintuitively from the perspective of much of the literature, on all eight observations (Hindus and Muslims on each of the four variables), the groups with "high religiosity" have higher scores on each of the four variables than do the groups with "low religiosity."

TABLE 5.4 The Great Similarity in India of Hindu, Muslim, Christian, and Sikh Support for Democracy

	All India (%)	Hindu (%)	Muslim (%)	Christian (%)	Sikh (%)
Democracy is always preferable	70	71	71	74	71
	(88)	(88)	(87)	(91)	(88)
Sometimes authoritarianism is preferable	4	4	4	3	4
No difference	6	6	7	5	6
Don't know/no answer	20	19	18	18	19
Total	100	100	100	100	100
Number of respondents	27,145	21,626	3103	838	687

Notes: Figures in parentheses are for valid responses if the "don't knows" are treated as missing data. According to a Pearson's Chi-Square test, the findings for all religious communities are statistically significant (p-value < .001). Thus, the probability of this occurring by chance is less than one in 1000.

Source: National Election Study, India: 2004.

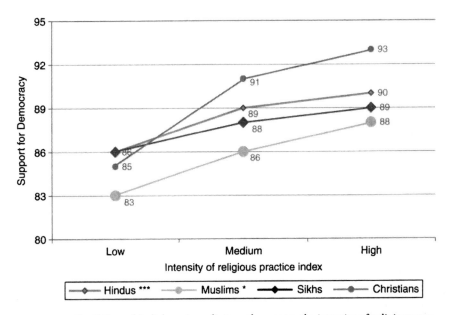

FIGURE 5.1 *In all four of India's major religions, the greater the intensity of religious practice, the greater the support for democracy.*

Notes: The analysis is based on valid answers in the *National Election Study, India: 2004.* Total n = 27,189. Valid responses for the table are: Hindus = 17,261; Muslims = 2549; Sikhs = 544; and Christians = 697. The findings for Hindus are statistically significant (Pearson's Chi-Square < .001), which means that the possibility of the findings occurring by chance are less than one in 1000. The findings for Muslims are also statistically significant (Pearson's Chi-Square < .050), which means that the possibility of the findings occurring by chance are less than one in 20. The findings for Sikhs and Christians are also positive but not statistically significant. In order to analyze further the impact of intensity of religious practice on support for democracy, we made a binary logistic regression model. In addition to the intensity of religious practice, we added as control variables efficacy of vote (Q21), membership of organizations other than caste or religious organization (Q19), whether the respondent voted or not in the 2004 parliamentary election (Q3), gender, respondent's education (B4), monthly household income (B19), and level of urbanity (B10). The coefficient on the index of religiosity is .138. Using the rule of four, we say that a one-unit increase in the index of religiosity (controlling for other factors) predicts approximately a 3.5-percent increase in the probability of support for democracy.

The findings of our surveys indicate that among all four major religions in "respect all" India, at the aggregate level, there is a relative consensus among devotees that both their practice of religion and their practice of democracy are integral and valued parts of their public and their private lives.

Somewhat similar findings about the relation between the intensity of religious practice and the support for democracy were found by Saiful Mujani, Indonesia's most prestigious public-opinion-poll specialist, in his doctoral dissertation at Ohio State University, "Religious Democrats: Democratic Culture and Muslim Political Participation in Post-Suharto Indonesia."[58] In his data and regressions, he found that high-practicing Muslims joined more organizations (both "bonding" among active Muslim citizens and "bridging" with secular citizens) than did low-practicing Muslims, that respondents who joined

TABLE 5.5 Relationship between Intensity of Religious Practice and Support for Political Institutions

		Low intensity (%)	Medium intensity (%)	High intensity (%)	Net gain from low to high
Trust in public institutions:	Hindus	31	35	38	+7
Respondents who reported that they had a high degree of trust in public institutions.	Muslims	39	40	48	+9
Satisfaction with "the way democracy works in India":	Hindus	76	82	80	+4
Respondents who reported that they are "very satisfied" or "satisfied."	Muslims	71	83	84	+13
Political efficacy:	Hindus	76	81	81	+5
Respondents who answered "Yes" to "Do you think your vote has an effect on how things are run in this country?"	Muslims	75	80	77	+2
Frequency of voting:	Hindus	64	76	79	+15
Respondents who reported that they had "voted in every election since they became eligible for voting."	Muslims	60	72	86	+26

Notes: The findings for "efficacy" and "trust," among both Hindus and Muslims, are statistically significant using the Pearson's Chi-Square test (p. value < .001), which means that the possibility of the findings occurring by chance are less than one in 1000.

Sources: *State of Democracy in South Asia Survey: 2005* for "trust" (Question C-13 battery), voting (Question C-8), "satisfaction" (Question C-12). "Efficacy" is based on the *National Election Study, India: 2004* (Question 21).

more organizations trusted people more than those who joined fewer, that respondents who trusted people more trusted the state more, and that respondents who trusted the state more trusted democracy more.

Surveys are not very abundant in Senegal, but those that we have are consistent with the account of relatively widespread tolerance of "other" religious groups, especially by the more religiously active. Three political scientists from the University of Connecticut interviewed 200 Islamic religious leaders and a national sample of 1500 respondents in Senegal. They constructed a tolerance measure based on responses to twelve questions. The religious leaders were by no means tolerant across the board; for example, only 12 percent of them were tolerant of "drug addicts." But 92 percent of religious leaders, in contrast with 78 percent of the general population, were tolerant of "people from another religious group."[59] Pew surveyed people in seventeen Muslim-majority countries about whether democracy "could work in their country or was only a

Western way." The country with the highest percentage of respondents who felt that democracy "can work here" was Senegal, with 87 percent.[60]

Conclusion

The use of the phrase "multiple secularisms" in the title of this chapter is not just a normative or methodological assertion but also an empirical claim. Secular patterns of democracy are not singular in their practice and values but are multiple. To support and clarify this claim, I have documented four distinct patterns of secularism: (1) "separatist," (2) "established religion," (3) "positive accommodation," and (4) "respect all, positive cooperation, and principled distance."

Let me conclude with some reflections about the third pattern, "positive accommodation," and the fourth pattern, "respect all, positive cooperation, and principled distance," to help us better understand how and why new patterns emerged in the past and may continue to emerge in the future. The "positive accommodation" pattern was historically constructed and negotiated in Europe over hundreds of years, initially as a way to accommodate conflicts *within* the Christian religions and later between Christianity and liberalism, both of which often distrusted, and attempted to curtail, the other. These accommodations often took the form of socially constructed institutional arrangements that, once created, often took on "path dependent" qualities, and were even conflated over time with fixed normative values. However, in the 21st century, many of the positive accommodation countries like Germany, Switzerland, Holland, and Belgium are experiencing growing difficulties accommodating new immigrants from religions, such as Muslims, who have not been a party to the highly negotiated, often even consociational, agreements. A particular, for some no doubt convenient, sticking point with Muslims was that a key vehicle for accommodating religions was to give them subsidies and space in the public sphere in their capacity as "hierarchically organized public corporations." As we have seen, this formula implicitly excluded most Muslim organizations because, owing to Islam's inherent, but not necessarily undemocratic, structures most of the Muslims in Europe are not in hierarchical organizations.

A salient distinctive quality of the countries that adopted the "respect all, positive cooperation, principled distance" model, particularly India and Indonesia, was that they were vastly more religiously heterogeneous than Holland, Belgium, Germany, or Switzerland, so if they were to accommodate religions they had to invent more inclusive formulas than Europe's "positive accommodation." This helps explain the origins of the "respect all" dimension.

Also, all three countries in the "respect all" set were newly independent and had to construct new constitutions, so the historically negotiated dimension of "positive accommodation" was not an available option. Conjuncturally, these politically constructed models at independence (particularly in India after the partition and in Indonesia threatened with the succession of some of the Christian outer islands) had to immediately take into consideration new religious threats to social peace and territorial integrity. As we saw, independence leaders in India, Indonesia, and Senegal created a new model to help them respond to a new set of challenges. Because these models were newly negotiated, there were fewer existing "path dependent" obstacles (such as the "hierarchically organized public corporation" requirement) to preclude innovative formulas of accommodation. In particular, as we have seen, the addition of the "positive cooperation" dimension of the model opened up the possibility of secular education ministries and religious leaders co- designing, co-funding, and co-recognizing some academic curricula that may have violated French or American separatist norms, but fully respected the twin tolerations and did not violate fundamental democratic principles.

Given what we have seen of the conjunctural and socially and politically constructed nature of all four patterns we have analyzed in this paper, it is highly probable that in our increasingly globalized and multi-cultural societies, new state-society-religion patterns will have to be constructed, and old ones reconstructed, in order to respond adequately to new contingencies and new challenges to the twin tolerations in modern democracies.

Notes

1. I develop, conceptually, empirically, and historically, the roles of the "twin tolerations" in Alfred Stepan, *Arguing Comparative Politics* (Oxford and New York: Oxford University Press, 2001), 213–255. For brevity, this chapter of *Arguing Comparative Politics,* "The World's Religious Systems and Democracy: Crafting the 'Twin Tolerations,'" will henceforth be referred to as Stepan, "The Twin Tolerations."

2. See S. N. Eisenstadt, "Multiple Modernities," *Daedalus* 129 (Winter 2000): 1–30; and Sudipta Kaviraj, "An Outline of a Revisionist Theory of Modernity," *European Journal of Sociology* 46, no. 3 (2005): 497–526.

3. See Robert Dahl, *Polyarchy: Participation and Opposition* (New Haven, Conn.: Yale University Press, 1971).

4. See Arend Lijphart, *Patterns of Democracy: Government Forms and Performance in Thirty-Six Countries* (New Haven, Conn.: Yale University Press, 1999).

5. See Juan J. Linz and Alfred Stepan, *Problems of Democratic Transitions and Consolidation: Southern Europe, South America, and Post-Communist Europe* (Baltimore, Md., and London: Johns Hopkins University Press, 1996), chap. 3.

6. Eisenstadt, "Multiple Modernities." The reference to the United States as the first case of a multiple modernity in the West is on p. 13. See also S. N. Eisenstadt, "The Reconstruction of Religious Arenas in the Framework of 'Multiple Modernities,'" *Millennium* 29, no. 3 (2000): 591–611.

7. Sudipta Kaviraj, "Modernity and Politics in India," *Daedalus* 129 (Winter 2000): 137–162.

8. Kaviraj, "An Outline of a Revisionist Theory of Modernity," *European Journal of Sociology* 46 (2005): 497–526.

9. See Stepan, "The Twin Tolerations," esp. 215–227.

10. See Stathis N. Kalyvas, *The Rise of Christian Democracy in Europe* (Ithaca, N.Y.: Cornell University Press, 1996).

11. For the history of the establishment of churches in America and for debates about the First Amendment, see A. J. Reichley, *Religion in American Public Life* (Washington, D.C.: Brookings Institution, 1985), 53–167.

12. See, for example, Joel S. Fetzer and J. Christopher Soper, *Muslims and the State in Britain, France, and Germany* (New York: Cambridge University Press, 2005).

13. Ahmet T. Kuru, "Secularism, State Policies, and Muslims in Europe: Analyzing French Exceptionalism," *Comparative Politics* 41, no. 1 (2008): 1–19.

14. On such funding of settlements in the West Bank by U.S.-based religious groups, see the extensively documented investigative story by Jim Rutenberg, Mike McIntyre, and Ethan Bronner, "Tax Exempt Funds Aiding Settlement in the West Bank," *New York Times*, July 6, 2010, 1A.

15. Some religious groups in France, such as Jehovah's Witnesses and Scientologists, have experienced problems with this issue.

16. See Ahmet T. Kuru, "Passive and Assertive Secularism: Historical Conditions, Ideological Struggles, and State Policies towards Religion," *World Politics* 59, no. 4 (2007): 568–594. See also Ahmet T. Kuru, *Secularism and State Policies toward Religion: The United States, France, and Turkey* (New York: Cambridge University Press, 2009), 161–235.

17. See Jonathan Fox, *A World Survey of Religion and the State* (Cambridge and New York: Cambridge University Press, 2008), tables 5.4 for France, 8.4 for Turkey, 9.2 for Senegal.

18. Ibid., table 8.4.

19. In 2000, Sweden began a process of disestablishment. Finland also has an established Orthodox Christian church to service its small Orthodox population.

20. Pippa Norris and Ronald Inglehart, *Sacred and Secular: Religion and Politics Worldwide* (New York: Cambridge University Press, 2004), 72.

21. The data are from the 2001 census of Northern Ireland.

22. Norris and Inglehart, *Sacred and Secular*, 72.

23. See John T. S. Madeley, "A Framework for the Comparative Analysis of Church-State Relations in Europe," *West European Politics* 26, no. 1 (2003): 23–50, esp. 45.

24. This is well documented in a series of papers that will be a part of Emily Beck's doctoral dissertation in the Political Science Department of Columbia University.

25. See the maps of mono-confessional and multiconfessional polities in western Europe in Madeley, "A Framework."

26. Gerhard Robbers, "Religion in the European Union Countries: Constitutional Foundations, Legislations, Religious Institutions and Religious Education; Country Report on Germany," in a book that has not yet been published in English, Ali Köse and Talip Küçükcan, eds., *Avrupa Birliği Ülkelerinde Din-Devlet İlişkileri* [State-Religion Relations in the European Union Members] (Istanbul: Center for Islamic Studies, 2008), 112; emphasis added. In this same collection, Rik Torfs, the author of the chapter on Belgium, "*Belçika*," which has many positive accommodationist features, makes very similar arguments: "The state positively promotes the free development of religious and institutional activities without interfering with their independence. In that sense, one might call this positive neutrality" (58). This collection is extremely useful. In 2005, when the EU

decided to start full membership negotiations with Turkey as a candidate country, Turkey, via the research wing of Diyanet, managed to get many of the most prestigious independent scholars on state-religion-society relations from twelve EU countries—such as Robbers from Germany, Grace Davie from the United Kingdom, Sophie van Bijsterveld from the Netherlands, and Silvio Ferrari from Italy—to write frank essays on the social, legal, and political status of religions in their own countries. I thank the editors for making all of the papers available to me.

27. Robbers, "Religion in the European Union Countries," 131.

28. Ibid., 120. In some, not all, Länder, the Jewish authorities have a similar arrangement. In positive accommodationist Switzerland, "most of the 26 cantons financially support a form of Catholicism or Protestant Christianity and collect taxes on behalf of whatever church or churches they support.... Religious education is standard in Swiss schools, generally in the majority denomination of the canton, but classes in other religions are usually offered and students may opt out of the classes." Fox, *A World Survey*, 131.

29. Robbers, "Religion in the European Union Countries," 121.

30. Ibid., 130.

31. See the classic book on the emergence of this type of consociational accommodation, Arend Lijphart, *The Politics of Accommodation: Pluralism and Democracy in the Netherlands*, rev. ed. (Berkeley: University of California Press, 1975), 47–52.

32. See Sophie van Bijsterveld, "Religion and Law in the Netherlands: Constitutional Foundations, Legislation, Religious Institutions and Religious Education," in Köse and Küçükcan, eds., *State and Religion in Europe*, 196.

33. See Sophie van Bijsterveld, "The Netherlands: Principled Pluralism," in Stephen V. Monsma and J. Christopher Soper, eds., *The Challenge of Pluralism: Church and State in Five Democracies* (New York: Rowman and Littlefield, 1997), 51–86, quotes from 65 and 73; emphasis added.

34. For comparisons of this set of non-Arab countries with large Muslim populations with Arab countries, see Alfred Stepan with Graeme Robertson, "An 'Arab' More Than 'Muslim' Electoral Gap," *Journal of Democracy* 14, no. 3 (July 2003): 30–44; and the debate about this article with our response, "Arab, Not Muslim Exceptionalism," *Journal of Democracy* 15, no. 4 (October 2004): 140–146.

35. I will frequently refer to this model simply as the "respect all" model. I am building on work on India of my colleague Rajeev Bhargava, particularly his idea of "principled distance." See Rajeev Bhargava, "The Distinctiveness of Indian Secularism," in T. N. Srinivasan, ed., *The Future of Secularism* (Oxford and Delhi: Oxford University Press, 2006), 20–53. For the moral and political theory behind India's secularism, see Rajeev Bhargava, "Political Secularism," in John S. Dryzek, Bonnie Honig, and Anne Phillips, eds., *The Oxford Handbook of Political Theory* (Oxford and New York: Oxford University Press, 2006), 636–655. See also Rajeev Bhargava, ed., *Secularism and Its Critics* (Oxford and Delhi: Oxford University Press, 1998), especially the articles by Bhargava, Akeel Bilgrami, and Amartya Sen.

36. More documentation and analysis for Senegal, India, and Indonesia can be found in Alfred Stepan, "Rituals of Respect: Sufis and Secularists in Senegal" (unpublished manuscript); Alfred Stepan, Juan J. Linz, and Yogendra Yadav, *Crafting "State-Nations": India and Other Multinational Democracies* (Baltimore, Md., and London: Johns Hopkins University Press, 2011), esp. chap. 2; Alfred Stepan, Juan J. Linz, and Yogendra Yadav,

"The Rise of 'State-Nations,'" *Journal of Democracy* 21, no. 3 (July 2010): 50–68; and Mirjam Künkler and Alfred Stepan, eds., *Democracy and Islam in Indonesia: Comparative Perspectives*, a forthcoming collection of papers from an April 2009 international conference at the Center for the Study of Democracy, Toleration, and Religion, Columbia University, New York.

37. Interestingly, the other two most highly ranked Muslim-majority countries on these two democracy indexes are Albania and Mali, and both have this same pattern of public religious holidays. Albania has large Roman Catholic and Orthodox Catholic religious minorities, which together are accorded five national holidays, whereas the Muslim majority has only three holidays. In Mali, the majority Muslim population receives four religious holidays, and the small Christian minority receives three; see "Worldwide Public Holidays," http://www.qppstudio.net/publicholidays.htm.

38. Constitution of Senegal, Me Doudou Ndoye, ed. (Dakar: EDJA, 2001), 48–49; my translation.

39. For a documented and convincing discussion of "France as a 'Muslim Power,'" see David Robinson, *Paths of Accommodation: Muslim Societies and French Colonial Authorities in Senegal and Mauritania, 1880–1920* (Athens: Ohio University Press, 2000), 75–96. See also Donal Cruise O'Brien, "Towards an 'Islamic Policy' in French West Africa," *Journal of African History* 8 (1967): 303–316.

40. Neither does Mali or Albania.

41. A basic book on the history and evolution of Pancasila is Azyumardi Azra, *Indonesia, Islam, and Democracy: Dynamics in a Global Context* (Jakarta: Solstice, 2006). An important work on the development of democratic Islamic thought, practices, and organizations in Indonesia is Mirjam Künkler, "Democratization, Islamic Thought and Social Movements: Coalitional Success and Failure in Indonesia and Iran," PhD dissertation in Political Science, Columbia University, New York, 2008. See esp. chap. 3, "How Pluralist Democracy Became the Consensual Discourse among Secular and Non-Secular Muslims in Indonesia."

42. The Indonesian state does not, however, officially recognize the small Jewish presence, the numerous animists within Indonesia's estimated 400 ethnic and language groups, or the variant of Islam called Ahmadiyah, which recognizes a prophet after Muhammad, and, indeed, the state recently was very slow to dispatch police to protect Ahmadiyah from threatened mob attacks.

43. Mohammad Amien Rais, *Putra Nasantara: Son of the Indonesian Archipelago* (Singapore: Singapore Press, 2003), 11. See also the interview with Amien Rais by Mirjam Künkler and Alfred Stepan, *Journal of International Affairs* 61, no. 1 (2007): 205–216.

44. In two long interviews I had with Wahid in September 1998 and October 2007, he paid particular attention to stressing these points. For diversity as a "sociological fact" and pluralism as a "political choice," in Indonesia in general and in the speeches and actions of Wahid, see Abdullahi Ahmed An-Na'im, "Indonesia: Realities of Diversity and Prospects of Pluralism," in his *Islam and the Secular State: Negotiating the Future of Shari'a* (Cambridge, Mass.: Harvard University Press, 2008), 223–266. For an analysis of Wahid's political discourse, see the chapter "Abdurrahman Wahid: Scholar-President," in John L. Esposito and John O. Voll, *Makers of Contemporary Islam* (Oxford: Oxford University Press, 2001), 199–216.

45. See, for example, the writings of the distinguished anthropologist who is a specialist on legal codes and practices in Indonesia and France, John Bowen, "Does French Islam

Have Borders? Dilemmas of Domestication in a Global Religion Field," *American Anthropologist*, 106, no. 1 (2004): 43–55; and *Why the French Don't Like Headscarves* (Princeton, N.J.: Princeton University Press, 2006).

46. D. E. Smith, "India as a Secular State," in Bhargava, ed., *Secularism and Its Critics*, 183, 189.

47. The Ministry of Religion building occupies an entire block in downtown Jakarta.

48. See Azyumardi Azra, Dina Afrianty, and Robert W. Hefner, "Pesantren and Madrassa: Muslim Schools and National Ideals in Indonesia," in Robert W. Hefner and Muhammad Zaman, eds., *Schooling Islam: The Culture and Politics of Modern Muslim Education* (Princeton, N.J.: Princeton University Press, 2007), 172–198. For recent analogous processes in the educational system in Senegal, see Stepan, "Rituals of Respect."

49. See Stepan, "The Twin Tolerations," 227–229.

50. See the long feature article in one of Senegal's leading newspapers, Habibou Bangré, "*Croisade muselmane contre l'excision: Les imams rétablissent la vérité sur cette tradition,*" *Walfadiri*, June 8, 2004.

51. Ibid. A similar social policy of public pledges renouncing foot binding in neighboring Chinese villages with high patterns of intermarriages proved useful.

52. See Abdoul Aziz Kebe, *Argumentaire religieux musulman pour l'abandon des MGF's* (Dakar: Organisation Mondiale de la Sante, 2003). Female circumcision is still a problem in Senegal, with an estimated 28 percent of women from the ages of fifteen to forty-nine having undergone FGM, according to UNICEF. The same source lists Egypt at 96 percent. Senegal's three contiguous Muslim-majority countries have much higher rates; Mali, 92 percent; Guinea, 95 percent; and Mauritania, 71 percent.

53. See note 35, above.

54. Donald Eugene Smith, *India as a Secular State* (Princeton, N.J.: Princeton University Press, 1963), 243.

55. The same question, using the same survey instrument, reveals that support for democracy by Muslims in India is approximately twice as high as that of Muslims in Pakistan. See Stepan, Linz, and Yadav, *Crafting "State Nations,"* chap. 2. These and other results demonstrate the great political contextuality of religion.

56. *State of the Nation Survey*, New Delhi, January 2007, Lokniti, CSDS, N = 15,373, questions B5, B3, B11, B6, B17.

57. National Election Study [India], CSDS, Delhi, 2004.

58. Saiful Mujani, "Religious Democrats: Democratic Culture and Muslim Political Participation in Post-Suharto Indonesia," PhD dissertation, Department of Political Science, Ohio State University, 2003.

59. See Richard Vengroff, Lucy Creevy, and Abdou Ndoye, "Islamic Leaders' Values and the Transition to Democracy: The Case of Senegal," unpublished ms., University of Connecticut, 2005.

60. See *The Pew Global Project Attitudes*, February 3, 2005. The report also says that Pew polled twelve Muslim-majority countries about whether it was "very important to live in a country with honest multiparty elections," and Senegal polled the highest.

6

Civilizational States, Secularisms, and Religions
Peter J. Katzenstein

This chapter[1] cuts against the grain of much writing on international relations. It does not start with the assumption that by privatizing religion, the Peace of Westphalia left international politics fully secular. Furthermore, it does not assume that secularism should be conceived of in the singular. Secularism in international relations is central to substantively different arguments about international relations—realist power politics, liberal cosmopolitanism, and Marxist class struggle. All three view religious conflicts as relics of a bygone era, a sideshow to the struggle over primacy, the coordination of conflicting objectives, and the dynamics of class conflict. There is something appealing and implausible about this view. Appealing is the search for simplification and a parsimonious understanding of international politics. Implausible are the denial of the continued relevance of religion for world politics and a view of secularism in the singular despite the fact that many aspects of secular politics—state, capitalism, and democracy—are so variegated empirically.

Bringing the state (in the singular) back into focus was the flag under which sociologically inclined scholars rallied in the early 1980s. After a couple of decades of writings about interest-group liberalism and Marxism, reemphasizing the importance of the state brought a welcome shift in perspective. This was less true for students of international relations and comparative politics who had never thrown the state out. Realists held firmly to the view that the state was the basic unit of analysis and that states were like units. Where realists saw only sameness, students of comparative politics saw the state in the plural. Varieties of social and political coalitions and state-society relations created different objectives and capacities for political action. In this view, states could be conceived of only in the plural.

Unraveling the mysteries of capitalism yielded the same conclusion. The project of Marxist international political economy was to understand the logic of Capitalism, with a capital C and in the singular. While liberal scholars focused on the convergences that industrialism, welfarism, and mass society were creating across the advanced industrial world, Marxists were pointing to the structural contradictions of capitalism, which they saw reflected in both domestic and international life. The empirical results suggested that capitalism conceived in the singular was not offering a sharp tool for understanding. A different cohort of scholars interested in comparative political economy developed an institutional argument so as to understand better what eventually came to be known as the varieties of capitalism. Welfare capitalism, developmental capitalism, neoliberal capitalism, and Leninist capitalism, among others, share one characteristic: they are capitalisms that take multiple institutional forms. And the differences in form are politically and economically consequential.

Finally, as with the state and capitalism, so with democracy. Nuanced conceptual and rich empirical studies of democratic politics yielded in the 1970s and 1980s one important conclusion. Democracy could be understood only in the plural. American polyarchy, for example, differed greatly from Britain's Westminster model of parliamentary government, multiple strands of consociational and corporatist democratic politics, and one-party-dominant democracies. The theory of democracy has yielded to an astonishing variety of models of democratic politics.

States, capitalisms, and democracies are variegated and complex and must be understood in their multiple manifestations. This conclusion is the result not of a playful postmodernism but of disciplined social-science research. If three core components of secular politics are not well conceptualized in the singular, why should secular politics in the international system?

Section 1 of this chapter explains why scholars of international relations focus on secularism in the singular and all but disregard religion in their analyses.[2] Seeking to show the intermingling of secularisms and religions in world politics, section 2 develops the concept of the "civilizational state" as an alternative to the "rational state."[3] Informed by the writings of Yasusuke Murakami, section 3 inquires into the topic of cultural commensurabilities in world politics.[4] Section 4 offers a brief conclusion.

1. International Relations Theory, Secularism, and Religion

International-relations scholarship in the United States has pivoted around the traditional divide between liberalism and realism. These two schools of thought were reformulated numerous times in the twentieth century to adjust to changing currents in world politics and new fashions in academia. Despite important agreements on some fundamental assumptions, they retain clearly discernible analytic and political commitments that make them distinct.[5] Commercial, political, and institutional versions of liberalism, for example, differ on the relative importance of trade, democratic institutions, and international institutions. Yet they all hold to the perfectibility of a secular international politics in a system that is fundamentally anarchic. Traditional realism, structural realism, and neoclassical realism differ on the role of nonmaterial capabilities and domestic politics for the international system and the foreign policies of states. But they are united in the insight that material capabilities matter greatly in an anarchic, secular system of states.

Liberalism is sweet common sense for many American scholars of international relations. For them, it remains an article of faith, so to speak, that secularization is the dominant trend characterizing the process of modernization. For Francis Fukuyama, history ended with what he saw as liberalism's decisive victory over fascism and communism as its two most serious ideological competitors in the twentieth century.[6] The end of the Cold War, Fukuyama argued, had left rationalist secularism without any serious ideological and political rivals. Yet the defeat of the Soviet Union was brought about not only by the high-tech arms race that the United States accelerated in the 1980s but also by the ideological challenges posed by a devout Polish pope hollowing the Soviet empire from within and fervent Islamicist *mujahideen* fighting it from without.

In the 1990s, other scholars argued the same point. Ernst Haas, for example, insists that liberal, secular nationalism can, but must not, produce progress.[7] Religion, like race and language, is a cultural building block of national identity that permits leaders to articulate a collective national vision to which mass publics respond for instrumental reasons. The triumph of liberalism is procedural rather than substantive. According to Haas, liberalism rejects fixed dogma in favor of rules that remain devoid of moral content and that permit vigorous debate and conflict among competing interests and values, none of which can claim inherent superiority. Diffuse reciprocity and compromise, not moral ends, are at the core of this procedural understanding of liberal, secular nationalism. Its story starts in the eighteenth century with the Enlightenment, the idea of progress, and the possibility of policy based on scientific reasoning. By the end of the twentieth century, liberal nationalism has transformed itself at least in part to a new kind of multilateral cosmopolitanism. The conjoining of the European welfare state with the European integration movement in the second half of the twentieth century is the prime case for Haas's vision of secular liberalism.

That vision, Haas argues, is challenged by the delayed and rapid modernization efforts undertaken under the banner of syncretist nationalism.[8] Syncretism affords religion a central role. Modernization thus does not yield progress by default, as Fukuyama argues. Significant modernization and rationalization can be achieved through nonliberal forms of nationalism that mobilize religion to the task of government at home and governance abroad. In the end, however, Haas remains convinced that it is the secular, liberal variant of nationalism that has the best historical record and holds forth the greatest promise for bringing about modernity.

Cultural realism is more open to acknowledge the importance of religion in world politics.[9] Samuel Huntington's political intuition differed sharply from Fukuyama's. Huntington's argument about the likelihood of a "clash of civilization" draws a pessimistic picture.[10] In Huntington's view, the historical turn of 1989 to 1991 did not end ideological rivalry but substituted one ideological conflict for another. For Huntington, civilizations with their different religious cores have become the relevant cultural context for states and nonstate actors alike. Activated by religion, civilizational clashes are for Huntington the defining characteristic of a new era of international politics.

Since their building blocks are variable constellations of religion, culture, language, values, traditions, and memories, Huntington concedes that civilizations cannot be defined easily and with any degree of precision. Like Doctor Dolittle's pushmi-pullyu, Huntington's argument appears to have two heads and thus can take on all comers. Under the wide umbrella of civilization, identities are contested and can be reconstructed quite easily through a politics that is forever in flux. Kemalist reformism thus can be explained within the context of Islam, as can significant reform efforts in Mexico, Australia, or Russia.[11] Yet this is not the central thrust of Huntington's argument, which stresses instead that the basic factors defining civilizations are objective and unchanging. Underneath civilizational multipolarity, Huntington thus discovers, ominously, a profound split between the "West" and the "rest."

In this formulation, cultural realism operates with static and totalizing concepts, such as "totalitarian, godless communism" and "democratic, Christian capitalism" during the Cold War and "Islam" and "Christianity" after the Cold War ended. Casting world politics in terms of such dualisms, or the generic "East" versus "West," yields an overly simplified and truncated view. Orientalist vocabulary recalls Oswald Spengler's warning that "the Yellow Peril" posed a great threat for Western civilization.[12] Such racial overtones are no longer common currency today. But as Edward Said argues, Orientalism remains fraught with ideological undercurrents that often seek to divide sharply between civilizational identities that in reality are highly variegated and blurred.[13] This is equally true of Occidentalism. Ian Buruma and Avishai Margalit show that Occidentalism can take a highly critical form focusing on the stipulated corrosive influences of the city, the bourgeois, reason, and feminism. Each of these concepts points to the alleged feebleness, greed, and decadence of the Occident.[14] Alternative accounts of Occidentalism underline instead only positive elements: the glory of Greece and Rome, Christianity, the Renaissance, the Enlightenment, and, finally, the French and Industrial Revolutions. Such accounts are to be found not only among those living in the West. Xiaomei Chen depicts an unremittingly favorable picture of the West prevailing in China during the first post-Mao decade.[15] The deep tension among different images of the "West" has brought into the open a deep chasm separating proponents of the "extreme West" on the American right and their domestic and European critics.[16] On the issue of Iraq, a fierce transatlantic disagreement pitted a European "Venus" against an American "Mars."[17] Evidently, there exists no stable and uncontested Western identity that clashes with the rest.

Could the "de-Westernization" of the United States also lead to its "de-Americanization"? Of all of the criticisms of his core claim, this is the one that Huntington took most seriously and that prompted him to write still another book.[18] Cultural and ethnic diversity is rapidly increasing in the United States. Muslims now outnumber Episcopalians and will soon outnumber Jews.[19] In a world where "our" Japanese can beat "their" Japanese, will "our" Muslims fight "theirs"? The social statistics of the United States belie the assertion of cultural homogeneity and coherence. The majority of the American population is projected to be nonwhite by 2050. Echoing European concerns about an Islamic demographic time bomb, Huntington is deeply worried about its Hispanic equivalent in the United States. The entangling of the United States and Mexico, Huntington argues, may well become the death knell for America with its Anglo-Protestant cultural core as we have come to know it.[20] In the analysis of cultural realism, the clash between homogeneous and coherent civilizations is inevitable. And so is, with a slight shift in perspective, the clash among groups inside civilizations.

Cultural realism offers a truncated analysis of world politics. It concludes that a clash will dominate over many other possible outcomes that also deserve close attention. These outcomes include, among others, absorption, hybridity, hegemony, rejection and resurgence, obliteration and genocide, isolation and suspicion, and cross-fertilization.[21] Other scholars have explored some of these avenues. Unlike Huntington, Karl Deutsch, for example, takes an entirely different view in analyzing the relations between "the West and the rest." The distinctiveness of the West, Deutsch argues, is greatest with respect to political and social institutions. Equally significant, virtually all Western traits can be found in one or more non-Western civilizations: "The peoples and culture of the West are like those of other regions, only more so. This is why the West and the rest of the world could learn from each other in the past and can continue to do so in the future."[22]

Analytical perspectives that draw on liberal secularism or cultural realism feel quite familiar. Yet both suffer from limitations that invite us to move beyond them. Secular liberalism looks to history as a teleological process. And cultural realism is undercut by the fact that diversity and difference, not unity and homogeneity, are at the core of civilizations and the collective identities they foster. This is not to argue that well-established concepts, such as efficiency and power, are unimportant in our understanding of the role of secularism and religion in world politics. Relative differences in power, understood as material capabilities, by themselves, do not yield a compelling answer to the mocking question that realists traditionally have posed to students of religion: "How many divisions has the pope?" After the end of the Cold War and the collapse of the Soviet empire, students of international relations are likely to give a very different answer from those they offered in the 1930s and 1940s and during the Cold War. Furthermore, efficiency, which figures prominently in liberal theories of world politics, does not engage well with many of the identities, motivations, and strategies of religious actors whose calculations can often not be reduced only to instrumental reasoning.[23]

Realist and liberal concepts are more useful in combination with others that seek to capture some of the ideas that motivate varieties of secular and religious politics. Specifically, they are more compelling if we graft them onto complementary sociological approaches. Constructivism, for example, as one variant of the sociological turn in international-relations theory, insists that the material world itself does not determine actor identities and interests; the creation of a social world through processes of interaction does. Social structures contain shared knowledge, material resources, and political practices; knowledgeable agents use these resources to construct variable and ever-changing norms and identities; and through practice, these agents change themselves and the structures in which they operate. Vendulka Kubálková, for example, has attempted to develop a theory of international political theology.[24] Following Nicholas Onuf, she has adopted a "rule-oriented" constructivism that focuses on rules as ordering the basic linguistic and nonlinguistic aspects of human existence.[25] Although she is interested in the productive effects of language, she does not reduce reality to text. Other analysts take somewhat different sociological approaches, displaying a bent for either more[26] or less[27] theoretical self-consciousness and positivist commitment. Such sociological approaches contradict many strands of realist and liberal international-relations scholarship. They do not give analytical primacy to actors, such as unitary, rational states, or particular levels of analysis, such as the international system. Because they are more open to alternative concepts, sociological approaches may help us shed more light on the dynamics of religious and secular forces in world politics.

2. Civilizational States

How can we conceive of the intermingling of secularisms and religions in contemporary world politics? As talk of Latin Christendom declined, references to European civilization became increasingly popular in the mid-eighteenth century. Historically rooted in religion, today's global civilization is marked by a belief in scientific and technological progress and human betterment. These beliefs are enacted in different civilizational states, embodying multiple modernities. The United States, Europe, China, Japan, and Islam are civilizational states or polities that are connected in the American imperium by processes, such as Americanization, Europeanization, Sinicization, Japanization, or

Islamicization and that are more (as in Sinicization) or less (as in Islamicization) regionally grounded. What do I mean by civilization, state and polities, civilizational process, and imperium?

Transcending individuals and societies, *civilizations* are social and operate at the broadest level of cultural identity in world politics. They are not fixed in space or time. Civilizations are both internally highly differentiated and culturally loosely integrated. Because they are differentiated, civilizational ideas and institutions transplant selectively, not wholesale. Because they are culturally integrated, civilizations can assume a reified identity when encountering other civilizations. Civilizations constitute a world that is neither a Hobbesian anarchy nor a Habermasian public sphere, neither empire nor cosmopolis.[28] Instead, it is a weakly institutionalized social order consisting of a variety of processes.

States are centers of political authority with distinct identities and institutions, endowed with the capacity of collectively mobilizing resources in the achievement of political objectives. States are not the only such centers of authority. *Polities* are broader centers of authority that are not necessarily territorially based.[29] States are often nested in such broader authorities, both older ones such as historical empires and newer ones such as emerging governance structures. Far from being unitary, states take on very different forms. Their hallmark, centralized territorial rule, persists today in many parts of the world, not unchallenged but as part of overlapping and intersecting networks of rules in which states hold a preeminent position. States are one of many sources of political identity and loyalty, among them nations, groups, movements, and localities. The degree of stateness is thus variable.[30] For example, stateness is high in the case of the United States and Japan; it is somewhat lower in the case of China, if we refer to China as the combination of the territorial state of China and the communities of overseas Chinese; it is still lower in the case of Europe's emerging polity; and it barely exists in the case of Islam. What varies also is the sociocultural embeddedness of the state. State policies and practices can be totally dominated by domestic norms, they might be guided by domestic rules, or they might be merely permissible under domestic rules and not constituted by them.[31] In contrast to rational conceptions of the efficient state, social conceptions posit a thicker context of state purpose. The international standing of civilizational states is determined by the perceived credibility of current power and prestige, the perceived salience of an active historical memory, and the prospect of an appealing, imagined future. If such appeals are acknowledged as politically authentic, civilizational states are consequential.

Civilizational states and the peoples they rule are engaged in practices that, in the aggregate, sum to *civilizational processes,* such as Americanization, Japanization, Sinicization, Europeanization, and Islamicization. Past scholarship has for the most part sought to capture the integrating aspects of such processes, as in Max Weber's "rationalization" or today's "globalization." At the same time, however, such processes are also differentiating. They shape politics, and are shaped by it, through different mechanisms, including outright imitation, selective adaptation, negotiation, and violent imposition. And they can be tracked in different empirical domains.

As was true of Rome, the American *imperium* joins territorial and nonterritorial power.[32] It combines traditional elements of an old-fashioned European- and American-style imperialism with elements of rule that are relatively new. The system of far-flung military bases and the power of the American military illustrate the importance of the territorial-military aspects of America's imperium. At the same time, the United States is also a central actor that is creating systems of nonterritorial rule, for example, in the evolution of governing mechanisms in financial markets or in the standards that help define the evolution of consumer society.

Randall Collins has provided an admirably pithy and highly plausible view of civilizations as zones of prestige that have one or several cultural centers.[33] The attractiveness of these zones of prestige radiates outward with variable strengths. Distances are not only geographic but take the form of networks of attraction that carry prestige through various channels, passing over or penetrating other civilizational zones. This conceptualization focuses our attention on social activity and cultural variety. It avoids regarding civilizations as cultural codes, as patterns that govern beliefs and institutions that are endowed with an enduring essence. Civilization is not an actor or an attribute of actors; it is a set of relationships and activities.

The power of a civilization depends on the practices that promote or diminish its magnetism. Such magnetism reflects creativity, typically shaped by rival positions and disagreements in stances that command attention. Competing schools of thought that are in vigorous debate and disagreement thus are crucial to civilizational prestige. Civilizations are marked by dialogue, debate, and disagreement that generate intellectual and artistic tension. In their engagement of the world, both attraction and propagation characterize zones of civilizational prestige that are composed of multiple, competing networks and distant connections. Such zones attract students and visitors of different kinds, some from very far away. Conversely, zones of high prestige also send out teachers and missionaries, both to civilizational peripheries and to other civilizations. Zones of prestige are not free-standing, monolithic, and unchanging essences. Diversity and active debate among rival positions spur creativity and stymie uniformity of opinion.

Civilizational ruptures can occur for many reasons, as they did in the relations between China and Japan during the Tokugawa period. In that case, as well as with the earlier Chinese resistance to the import of Indian Buddhism, cultural resistance was not derivative of a broader struggle against geopolitical and economic hegemony. This contrasts with the case of anti- and postcolonial movements in the second half of the twentieth century. Then the shift away from European- and Western-centered cultural domination in many parts of the world typically was also a move against the cultural imperialism of a civilizational zone of prestige that, together with its political preeminence, had lost much of its cultural magnetism. Conversely, struggles for political liberation, such as the Indian independence movement, and moves for economic advancement, such as Japan's rise after 1945, have occurred without a simultaneous rejection of the cultural imports of existing zones of civilizational prestige. The dynamics of civilizational politics cannot be reduced simply to political or economic factors.

This is confirmed by those historical instances in which militarily weak or defeated parts of the world that were economically lagging remained zones of civilizational prestige with deep sources of attraction to many members of the military or economic centers of domination. Ancient Greece and twentieth-century France are good examples. Despite Rome's military conquest, Greek civilization did not lose its prestige and absorbed Rome culturally. Greece had institutionalized networks of opposing schools of thought and creativity in a system of higher education that fostered the kind of intellectual rivalries that created cultural attraction; Rome did not. Twentieth-century France offers another example of a zone of civilizational prestige that persisted as France relinquished its central position in the global and European capitalist system. Despite this slide, Paris has remained an important center of intellectual creativity and fashion in literary theory, philosophy, and parts of the social sciences. In sharp contrast to the relatively isolated, world-class universities that emerged in the United States, Paris had developed intersecting networks of intellectuals who focused on academic subjects and connected their subjects to a broader intellectual life and the worlds of high-culture entertainment, journalism, and politics. In the natural sciences and engineering, in sharp contrast, the links among university-based research, government, and the world of corporate or start-up capitalism were more developed and vibrant in the United States than in France. In contrast to France, the infrastructure of military and economic primacy was much better served by the evolving American than the French pattern of creativity.

Cultural prestige and military or economic primacy thus should not be equated unthinkingly. Robert Gilpin argues quite correctly that numerous factors such as respect and common interest underlie the prestige of a state as the everyday currency of international relations. "Ultimately, however, the hierarchy of prestige in an international system rests on economic and military power . . . the fact that the existing distribution of power and the hierarchy of prestige can sometimes be in conflict with one another is an important factor in international political change."[34] Even in such situations, however, it seems plausible to assume that struggles for military and economic catch-up will involve a good deal of emulation of the practices that characterize zones of civilizational prestige. And emulation and rejection are often deeply intertwined. The cultural dynamic in such processes often reflects the intellectual interests and career aspirations of elites no longer dependent on travel to or imports from zones of prestige and eager, as well as able, to exploit and build up further the creativity of a zone that is no longer a civilizational periphery. For this to happen, two conditions must be met. The material conditions for cultural production must have advanced to a threshold level. And rival schools of thought and creativity must have come into being to create vibrant debate within this emerging zone of prestige, as well as between it and the former center from which it is beginning to break away.

In his voluminous writings on civilizations, Shmuel Eisenstadt's perspective complements that of Collins. Eisenstadt starts with a key distinction between two types of civilizations. Axial-age civilizations emerged together with the major world religions around the sixth century BCE. The civilization of modernity, by way of contrast, is a product of the very recent past, starting with the European Enlightenment and the scientific and technological revolution.

Eisenstadt takes the concept of the axial age from Karl Jaspers.[35] It denotes a formative period in world history when a number of powerful cultural developments occurred independently in China, India, Iran, Palestine, and Greece. Humankind then moved from an instinctual disposition to a self-reflexive striving for transcendence and self-determination. For Jaspers and Eisenstadt, the sixth century BCE is an axis that divides history, a transformative break brought about by the appearance of the world's great religions and the onset of the spiritualization of humankind. Jaspers's argument was anchored in eighteenth- and nineteenth-century German philosophy and social theory (Fichte, Schelling, and Hegel) and its preoccupation with autonomous human self-direction (Kant) and cultural creativity (Herder). In the twentieth century, Weber's sociology of world religions, Scheler's philosophical anthropology, and Simmel's argument of a transformative turn to the ideational in human life all were important precursors to Jaspers's insights. In all of these formulations, the autonomous role assigned to ideational factors is the same as in Jaspers:[36] a shift in religion from serving as a tool to satisfy human needs to a guide for following divine norms (Weber); a move from adaptive rationality and practical intelligence to the capacity for self-consciousness and self-reflection that distinguishes between essence and existence (Scheler); and the elevation of the realm of human freedom above the realm of human purpose (Simmel).

Eisenstadt's comparative analyses of axial-age civilizations is important for his core argument: the delayed impact that the different religions embodied in these civilizations had on the eventual emergence of one global civilization containing multiple modernities.[37] Following Max Weber, Eisenstadt argues that the different religious cores and cultural programs of the axial-age civilizations are historically grounded and continually reconstructed traditions. The religious cores of civilizations thus continue to have a strong impact on the unending restructuring of their core states. Eisenstadt dissents from

Weber's Eurocentrism by insisting that this reconstruction is shaped in all civilizations by specific antinomies: transcendental and mundane, universalistic and particularistic, totalistic and pluralistic, orthodox and heterodox. And these antinomies motivate political struggles that have a strong impact on political institutions, social and economic structures, and collective identities. All axial-age civilizations have generated proto-fundamentalist movements. In the West, Jacobinism became an oppositional movement in European civilization that exploded in the twentieth century under the banners of communism and fascism. Modern fundamentalism in non-Western civilizations combines the impact of Western Jacobinism with indigenous fundamentalist movements. Jacobin impulses in modernity thus are not passing phenomena in the history of civilizations. They are permanent features. Fundamentalism is an engine of change in all civilizations and a core aspect of the civilization of modernity.

The first modern civilization was western European. Based on the Enlightenment and crystallized politically in the American and French Revolutions, it develops in the specific context of European Christianity. Its cultural core is a bundle of cognitive and moral imperatives for more individual autonomy, less traditional constraints, and more control over nature. The first modernity was constructed and reconstructed in the specific context of Judeo-Greek-Christian cultural universalism and the political pluralism in its center-periphery relations, social movements, and political protest. Western European modernity spread to central and eastern Europe, North and South America, and other non-European civilizations. For Eisenstadt, the civilization of modernity is defined not by being taken for granted but by becoming a focal point of contestation, an object of uninterrupted conflict engaging both pre- and postmodern protest movements. The civilization of modernity embodies a multiplicity of different cultural programs and institutions of modernity that derive from the interaction between western European modernity and the different civilizations of the axial age.

Modern societies are not converging on a common path involving capitalist industrialism, political democracy, modern welfare regimes, and pluralizing secularisms. Instead, the different religious traditions act as cultural sources for the enactment of different programs of modernity. For example, western European modernity was transformed in the United States under the specific circumstances of a settler and immigrant society. The continued relevance of fundamentalist movements have had a profound impact on the multiple traditions and various dimensions of social structure, political institutions, and collective identity of the American state. A second example is offered by Japan's reconstruction of modernity. Japan is the only civilization that did not experience a break in the axial age. It is based on specific patterns of emulation and selection that evolved a distinctive set of protest movements, social structures, and collective identities. Based on a deeply anchored syncretism of religious belief systems, since the Meiji revolution, Japanese civilization has been highly eclectic in the values it has adopted and flexible in the interpretation of the dramatic shifts in political context it has confronted.

The legacies of different world religions thus create multiple modernities as sources of cultural innovation. In the evolution of the socioeconomic, political-legal, and technical-scientific dimensions of the civilization of modernity, forces of convergence are always balanced against forces of divergence. Modernity is inescapably multiple and undergoing a constant process of reinvention in which all traditional elements that rebel against it have themselves a modern, Jacobin character.

3. Cultural Commensurabilities

We live in a civilization of globalization that creates convergences around some of the values of modernity and is marked by divergences that derive from the enactment of cultural programs grounded in different religious traditions. This condition invites two problematic responses. To argue, as some do, that the global world is flat is to follow the example of the one-eyed Nelson at the Battle of Copenhagen (April 2, 1802)—reversing the telescope and putting it on one's blind eye. (Nelson knew what he was doing; this is less certain of today's breathless admirers of a new, brave and global world.) Conversely, to deny the force and power of globalization in its various manifestations, as some of the critics of globalization do, is to play Peter Pan with reality, closing one's eyes and wishing really hard.

The prospect for cultural commensurabilities in the relations between civilizational states is unavoidably shaped by both homogenizing and differentiating tendencies. Commensurabilities cannot emerge simply from the growth of community and universal standards as defined by science. And commensurabilities are not denied simply by the existence of diverging legacies, religious and otherwise. They emerge instead from the partial overlaps of the multiple secular and religious traditions that mark all civilizational states. Adapting Murakami's[38] and Michael Mann's[39] terminology, that partial overlap creates space for what I call here a polymorphic globalism. In such a globalism, various intersections of secularisms and religions are created through never-ending processes of mutual cooperation, adaptation, coordination, and conflict.

Two such intersections command attention. The first pits the secular world against the religious world. Both of these worlds have profound impacts on world politics. Both are based on transcendental thought. The religious world holds to an unquestioned belief in the divine. The secular world has an unshaken belief in the attainability of ultimate truth. Each seeks to deny or undermine the existence of the other. And both have offered radically different foundations to different world orders in history.

Andrew Phillips inquires into the constitution, operation, and eventual decay of two such world orders: Latin Christendom before the mid-seventeenth century and the Sinocentric world order in the nineteenth century.[40] Latin Christendom and its decaying canon law were undermined by the confessional splintering that accompanied the Protestant Reformation. Sectarian violence increased at the very time that technological innovations increased the cost, scale, and destructiveness of warfare. After Habsburg had failed to shore up a unified Christendom along imperial lines, Europe's princes began enforcing confessional conformity in their own realms. Religious heresy came to be equated with political treachery, and a century of warfare ensued. At its end, the Westphalian system of sovereign states began the attempt of separating an international, secular order from private, religious ones.

The nineteenth-century Sinocentric world order confronted not only endogenous but also exogenous shocks. Dynastic decline was accelerated by millenarian peasant rebellions and an incipient military revolution that destroyed the East Asian world order and plunged China and much of the region into a century of upheaval. Emboldened by a revolution in naval warfare, imperialist Western powers opened China by force to satisfy their commercial and cultural interests. The Taiping rebellion was a puritanical millennial movement that incorporated evangelical Christianity into Chinese folk religion, thus creating a ferocious insurgency. Although it was ultimately defeated, this rebellion hollowed out the Chinese state by accelerating the unraveling of China's system of centralized control and thus opened the path toward the system's ultimate demise, civil war, Japanese occupation, and, after a bloody civil war, the Communist seizure of power.

Is today's international order likely to go the way of Latin Christendom and the Sinocentric world? The intermingling of secular and religious elements in contemporary world politics is not just a matter of the different types of actors—state versus nonstate, secular versus religious—vying for primacy. It is also a matter of the principles that constitute contemporary world politics. Do secular or religious elements provide the core organizing principles?[41] Although the Westphalian system is organized along secular lines, the weakening of a large number of states in recent decades has given more political space to religious actors. And in seeking to substitute religious for secular principles in the organization of world politics, some of these actors pose a radical challenge to secular authorities. The current wave of jihadist politics is one such effort. It does not seek to advance its preferred outcomes within the existing Westphalian system. It wants to create a new order. The secular state system is organized around multiple sovereign centers of authority that respect territorial borders, subscribe to the sanctity of law and the legitimacy of international organizations, and deny that there exists one single truth governing world politics. A religious world order would recognize only one center of authority, might not respect territorial borders, would deny the sanctity of law and the legitimacy of international organizations, and would insist on the existence of only one source of divine truth. Calling for such an order poses a systemic and total threat, not national or regional and partial ones. Today, there is no state seeking to effect such a dramatic change, and only a few nonstate actors, among them the al-Qaeda-led jihadist movement and, according to Mendelsohn, possibly Hizb ut-Tahrir.[42]

Polymorphic globalism is possible also at a second and less familiar intersection that is of particular interest to Murakami in his magisterial book.[43] Rather than dividing secularism from religion, Murakami underlines the similarities in the transcendental tendencies of historical religions *and* modern science in the West and contrasts their revolutionary aspirations and impact with the conservative historiological and hermeneutic tendencies of East Asian civilizations. The former is possessed by the belief in progress. The latter remains firmly grounded in the world of the profane, which lends itself to limitless reinterpretations and living in multiple realities.

Murakami argues that polymorphic liberalism is based on hermeneutic, not transcendental, reflection. In developing his argument, Murakami follows Weber in his sociological treatment of historical religions. Distinctive of Christianity and the Western civilizations based on it is a transcendental orientation. Divided into a high-level, intellectual and a low-brow, popular form, Eastern religions and civilizations lack this transcendental orientation. The coexistence of various religions in Japan is an example of the hermeneutic principle of reflexive action. For Murakami, a decline in progressive and a rise in polymorphic liberalism are not the end of history. They are merely the end of a historical era dominated by Western states—specifically, two great empires, British and American, that have dominated world politics during the last two and a half centuries. History will continue, sustained by the dialectical relations between two kinds of reflexive practices: transcendental, scientific-religious on the one hand and hermeneutic, historical-practical on the other. Flirting with an essentialist view of East and West, Murakami sees reflexive action shaped by two axes crossing almost at right angles: religion and science on the one hand, history and practice on the other.

For Murakami, the religions that are part of the Judeo-Christian tradition have an absolute character, promise salvation in the afterlife, and are prone to violence. In their high-brow intellectual and low-brow popular forms, Eastern religions are marked instead by syncretism, promise salvation in the earthly life, and tend toward peaceful coexistence. The prospect for cultural commensurability in a polymorphic globalism, according to Murakami, depends on a partial move away from universal justice-based standards and a transcendental style of thought in a world dominated by the West to accommodate contextual, rule-based standards and a hermeneutic style of thought in a world inhabited also by East Asian and, we might add, a number of other civilizational states.

Polymorphic globalism as the institutional order for world politics is not captured well by the combination of philosophical speculation and psychological intuition that characterizes Murakami's work. It is served better by an institutional perspective that John Meyer has provided.[44] Meyer argues that the culture of Latin Christendom has shaped the organizational form, rather than the substance, of a secular world polity. Christianity brought together both strong, local mobilization of individual effort and general, universalistic long-distance relationships. Christianity offered an institutional model of collective life that accorded political prominence to states as ideologically validated units. It thus avoided global segmentation and disintegration. For many centuries, the Church owned much of the world's productive land, provided the ideology that defined the content of the political practices of princes and justified the management of the church's vast worldly affairs. Christianity offered a general civilizational frame that brought together both elites and mass publics, as well as the organizational life that was central and peripheral to the world polity. It created and sustained the political and economic vitality and imperialist thrust of the West.

Karl Deutsch has provided a compelling account of why the civilization of Latin Christendom was able to unite and why subsequently it was fated to split apart.[45] He argues that the spiritual, linguistic, and cultural unity of medieval Christendom—its common Latin language, the shared legal and spiritual authority of the pope, the common political leadership provided by the emperors of the Holy Roman Empire, the collective enterprise of the crusades, and the common style of Romanesque and Gothic art and architecture—was a transitory stage in history that was destroyed by the very forces that gave rise to it.

Scarcity was the economic foundation of the international civilization of Latin Christendom—scarcity in goods, services, and skilled personnel. Scarcity permitted the growth of a thin web of supranational trading communities sharing in a common language, customs, sprit, laws, traditions, and family connections. And in this web, specialized nodes of productive skill sets arose that diffused over long distances—provided, for example, by Irish monks, German knights, Lombard traders, French master builders, and Flemish peasants knowledgeable about advanced agricultural techniques. While at the local level, the linguistic fractionalization of an immobile peasantry persisted, the thin web of supranationalism created the conditions for a superficial internationalization of several civilizations knit together by commerce, intellectual life, and politics. Deutsch identifies three major European civilizations: Latin Christianity in western and central Europe, Byzantium in southeastern Europe, and Islam on the Iberian Peninsula and in the Middle East. And he includes two trading people—Jews with a pan-European and Vikings with a northern European presence—which had incomplete civilizational traits in that they lacked adequate contact with advanced skills and centers of production. By the thirteenth century, four of these civilizations had given way to Latin Christendom. Yet increasing contacts among village, manor, and town eventually gave rise to the conditions that led to the demise of Latin Christendom, as the rate of national mobilization began to outpace the rate of international assimilation in subsequent periods of the rise of modern nationalism.

Deutsch ends his discussion with two scenarios. In the first, the world would try to return to the medieval unity of thin internationalism, based on a rigid system of social and political stratification around continentwide or worldwide civilizational barriers of entry of the diverse and unassimilated majority of humankind into conditions of economic advancement. In the second, the world would go through a prolonged period of internationalization and globalization that would spread economic advancement across the globe and permit the flowering of national cultures and languages into an era marked by a rapid rise in social mobilization and national differentiation. Nazi victory in World War II might have advanced the first scenario around the concepts of "master race" and "high culture." Allied victory created instead the global civilization of modernity, with its characteristic mixture of secular and religious elements in world politics, with nationalism often playing the role of secular religion.

With the desacralization of Christianity and the rise of science and technology since the eighteenth century, the content of the emerging global polity has become more secular than religious. Yet the historical foundations of that polity and the continued or renewed vibrancy of several of the world's major religions have made religion once again an increasingly important part of world politics in recent decades. The commensurability of culture that interests Murakami is rooted in the legacy of a diffusion of organizational forms and institutional practices in a world marked by the continued relevance of religious beliefs.

Cultural commensurabilities result from global social processes that derive from the institutional model created by Christianity's impact on other civilizations—including institutionally differing models of modern statehood, contemporary varieties of market capitalism, and different democratic regimes. The emergence of such a global context—constituting, transforming, and reforming the identities and norms that define political interests—makes cultural commensurability an important link in the relations between different civilizational states.

4. Conclusion

To those who scan the headlines of the daily news and to the readers of Mark Juergensmeyer's analysis of religious violence in world politics, the need for examining the interaction among secularism, religion, and international relations is self-evident.[46] Yet international-relations scholarship has barely begun this task, as the rejection of religion "seems to be inscribed in the genetic code of the discipline of IR."[47] Since the main actors, purposes, and constitutive practices of the modern international state system were established at the end of the wars of religion in Europe, Westphalia has become a shorthand for an interstate system that was assumed to have banished religion to the domestic and private realm.[48] The principle of *cuius regio eius religio* and the doctrine and practice of state neutrality on religious matters in Europe supposedly set the tone worldwide.[49] Religious pluralism among states eventually became the rule, as did the principle of noninterference in domestic affairs.

This is a skewed reading not only of European politics but also of the principles of Westphalia. The historical evolution from an international politics dominated by religion to a secular state system was anything but smooth and simple. Historians such as Anthony Marx and Linda Colley argue that strong exclusionary religious elements were present at the birth of modern states, such as Spain and Britain, convulsed, respectively, by the Spanish Inquisition and the Protestant Reformation.[50] Religious conflict mobilized people into politics and gave leaders an opportunity to consolidate power. European states such as Britain, Sweden, and the Netherlands saw themselves as the new Israel. Whether religion is also a bedrock of modern nationalism is more controversial.[51] It was only after the French Revolution, as Eugen Weber argues, that peasants were made into Frenchmen, as only about a quarter of France's population actually spoke French in 1789.[52] Yet language and the printing press as the source of modern national consciousness might not be the beginning of the history of nationalism. Deutsch's argument makes us ponder whether developments that led to the breakdown of Latin Christendom perhaps helped create the modern secular state system on the back of a religiously infused, bloody-minded proto-nationalism. Intent on securing absolute power over their subjects, European states both mobilized religious passions and privatized religion.[53] Secularization and religion thus were deeply entangled at the outset of the modern state system and have remained so ever since, illustrated by the state-imposed solution of religious depoliticization through privatization. The sociological turn in international-relations theory makes it possible to deploy now commonly accepted categories of analysis—culture, identity, norm, idea, ideology—to probe once more the connections between secularism and religion in international politics.

Our conventional understanding of the origins of a secular international politics has concealed the continued relevance of religious motivations, often cast in the guise of civilizational language. For example, Gerrit Gong's analysis of the standards of civilization that informed state practices in the nineteenth century was predicated on Christian, white, male notions of who was considered to be a human.[54] And a burgeoning literature on sovereignty demonstrates that the canonical view of sovereign states governed by the principle of nonintervention is bad history.[55] Many elements of the secular relations among sovereign states have religious roots.[56] James Kurth, for example, traces the antecedents of the contemporary human-rights revolution, especially in Europe, to the missionary zeal of Protestantism of centuries past.[57] And in its war on terror, America's religiously rooted sense of nationalism has become a defining element. Varieties of secularisms and religions remain a vital force in world politics and the foreign policies of the civilizational state we call America.

Notes

1. I would like to thank all of the participants at the various SSRC workshops that have led to this book's publication for their comments, criticisms, and suggestions, which have helped to improve this chapter. Blame for remaining weaknesses lies with me only.

2. Section 1 draws on, deepens and extends a line of argument developed first in Peter J. Katzenstein, "Multiple Modernities as Limits to Secular Europeanization?" in Timothy A. Byrnes and Peter J. Katzenstein, eds., *Religion in an Expanding Europe* (Cambridge: Cambridge University Press, 2006), 1–33.

3. Some of the ideas in Section 2 draw on arguments developed in greater depth in Peter J. Katzenstein, "A World of Plural and Pluralist Civilizations: Multiple Actors, Traditions and Practices," in Peter J. Katzenstein, ed., *Civilizational Politics in World Affairs: Plural and Pluralist Perspectives* (New York: Routledge, 2009), 1–40.

4. Section 3 builds on Peter J. Katzenstein, "The Cultural Foundations of Murakami's Polymorphic Liberalism," in Kozo Yamamura, ed., *A Vision of a New Liberalism? Critical Essays on Murakami's Anticlassical Analysis* (Stanford, Calif.: Stanford University Press, 1997), 23–40.

5. Elizabeth Shakman Hurd, *The Politics of Secularism in International Relations* (Princeton, N.J.: Princeton University Press, 2008). Elizabeth Shakman Hurd, "The Political Authority of Secularism in International Relations," *European Journal of International Relations* 10, no. 2 (2004): 235–262. Peter J. Katzenstein, "Introduction: Alternative Perspectives on National Security," in Peter J. Katzenstein, ed., *The Culture of National Security: Norms and Identity in World Politics* (New York: Columbia University Press, 1996), 1–32.

6. Francis Fukuyama, *The End of History and the Last Man* (New York: Free Press, 1992). Francis Fukuyama, "The End of History?" *National Interest* 16 (Summer 1989): 3–18.

7. Ernst Haas, *Nationalism, Liberalism, and Progress: The Dismal Fate of New Nations,* vol. 2 (Ithaca, N.Y.: Cornell University Press, 2000). Ernst Haas, *Nationalism, Liberalism, and Progress: The Rise and Decline of Nationalism,* vol. 1 (Ithaca, N.Y.: Cornell University Press, 1997).

8. Haas, *Nationalism*, vol. 2.

9. Alastair Iain Johnston, *Cultural Realism: Strategic Culture in Chinese History* (Princeton, N.J.: Princeton University Press, 1995). Henry R. Nau, *At Home Abroad: Identity and Power in American Foreign Policy* (Ithaca, N.Y.: Cornell University Press, 2002). See also Reinhold Niebuhr, *Christianity and Power Politics* (New York: Scribner's, 1940). Douglas Johnston, ed., *Faith-Based Diplomacy: Trumping Realpolitik* (Oxford: Oxford University Press, 2003).

10. Samuel P. Huntington, "The Clash of Civilizations?" *Foreign Affairs* 72, no. 3 (Summer 1993): 22–49. Samuel P. Huntington, *The Clash of Civilizations and the Remaking of World Order* (New York: Simon & Schuster, 1996).

11. Huntington, "The Clash of Civilizations?" 24, 42–44, 48.

12. Oswald Spengler, *Jahr der Entscheidung* (Munich: C. H. Beck, 1933).

13. Edward W. Said, *Orientalism* (New York: Pantheon, 1978).

14. Ian Buruma and Avishai Margalit, *Occidentalism: The West in the Eyes of Its Enemies* (New York: Penguin, 2004).

15. Xiaomei Chen, *Occidentalism: A Theory of Counter-Discourse in Post-Mao China*, 2nd ed. (Lanham, Md.: Rowman & Littlefield, 2002).

16. Jacinta O'Hagan, *Conceptualizing the West in International Relations: From Spengler to Said* (New York: Palgrave, 2002).

17. Robert Kagan, *Of Paradise and Power: America and Europe in the New World Order* (New York: Knopf, 2003).

18. Samuel P. Huntington, "The Hispanic Challenge," *Foreign Policy* (March-April 2004): 31–45. Samuel P. Huntington, *Who Are We? The Challenges to America's National Identity* (New York: Simon & Schuster, 2004).

19. Susanne Rudolph, "Introduction: Religion, States, and Transnational Civil Society," in Susanne Hoeber Rudolph and James Piscatori, eds., *Transnational Religion and Fading States* (Boulder, Colo.: Westview, 1997), 3.

20. In developing this pessimistic analysis of America, Huntington contradicts an argument he made earlier when he wrote that "the cultural distance between Mexico and the United States is far less than that between Turkey and Europe." See Huntington, *The Clash of Civilizations*, 150.

21. Donald J. Puchala, "International Encounters of Another Kind," paper prepared for the 35th Annual Convention of the International Studies Association, Washington, D.C., March 30–April 2, 1994.

22. Karl W. Deutsch, "On Nationalism, World Regions, and the Nature of the West," in Per Torsvik, ed., *Mobilization, Center-Periphery Structures and Nation-Building: A Volume in Commemoration of Stein Rokkan* (Bergen: Universitetsforlaget, 1981), 86.

23. Scott Thomas, "Religious Resurgence, Postmodernism and World Politics," in John L. Esposito and Michael Watson, eds., *Religion and Global Order* (Cardiff: University of Wales Press, 2000). Susanne Rudolph, "Dehomogenizing Religious Formations," in Rudolph and Piscatori, eds., *Transnational Religion*, 243–261.

24. Vendulka Kubálková, "Towards an International Political Theology," *Millennium* 29, no. 3 (2000): 686, 688, 693.

25. Nicholas Greenwood Onuf, *World of Our Making: Rules and Rule in Social Theory and International Relations* (Columbia: University of South Carolina Press, 1989).

26. See Gabriel A. Almond, R. Scott Appleby, and Emmanuel Sivan, eds., *Strong Religion: The Rise of Fundamentalism around the World* (Chicago: University of Chicago Press, 2003).

27. John L. Esposito and Michael Watson, eds., *Religion and Global Order* (Cardiff: University of Wales Press, 2000).

28. Fiona B. Adamson, "Global Liberalism versus Political Islam: Competing Ideological Frames in International Politics," *International Studies Review* 7 (2005): 547–569. Fred Dallmayr, "Empire or Cosmopolis? Civilization at the Crossroads," *Globalization* 2, no. 1 (2005): 14–30.

29. Yale H. Ferguson and Richard W. Mansbach, *Polities: Authority, Identities, and Change* (Columbia: University of South Carolina Press, 1996). Yale H. Ferguson, Richard W. Mansbach, et al., "What Is a Polity? A Roundtable," *International Studies Review* 2, no. 1 (Spring 2000): 3–31.

30. J. P. Nettl, "The State as a Conceptual Variable," *World Politics* 20, no. 4 (July 1968): 559–592.

31. Bruce Andrews, "Social Rules and the State as a Social Actor," *World Politics* 27, no. 4 (July 1975): 521–540.

32. Peter J. Katzenstein, *A World of Regions: Asia and Europe in the American Imperium* (Ithaca, N.Y.: Cornell University Press, 2005), 2–6. J. S. Richardson, "Imperium Romanum: Empire and the Language of Power," *Journal of Roman Studies* 81 (1991): 1–9.

33. See Randall Collins, "Civilizations as Zones of Prestige and Social Contact," in Saïd Amir Arjomand and Edward A. Tiryakian, eds., *Rethinking Civilizational Analysis* (Thousand Oaks, Calif.: Sage, 2004), 132–147. Randall Collins, "The Sociology of Philosophies: A Précis," *Philosophy of the Social Sciences* 30 (2000): 157–201. Randall Collins, *Macro-History: Essays in Sociology of the Long* Run (Stanford, Calif.: Stanford University Press, 1999). Randall Collins, *The Sociology of Philosophies: A Global Theory of Intellectual Change* (Cambridge, Mass.: Harvard University Press, 1998).

34. Robert Gilpin, *War and Change in World Politics* (New York: Cambridge University Press, 1981), 30–31.

35. Karl Jaspers, *The Origin and the Goal of History* (London: Routledge & Kegan, 1953). Donald N. Levine, "Note on the Concept of an Axial Turning in Human History," in Arjomand and Tiryakian, eds., *Rethinking Civilizational Analysis*, 67–70. Donald N. Levine, *Visions of the Sociological Tradition* (Chicago: University of Chicago Press, 1995).

36. Levine, "Note on the Concept" and *Visions.*

37. See Shmuel N. Eisenstadt, *Comparative Civilizations and Multiple Modernities*, 2 vols. (Leiden: Brill, 2003); "Multiple Modernities," *Daedalus* 129, no. 1 (Winter 2002): 1–29; *Fundamentalism, Sectarianism, and Revolution: The Jacobin Dimension of Modernity* (Cambridge: Cambridge University Press, 1999); *Paradoxes of Democracy, Fragility, Continuity, and Change* (Baltimore, Md.: Johns Hopkins University Press, 1999); *Japanese Civilization: A Comparative View* (Chicago: University of Chicago Press, 1996); *Jewish Civilization: The Jewish Historical Experience in Comparative Perspective* (Albany, N.Y.: SUNY Press, 1992); *European Civilization in Comparative Perspective* (Oslo: Norwegian University Press, 1987); and Shmuel N. Eisenstadt, ed., *The Origins and Diversity of Axial-Age Civilizations* (Albany, N.Y.: SUNY Press, 1986). My summary of Eisenstadt's encompassing and voluminous thought is indebted to the discussion in Willfried Spohn, "Eisenstadt on Civilizations and Multiple Modernity," *European Journal of Social Theory* 4, no. 4 (2001): 499–508. Eisenstadt's scholarship on this topic is a partial revision of his own writings on modernization dating back to the 1950s and 1960s and a forceful dissent from contemporary globalization theory and the philosophical discourse on modernity and postmodernity.

38. Yasusuke Murakami, *An Anti-Classical Political-Economic Analysis* (Stanford, Calif.: Stanford University Press, 1996). See also Yamamura, ed., *A Vision of a New Liberalism?*

39. Michael Mann, *The Sources of Social Power: The Rise of Classes and Nation-States, 1760–1914* (Cambridge: Cambridge University Press, 1993), 44–91.

40. Andrew Phillips, "Soldiers of God—War, Faith, Empire, and the Transformation of International Orders from Calvin to Al Qaeda," PhD dissertation, Government Department, Cornell University, 2008.

41. Barak Mendelsohn, "God vs. Westphalia: The Longer World War," paper prepared for the 48th Annual Convention of the International Studies Association, Chicago, February 28–March 3, 2007.

42. Ibid., 23–45.

43. Murakami, *An Anti-Classical Political-Economic Analysis*.

44. John W. Meyer, "Conceptions of Christendom: Notes on the Distinctiveness of the West," in Melvin Kohn, ed., (Newbury Park, Calif.: Sage, 1989), 395–413.

45. Karl W. Deutsch, "Medieval Unity and the Economic Conditions for an International Civilization," *Canadian Journal of Economic and Political Science* 10, no. 1 (February 1944): 18–35.

46. Mark Juergensmeyer, *Terror in the Mind of God: The Global Rise of Religious Violence* (Berkeley: University of California Press, 2000).

47. Pavlos Hatzopoulos and Fabio Petito, "The Return from Exile: An Introduction," in Fabio Petito and Pavlos Hatzopoulos, eds., *Religion in International Relations: The Return from Exile* (New York: Palgrave, 2003), 1.

48. Daniel Philpott, *Revolutions in Sovereignty: How Ideas Shaped Modern International Relations* (Princeton, N.J.: Princeton University Press, 2001); and "The Religious Roots of Modern International Relations," *World Politics* 52, no. 2 (2000): 206–245.

49. John T. S. Madeley, "European Liberal Democracy and the Principle of State Religious Neutrality," in John T. S. Madeley and Zsolt Enyedi, eds., *Church and State in Contemporary Europe: The Chimera of Neutrality* (London: Frank Cass, 2003), 1–22; and "A Framework for the Comparative Analysis of Church-State Relations in Europe," in Madeley and Enyedi, eds., *Church and State in Contemporary Europe*, 23–50.

50. See Anthony W. Marx, *Faith in Nation: Exclusionary Origins of Nationalism* (New York: Oxford University Press, 2003); and Linda Colley, *Britons: Forging the Nation 1707–1837* (New Haven, Conn.: Yale University Press, 1992).

51. Alexander Stille, "Historians Trace an Unholy Alliance: Religion as the Root of Nationalist Feeling," *New York Times*, May 31 2004, B9, B11.

52. Eugen Weber, *Peasants into Frenchmen: The Modernization of Rural France, 1870–1914* (Stanford, Calif.: Stanford University Press, 1976).

53. William T. Cavanaugh, "'A Fire Strong Enough to Consume the House': The Wars of Religion and the Rise of the State," *Modern Theology* 11, no. 4 (October 1995): 397–420.

54. Gerrit W. Gong, *The Standard of "Civilization" in International Society* (Oxford: Clarendon, 1994). See also Martha Finnemore, "Constructing Norms of Humanitarian Intervention," in Katzenstein, ed. *The Culture of National Security*, 153–185.

55. Stephen D. Krasner, *Sovereignty: Organized Hypocrisy* (Princeton, N.J.: Princeton University Press, 1999); and Stephen D. Krasner, ed., *Problematic Sovereignty: Contested Rules and Political Possibilities* (New York: Columbia University Press, 2001).

56. Carl Schmitt, *Political Theology: Four Chapters on the Concept of Sovereignty* (Cambridge, Mass.: MIT Press, 1985 [1922]).

57. James Kurth, "Religion and Globalization," 1998 Templeton Lecture on Religion and World Affairs, Foreign Policy Research Institute, May 1998.

7

A Suspension of (Dis)Belief:
The Secular-Religious Binary and
the Study of International Relations*
Elizabeth Shakman Hurd

Today Egypt is being challenged over the fundamental structure of the field in which the secular and the religious are defined and contested. The structure of this field under Mubarak served to legitimize certain parties, institutions, and forms of collective identification. It allowed certain kinds of political practice, such as vigorous antiterror laws and violent repression of opponents of Mubarak's regime, while disallowing others, such as full political participation by parties designated by that regime as religious. These distinctions were enacted legally: revisions to Article 5 of the Egyptian constitution enacted in 2006 prohibited political activity based in any way upon religion, effectively banning the Muslim Brotherhood from participating in Egyptian politics.[1]

This was not only an internal affair. The United States stood forcefully and famously behind this state-instituted and highly securitized secular/religious oppositional binary as a means of defending its interests in the region, defined primarily as ensuring Israeli security, pursuing the war on terror, and guaranteeing access to oil. In a 2005 speech at the American University in Cairo, former secretary of state Condoleezza Rice remarked: "our goal here is to encourage the Egyptian government, within its own laws and hopefully within a process and a context that is ever more reforming, to engage with civil society, with the people of Egypt for elections that can be free and fair. But we have not engaged the Muslim Brotherhood and we don't—we won't."[2]

According to Samer Shehata and Joshua Stacher, the Bush administration further hardened this position after Rice's visit. After Egypt's 2005 parliamentary elections, in which the MB gained one-fifth of the seats in parliament, U.S. pressure on the Mubarak regime decreased and then ceased entirely after Hamas's victory in 2006. Washington remained silent as the Mubarak regime arrested hundreds of Brothers and transferred dozens to military courts.[3] In early 2011, a powerful anti-Mubarak coalition representing a diverse cross-section of the Egyptian people overturned this entire structure of domination. Rami

Khouri, the eminent Lebanese journalist, described this momentous change as "the unraveling of the post-colonial order that the British and French created in the Arab world in the 1920s and 30s and then sustained—with American and Soviet assistance—for most of the last half century."[4] The degree to which decision makers in the United States and Europe will cling to the familiar securitization of secular/religious politics in the name of regional security and order in the wake of the democratizing transformations in Egypt and elsewhere in the region remains uncertain.

The object of this book is to rethink the categories of the secular and the religious in a world in which the limitations of these categories are becoming increasingly clear with each day that passes. With this in mind, this chapter interrogates the relation between two fundamental terms used to study these questions, the secular and the religious. I refer to the division of labor between these two categories as the secular/religious binary. This binary is often perceived as something that is understood intuitively, especially by social scientists. As Linell E. Cady observes, "the conventional story of secularization authorizes a bifurcated spatialized picture of the religion/secular landscape, identifying religion with the supernatural, the irrational, and the outdated, as it positions the secular in relationship to science, reason, and modernity."[5] This chapter politicizes the secular/religious binary, using examples from recent world politics to illustrate the argument.

A Suspension of (Dis)Belief

Most academic discussions in political science and international relations presuppose a fixed definition of the secular and the religious and proceed from there. Most realist, liberal, English school, feminist, and historical-materialist approaches to international relations treat religion as either private by prior assumption or a cultural relic to be handled by anthropologists. Even constructivists, known for their attention to historical contingency and social identity, have paid scant attention to the politics of secularism and religion, focusing instead on the interaction of preexisting state units to explain how international norms influence state interests and identity or looking at the social construction of states and the state system with religion left out of the picture.

This disciplinary convention fixes in advance key definitions and terms of inquiry, with some of the most vital aspects of contemporary world politics systematically excluded from consideration. The presumption that religion has been privatized and is no longer operative in modern politics or that its influence can be neatly encapsulated in anthropological studies of a particular religious tradition and its external influence on politics has led scholars of international relations to miss or misconstrue some of the most significant political developments of our time. This narrow vision is in part attributable to a rigid and dehistoricized secular/religious binary that prestructures the field of academic political science and international relations. This academic practice, in turn, mirrors and reinforces particular kinds of limits on political practice, as suggested by the Egyptian example. Expressed and reproduced through both forms of practice, this binary polices the borders of what counts as politics and what counts as religion and how they relate to each other. It has played a critical role in the global production of knowledge. As Alasdair MacIntyre has observed of the fluid relation between theory and practice, "there ought not to be two histories, one of political and moral action and one of political and moral theorizing, because there were not two pasts, one populated only by actions, the other only by theories. Every action is the bearer and expression of more or less theory-laden beliefs and concepts; every piece of theorizing and every expression of belief is a political and moral action."[6]

To be clear, I do not want to suggest that the categories of the secular and the religious fluctuate so wildly that they lack any analytical, political, or metaphysical salience, depending on one's perspective, but, rather, that from the perspective of deep pluralism that underlies my argument, these categories cannot be taken for granted in their fixity.[7] Failing to account for the power and limitations of the category of the secular and its shifting and contested relation not only to religion but to other political phenomena cast in opposition to it risks imposing a simplistic and distorted template on world politics. A rigid secular/religious divide stabilizes particular, historically contingent, and often hegemonic definitions of both politics and religion. This makes life easier for social scientists looking for answers in the short run but is costly in a world in which the way these categories come to be defined, what they come to represent and not represent, is critical to understanding how they operate politically.

At the same time, the category of religion is no more obvious than the category of the secular.[8] Reconsidering the fixity of the secular/religious binary opens new epistemological spaces for the identification of forms and locations of politics that fall off the radar screen of conventional secular rationalist approaches to politics and conventional religious approaches to politics. It makes room for alternative instantiations of the secular/religious divide to work their way into political theory and practice, as is occurring today in Turkey and is discussed below.[9]

A second qualification is that not all social scientists are cut from a single mold, and the degree to which any individual, institution, party, state, or international organization unthinkingly reproduces any particular secular/religious binary varies. It would be inaccurate to suggest that everyone approaches these questions in the same way. Yet particular varieties of secularism, like varieties of religion, have had an organizing influence on the ways in which most Europeans and Americans define and relate to basic categorizations involving religion and politics. These categorizations also change over time, as Charles Taylor argues in chapter 1 of this book, with the secular coming to refer in our time to that pertaining to a self-sufficient immanent sphere. The practices, institutions, and ways of being designated as secular sustain and shape the contours of public life and the modern organization of social-scientific knowledge. These traditions do not merely reflect social reality; they help to construct it.[10] They embody attitudes, sensibilities, and habits that facilitate closure and agreement around cultural, political, and legal settlements of the separation of church and state, the definition of religion, and what constitutes normal politics. There is in many contexts an identifiable secular "pattern of political rule,"[11] helping to generate and sustain the category of religion and setting preconditions for particular kinds of academic and political practice.

The unthinking adoption of a rigid secular/religious binary in the social sciences has had at least three consequences for the study of world politics. First, social scientists are encouraged to define research questions, select methods, and present results that fall squarely into the "secular" half of the binary, understood as the domain of rational humanism. They are taught to avoid religion, the domain of the supernatural, superstitious, otherworldly, metaphysical, and so forth. This encourages social scientists to approach religion either not at all or as a particular, emotive (as opposed to secular, rational, and universal) dimension of politics alongside others such as gender, caste, and (at times) nation.[12] The secular/religious binary operates such that *not* to be secular is to be emotional, irrational, unpredictable, and behind the march of progress. Quietly at work here is the notion that only the West, with its narrative of secularization, has found its way out of the woods, while other civilizations continue to cast about in a desperate search to answer the questions that the West resolved centuries ago.[13] Lodged within this narrative is the assumption that the secular is the natural domain of rational self-interest and universalist ethics.[14] The secular thus comes to stand not only in an oppositional relation to religion but also as the natural counterpart to other dimensions of politics that do not fit comfortably within the categories of either rational self-interest or universalist ethics.

This suggests that the secular is a more powerful and capacious category than one might assume when it is taken to stand only in contradistinction to the religious. Loosening the hold of a fixed secular/religious binary opens up a broader field of inquiry into modern formations of authority than may be apparent at the outset. The secular grounds and secures a place for the good, rational, and universal in Western moral order, which is then opposed to series of nonrational or irrational particularisms, aberrations, or variations. Religion often, though not always, appears as one of these particularisms. It is not the only candidate: institutions and identities associated with (ethnic as opposed to civic) nationalism, race, caste, and gender all have been cast in an oppositional relation to secular rational self-interest and/or universalist ethics. This is the sense in which it is possible to glimpse the capacious power of the category of the secular above and beyond its extraordinary capacity to define and delimit the religious. I return to this below.

A second consequence of the naturalization of the secular/religious binary is that the study of religion and politics tends to focus not on secularism in relation to religion or the other categories discussed above (the binary has effectively segregated these categories) but on predefined religious traditions taken as independent objects of inquiry and the degree to which they infiltrate or influence politics. This division of labor divides inquiry into mainstream (secular) studies on the one hand and studies of religion or religion and politics on the other. A fixed understanding of religion in relation to the secular supports an understanding of the secular as that which is associated with normal, rational politics. Religion becomes a repository for a range of nonrational and nonuniversal dimensions of politics that fall outside the range of "normal" politics, including belief, culture, tradition, mood, and emotion.

A third consequence of the stabilization of the binary is that a particular (often monotheistic) definition of religion is often taken as the norm. This definition constructs an object of study and defines religious actors and institutions according to a particular set of parameters. These limitations press those trained in the traditions of European and American international-relations scholarship to read the world in a particular way, with an emphasis on European religious history and experience, and to misconstrue or miss entirely a whole spectrum of political actors, histories, and processes. Perhaps most significant among these are the intense political struggles, historical contingencies, religious ambivalences, and philosophical uncertainties surrounding the practices associated with and legitimized by claims to the secular itself.

The study of religion, secularism, and international affairs requires a suspension of (dis)belief to address these limitations and move toward new paradigms for the study of religion and politics.[15] It requires suspending disbelief in the particularity of the secular (or suspending one's belief in the universalizing potential of the secularization narrative, depending on how you look at it) and approaching the secular/religious binary not as fixed but as shifting, evolving, and elusive. This suspension of (dis)belief can be uncomfortable for those socialized in Euro-American secularisms, which are kept afloat by a high degree of certainty surrounding the stability of these categories. But I hope to show that it is worth the effort. Suspending the assumption that any secular/religious binary is fixed and universal and approaching it as an unstable, historically contingent construct that is capable of sustaining a broad discursive field that goes beyond the maintenance of a distinction between the secular and the religious allows the ground that supports this distinction to shift in intellectually fruitful directions.

And the ground is shifting. Developments in late-modern international relations, such as increasing pluralization within societies, rising global interdependence, the retreat of Christendom,[16] the questioning of the universality of the Enlightenment, and a rise in religiously inspired forms of collective political identification, demand a destabilization of the fundamental terms and binaries (secular rational versus religious irrational, philosophical versus theological, reason versus faith) that have structured inquiry on this subject for decades.[17] Understanding the politics of secularism requires this suspension of (dis)belief. Like their counterparts in philosophy and political theory, international relations theorists need to hone their capacity to pose research questions that do not presuppose fixed definitions of these terms or relations between them. What claims to the secular and the religious signify in different circumstances and what political effects these claims have in various settings are precisely what needs to be explored.

Politicizing and Historicizing Secularism

How a researcher identifies an object of inquiry, the kinds of questions posed, and the methods chosen are determined in part by his or her presuppositions about the secular/religious binary. Charles Taylor alludes to this in his discussion of the "unthought" underpinning secularization theory: "Much of the sociology/history of secularization has been affected/shaped by an 'unthought,' which is related in a more complex way to the outlook of the author in question, that is, not simply as a polemical extension of one's views, but in the more subtle way that one's own framework beliefs and values can constrict one's theoretical imagination."[18] Most international relations scholars operate from within a secularist "unthought" that predisposes them toward questions, actors, institutions, and processes presumed to be nonreligious or irreligious. Others, swimming against this tide, focus explicitly on religious questions, actors, institutions, challenges, and processes, conventionally understood. In both cases, the relation between the secular and the religious is presumed to be stable. An ontologically fixed understanding of what is secular and what is religious underlies and is reinforced both by analysts concerned with secular actors, institutions, and processes and by those focusing on religious actors, institutions, and processes. A corollary to this is the assumption that religious actors and institutions progress in a linear fashion away from the religious and toward the secular. This developmentalist teleology, also influential in the literature on democratization,[19] is an important component of the modern social imaginary, and analyses of religion and politics are not immune from its influence.

To move beyond this mode of inquiry and account for the co-constitutive relation between the secular and the religious and the power relations reflected in the division between them, it will not do simply to incorporate religious actors, variables, viewpoints, institutions, or practices into otherwise untouched secular analyses. This "add and stir" approach misses the point, because adding a religious viewpoint, variable, or actor does not compensate for the fact that the basic categories structuring the analysis remain untouched. As other contributors to this book have emphasized, it is the unreflective reliance on these basic categories that needs to be overcome in order to make the transition into the modes of apprehending the world required to understand contemporary global politics. The task is to develop research questions that neither default without explanation to a conventional secular or religious perspective, thereby reproducing the very categories and distinctions that need interrogation, nor succumb to the assumption that there is a naturally occurring, linear progression out of the religious and into the secular.

This requires navigating the history and politics of the secular/religious binary. As both the more secularly and more religiously inclined discover along the way, it is nearly impossible to avoid engagement with the spaces that lie between these two points of entry (confounding their supposed epistemological integrity) and, more fundamentally, with the broader field that underlies and sustains this complex and unstable binary itself.[20] Studying religion and international affairs requires an engagement with the secular because the definition of religion, of religious actors, of religious subjectivities and institutions is bound up with and animated by particular (and often variable) assumptions about and historical practices associated with various forms of secularism. Studying secularism and international affairs requires an engagement with the religious because various forms of secularism carry within them particular assumptions about, definitions of, and practices associated with (both in terms of contemporary practices and as historical legacies) religion. Talal Asad has argued most convincingly in favor of the interrelatedness of these categories; as Gil Anidjar observes, "no one has done more than Asad (and arguably, Said) to show *in the same gesture* the urgency of reflecting on religion and the religious *as well as* on the secular and all its ensuing distinctions."[21]

To take the secular/religious distinction, presumably one's own or the disciplinary norm, for granted is to miss the influence of varieties of secularism in international relations. International-relations scholars need to attend to how the terms of this distinction prestructure political theory and practice. Conventional negotiations of the secular/religious distinction in the discipline of international relations presume a fixed definition of the secular and, correspondingly, the religious. This rules out identifying and framing objects of study that require historicization and politicization of the secular/religious binary to appear in the researcher's field of vision. To open these spaces requires letting go of the notion that the secular/religious distinction is fixed, secure, and universal—a presupposition that Taylor, Connolly, and Anidjar have identified, in different ways, as part of the complex humanist inheritance of Latin Christendom. Acknowledging the historical and political contingencies of this binary leads to a critical reexamination of the assumptions embedded in hypotheses, empirical tests, and research findings in international-relations scholarship.

Let me give some examples. First, historicizing the binary makes it possible to access the assumptions that sustain different varieties of secularism and analyze the political consequences for foreign policy and international relations. This was the task of my book *The Politics of Secularism in International Relations*. The book analyzes how certain state (and suprastate) institutions organize, settle, and institutionalize—politically, legally, culturally—public settlements involving the relation between religion and politics. It identifies the contours and contents of the forms of secularism that have become hegemonic in particular times and places and argues that these broad and contested settlements are embedded in the creation and reproduction of national and supranational forms of collective identity, reflected and reproduced in legal, religious political traditions and institutions and sustained and transformed through everyday practices, lived experiences, and dispositions. It then seeks to determine how these public settlements influence how political collectivities represent and interact with other state or suprastate actors in the international system. Shared interests, identities, and traditions involving religion and politics developed at the state and regional level are influential at the systemic level; in particular, domestic negotiations of the secular and the religious in Europe and the United States have influenced the ways Europeans and Americans relate to the Middle East and North Africa. In Europe, the United States, and to varying degrees elsewhere, two sets of shared dispositions involving the relation between religion and politics have crystallized into two traditions of secularism: laicism and what I call "Judeo-Christian" secularism.[22] Briefly, laicism insists on a rigid separation between what it designates as religion and secular law, institutions, and politics, while Judeo-Christian secularism calls for a less rigid accommodation of Christian, and eventually what came to be referred to as "Judeo-Christian," tradition in secular law, institutions, and politics. These shared systems of belief and practice form part of the cultural and religious backdrop out of which Europeans and Americans engage in international relations. They are powerful collective dispositions that shape modern sensibilities, habits, laws, and institutions concerning the meaning of the religious and its relationship to the political.

Second, the identities and scope of activities of many transnational actors, including relief organizations, terrorists, missionaries, political parties, the Catholic church, human-rights activists, and environmentalist networks, cannot be represented within the terms of a fixed secular/religious binary. Politicizing and historicizing the binary make it possible to access interdependencies and interplay between secular and religious ideas, actors, and institutions and to understand how they transform one another while contributing to modern forms of social and political order. Taking AIDS policy in Senegal as an example, Alfred Stepan has shown that Senegalese political leaders have adopted multiple strategies to fight AIDS, including enlisting religious leaders, training them, and ensuring that HIV/AIDS is an issue in Friday prayers, on TV and radio, and in religious teaching programs.[23] Since the early 1980s, as a result of these efforts, the HIV/AIDS rate in Senegal has been less than

1 percent. It is not possible to understand these developments without reconsidering the secular/religious binary; looking only at so-called secular political actors or so-called religious actors systematically biases the account and leaves out some of the most interesting aspects of these developments, including how interactions between religious actors and their secular counterparts change both of them. Approaching this question in terms of a broader field of practice that is not defined by the secular/religious binary makes it possible to look at how various ideas, institutions, and actors interact, deconstructing and reconstructing each other, while expanding or contracting what Stepan identifies as spaces of conflict and tolerance.

The same holds for the study of missionary activities. Focusing exclusively on so-called secular themes, actors, and institutions misses early American Protestant missionaries' contribution to defining what it meant to be an American, and not just a religious American, in early America. Politicizing and historicizing the secular/religious distinction opens space for consideration of religious actors that have remained on the margins of the discussion. Early American nationalism, like its contemporary counterpart, cannot be fully understood in purely secular terms, as it was (and remains) an amalgam of anti-Islamic Orientalism, ideals of Christian superiority, and an American approach to government.[24] This approach to American foreign relations leads to a richer and more nuanced account of how the secular, the religious, and the political interweave, interact, and modify one another. It also makes it possible to see how religious traditions are rephrased and resonate within American politics and foreign policy, including contemporary notions of the "rogue state" and the Islamist terrorist and depictions of Islam as a "false religion."[25]

The Politics of Secularism and American Opposition to Iran

Politicizing the secular/religious binary changes the interpretive filter used to process key events and processes in global politics. This section illustrates the implications of this argument with a closer look at two cases from *The Politics of Secularism in International Relations*: American reactions to the Iranian revolution of 1978–79 and the rise of the Justice and Development party in Turkey.

The most powerful American condemnation of the Iranian Revolution on cultural and religious grounds occurred when secularists of different types came to the same conclusion about developments in Iran in 1978–79, though for different reasons. In both laicist and Judeo-Christian secularist accounts, in the former because of its inexplicable and irrational revolt against modernization and in the latter because of the resurgence of Islam and its alleged theocratic proclivities, the Iranian Revolution was depicted as a setback for civilization. In both cases, as Richard Cottam argues, "the Khomeini phenomenon was

explained as a consequence of the shah's having moved too quickly for the ignorant, barely aware Iranian to be able to follow his lead."[26] This account became
the standard bearer among U.S. representations of the revolution. For laicists,
because the revolution imported (any) *religion* directly into a modernizing public
sphere in which the former was unwelcome, it was a defeat for the progress of
universal values and civilization. For Judeo-Christian secularists, because the
revolution imported *Islam* into a modernizing public sphere in which the former
was unwelcome, it represented a defeat for the progress of *Western* values and
civilization. Working in tandem and combined at different moments with the
influence of material and strategic interests in the region, the tenacity of these
two varieties of secularism in the American political imagination helps to explain
the vehemence of American opposition to the Iranian Revolution.

The American response to the revolution also illustrates the ways in which
particular varieties of secularism become embedded in the creation and
reproduction of national identities. In addition to activating preexisting
American cultural and religious presuppositions about religion and politics,
the Iranian Revolution represented a direct affront to a powerful set of connections among American national identity, secularism, and democracy. Secular,
rational, democratic American national identity was secured in part through
opposition to theocratic, irrational, tyrannical Iran. This illustrates my earlier
point that the secular often comes to stand in for the rational and universal in
distinction to the irrational and particular, reproducing a series of distinctions
that go beyond secular/religious, such that the nonsecular is defined (and
rejected) as antimodern, antiuniversalist, antirational, and also, in this case,
anti-American.

In rejecting the attempt to impose authoritarian secularism in Iran, the
revolution called into question this foundational connection among secular
modernization, secular universalism, rational politics, and democratization.
It disrupted the secular-rational-universalist/religious-irrational-particularist
division of labor. Indeed, one of the central messages of the revolutionaries
was that in prerevolutionary Iran, these principles had been working at
odds—secular rationalism and modernization had led to repression and not
to democratization. The shah was secular yet undemocratic. Secular modernization had served as a legitimizing principle for the suppression of local
politics and practice.[27] In challenging Western assumptions about securaliza-
tion and its allegedly irrefutable connection to rational universalism and
democratization, the revolution called attention to the fact that the secular/
religious binary is not fixed but rather socially and historically constructed. It
can be constructed differently in different historical circumstances, with
varying implications for democratization. The revolution demonstrated that
secularism is not always a stand-in for rational universalism but is instanti-
ated differently in different circumstances. By illustrating the contingent
nature of the secularist settlement in Iran, the revolution made explicit the

essentially contested and politicized nature of secularist settlements everywhere, including in the United States.[28] By confirming the contingent relationship between secularization and democratization in Iran, the revolution called attention to the contested and controversial relation among religion, democracy, and national identity in the United States. The revolution presented a challenge to American national identity insofar as the latter is anchored in a powerful series of assumptions about the pregiven and nonnegotiable compatibility among modernity, secular universalism, and democratization.

One consequence for international politics of this perceived affront to the American democratic, secularist settlement was that in the United States from 1979 onward, to stand for a (laicist or Judeo-Christian) secular and democratic United States was to oppose an (Islamic) theocratic and authoritarian Iran. Representing Islam and the Iranians as a threat to modern American civilization was a performative gesture cementing the connection among American national identity, (laicist and Judeo-Christian) secularism, and democracy in opposition to Iranian (Islamic) theocracy and tyranny. A secularist version of what Michael Dillon calls a *horror alieni*[29] surfaced on the American political landscape at the time of the revolution, seeking to disassociate the United States from the injustices of the shah's secular yet undemocratic regime, to divest American identity of everything enigmatic and strange (Islam), and to shore up American nationalism as universalist, democratic, laicist, Christian, and secular. This helps to explain the intensity of the American response to the revolution and the long life span of American opposition to postrevolutionary Iran. The antagonism results not only from clashing economic and strategic interests in the Middle East, although these factors were and remain significant. It is part of a process of securing a complex and hybrid identity of the United States as secular, Christian, and democratic in opposition to a particular figure of Iran. It was not just that in order to defend American national interests, one needed to be opposed to Iran but that in order to *be* a real American, one needed to oppose Iran. Anti-Iranianism became at least in part constitutive of American identity, which is inhabited by powerful assumptions about the relationship among modernity, secularism, and democracy. The American reaction to the revolution made these assumptions explicit. Anti-Iranianism was, and to some extent remains today, what constructivists in international relations refer to as a constitutive norm.

The Politics of Secularism and the Challenge to Turkish Kemalism

Nowhere has a particular secular/religious distinction been defended with the vigor of the Turkish Kemalist establishment and its supporters. For this reason, it is not possible to understand recent political developments in Turkish politics, and specifically the rise of the AK Party (Adalet ve Kalkınma Partisi, or Justice and Development Party) without politicizing and historicizing the secular/religious distinction. From a Kemalist perspective, the AKP appears as a threat to democratic politics to be repressed at any cost. Reconsidering the rigid secular/religious binary that animates Kemalist practice, however, allows us to tell a different story about the AKP's ascent in Turkish politics.[30]

In 1997, the National Security Council forced Necmettin Erbakan, the leader of RP (Refah Partisi, or Welfare Party, the AKP's predecessor), to accept eighteen "recommendations" reaffirming the secular nature of the Turkish state and designating political Islam the top national security concern. The military briefed governmental, judicial, and nongovernmental organizations on the presence of an "Islamic threat" in Turkey, and Erbakan resigned on June 18, 1997. In this "soft coup," the army enjoyed the backing of the Kemalist establishment, including much of the military, civil service, and intelligentsia. In January 1998, the Turkish Constitutional Court banned the RP, expelled Erbakan from Parliament, tried him for sedition, banned him from politics for five years, and seized the party's assets. The court argued that "laicism is not only a separation between religion and politics but also a necessary division between religion and society."[31] Defying the official ban, the RP was succeeded by the Virtue (Fazilet) Party, which was in turn banned in June 2001, charged with serving as a "center for antisecular activities." Virtue split into two factions: conservatives led by Necmettin Erbakan became the Felicity (Saadet) Party, and reformists under Recep Tayyip Erdogan became the AKP. In national elections on November 3, 2002, the AKP received 34 percent of the vote, far more than any other party and enough to form a government and nominate a prime minister. While some contend that the AKP renegotiated the Kemalist settlement since taking power in late 2002, others counter that the party distanced itself from its previous commitments so as to render its challenge to Kemalism less substantial or nonexistent. In any case, despite considerable trepidation on the part of the military and its Western allies concerning the Islamicization of Turkish politics, the party has not imposed Islamic law. It has endorsed what some describe as a conservative democratic and others a "Muslimhood" model in which "religious ethics inspire public service but overt religiosity is not part of an individual's public political identity."[32]

Yet suspicions of the party continue to circulate and even to define Turkish politics. In spring 2006, former president Süleyman Demirel suggested that the AKP "remained under suspicion of 'dissimulation' (*takiye*), a reference to its failure to convince the entire public that it has fully acquiesced in the secularism of Atatürk."[33] In April 2007, President Ahmet Necdet Sezer warned that the country's secular system "faces its greatest threat since the founding of the republic in 1923" and proclaimed that all state organs, including the military, had a duty to protect the system.[34] Hundreds of thousands of supporters of Kemalism demonstrated in Ankara and then Istanbul at the end of April 2007. When the AKP announced its candidate for president, Abdullah Gül, the opposition deputies boycotted the election in Parliament,[35] and the military posted a declaration on its official Web site (referred to as an "e-coup") suggesting that "some circles who have been carrying out endless efforts to disturb fundamental values of the Republic of Turkey, especially secularism, have escalated their efforts recently" and that the military is the "definite defender of secularism" and "will show its stance clearly when needed."[36]

Kemalists (represented prominently but not exclusively by the Turkish military) portray the destabilization of the Kemalist secular/religious binary and renegotiation of Turkish *laiklik* as a lurking danger to be suppressed in defense of democratic (read Kemalist) norms and institutions. The Kemalist establishment and its allies abroad, including the United States, have been wary of the rise of Islamic political identification symbolized by the party.[37] A rigid secular/religious binary, in which Kemalism has sought to monopolize the "secular" side of the binary and designated rival political actors as "religious" as a means of delegitimizing them, has been a powerful force in Turkish politics, as it was in Egypt under Mubarak. Seen from within this binary, any challenge to Kemalism with any relation to Islamic political identification is indicted as backsliding away from modernization and toward archaic forms of political order that threaten domestic and regional stability and security. From this perspective, religion in general, and Islam in particular, is "a remnant of underdevelopment that is bound to disappear with industrialization and urbanization."[38]

Not only Kemalists but also many others take this perspective as normal and natural. The secular comes to stand in for modern, rational politics not only in opposition to *religion* per se but also as distinguished from other forms of dissenting politics that do not fit a particular understanding of what it means to be modern and democratic. This mind-set contributed to a July 31, 2001, decision by the European Court of Human Rights to support the Turkish establishment's suppression of the Welfare Party.[39] The court ruled 4-3 that the government's action to ban the party did not violate human rights because Turkey had legitimate concerns about the party's threatening its democratic society.[40] The majority argued that the party leadership's intention to establish Islamic law conflicted with values embodied in the European Convention on Human Rights and that statements by the leadership suggested that it might resort to force in order to gain and retain power.[41] The following excerpt from the summary of the judgment of the court's decision indicates that the majority subscribed to a Kemalist secular/religious distinction in which a party must either support the particular, state-sponsored version of laicism (Kemalism) *or* represent a threat to democratic politics:

> The Court held that the sanctions imposed on the applicants could reasonably be considered to meet a pressing social need for the protection of democratic society, since, *on the pretext of giving a different meaning to the principle of secularism,* the leaders of the Refah Partisi had declared

their intention to establish a plurality of legal systems based on differences in religious belief, to institute Islamic law (the *Sharia*), a system of law that was in marked contrast to the values embodied in the Convention. They had also left in doubt their position regarding recourse to force in order to come to power and, more particularly, to retain power.

The Court considered that even if States' margin of appreciation was narrow in the area of the dissolution of political parties, since pluralism of ideas and parties was an inherent element of democracy, the State concerned could reasonably prevent the implementation of such a political programme, which was incompatible with Convention norms, before it was given effect through specific acts that might jeopardise civil peace and the country's democratic regime.[42]

Yet the RP was a complex phenomenon insofar as it contained significant elements that did not advocate a radical stance against the West, democracy, or the concept of secularism, although it did oppose the *Kemalist* instantiation of secularism.[43] These complexities, and the possibility (expressed to a lesser degree in Refah's policies and rhetoric and to a greater degree by its successor AKP) that one could oppose Kemalism while supporting a different *form* of secularism, escaped the categorizations available to European and Turkish judicial authorities sitting on both the Turkish Constitutional Court and the European Court of Human Rights. Working out of a secular/religious binary defined by Kemalist practice and informed by European traditions of secularism upon which Kemalism had been loosely modeled nearly a century earlier, the courts presumed that the alternative to benevolent secular democracy (in its Kemalist form) would be menacing antimodern Islamic theocracy (overturning Kemalism). The judges dismissed the possibility of a reformulated secularism as a "pretext," arguing that the real intention of the party was to "institute Islamic law." They viewed Kemalism in its current form as the closest approximation to secularism available and took it to be a universal good, or at least a decent approximation of the "values embodied in the Convention." In short, they both subscribed to and reproduced a rigid Kemalist construal of the secular/religious distinction.

My reading of developments in Turkey politicizes the Kemalist secular/religious distinction. The rise of Islamic political identification in Turkey represents not a return to a fixed, antimodern Islamic tradition but a renegotiation of the Kemalist settlement including the secular/religious distinction and a vast array of juridical, institutional, and everyday practices that undergird and reproduce it. This becomes apparent when the Kemalist secular/religious distinction is made part of the object of inquiry rather than being taken for granted. To return to the overarching argument of this chapter, developments in Turkey demand a destabilization of the fundamental terms and binaries (secular versus religious, philosophical versus theological) that structure political inquiry. This recovers the conceptual space needed to develop research questions about secularism, religion, and politics that do not presuppose fixed definitions of these terms or relations among them. What claims to the secular or the religious signify in Turkey and what moral and political effects these claims have in this particular case are questions to be explored.

This approach also reveals the extent to which the Kemalist settlement reproduces a particular relationship to, and control over, what the state defines as (a particular Sunni-Hanefi form of) Islam. Kemalist practice is constantly defining and controlling religion. The Kemalist power centers of the state, to the extent that they remain powerful, are forced to "theologize" the religions that they oversee. By this I mean that the state, like other secular states, must play the theologian, discourse and reason theologically, and speculate in theology. The Turkish state controls all of the 80,000 mosques in Turkey and employs their imams as state functionaries. Sunni Hanefi Islam is the doctrine of the State Directorate of Religious Affairs (DRA). Other sects, including the Alevis, which make up 20 to 30 percent of the Turkish population, are not recognized by the state.[44]

The rise to political prominence of differently configured forms of religiopolitical identity and practice in Turkey is part of a public struggle against and around authoritative Kemalist designations of the secular/religious binary authorized and enforced by state authorities since the founding of the Republic. These dissenting forms of politics represent a challenge to Kemalist attempts to define and regulate the division among the secular, the religious, and the political. They contest Kemalist attempts to theologize religion. These challenges are a series of efforts to grant cultural and political legitimacy to alternative models of religious separation and accommodation. They are working out of a different instantiation of the secular/religious distinction, not to jettison this distinction altogether, as some critics have suggested, but to refashion it.

Politicizing the secular/religious binary may allow us to see developments in Turkey through the lens of what Stepan calls the "twin tolerations," defined as "the minimal boundaries of freedom of action that must somehow be crafted for political institutions vis-à-vis religious authorities, and for religious individuals and groups vis-à-vis political institutions."[45] As Stepan concludes, "when we consider the question of non-Western religions and their relationship to democracy, it would seem appropriate not to assume univocality but to explore whether these doctrines contain multivocal components that are usable for (or at least compatible with) the construction of the twin tolerations."[46] The challenge to Kemalism testifies both to the inability of the Kemalists to monopolize the secular/religious distinction and to the multivocality of Islamic tradition and its potential compatibility with the twin tolerations. The drive to remake the Kemalist public realm is a contestation of an authoritative secularist tradition that has been authorized and regulated by state authorities since the founding of the Turkish Republic in 1923. This contest involves whether the secular/religious distinction that underlies and animates Kemalism will remain hegemonic or will be refashioned. After the elections of July 2007 and Gül's election to the presidency in August 2007, the latter appears more likely.

Conclusion

Secularisms differ from one another, particularly those that arose not out of Christianity, as did dominant strains of European and American secularisms (such as French *laïcité*, famously dubbed *catholaïcité* by French philosopher and sociologist Edgar Morin),[47] but out of, through, and against other religious traditions. To study the secular and the religious in world politics requires a suspension of (dis)belief, a reconsideration of the political, philosophical, and religious certainties sustaining the rigid secular/religious binary that has underwritten most social-scientific scholarship to date. Politicizing and historicizing this binary is the first step toward research questions that do not presuppose rigid definitions of the secular and the religious or relations between them. Secular/ religious binaries are contingent constructs that draw sustenance from different guiding assumptions, beliefs, and faiths—theistic, polytheistic, nontheistic— about the world both seen and unseen.

In politicizing and historicizing this binary, this chapter has drawn attention to dimensions of politics and forms of political authority, including the power exercised by the category of the secular itself, which would otherwise fall outside the epistemological reach of the conventional toolkit of social science. This shift in paradigm brings new insights to the field of international relations. It makes it possible to see the world more fully, not necessarily to reject rationalism as such but to embed it within something bigger.

Notes

* I would like to thank the members of the SSRC Working Group on Religion, Secularism & International Affairs for their commentary on and contributions to this chapter.

1. Samer Shehata and Joshua Stacher, "Boxing in the Brothers," *Middle East Report*, August 8, 2007, http://www.merip.org/mero/mero080807.html.

2. Condoleezza Rice, "Question and Answer at the American University in Cairo," June 20, 2005.

3. Shehata and Stacher, "Boxing in the Brothers."

4. Rami G. Khouri, "The Arab Freedom Epic." Agence Globale, February 2, 2011, http://www.agenceglobal.com/article.asp?id=2492.

5. Linell E. Cady, "Royce, Dewey, and the Religion/Secular Classification: Toward a Kaleidoscopic Model," *American Journal of Theology & Philosophy* 29, no. 3 (September 2008): 243–244.

6. Alasdair MacIntyre, *After Virtue: A Study in Moral Theory*, 2nd ed. (Notre Dame, Ind.: University of Notre Dame Press, 1997), 61.

7. On deep pluralism, see William E. Connolly, *Pluralism* (Durham, N.C.: Duke University Press, 2005).

8. See Timothy Fitzgerald, *Discourse on Civility and Barbarity: A Critical History of Religion and Related Categories* (New York: Oxford University Press, 2007); and Talal Asad, *Genealogies of Religion: Discipline and Reasons of Power in Christianity and Islam* (Baltimore, Md.: Johns Hopkins University Press, 1993).

9. This attempt to open new epistemological and political spaces may be contrasted with Pope Benedict XVI's reassertion of the spiritual supremacy of the Vatican, in which he called for believers to return to the "true faith" and harden their suspicion of Protestants, atheists, Muslims, pluralists, Jews, secularists, and others who (allegedly) threaten that faith. See Robert Marquand, "A Church's Assertive Shift toward Tradition," *Christian Science Monitor*, July 18, 2007, http://www.csmonitor.com/2007/0718/p01s05-lire.html.

10. This argument is from chap. 2, "Varieties of Secularism," of my book, Elizabeth Shakman Hurd, *The Politics of Secularism in International Relations* (Princeton, N.J.: Princeton University Press, 2008). Excerpts from the book are reprinted here with permission of Princeton University Press.

11. Talal Asad, "Responses," in David Scott and Charles Hirschkind, eds., *Powers of the Secular Modern: Talal Asad and His Interlocutors* (Stanford, Calif.: Stanford University Press, 2006), 219.

12. For a discussion of emotion and affect in international relations that bears on the power of the secular to secure particular forms of modern moral order, see Andrew A. G. Ross, "Coming in from the Cold: Constructivism and Emotions," *European Journal of International Relations* 12, no. 2 (2006): 197–222.

13. See Mark Lilla, *The Stillborn God: Religion, Politics, and the Modern West* (New York: Knopf, 2007).

14. I thank Craig Calhoun for encouraging me to develop this argument.

15. Poet and philosopher Samuel Taylor Coleridge coined the term "suspension of disbelief" in his *Biographia Literaria* (1817), in the context of the creation and reading of poetry, to refer to "the voluntary witholding of skepticism on the part of the reader with regard to incredible characters and events." In coining the term, Coleridge was describing preparations for a collaboration with William Wordsworth, *Lyrical Ballads* (1798): "it was agreed, that my endeavors should be directed to persons and characters supernatural, or at least romantic, yet so as to transfer from our inward nature a human interest and a semblance of truth sufficient to procure for these shadows of imagination that willing suspension of disbelief for the moment, which constitutes poetic faith. Mr. Wordsworth on the other hand was to propose to himself as his object, to give the charm of novelty to things of every day, and to excite a feeling analogous to the supernatural, by awakening the mind's attention from the lethargy of custom, and directing it to the loveliness and the wonders of the world before us." William Safire observed of this statement, "the context is an eye-opener.…Wordsworth delivered in his area…'to give the charm of novelty to things of every day'…and Coleridge worked the other side of the street." William Safire, "On Language," *New York Times Magazine*, October 7, 2007, 16.

16. See Charles Taylor, *A Secular Age* (Cambridge, Mass.: Harvard University Press, 2007), chap. 14, "Religion Today."

17. William Connolly describes a world in which, "first, the acceleration of tempo compresses distance and intensifies interdependence, second, no more than thirty percent of human beings call themselves Christian, and, third, secular intellectualism provides too

thin a gruel to serve as the neutral matrix to regulate relations between faiths." William E. Connolly, "Catholicism and Philosophy: A Nontheistic Appreciation," in Ruth Abbey, ed., *Charles Taylor* (Cambridge: Cambridge University Press, 2004), 178.

18. Taylor, *A Secular Age*, 428.

19. In Jillian Schwedler's critique of the transitions to democracy literature, she argues that "scholars should abandon the notion that the 'space' between authoritarianism and democracy is characterized by a continuum of stages from primitive, traditional, or patriarchal systems of rule (authoritarianism) to modern, rational-legal systems of rule (democracy)." Jillian Schwedler, *Faith in Moderation: Islamist Parties in Jordan and Yemen* (Cambridge: Cambridge University Press, 2006), 6.

20. See Taylor, *A Secular Age*; Talal Asad, *Formations of the Secular: Christianity, Islam, Modernity* (Stanford, Calif.: Stanford University Press, 2003); and William E. Connolly, *Why I Am Not a Secularist* (Minneapolis: University of Minnesota Press, 1999).

21. Gil Anidjar, "Secularism," *Critical Inquiry* 33 (Autumn 2006): 57–58. See Asad, *Formations of the Secular;* and Edward Said, *The World, the Text, and the Critic* (Cambridge, Mass.: Harvard University Press, 1983).

22. For an explanation of my use of the term "Judeo-Christian" secularism that goes beyond the discussion in this book, see Elizabeth Shakman Hurd, "Secularism and International Relations Theory," in Jack Snyder, ed., *Religion and International Relations Theory* (New York: Columbia University Press, 2011).

23. Alfred Stepan, "Rituals of Respect: Sufis and Secularists in Senegal" (unpublished manuscript).

24. Timothy Worthington Marr, *Imagining Ishmael: Studies of Islamic Orientalism in America from the Puritans to Melville* (Ann Arbor, Mich.: UMI, 1998), 87; see also Timothy Worthington Marr, *The Cultural Roots of American Islamicism* (Cambridge: Cambridge University Press, 2006).

25. Marr, *Imagining Ishmael*, 92. See also Richard Falk, "False Universalism and the Geopolitics of Exclusion: The Case of Islam," *Third World Quarterly* 18, no. 1 (March 1997): 7–23.

26. Richard W. Cottam, *Iran and the United States: A Cold War Case Study* (Pittsburgh, Pa.: University of Pittsburgh Press, 1988), 13.

27. Ali Mirsepassi, *Intellectual Discourse and the Politics of Modernization: Negotiating Modernity in Iran* (Cambridge: Cambridge University Press, 2000).

28. For a comparative and global study of the history and politics of secularism in France, India, the United States, and Turkey, see Linell E. Cady and Elizabeth Shakman Hurd, eds., *Comparative Secularisms in a Global Age* (New York: Palgrave Macmillan, 2010).

29. Michael Dillon, "The Scandal of the Refugee: Some Reflections on the 'Inter' of International Relations and Continental Thought," in David Campbell and Michael J. Shapiro, eds., *Moral Spaces: Rethinking Ethics and World Politics* (Minneapolis: University of Minnesota, 1999), 104.

30. For a more detailed account, see "Contested Secularisms in Turkey and Iran," chap. 4 of Hurd, *The Politics of Secularism,* 65–83.

31. M. Hakan Yavuz, "Cleansing Islam from the Public Sphere," *Journal of International Affairs* 54, no. 1 (Fall 2000): 38.

32. Jenny White, "Turkey's New 'Muslimhood': The End of 'Islamism'?" *Congress Monthly* (November/December 2003): 6–9.

33. Gamze Çavdar, "Behind Turkey's Presidential Battle," *Middle East Report Online*, May 7, 2007, http://www.merip.org/mero/mero050707.html.

34. Ibid., citing the Turkish daily *Milliyet,* April 13, 2007.

35. The opposition asserted (without precedent) that a quorum of three-quarters of MPs had to be present for the vote to proceed and took their objection to Turkey's constitutional court, which annulled the first round of voting on May 1, 2007, a verdict described by Prime Minister Erdogan as a "bullet fired at the heart of democracy." Gül withdrew his candidacy five days later, after another failed round of voting. Andrew Finkel, "Turkey: Torn between God and State," *Le Monde Diplomatique* (May 2007), http://mondediplo.com/2007/05/02turkey.

36. Çavdar, "Behind Turkey's Presidential Battle," citing *Milliyet,* April 28, 2007. Çavdar notes that "the government issued a counter-statement reminding the general staff that they are government employees and that, in democracies, it is not acceptable for the armed forces to intervene in politics."

37. The Turkish military had the full support of Israel and the United States in the 1998 ouster of the Erbakan government. See M. Hakan Yavuz, *Islamic Political Identity in Turkey* (New York: Oxford University Press, 2003), 254.

38. Haldun Gülalp, "Globalizing Postmodernism: Islamist and Western Social Theory," *Economy and Society* 26, no. 3 (August 1997): 431.

39. Although the European Court of Human Rights is not an official EU institution, its decisions are regarded as significant in Turkey at a time when Turkey is seeking accession to the European Union.

40. Judges from France, Turkey, Norway, and Albania supported the majority opinion, and judges from Austria, Cyprus, and Britain dissented.

41. Human Rights Watch World Report 2002: Turkey, http://www.hrw.org/wr2k2/europe19.html.

42. Press release issued by the Registrar of the European Court of Human Rights, "Judgment in the Case of Refah Partisi (the Welfare Party) Erbakan, Kazan and Tekdal v. Turkey," issued July 31, 2001.

43. Nilüfer Gole, "Authoritarian Secularism and Islamist Politics: The Case of Turkey," in Augustus Richard Norton, ed., *Civil Society in the Middle East*, vol. 1 (New York: Brill, 1995), 38–39.

44. Hakan Yavuz, "Islam and Europeanization in Turkish-Muslim Socio-Political Movements," in Peter J. Katzenstein and Timothy Byrnes, eds., *Religion in an Expanding Europe* (Cambridge: Cambridge University Press), 240.

45. Alfred Stepan, "Religion, Democracy, and the 'Twin Tolerations,'" in Larry Diamond, Marc F. Plattner, and Philip J. Costopoulos, eds., *World Religions and Democracy* (Baltimore, Md.: Johns Hopkins University Press, 2005), 3. For a more detailed discussion of the twin tolerations, see Alfred Stepan, *Arguing Comparative Politics* (New York: Oxford University Press), 213–254.

46. Stepan, "Religion, Democracy, and the 'Twin Tolerations,'" 44.

47. Yolande Jansen, "Laïcité, or the Politics of Republican Secularism," in Hent de Vries and Lawrence E. Sullivan, eds., *Political Theologies: Public Religions in a Post-Secular World* (New York: Fordham University Press, 2006), 478–480.

8

Rethinking the Secular and Religious Aspects of Violence
Mark Juergensmeyer

Behind many of the strident new religious movements that have arisen around the world in recent years lie some common themes. Regardless of their religious tradition—from Islamic jihadist militants to Jewish anti-Arab activists to Christian militia in the United States—the activists involved in these movements are parts of communities that perceive themselves to be fragile, vulnerable, and under siege from a hostile secular world.

These movements are political as well as cultural, in that they share a common ideological perception that the secular state is the enemy. Their supporters have lost faith in secular nationalism and regard the secular state as an insufficient agency to protect their communities or provide the moral, political, economic, and social strength to nurture them. In scores of interviews with political activists around the world, I have found a frequent motivating cause, not a yearning for a specific political goal but the gnawing sense of a loss of identity and control in the modern world.

This sense of social malaise is not a religious problem, but in many contemporary movements of political activism, religion has become the ideology of protest.[1] Particular religious images and themes are marshaled to resist what are imagined to be the enemies of traditional culture and identities: global secular systems and their secular nation-state supporters. Why are social and political tensions in the twenty-first century imagined as confrontations between religion and secularism?

This is an interesting question. One answer is that this problem has been created by secularism as much as by religion. Or to put it another way, it has been generated by the construction of the idea of a secular social order that marginalizes religious values, practices, and identities and creates a potential scapegoat for social and cultural frustrations. When individuals feel marginalized, for whatever reason, they can imagine that their situations are fostered by an alienating secular state.

In each of the recent cases of violent religious activism, the supporters who have embraced these radical antistate religious ideologies have felt personally upset with what they regard as the oppression of the secular state. They experience this oppression as an assault on their pride and feel insulted and shamed as a result. The failures of contemporary society—though economic, political, and cultural—are often experienced in personal ways as humiliation and alienation, as a loss of selfhood. The secular state is the imagined enemy, and regimes that are corrupt or inept or militant contribute to their own demonic self-images. Acts of violence against the secular state become symbolic expressions of empowerment and attempts to claim leverage in a public arena that is perceived as hostile and marginalizing. Thus, these acts need to be taken seriously as calls for inclusion in an alienating global world.

In thinking about the way that the activists I interviewed described the role of religion, I have come to an unsettling conclusion. It is not religion that is the cause of much of the violence associated with it—as if religion were an entity that could do things by itself—but the way that the activists and their foes have come to think about religion. In particular, the problem lies in the idea that there is something called "religion" that is excluded from public life and "secularism" that dominates the public sphere. Behind this notion is the distinction between things religious and secular that has been a habit of thought since the Enlightenment. This image of a bifurcated religious and secular world has caught on in virtually every society—today in Asia and the Muslim world, as well as the West—and it has become linked with social and cultural tensions that from time to time erupt in public violence. In one of history's great ironies, the political construction of secular nationalism—meant to bring peace and civility to social life—has in this period of late modernity become a contested idea and a source of conflict and critique.

The Rise of the Secular State

It is not entirely clear how this imagined bifurcation between the secular world and the religious world came about. It is usually described as being an invention of the European Enlightenment, but there were precedents. According to some accounts, secular nationalism was promoted in thirteenth-century France and England in order to buttress the authority of secular rulers after the clergy had been removed from political power earlier in the century. In the fourteenth and fifteenth centuries, there was a reaction against central secular-national governments; the next great wave of laicization occurred in the sixteenth century.[2] Challenges to the divine right to rule in Europe reach back at least to the twelfth century, when John of Salisbury, who is sometimes regarded as the first modern political philosopher, held that rulers should be subject to charges of treason and could be overthrown—violently if necessary—if they violated their public trust; and William of Ockham, in the fourteenth century, argued that a "secular ruler need not submit to spiritual power."[3] But despite these earlier examples, the most complete expression of the independence of what is imagined to be a secular state is to be found in the political manifestation of the Enlightenment view of social order.

The role of religion in Enlightenment thought is complicated.[4] Although John Locke and Jean-Jacques Rousseau had religious sensibilities and allowed for a divine order that made the rights of humans possible, these ideas did not directly buttress the power of the church and its priestly administrators. Although he advocated the "reasonableness" of Christianity, Locke's ideas of the origins of a civil community had virtually no connection to the communities of church and Christendom. Because humans are "equal and independent" before God, Locke argued, they have the sole right to exercise the power of the law of nature, and the only way in which an individual can be deprived of his or her liberty is "by agreeing with other Men to joyn and unite into a community, for their comfortable, safe, and peacable living one amongst another."[5] And Rousseau's social-contract theories required little commitment to religious belief. According to Rousseau, a social contract is a tacit admission by the people that they need to be ruled and an expression of their willingness to relinquish some of their rights and freedoms to the state in exchange for its administrative protection. It is an exchange of what Rousseau calls one's "natural liberty" for the security and justice provided through "civil liberty."[6] Rousseau implied that the state does not need the church to grant it moral legitimacy; the people grant it a legitimacy on their own through a divine right that is directly invested in them as a part of the God-given natural order. Their secular concepts of nation and state had the effect of taking religion—at least church religion—out of public life.

The medieval church once possessed "many aspects of a state," as one historian put it, and it commanded more political power "than most of its secular rivals."[7] By the mid-nineteenth century, however, Christian churches had ceased to have much influence on European or American politics. The church—the great medieval monument of Christendom, with all of its social and political diversity—had been replaced by churches: various denominations of Protestantism and a largely depoliticized version of Roman Catholicism. These churches functioned like religious clubs, voluntary associations for the spiritual edification of individuals in their leisure time, rarely cognizant of the social and political world around them.[8]

The Enlightenment ushered in a new way of thinking about religion—a narrower definition of the term which encompassed institutions and beliefs that were regarded as problematic and conceptually separated them from the rest of social life, which was identified by a new term, "secular." What many people in Europe were afraid of at the time was the economic and political power of the clergy and the fanaticism associated with the terrible wars of religion of the sixteenth and seventeenth centuries. These would be controlled in a society in which "religion" had its limitations within "secular" society.

At the same time that religion in the West was becoming less political, its secular nationalism was becoming more religious. It became clothed in romantic and xenophobic images that would have startled its Enlightenment forebears. The French Revolution, the model for much of the nationalist fervor that developed in the nineteenth century, infused a religious zeal into revolutionary democracy; the revolution took on the trappings of church religion in the priestly power meted out to its demagogic leaders and in the slavish devotion to what it called the temple of reason. According to Alexis de Tocqueville, the French Revolution "assumed many of the aspects of a religious revolution."[9] The American Revolution also had a religious side: many of its leaders had been influenced by eighteenth-century Deism, a religion of science and natural law that was "devoted to exposing [church] religion to the light of knowledge."[10] As in France, American nationalism developed its own religious characteristics, blending the ideals of secular nationalism and the symbols of Christianity into what has been called "civil religion."[11]

The nineteenth century saw the fulfillment of Tocqueville's prophecy that the "strange religion" of secular nationalism would, "like Islam, overrun the whole world with its apostles, militants, and martyrs."[12] It spread throughout the world with an almost missionary zeal and was shipped to the newly colonized areas of Asia, Africa, and Latin America as part of the ideological freight of colonialism. It became the ideological partner of what came to be known as nation-building. As the colonizing governments provided their colonies with the political and economic infrastructures to turn territories into nation-states, the ideology of secular nationalism emerged as a by-product. As it had in the West during previous centuries, secular nationalism in the colonized countries during the nineteenth and twentieth centuries came to represent one side of a great encounter between two vastly different ways of perceiving the sociopolitical order and the relationship of the individual to the state—one informed by religion, the other by a notion of a secular compact.

In the West, this encounter and the ideological, economic, and political transitions that accompanied it took place over many years, uncomplicated by the intrusion of foreign control of a colonial or neocolonial sort. The new nations of the twentieth and twenty-first centuries, however, have had to confront the same challenges in a short period of time and simultaneously contend with new forms of politics forced on them as by-products of colonial rule. As in the West, however, the challenge they have faced is fundamental; it involves the encounter between an old religious worldview and a new one shaped by secular nationalism.

When Europeans colonized the rest of the world, they were often sustained by a desire to make the rest of the world like themselves.[13] Even when empires became economically burdensome, the cultural mission seemed to justify the effort. The commitment of colonial administrators to a secular-nationalist vision explains why they were often so hostile to the Christian missionaries who tagged along behind them: the missionaries were the liberal colonizers' competitors. In general, the church's old religious ideology was a threat to the new secular ideology that most colonial rulers wished to present as characteristic of the West.[14]

In the mid-twentieth century, when the colonial powers retreated, they left behind the geographical boundaries they had drawn and the political institutions they had fashioned. The borders of most Third World nations, which were created as administrative units of the Ottoman, Hapsburg, French, and British empires, continued to survive after independence, even if they failed to follow the natural divisions between ethnic and linguistic communities. By the middle of the twentieth century, it seemed as if the cultural goals of the colonial era had been reached; although the political ties were severed, the new nations retained all of the accoutrements of Westernized countries.

The only substantial empire that remained virtually intact until 1990 was the Soviet Union. It was based on a different vision of political order, of course, one in which international socialism was supposed to replace a network of capitalist nations. Yet the perception of many members of the Soviet states was that their nations were not so much integral units in a new internationalism as colonies in a secular Russian version of imperialism. This reality became dramatically clear after the breakup of the Soviet Union and its sphere of influence in the early 1990s, when old ethnic and national loyalties sprang to the fore.

The Golden Age of Secular Nationalism, 1945–1990

In the middle of the twentieth century, when many colonies in the developing world gained political independence, Europeans and Americans often wrote with an almost religious fervor about what they regarded as these new nations' freedom—by which they meant the spread of nationalism throughout the world. Invariably, they meant a secular nationalism: new nations that elicited loyalties forged entirely from a sense of territorial citizenship. These secular-nationalist loyalties were based on the idea that the legitimacy of the state was rooted in the will of the people in a particular geographic region and divorced from any religious sanction.[15]

In the mid-twentieth century, the new global reach of secular nationalism was justified by what it was—and what it was not. It distanced itself especially from the old ethnic and religious identities that had made nations parochial and quarrelsome in the past. The major exception was the creation of the state of Israel in 1948 as a safe haven for Jews, but even in this case, the nation's constitution was firmly secular, and Israeli citizenship was open to people of all religious backgrounds—not only Jews but also Christians and Muslims. In general, mid-twentieth-century scholars viewed the spread of secular nation-alism in a hopeful, almost eschatological light: it was ushering in a new future. It meant, in essence, the emergence of mini-Americas all over the world.

European and American scholars in the mid-1950s embraced the new global nation-state era with unbridled joy. At that time, Hans Kohn, his generation's best-known historian of nationalism, could brazenly assert that the twentieth century was unique: "It is the first period in history in which the whole of man-kind has accepted one and the same political attitude, that of nationalism."[16] In his telling, the concept had its origins in antiquity. It was presaged by ancient Hebrews and fully enunciated by ancient Greeks. Inexplicably, however, the concept stagnated for almost 2000 years, according to Kohn's account, until suddenly it took off in earnest in England, "the first modern nation," during the seventeenth century.[17] By the time of his writing, in the mid-twentieth century, he cheerfully observed that the whole world had responded to "the awakening of nationalism and liberty."[18]

Not only Western academics but also a good number of new leaders—espe-cially those in the emerging nations created out of former colonial empires—were swept up by the vision of a world of free and equal secular nations. The concept of secular nationalism gave them an ideological justification for being, and the electorate that subscribed to it provided them with power bases from which they could vault into positions of leadership ahead of traditional ethnic and religious figures. But secularism was more than just a political issue; it was also a matter of personal identity. A new kind of person had come into existence: the "Indian nationalist" or "Ceylonese nationalist" who had an abid-ing faith in a secular nationalism identified with his or her homeland. Perhaps none exemplified this new spirit more than Gamal Abdel Nasser of Egypt and Jawaharlal Nehru of India. According to Nehru, "there is no going back" to a past full of religious identities, for the modern, secular "spirit of the age" will inevitably triumph throughout the world.[19]

There was a cheerful optimism among the followers of Nehru after India's independence, political scientist Donald Smith writes: "The Indian nationalist felt compelled to assert that India was a nation," even though some "embar-rassing facts"—such as divisive regional and religious loyalties—had to be glossed over.[20] The reason for this compulsion, according to Smith, was that such people could not think of themselves as modern persons without a national identity. "In the modern world," Smith writes, "nationality and nationalism were the basic premises of political life, and it seemed absolutely *improper* for India to be without a nationality."[21] A similar attitude predominated in many other new nations, at least at the beginning.

Leaders of minority religious communities—such as Hindu Tamils in Ceylon and Coptic Christians in Egypt—seemed especially eager to embrace secular nationalism, because a secular nation-state would ensure that the public life of the country would not be dominated completely by the majority religious community. In India, where the Congress Party became the standard bearer of Nehru's vision, the party's most reliable supporters were those at the margins of Hindu society—untouchables and Muslims—who had the most to fear from an intolerant religious majority.

The main carriers of the banner of secular nationalism in these newly independent countries, however, were not members of any religious community at all, at least in a traditional sense. Rather, they were members of the urban educated elite. For many of them, embracing a secular form of nationalism was a way of promoting its major premise—freedom from the parochial identities of the past—and thereby avoiding the obstacles that religious loyalties create for a country's political goals. By implication, political power based on religious values and traditional communities held no authority.

The problem, however, was that in asserting that the nationalism of their country was secular, the new nationalists had to have faith in a secular culture that was at least as compelling as a sacred one. That meant, on a social level, believing that secular nationalism could triumph over what they thought of as "religion." It could also mean making secular nationalism a suprareligion of its own, which a society could aspire to beyond any single religious allegiance. In India, for example, political identity based on religious affiliation was termed communalism. In the view of Nehru and other secular nationalists, religion was the chief competitor of an even higher object of loyalty: secular India. Nehru implored his countrymen to get rid of what he called "that narrowing religious outlook" and to adopt a modern, nationalist viewpoint.[22]

The secular nationalists' attempts to give their ideologies an antireligious or a suprareligious force were encouraged, perhaps unwittingly, by their Western mentors. The words used to define nationalism by Western political leaders and such scholars as Kohn always implied not only that it was secular but also that it was competitive with what they defined as religion and ultimately superior to it. "Nationalism [by which he meant secular nationalism] is a state of mind," Kohn wrote, "in which the supreme loyalty of the individual is felt to be due the nation-state."[23] And he boldly asserted that secular nationalism had replaced religion in its influence: "An understanding of nationalism and its implications for modern history and for our time appears as fundamental today as an understanding of religion would have been for thirteenth century Christendom."[24]

Rupert Emerson's influential *From Empire to Nation,* written several years later, shared the same exciting vision of a secular nationalism that "sweeps out [from Europe] to embrace the whole wide world."[25] Emerson acknowledged, however, that although in the European experience, "the rise of nationalism [again, secular nationalism] coincided with a decline in the hold of religion," in other parts of the world, such as Asia, as secular nationalism "moved on" and enveloped these regions, "the religious issue pressed more clearly to the fore again."[26] Nonetheless, he anticipated that the "religious issue" would never again impede the progress of secular nationalism, which he saw as the West's gift to the world. The feeling that in some instances, this gift had been forced on the new nations without their asking was noted by Emerson, who acknowledged that "the rise of nationalism among non-European peoples" was a consequence of "the imperial spread of Western European civilization over the face of the earth."

The outcome, in his view, was nonetheless laudable: "With revolutionary dynamism...civilization has thrust elements of essential identity on peoples everywhere....The global impact of the West has...run common threads through the variegated social fabrics of mankind, [and it] has scored an extraordinary triumph."[27]

When Kohn and Emerson used the term "nationalism," they had in mind not just a secular political ideology and a religiously neutral national identity but also a particular form of political organization: the modern European and American nation-state. In such an organization, individuals are linked to a centralized, all-embracing democratic political system that is unaffected by any other affiliations, be they ethnic, cultural, or religious. That linkage is sealed by an emotional sense of identification with a geographical area and a loyalty to a particular people, an identity that is part of the feeling of nationalism. This affective dimension of nationalism is important to keep in mind, especially in comparing secular nationalism with the Enlightenment idea of religion. In the 1980s, social theorist Anthony Giddens described nationalism in just this way—as conveying not only the ideas and "beliefs" about political order but also the "psychological" and "symbolic" element in political and economic relationships.[28] Scholars such as Kohn and Emerson recognized this affective dimension of nationalism early on; they felt it appropriate that the secular nation adopt what Charles Taylor has described as the cultural sensibility of secularism and what might also be called the spirit of secular nationalism.[29]

The Religious Challenge to the Secular State in the Twenty-First Century

Since the modern nation-state has been presented to the world as a secular institution, the criticism of it has often been clothed in religious language. In the contemporary era, the "crisis of legitimation" that Jürgen Habermas has observed in social institutions has led to a rejection of the optimistic premises of secular politics.[30] The legitimacy of the secular nation-state has been eroded by several factors, including a resurgent new wave of anticolonialism, the corrosive power of globalized economic and communication systems, and the corruption and incompetence of secular leaders. In many parts of the world, the failure of the secular state began to be attributed to secularism itself. This raised what Talal Asad describes as its twin concept, the newly created idea of "religion," to a position of political influence. In earlier decades, traditional leaders and cultural institutions seldom played a political role, although when they did become involved, it was often to critique specific social issues of the state rather than to challenge the credibility of the entire political system.[31]

Contemporary religious politics, then, is quite a new development. It is the result of an almost Hegelian dialectic between what has been imagined by most citizens of the modern world to be two competing frameworks of social order: secular nationalism (allied with the nation-state) and the Enlightenment idea of religion (allied with large ethnic communities, some of them transnational). The clashes between the two have often been destructive, but they have also offered possibilities for accommodation. In some cases, these encounters have given birth to a synthesis in which cultural ideas and institutions have become the allies of a new kind of nation-state. At the same time, other liaisons with contemporary political trends have led to a different vision: religious versions of a transnationalism that would supplant the nation-state world.

The rivalry between secular nationalism and cultural identities makes little sense in the modern West, where the idea of religion has been conceptually confined to personal piety, religious institutions, and theological ideas. But it makes sense in traditional societies around the world, in which the cultural and moral elements of religious imagination are viewed as an integral part of social and political life.

Perhaps it is useful, then, to think of religion in two senses, in Enlightenment and non-Enlightenment ways of thinking. The first, the Enlightenment view, is the narrow idea of religious institutions and beliefs contrasted with secular social values in the modern West. The other, the more traditional view, is a broad framework of thinking and acting that involves moral values, traditional customs, and publically articulated spiritual sensibility. The latter, traditional view of "religion" (or, rather, the religious worldview) includes much of what the secular West regards as public virtue and purposeful social life—values shared by most thoughtful and concerned citizens within a society.

Thus, the elusive term "religion," in the broad sense, can point to a moral sensibility toward the social order that in many ways is remarkably similar to the civic values of those who feel most ardently about secularism. This is especially so in the non-Western world. In traditional India, for instance, the English term "religion" might be translated as the word for moral order (*dharma*), as well as for belief (*mazhab*), fellowship (*panth*), or community (*qaum*). As *dharma*, Hindu thought is like political or social theory, the basis of a just society. The Enlightenment thinkers who were most insistent on secularism did not see religion in this way; what they saw was an arrogant religious hierarchy keeping the masses enslaved to superstition in order to avoid justice and reason. They thought of religion as competitive with Enlightenment values, yet religion as *dharma* looks very much like that moral ground on which the Enlightenment thinkers were able to build the edifice of a just society. In ways that might surprise them, religion—at least in its broad sense, as a conveyor of public values—and secularism as a social ideology might well be two ways of talking about the same thing.

Because the functions of traditional religious and secular social values are so similar, it might be useful to designate a general category that includes both terms, a "genus" of which this kind of religion and secularism are the two competing "species." Wilfred Cantwell Smith recommended enlarging the idea of "traditions" to include both religious and secular humanist traditions; Benedict Anderson suggested "imagined communities" for all national societies; and Ninian Smart offered "worldviews" as the common term for nationalism, socialism, and religion.[32] Elsewhere, I have suggested the phrase "ideologies of order," even though the term is freighted with meanings attached to it by Karl Marx and Karl Mannheim, and a great deal of controversy lingers over its interpretation.[33] The term originated in the late eighteenth century in the context of the rise of secular nationalism.[34] A group of French *idéologues*, as they called themselves, sought to build a science of ideas based on the theories of Francis Bacon, Thomas Hobbes, John Locke, and René Descartes that would be sufficiently comprehensive to replace religion, in the broad sense, and provide a moral weight to public values that would counter the violent excesses of the French Revolution. According to one of the *idéologues*, Destutt de Tracy, whose book *Elements of Ideology* introduced the term "ideology" to the world, "logic" was to be the sole basis of "the moral and political sciences."[35] The French originators of the term "ideology" would be surprised at the way it has come to be redefined, especially in contemporary conversations, where it is often treated as an explanatory system that is specifically nonscientific.

In proposing a "science of ideas" as a replacement for religion, the *idéologues* were putting what they called ideology and what we call religion (in the broad sense) on an equal plane. Perhaps Clifford Geertz, among modern users of the term, has come closest to its original meaning by speaking of ideology as a "cultural system."[36] Geertz includes both religious and political cultural systems within this framework, as well as the many cultural systems that do not distinguish between religion and politics. Religion and secular nationalism could both be considered cultural systems in Geertz's sense of the word, and thus, as he uses it, they are ideologies. Both conceive of the world in coherent, manageable ways; both suggest that there are levels of meaning beneath the day-to-day world that give coherence to things unseen; and both provide the authority that gives the social and political order its reason for being. In doing so, they define for the individual the right way of being in the world and relate persons to the social whole.

Secular nationalism is a social form of secularism that locates an individual within the universe. The idea of a secular nation ties him or her to a particular place and a particular history. A number of social scientists have argued that the phenomenon of secular nationalism is linked to the innate need of individuals for a sense of community. Recently, John Lie has posited that the idea of a common "peoplehood"—often construed in ethnic or religious terms—is essential for the modern idea of a nation.[37] Earlier, Karl Deutsch pointed out the importance of systems of communication in fostering a sense of nationalism.[38] Ernest Gellner argued that the political and economic network of a nation-state can function only in a spirit of nationalism based on a homogeneous culture, a unified pattern of communication, and a common system of education.[39] Other social scientists have stressed the psychological aspect of national identity: the sense of historical location that is engendered when individuals feel they have a larger, national history.[40]

But behind these notions of community is the stern image of social order. Nationalism involves loyalty to an authority that, as Max Weber observed, holds a monopoly over the "legitimate use of physical force" in a given society.[41] Giddens describes nationalism as the "cultural sensibility of sovereignty," implying that, in part, the awareness of being subject to an authority—an authority invested with the power of life and death—gives nationalism its potency.[42] Secular nationalism, therefore, involves not only an attachment to a spirit of social order but also an act of submission to an ordering agent.

Scholarly attempts to define religion also stress the importance of order, although in a post-Enlightenment context in which religion is thought of in the narrower sense, the orderliness is primarily metaphysical rather than political or social. In providing its adherents with a sense of conceptual order, religion often deals with the existential problem of disorder. The disorderliness of ordinary life is contrasted with a substantial, unchanging divine order.[43] Geertz saw religion as the effort to integrate everyday reality into a pattern of coherence at a deeper level.[44] Robert Bellah also described religion as an attempt to reach beyond ordinary phenomena in a "risk of faith" that allows people to act "in the face of uncertainty and unpredictability" on the basis of a higher order of reality.[45] This attitude of faith, according to Peter Berger, is an affirmation of the sacred, which acts as a doorway to a truth more certain than that of this world.[46] Louis Dupré prefers to avoid the term "sacred" but integrates elements of both Berger's and Bellah's definitions in his description of religion as "a commitment to the transcendent as to another reality."[47] In all of these cases, there is a tension between this imperfect, disorderly world and a perfected, orderly one to be found in a higher, transcendent state or in a cumulative moment in time. As Émile Durkheim, whose ideas are fundamental to each of these thinkers, was adamant in observing, religion has a more encompassing force than can be suggested by any dichotomization of the sacred and the profane. To Durkheim, the religious point of view includes both the notion that there is such a dichotomy and the belief that the sacred side will always, ultimately, reign supreme.[48]

Even on the metaphysical level, religion, like secular nationalism, can provide the moral and spiritual glue that holds together broad communities. Members of these communities—secular or religious—share a tradition, a particular worldview, in which the essential conflict between appearance and deeper reality is described in specific and characteristically cultural terms. This deeper reality has a degree of permanence and order quite unobtainable by ordinary means. The conflict between the two levels of reality is what both religion and secular nationalism are about: the language of both contains images of chaos, as well as tranquil order, holding out the hope that, despite appearances to the contrary, order will eventually triumph and disorder will be contained. Because religion (in both broad and narrow senses) and secular nationalism are ideologies of order, they are potential rivals.[49] Either can claim to be the guarantor of orderliness within a society; either can claim to be the ultimate authority for social order. Such claims carry with them an extraordinary degree of power, for contained within them is the right to give moral sanction for life-and-death decisions, including the right to kill. When either secular nationalism or religion assumes that role by itself, it reduces the other to a peripheral social role.

Religious Violence as a Response to Secular Nationalism

The rejection of secular nationalism is often violent. The reason for this is not only that those who challenge the secular state are eager to assume their own positions of power in public life. They are also challenging the right of the secular state to the legitimacy provided by its monopoly on the use of violence to maintain public order. The creation of "religion" in juxtaposition to "secular" provides the potential for those identified with this kind of religion to utilize the same force of power that the secular state has used to maintain its order.

Thus, the religious critique of secular nationalism contains a challenge to the source of social power on which secular public order is based: absolute control undergirded by the moral sanction of political violence. Ascribing to an alternative ideology of public order—the imagined idea of religion—gives one the ability to be violent. In the modern world, the secular state, and the state alone, has been given the power to kill legitimately, albeit for limited purposes: military defense, police protection, and capital punishment. Yet all the rest of the state's power to persuade and to shape the social order is derived from this fundamental power. In Weber's view, the monopoly over legitimate violence in a society lies behind all other claims to political authority.[50] In challenging the state, today's religious activists, wherever they assert themselves around the world, reclaim the traditional right of religious authorities to say when violence is moral and when it is not.

Situations of social conflict provide contexts in which religious authority is called upon to sanction killing. This is especially true in the case of conflicts that involve issues of identity, loyalty, and communal solidarity. Religious identities may be a factor in movements of mobilization, separatism, and the establishment of new states. It is interesting to note, in this regard, that the best-known incidents in which religious language and authorities have played a role in the contemporary world have occurred in places where it is difficult to define or accept the idea of a nation-state. At the end of the twentieth century, these places included Palestine, the Punjab, and Sri Lanka; in the first decade of the twenty-first century, they included Iraq, Somalia, and Lebanon, areas where uncertainties abound about what the state should be and which elements of society should lead it. In these instances, religious loyalties have often provided the basis for a new national consensus and a new kind of leadership.

Cultural practices and ideas related to Islam, Judaism, and Christianity have provided religious alternatives to secular ideology as the basis of nationalism, and political images from their religious history have provided resources for thinking of modern religion in political terms. This is also true of Hinduism, Sikhism, and, perhaps most surprisingly, Buddhism. In Thailand, for example, Buddhist political activists recall that the king must be a monk before assuming political power—he must be a "world renouncer" before he can become a "world conqueror," as Stanley Tambiah has put it.[51] Burmese leaders established a Buddhist socialism, guided by a curious syncretic mix of Marxist and Buddhist ideas, and even the protests against that order in Burma (renamed Myanmar) had a religious character: many of the demonstrations in the streets were led by Buddhist monks.[52] Thus, in most traditional religious societies, including Buddhist ones, "religion," as Donald Smith puts it, "answers the question of political legitimacy."[53] In the modern West, that legitimacy is provided by nationalism, a secular nationalism. But even there, religious justifications wait in the wings, potential challenges to the nationalism based on secular assumptions. Perhaps nothing indicates this potential more than the persistence of religious politics in American society, including the rise of the Christian militia and the American religious right.[54] The justification for social order may be couched in secular or religious terms, and both require a faith in the unitary nature of a society that can authenticate both political rebellion and political rule.

When I interviewed Sunni mullahs in Iraq in 2004 after the U.S. invasion of their country, they told me that opposition to U.S. occupation was because they regarded America as the enemy of Islam. What was striking to me about this comparison was that they were equating the two and perceived that a secular state was in competition with what is regarded as a religion. This would have startled many of the twentieth-century proponents of secular nationalism. In the 1950s and '60s, scholars such as Kohn and Emerson and nationalist leaders such as Nasser and Nehru regarded secular nationalism as superior to religion, in large measure because they thought it was categorically different.

Yet it is clear that the belief in secular nationalism required a great deal of faith, even though the idea was not couched in the rhetoric of religion. The terms in which it was presented were the grandly visionary ones associated with spiritual values. As early as Tocqueville, comparisons have been made between secular nationalism and religion.[55] After the global rise of secular nationalism at the end of World War II, quite a few scholars observed that there was a similarity between the ideological characteristics of secular nationalism and the modern idea of religion—both of which embraced "a doctrine of destiny," as one scholar observed.[56] Some took this way of viewing secular nationalism a step further and stated flatly, as did an author writing in 1960, that secular nationalism is "a religion."[57] A scholar of comparative religion, Ninian Smart, specified the characteristics that make secular nationalism akin to a certain kind of religion, "a tribal religion."[58] Employing six criteria to define the term, he concluded that secular nationalism measured up on all counts: on doctrine, myth, ethics, ritual, experience, and social organization.

The two inventions of modernity—secular nationalism and religion—both serve the ethical function of providing an overarching framework of moral order, a framework that commands ultimate loyalty from those who subscribe to it. And although the modern assumption is that nationalism is a moral order for the public realm and religion for the private realm, both provide moral sanction to martyrdom and violence. As a result, the modern idea of religion is a potential revolutionary construct, for it can provide a justification for violence that would challenge the power of the secular state.

Although it may be true that other entities, such as the Mafia and the Ku Klux Klan, also sanction violence, they are able to do so convincingly only because they are regarded by their followers as (respectively) quasi-governmental or quasi-religious organizations. Since the line between secular nationalism and religion has always been quite thin—the public and private notions of modern moral order—they have sometimes emerged as rivals. Both are expressions of faith, both involve an identity with and a loyalty to a large community, and both insist on the ultimate moral legitimacy of the authority invested in the leadership of that community.

Benedict Anderson, in observing the ease with which secular nationalism is able to justify mass killings, finds a strong affinity between "nationalist imagining" and "religious imagining." The rise of secular nationalism in world history, as Anderson observes, has been an extension of "the large cultural systems that preceded it, out of which—as well as against which—it came into being."[59] Secular nationalism often evokes an almost religious response, and it frequently appears as a kind of "cultural nationalism" in the way that Howard Wriggins once described Sinhalese national sentiments.[60] It not only encompasses the shared cultural values of people within existing, or potentially existing, national boundaries but also evokes a cultural response of its own.

This similarity between secular and religious imaginings in the implementation of public acts of violence enforces the idea asserted by many present-day religious activists that religion can provide a justification for the power, based on violence, that is the basis of modern politics. And why not? If secularism, as an imagined concept of social order, is capable of providing the ideological legitimacy to modern political communities, this same legitimizing function can be extended to secularism's twin concept, the idea of religion. The religious activists of today are unwittingly modern, therefore, because they accept the same secularist notion that there is a fundamental distinction between secular and religious realms. Religious activists think that they are simply reclaiming the political power of the state in the name of religion. It might be a workable arrangement in a premodern world where religious sensibilities were intertwined with a broad sense of moral order, and a religion-based polity could embrace a varied and pluralistic society.

The irony is that the modern idea of religion is much narrower than that, consisting of doctrines and communities that have been marginalized by secularism and that in some cases seek revenge. The Frankenstein of religion created in the Enlightenment imagination has risen up to claim the Enlightenment's proudest achievement, the nation-state. The tragedy is that the challenge to the secular order that emerges from this kind of religious nationalism shakes the foundations of political power in ways that are often strident and violent.

Notes

1. See Mark Juergensmeyer, "Is Religion the Problem?" *Hedgehog Review* 6, no. 1 (Spring 2004): 21–33; and Mark Juergensmeyer, *Global Rebellion: Religious Challenges to the Secular State* (Berkeley: University of California Press, 2008), where many of the ideas in this essay first appeared.

2. Joseph Strayer, *Medieval Statecraft and the Perspectives of History* (Princeton, N.J.: Princeton University Press, 1971), 262–265.

3. See Sidney R. Packard, *Twelfth-Century Europe: An Interpretive Essay* (Amherst: University of Massachusetts Press, 1973), 193–201; and Thomas Molnar, "The Medieval Beginnings of Political Secularization," in George W. Carey and James V. Schall, eds., *Essays on Christianity and Political Philosophy* (Lanham, Md.: University Press of America, 1985), 43.

4. See, for instance, Jonathan Sheehan, "Enlightenment, Religion, and the Enigma of Secularization," *American Historical Review* 108, no.4 (October 2003): 1061–1080; and David Sorkin, *The Religious Enlightenment: Protestants, Jews, and Catholics from London to Vienna* (Princeton, N.J.: Princeton University Press, 2009).

5. John Locke, "Of the Beginnings of Political Societies," *The Second Treatise on Government* (New York: Cambridge University Press, 1960), 375.

6. Jean-Jacques Rousseau, "On the Civil State," *The Social Contract* (New York: Pocket, 1967), 23.

7. Strayer, *Medieval Statecraft*, 323.

8. Although the churches supported a number of secular reforms in the nineteenth and twentieth centuries, religion in the West largely fit Whitehead's description: it was what "an individual does with his own solitariness." Alfred North Whitehead, *Religion in the Making*, in F. S. C. Northrup and Mason W. Gross, eds., *Alfred North Whitehead: An Anthology* (New York: Macmillan, 1961), 472.

9. Alexis de Tocqueville, *The Old Regime and the French Revolution*, trans. Stuart Gilbert (New York: Doubleday, Anchor, 1955), 11. See also John McManners, *The French Revolution and the Church* (Westport, Conn.: Greenwood, 1969).

10. Ernst Cassirer, *The Philosophy of the Enlightenment* (Boston: Beacon, 1955), 171. Among the devotees of Deism were Thomas Jefferson, Benjamin Franklin, and other founding fathers of the United States.

11. Robert Bellah, "Civil Religion in America," *Daedalus* 96, no. 1 (Winter 1967): 1–22.

12. Tocqueville, *The Old Regime*, 13.

13. Liberal politicians within the colonial governments were much more insistent on imparting notions of Western political order than were the conservatives. In the heyday of British control of India, for instance, the position of Whigs such as William Gladstone was that the presence of the British was "to promote the political training of our fellow-subjects"; quoted in H. C. G. Matthew, *Gladstone, 1809–1874*, vol. 1 (Oxford: Clarendon, 1986), 188. Conservatives such as Benjamin Disraeli, however, felt that the British should "respect and maintain" the traditional practices of the colonies, including "the laws and customs, the property and religion"; from a speech delivered after the Sepoy Rebellion in India in 1857, quoted in William Monypenny and George Buckle, *The Life of Disraeli, 1: 1804–1859* (London: John Murton, 1929), 1488–1489. In the end, the liberal vision caught on, even among the educated Indian elite, and the notion of a British-style secular nationalism in India was born.

14. Not all missionary efforts were so despised, however. The Anglicans were sometimes seen as partners in the West's civilizing role. Activist, Evangelical missionaries were considered more of a threat.

15. Anthony Giddens, *The Nation-State and Violence*, vol. 2 of *A Contemporary Critique of Historical Materialism* (Berkeley: University of California Press, 1985), 2: 4. For the idea of nationalism and the nation-state, see also Ernest Gellner, *Nations and Nationalism* (Oxford: Basil Blackwell, 1983); and Craig Calhoun, *Nationalism* (Minneapolis: University of Minnesota Press, 1998).

16. Hans Kohn, *Nationalism: Its Meaning and History* (Princeton, N.J.: D. Van Nostrand, 1955), 89.

17. Ibid., 16.

18. Ibid.

19. Jawaharlal Nehru, *The Discovery of India* (New York: John Day, 1946), 531–532.

20. Donald Eugene Smith, *India as a Secular State* (Princeton, N.J.: Princeton University Press, 1963), 140.

21. Ibid., 141.

22. Nehru, *The Discovery of India*, 531.

23. Kohn, *Nationalism*, 9.

24. Ibid., 4.

25. Rupert Emerson, *From Empire to Nation: The Rise to Self-Assertion of Asian and African Peoples* (Boston: Beacon, 1960), 158.

26. Ibid.

27. Ibid., vii.

28. Giddens, *The Nation-State*, 2: 215–216.

29. Charles Taylor, *A Secular Age* (Cambridge, Mass.: Harvard University Press, 2007).

30. Jürgen Habermas, *Legitimation Crisis*, trans. Thomas McCarthy (Boston: Beacon, 1975).

31. Gerald Larson describes the relation between religion and nationalism as ambivalent. Although the global system relies on nation-states that need religion for their legitimacy, the "religionization" of politics can challenge secular nationalism and call into question the global nature of the nation-state system. Gerald Larson, "Fast Falls the Eventide: India's Anguish over Religion," paper presented at a conference on Religion and Nationalism, University of California, Santa Barbara, April 21, 1989.

32. Wilfred Cantwell Smith, *The Meaning and End of Religion* (New York: Macmillan, 1962); Benedict Anderson, *Imagined Communities: Reflections on the Origin and Spread of Nationalism* (London: Verso, 1983); Ninian Smart, *Worldviews: Crosscultural Explorations of Human Beliefs* (New York: Scribner's, 1983).

33. See Karl Marx and Friedrich Engels, *The German Ideology*, ed. R. Pascal (New York: International, 1939); and Karl Mannheim, *Ideology and Utopia* (New York: Harcourt, Brace & World, 1936). For a discussion of the contemporary meaning of ideology, see David Apter, ed., *Ideology and Discontent* (New York: Free Press, 1964); and Chaim I. Waxman, ed., *The End of Ideology Debate* (New York: Simon & Schuster, 1964).

34. Richard H. Cox, *Ideology, Politics, and Political Theory* (Belmont, Calif.: Wadsworth, 1969).

35. Quoted in ibid., 17.

36. Clifford Geertz, "Ideology as a Cultural System," in Apter, ed., *Ideology and Discontent*.

37. John Lie, *Modern Peoplehood.* (Cambridge, Mass.: Harvard University Press, 2007).

38. Karl Deutsch, *Nationalism and Social Communication* (Cambridge, Mass.: MIT Press, 1966).

39. Ernest Gellner, *Nations and Nationalism* (Oxford: Basil Blackwell, 1983), 140.

40. Anthony D. Smith, *Nationalism in the Twentieth Century* (Oxford: Martin Robertson, 1979), 3. See also L. Doob, *Patriotism and Nationalism* (New Haven, Conn.: Yale University Press, 1964).

41. Max Weber, "Politics as a Vocation," in Hans H. Gerth and C. Wright Mills, eds., *From Max Weber: Essays in Sociology* (New York: Oxford University Press, 1946), 78. Regarding the state's monopoly on violence, see John Breuilly, *Nationalism and the State* (Manchester, U.K.: Manchester University Press, 1982); and Anthony D. Smith, *Theories of Nationalism* (London: Duckworth, 1971).

42. Giddens, *The Nation-State*, 219.

43. The notion of religion as a conceptual mechanism that brings order to the disorderly areas of life is a theme of such structuralists as Claude Lévi-Strauss and Mary Douglas and the adherents of René Girard's mimetic theory. For mimetic theory, see Jean-Pierre Dupuy, *Ordres et désordres: Enquêtes sur un nouveau paradigme* (Paris: Éditions du Seuil, 1982); and Paisley Livingston, ed., *Disorder and Order: Proceedings of the Stanford International Symposium (September 14–16, 1981), Stanford Literature Studies* 1 (Saratoga, Calif.: Anma Libri, 1984).

44. Geertz defines religion as "a system of symbols which acts to establish powerful, pervasive and long-lasting moods and motivations in men by formulating conceptions of a general order of existence and clothing these conceptions with such an aura of factuality that the moods and motivations seem uniquely realistic." Clifford Geertz, "Religion as a

Cultural System," in William A. Lessa and Evon Z. Vogt, eds., *Reader in Comparative Religion: An Anthropological Approach*, 3d ed. (New York: Harper & Row, 1972), 168.

45. Robert N. Bellah, "Transcendence in Contemporary Piety," in Donald R. Cutler, ed., *The Religious Situation: 1969* (Boston: Beacon, 1969), 907.

46. Peter Berger, *The Heretical Imperative* (New York: Doubleday, 1980), 38. See also Peter Berger, *The Sacred Canopy: Elements of a Sociological Theory of Religion* (Garden City, N.Y.: Doubleday, 1967).

47. Louis Dupré, *Transcendent Selfhood: The Loss and Rediscovery of the Inner Life* (New York: Seabury, 1976), 26. For a discussion of Berger's and Dupré's definitions, see Mary Douglas, "The Effects of Modernization on Religious Change," *Daedalus* 111, no. 1 (Winter 1982): 1–19.

48. Durkheim describes the dichotomy between the sacred and the profane in religion in the following way: "In all the history of human thought there exists no other example of two categories of things so profoundly differentiated or so radically opposed to one another.... The sacred and the profane have always and everywhere been conceived by the human mind as two distinct classes, as two worlds between which there is nothing in common.... In different religions, this opposition has been conceived in different ways." Émile Durkheim, *The Elementary Forms of the Religious Life*, trans. Joseph Ward Swain (London: Allen & Unwin, 1976 [1915]), 38–39.

49. Although I use the term "religion" (as in "the Christian religion"), in general I agree with Smith, who suggested some years ago that the noun "religion" might well be banished from our vocabulary because it implies a thing—a codified structure of beliefs and practices. He suggested that we restrict ourselves to using the adjective "religious." Smith, *The Meaning and End of Religion*, 119–153.

50. Weber, "Politics as a Vocation," 78.

51. Stanley J. Tambiah, *World Conqueror and World Renouncer: A Study of Buddhism and Polity in Thailand against a Historical Background* (Cambridge: Cambridge University Press, 1976). For a useful overview of Theravada society, see Donald K. Swearer, *Buddhism and Society in Southeast Asia* (Chambersburg, Pa.: Anima, 1981). For the role of monks in Thai politics, see Somboon Suksamran, *Buddhism and Politics in Thailand: A Study of Socio-political Change and Political Activism of the Thai Sangha* (Singapore: Institute of Southeast Asian Studies, 1982); and Charles F. Keyes, *Thailand: Buddhist Kingdom as Modern Nation-State* (Boulder, Colo.: Westview, 1987).

52. For the background of religious nationalism in Burma (Myanmar), see Donald Eugene Smith, ed., *Religion and Politics in Burma* (Princeton, N.J.: Princeton University Press, 1965); E. Sarkisyanz, *Buddhist Backgrounds of the Burmese Revolution* (The Hague: Martinus Nijhoff, 1965); and Heinz Bechert, "Buddhism and Mass Politics in Burma and Ceylon," in Donald Eugene Smith, ed., *Religion and Political Modernization* (New Haven, Conn.: Yale University Press, 1974), 147–167. For a somewhat opposing point of view— that there is relatively little Buddhist influence on Burmese nationalism—see the chapter on Burma in Fred R. von der Mehden, *Religion and Nationalism in Southeast Asia: Burma, Indonesia, the Philippines* (Madison: University of Wisconsin Press, 1963); and Fred R. von der Mehden, "Secularization of Buddhist Polities: Burma and Thailand" in Smith, ed., *Religion and Political Modernization*, 49–66.

53. Donald Eugene Smith, ed., *Religion, Politics, and Social Change in the Third World: A Sourcebook* (New York: Free Press, 1971), 11.

54. See Walter H. Capps, *The New Religious Right: Piety, Patriotism, and Politics* (Columbia: University of South Carolina Press, 1990); Randall Balmer, *Mine Eyes Have Seen the Glory: A Journey into the Evangelical Subculture in America* (New York: Oxford University Press, 1989); and Bruce B. Lawrence, *Defenders of God: The Fundamentalist Revolt against the Modern Age* (New York: Harper & Row, 1989).

55. Tocqueville, *The Old Regime*, 11.

56. Arlie J. Hoover, *The Gospel of Nationalism: German Patriotic Preaching from Napoleon to Versailles* (Stuttgart: Franz Steiner Verlag, 1986), 3.

57. Carlton J. H. Hayes, *Nationalism: A Religion* (New York: Macmillan, 1960).

58. Ninian Smart, "Religion, Myth, and Nationalism," in Peter H. Merkl and Ninian Smart, eds., *Religion and Politics in the Modern World* (New York: New York University Press, 1983), 27. For another comparison of nationalism and religion, see Hoover, *The Gospel of Nationalism*, 3–4.

59. Anderson, *Imagined Communities*, 18.

60. W. Howard Wriggins, *Ceylon: Dilemmas of a New Nation* (Princeton, N.J.: Princeton University Press, 1960), 169.

9

Religious Humanitarianism and the Global Politics of Secularism
Cecelia Lynch

The director of a Christian transnational humanitarian organization asserts that the "development model" is more rooted in Gospel teachings than the "charity model." A new wave of Muslim NGO activists from Somalia, Iraq, and Palestine call themselves secular, and some Iraqi Muslims reject the labels of "Sunni" and "Shi'a." Up to 80 percent of people in some African countries practice "traditional religion," often along with Christianity or Islam, although debate continues about whether such practices constitute "religion" or some other category of ritualized beliefs.

How do we make sense of these and other examples within existing religious/secular categories? What are the parameters of our "secular age" within the "desecularization of the world"?[1] This question might be posed in the inverse by many authors in this book, in order to ask about the parameters of desecularization within our secular age. Given the constitutive nature of my argument, however, I note the interchangeability of the question.

This chapter questions the boundaries between the secular and the religious in international affairs. In particular, it assesses how these categories work to produce assumptions about the nature of religious and secular beliefs and actions and whether they provide adequate conceptual space to capture the kinds of practices and understandings of contemporary religious humanitarians. The boundaries between the religious and the secular are often assumed to be fixed, although the contributions to this book demonstrate that they are anything but. I draw on in-depth interviews of activists from nongovernmental organizations (NGOs) working on humanitarianism broadly conceived in Central and East Africa, the Middle East, Geneva, New York, and Southern California, to analyze the implications of contemporary religious/secular intersections for international affairs.[2] The interpretations and actions that result are often construed as inherently "religious" or inherently "secular." I argue, however, that religious ethics and action in a secular world, or secular ethics and action in a religious world, are constitutive constructs.[3] They rework each other constantly, but the intersection of local contexts with global discourses and practices, including those of the "war on terror" and the liberal market, produces trends that can be identified and analyzed.

The "global war on terror" (GWOT), for example, conditions religious/secular boundaries in local contexts, and vice versa. Western policy makers assert that the rise of radical forms of Islam necessitated the GWOT; critics assert that the war on terror exacerbated the rise of radical Islam. Meanwhile, mosques remain important arenas for the articulation of ethics and the provision of social welfare in ways that do not necessarily fit the categories of either "radical" or "moderate." As a counterpoint, GWOT practices shape the discourses of Muslim humanitarian NGO activists who seek validation and funding from Western donors.

Liberal market economic practices also condition how religious actors conceptualize their work, as well as which issues they prioritize. Both religious and secular NGOs use a globalized "NGO-speak" to articulate their objectives, assess results, and seek donor funding. Moreover, discourses of economic efficiency pushed by donor communities in health-related humanitarian fields must be taken into account to understand the hierarchy of issues that faith-based NGOs (also called FBOs) seek to address.

Finally, the religious/secular binary is problematic in dealing with the varieties of syncretism produced by the intersection of "traditional" and "world" religions. Weberian predictions that traditions based on "magic" would give way to "rationalized" world religions have not come to pass. Instead, technology and science intersect with human rights and tradition to create enduring yet dynamic relationships between local and world religions. These relationships continue to highlight the unstable nature of distinctions among religious traditions, with important implications for the religious/secular binary.

The Nature of the Secular and the Religious

Binaries such as sacred/profane, transcendence/immanence, private/public, premodern/modern, and illiberal/liberal all grasp at distinctions between the religious and the secular. José Casanova traces one use of the term "secular" to refer to those clerics who "left the cloister to return to the 'world' and its temptations" and "secularization" as the legal procedure in medieval canon law by which they did so. He notes that "secularization" also refers to the historical process by which the emergent state appropriated the massive wealth of the church following the Reformation.[4] Talal Asad traces the terms "secularism" and "secularist" to mid-nineteenth-century free thinkers attempting to avoid the charge of "infidel" in predominantly Christian England.[5] Thus, the nature of the secular, seen through these processes, refers to stances produced by yet taken against the formidable background of Christian institutions, thought, and expectations and to the emergent distinctions between public and private social, economic, and political categories.

Asad has also famously highlighted the conditions of possibility for the category of "religion," situating it within the historical shifts that concretized the spheres of public and private during the Enlightenment.[6] But Casanova also reminds us that the line between the "City of God" and the "City of Man," or the duality of the spiritual and the temporal, remained ambiguous and flexible throughout the pre-modern era.[7] In the context of contemporary politics, Salvatore and LeVine et al. show that the categories of "public sphere" and "Islamic law," thought to be paradigmatic illustrations of the secular and the religious, respectively, constitute a range of public/private social forms in Muslim-majority societies.[8]

We are left, then, with questions about the foundations and ongoing constitution of the secular and religious, both historically and today. Some scholars argue that secularism is most productively viewed as a modern extension of Christianity, others that it is more symbiotically tied to different logics and mechanisms of liberal modernity.[9] Others broaden the scope conditions of what constitutes both the secular and the religious. The concept of "multiple modernities" has been taken up by a number of scholars, and several note a "theopolitical range" of secular/religious possibility.[10] Movement on this range underlies multiple possibilities of ethics and action, as well as a wide range of theological stances toward "otherness," from exclusivity to pluralism and syncretism.[11]

Each of these conceptualizations is helpful for challenging the simplistic dichotomies in the field of international relations that rest on essentialized understandings of religious and secular identities, interests, motivations, and actions. These dichotomies tend to promote the view that all religious belief and action is exclusivist and that a unified secularism represents the normative standard for global ethics and action. However, the question remains whether we can legitimately refer to some practices and ethics as "religious" and others as "secular," both historically and in the present. Charles Taylor adopts and refines a classical separation between the religious as "transcendent" and the secular as "immanent," in order to argue that what characterizes and distinguishes our secular age from previous ones is the condition in which transcendent modes of belief represent one option among many (at least in Western society). Moreover, as opposed to previous eras, belief in the transcendent, in something beyond human flourishing, is no longer the default option.[12] Yet others draw attention to the shifting and contingent nature of the religious and the secular, whether or not they subscribe to Taylor's historical narrative.[13]

In this chapter, I am interested in how religious humanitarian actors today engage with these categories in different parts of the world, in ways that may or may not align with the options as seen by Taylor and others. In particular, what work do claims about the religious and the secular accomplish when people employ them to describe the ethical imperatives that compel them to act? I want to acknowledge the power of "liberal secularism," in its Enlightenment, market, and statist manifestations, to shape the understandings and actions of contemporary religious humanitarians. Nonetheless, I also want to keep open the possibility of new forms of agency and ethics that might instantiate types of religious/secular inclusion that are problematic for liberal categories. To address these issues, I take a first cut at analyzing phenomena I encountered through research in Cameroon, Kenya, Ghana, Jordan, the West Bank, New York, and Geneva, paying attention to the construction of the religious and the secular in the midst of intersections among global-market and war-on-terror discourses and transnational and local humanitarian configurations of the religious and the secular.

Challenging the Religious/Secular Binary:Humanitarian NGOs

Humanitarianism in both its secular and religious guises has a long history. The intersection of religious and secular humanitarianism can be traced to the creation of European missions during the eras of colonization of the Americas, Asia, and Africa. In these cases, conversion went hand-in-hand with "secular" conquest and colonization, encompassing wide-ranging efforts to institutionalize (the colonizers') methods of health care, education, mineral extraction, and agricultural techniques. Those—usually religious—actors operating from a humanitarian sensibility believed that such "modern" techniques would ameliorate the living conditions of local peoples. Some, like the Dominican bishop Bartolomé de las Casas, questioned the unintended effects of their actions or probed more deeply into the ethics of otherness; others internalized the belief that political, as well as social and economic control, was a just, natural, and/ or necessary component of the evolution and progress of peoples. Likewise, political authorities and colonial governors used religious justifications in combination with balance-of-power logics to legitimize their conquest and control.

In the nineteenth century, however, a new form of humanitarianism emerged that attempted to shed an intimate connection with power politics and focus instead on the apolitical amelioration of suffering. Originating during the Crimean War with the work of Florence Nightingale and then Henri Dunant, this new species of humanitarian most often held religious sensibilities (which informed and motivated their actions) but promoted a "selfless" vocation of service to victims of battle, famine, and disease. Dunant created the nonsectarian International Committee of the Red Cross, still the primary nongovernmental provider of assistance all over the world today. Despite the intentionally apolitical character of the ICRC, however, even this form of humanitarianism required an international legal framework that still rests on a minimum degree of cooperation with governments.[14] Moreover, in an acknowledgment that religion plays a role in even "secular" humanitarian structures, in 1929, the ICRC split into two networks, the Red Cross and Red Crescent societies, to reflect dissatisfaction in former Ottoman territories with the symbolism of the cross. Debate about whether the ICRC can adopt a new, universal symbol that does not carry political, cultural, and religious connotations continues (see, for example, "The Emblem Debate" on the International Federation's Web site).[15]

Religious humanitarians today view themselves by and large as apolitical providers of succor, following in the footsteps of Dunant, even while they continually debate—along with secular humanitarians—the pragmatic consequences of their attempts not to take sides in conflicts. They are intimately concerned with "human flourishing" under some of the most difficult conditions imaginable—famine, genocide, systematic rape, disease, and the hopelessness generated by institutionalized oppression and poverty. And they differ considerably with regard to whether they encourage aid recipients to adopt their religious and cultural sensibilities along with material forms of aid.

Religious humanitarian organizations also operate in a context in which civil society organizations writ large have become an indispensable component of global governance mechanisms.[16] Scholars increasingly point out that the discourses and practices of global economic and political liberalism enable and even necessitate NGO growth and inclusion in providing health care, development services, disaster relief, and conflict-resolution procedures, especially after the end of the Cold War, in conjunction with the retreat of the state in all of these domains.[17] Third World states, as a result, sometimes welcome and often institutionalize or legalize the role of NGOs operating in their territories. Both Kenya and Cameroon, for example, created legal mechanisms to regulate and coordinate NGOs in 1990,[18] reflecting the rapid proliferation of NGOs at that time, as well as questions about the state's capacity to manage them.

The Multiple Effects of the War on Terror

In the field of international relations, the contemporary fascination with religion is intimately tied to ever-present concerns about the causes of violence. Consequently, studies attempting to evaluate the "rise of radical Islam" continue to proliferate. One response to the single-minded preoccupation with this religious tradition is to highlight the Muslim leaders and social groups that do not fit "extremist" labels and categorize (and promote) them as "moderate."[19] Another is to demonstrate that violence can (but need not) emanate from adherents of any religion.[20] Digging into the worldviews promoted by religious adherents, in this view, yields multiple modernities.[21]

Complementing this research is comparative and ethnographic work on individual Islamic religious organizations and NGOs.[22] Clark, for example, shows the middle-class character of Islamic social welfare in her study of Jordan, Egypt, and Yemen. Sparre and Petersen trace the relationship between new youth organizations and older organizations such as the Muslim Brotherhood in providing solutions to poverty, including micro-finance, education, charity, and development. Both types of work respond to the politicization of Islam by delving deeply into nationally based and explicitly Islamic networks of aid. Sparre and Petersen, for example, find "a fluid continuum between the extreme poles of radical Islamist ideologies and liberal-secular versions of personal religiosity."

Yet another possible phenomenon shaped by the intersection of GWOT discourses (along with liberal donor imperatives, discussed below) with local practices is illustrated by the NGO workers from very different Muslim-majority societies in the midst of ongoing, violent conflict (Palestine, Iraq, Somalia) who self-identify as secular. In my research, I expected to find Muslim NGO activists who could describe a range of ways in which their understandings of Islam motivated their humanitarian actions. I did hear some of these explanations, but on a more consistent basis, I heard activists who described themselves first as secular and second (or sometimes a distant third) as Muslim and who more often than not backed away from the opportunity to link their ethical motivations to religious sensibilities. This was true, in differing ways, of NGO workers in local humanitarian assistance (development, human rights, and advocacy) groups operating in Palestine, Iraq, and Somalia. It was also in contrast with representatives of the local Christian NGOs operating in Palestine and the local and transnational Christian and Islamic NGOs operating in all three contexts. NGO representatives from Palestine, Iraq, and Somalia operate within and against the constraints placed on them by the war on terror. NGOs from Somalia also attempt to attract the support of Western donor agencies, while the United States must support Iraqi NGOs as part of its war strategy. In partial contrast, Palestinian NGOs enjoy the support of "progressive" religious organizations, especially in Christian churches, in the United States and Europe (and to a lesser extent, Israel). I relate three examples of how these global/local intersections shape "secularized" identities, drawn from interviews with NGO activists in each of these societies.

In Nairobi, I met representatives of a dozen Somali NGOs (ten men and two women) as they sat around a conference table in a UN office. I was introduced to them after they had spent a long day together discussing their problems in achieving their goals and debating how to get Western donors to take them seriously.[23] As a result, by the time I entered the room, they had had time to vent their frustrations about how to provide aid in the midst of the renewed fighting at home, as well as their struggles with donors abroad.

A Web search before my arrival in East Africa revealed a list of more than 850 local Somali NGOs affiliated with the East Africa UN office. Each town had an affiliated youth group, women's committee, business organization, farmers' collective, and educational organization. The people I met all represented organizations founded between 1991 and 2007, itself a sign of the globalizing force of the NGO phenomenon. After I described my research project, several people in the room demanded to know what was in the research for them. How would it help them get money to do their work? They were unanimous in arguing that strengthening civil-society groups was imperative to foster peace and democracy, but they complained that nobody wanted to entrust them with the task. They argued that even UN agency workers refused to enter areas outside Mogadishu (for example, in the Juba province of the southwestern region, which borders Kenya), even though people in the room from that region said that travel there was safe at the time (when I returned in 2008, some of the same people provided very different assessments of safety). No NGO representatives in the room identified themselves or their organizations as Muslim during the initial introductions, even though Islam is the religion of 97 percent of the Somali population.

Although at first, people seemed reluctant to discuss the impact of religion on their work, some eventually began to relate pervasive fears of Islam to their reluctance. As one man put it, what would happen if he appeared before UN agencies or Western aid organizations in clothing that identified him as Muslim? He said it would send the wrong message to potential donors, who would assume that he was a "radical" and therefore dangerous.

A few days later, down the hall from the Somali NGO meeting, two representatives from European NGOs (one actually a "GONGO," or government-supported NGO) who worked in Somalia discussed the ongoing warfare and the technical requirements of coordinating and delivering aid. They also acknowledged their lack of trust in local "briefcase NGOs," which, they feared, might disappear after receiving donor money. In still other interviews, local representatives of two transnational Evangelical Christian organizations said separately that their organizations were looking for ways to work in Somalia. Funding was not a problem for either of these groups, as each possessed an extensive donor base through corporations, Western governments, and their faith-based constituencies. However, both admitted that their presence would likely not be welcomed, given the overwhelming Muslim majority in Somali society. Evangelical Christians, therefore, do not face the same obstacles to legitimacy vis-à-vis Western donors (or GWOT discourses) confronted by Somali NGOs, although they do face the obstacle of religious difference in the local Somali context.

Iraqi society, in contrast with Somali society, has long been acclaimed for its high level of education and its "secular" character before 2003, including under the regime of Saddam Hussein. In Iraq, as in other countries, NGOs have proliferated in recent years, particularly since the U.S. invasion. Approximately twenty Iraqi human-rights, women's-rights, health, and development NGO representatives attended a December 2007 conference in Amman to create an "Arab nonviolence network" (additional Arab participants came from Palestine, Syria, Lebanon, and Jordan). In addition to attending the conference and observing the proceedings, I interviewed six of the Iraqi representatives. Outside of the conference, I also interviewed the public-relations officer of a consortium of transnational NGOs operating in Iraq (with headquarters in Amman) and several other transnational NGOs and IGOs working in Iraq or assisting with Iraqi refugees in Jordan.

Postoccupation anxieties about religion in Iraq, constructed in tandem with GWOT discourses, emphasize sectarian divisions between Shi'as and Sunnis as a major cause of bloodshed. These anxieties, as well as "solutions" in the form of dividing the country into autonomous regions, do, in fact, work to essentialize religious identities, mimicking the processes narrated by David Campbell in his analysis of Bosnia during the 1990s.[24] Dynamics at the Amman conference, however, demonstrated Iraqi NGO representatives' resistance to religious categorization.

One of the most interesting moments of the conference came early on, during the introductions. One man identified himself as a member of the Mahdi movement (under the umbrella of Shi'a leader Moqtada al Sadr). At that point, an imam from Syria challenged the legitimacy of his participation, asking if he genuinely considered himself to be nonviolent. The first man responded that the Mahdi movement had taken the lead in promoting a cease-fire during the summer of 2007 and that advocates of nonviolence in the movement such as himself should be supported in order to maintain it.

The man sitting next to me then stood up. He had already introduced himself as the director of a human-rights NGO, but now he identified himself as Sunni to add legitimacy to his point. He protested the challenge to his compatriot, saying that he was tired of being divided by others; his colleague had every right to be there; they were all Iraqis. All of the Iraqi NGO representatives at the conference, selected to represent every part of the country, spontaneously and loudly clapped.

This incident occurred the day after an interview with two representatives of a Western-based, transnational Christian NGO (one from Sudan, the other from Jordan), who remarked that what they noticed in working with Iraqis was their insistence on not being divided by or labeled according to the religious categories of Shi'a and Sunni. In subsequent interviews with Iraqi NGO representatives at the Amman conference, I asked about the incident described above, as well as about the content of religious identities. One woman, who represented an educational NGO in south-central Iraq, said that her father was Sunni and her mother Shi'a. She followed her father's tradition, but the categories had never been important to her or her family. Another woman, who founded an NGO in 2003 to work against the rise in domestic violence against women (caused, she said, by the fact that men had nothing to do after the invasion destroyed the possibility of employment), said that she was Shi'a but protested that people tended not to notice religious difference before the war. This sentiment was repeated by two other men who worked for human-rights NGOs in the north. A Kurdish man partially dissented but still noted that the primary issue for Iraqi Kurds such as himself was fair treatment and significant autonomy within (rather than outside of) Iraq.

These NGO representatives all identified themselves as Muslims but almost always as "secular Muslims." All operated on the front lines of the alleged war on terror; several talked about family members and fellow NGO workers killed by both U.S. and opposition forces, and one described his multiple imprisonments by the U.S. occupational authorities. GWOT discourses thus affected their every move, but many were also heavily dependent on U.S. government funding for their organizations. At least one (who had been imprisoned by U.S. occupation authorities) was supported for a time by the Republican Party, and several were funded at the time of my interviews by the National Democratic Institute.

These Iraqi NGO representatives appeared to share several tacit understandings that shaped their constructions of the religious versus the secular. First, they were determined not to have their religious beliefs and practices defined or reified by others. Second, they claimed an "Iraqi" identity, while at the same time delegitimizing religious divisions. In so doing, they appeared to relegate their "religious" beliefs and practices to the private sphere, even as they struggled to cope with public manifestations and impositions of religious identity.

The Amman nonviolence network conference also included a large number of Palestinian NGO representatives. Palestinian activists are often equated with militant varieties of Islam, even though Palestine was historically a multireligious society. The Palestinian Christian population, however, which includes a variety of Orthodox, Anglican, Roman Catholic, and Protestant sects, has declined precipitously in the past generation, now making up approximately 2 percent of Palestinian society. Sabeel, an ecumenical Christian NGO promoting liberation theology that is based outside of Jerusalem and supports a nonviolent alternative to the Israeli-Palestinian conflict, documents the decline in several of its publications.[25]

The Muslim Palestinian NGO representatives I spoke with at the Amman conference, along with others interviewed later in Bethlehem and Jerusalem, seemed uninterested in relating their activities (which included promoting human rights and documenting abuses, resisting the construction of the barrier wall, and setting up job opportunities in communal olive cultivation and traditional crafts) to religious motivations or Islamic principles. In Amman, the Palestinian cohort was the most adamant in insisting on the right to a tactical rather than an absolute or a principled definition of nonviolence. They argued consistently that in the context of occupation, they could not compel their co-activists to forgo strategies to which they were entitled under international humanitarian law. At the conference, Palestinian NGO representatives consistently appealed to international legal discourses regarding rights to resist foreign occupation and ethnic cleansing, leaving open the methods by which such resistance might take place.[26]

Later, in Bethlehem, I interviewed several members of an interfaith Palestinian NGO that promoted nonviolence. When I asked about their religious backgrounds, two (one a cofounder of the group) said that they were Muslim but asserted that there was little, if any, connection between their Islamic upbringing and their current NGO activities. They described their struggle against occupation in political, not religious, terms (although they did not support any particular political party). This was in contrast with another leader of the group, a Christian, who immediately linked his work for justice to Christian interpretations of nonviolence and resistance to oppression.

In each of these cases, the Somali, Iraqi, and Palestinian NGO activists claimed predominantly secular identities. "Yes, I'm a Muslim, but I'm secular," was a statement made frequently by activists from all three regions. The work of the secular in these cases must be seen against the background of Western anxieties regarding Islam in the global war on terror. The secular also works in these cases to create spaces for appeals to Western donors on the part of Somalis (even though such appeals have not proven successful in most cases) and "progressive" Christian sympathizers on the part of Palestinians. Finally, it works to legitimize appeals to international legal norms. Yet there were also differences in these claims, depending on contextual factors and individual sentiments, as well as activists' varying resistances to the global discourses on liberalism and terror. This combination of local interpretations of and resistances to the external imposition of identity leaves room for new secular/religious possibilities.

The Influence of Liberal Market Practices

Liberal market practices, as well as GWOT discourses, reconfigure secular/religious assumptions and boundaries. As a number of scholars argue, the Foucauldian concept of governmentality is useful for understanding the explosive rise of NGO humanitarian activities in the context of contemporary neoliberalism.[27] Governmentality highlights how contemporary governance mechanisms interpellated by states and international organizations facilitate and even require the expansion of NGOs into "issues hitherto held to be the responsibility of authorized governmental agencies."[28] Increasingly, foreign aid is channeled through NGOs, including faith-based organizations. In turn,

NGO-run clinics, schools, and community programs represent considerable percentages of health care, education, and other basic services. One analysis, for example, estimates that by 1999, NGOs in Kenya contributed three times the funds to rural water schemes as the World Bank and provided between 45 percent and 50 percent of all health-care services.[29]

According to the governmentality paradigm, however, such influence by NGOs does not translate into independence for civil-society actors, who must constantly demonstrate their worthiness to assume the functions previously allocated to the state, by carrying out their tasks "in accordance with the appropriate (or approved) model of action."[30] Approved models of action include results-oriented market discourses that value and prioritize accountability, efficiency, results, and "sustainability" (referring not to ecological sensitivity but to the ability to wean local programs from transnational sources of funding). States, international organizations, and NGOs, including FBOs, reproduce these discourses through their programming, marketing techniques, and annual reports.

For example, donors and NGOs have created a globalized discourse that requires recipient organizations to mold their work into buzz-word categories such as "training," "capacity-building," and "partnership." Training refers broadly to the merging of technical abilities and education, in the belief that such knowledge solves problems ranging from hunger to disease to conflict. Capacity-building refers to mobilizing this knowledge and material resources into self-sustaining and locally led programs. Partnership indicates both collaboration among different groups on a local level and creating solid NGO-donor-IGO (intergovernmental organization) relationships. The focus on partnership, however, also hints at the inefficiencies resulting when the ever-proliferating NGOs trip over one another's work and their need to demonstrate outside donor support. The latter can paradoxically work against the goal of capacity-building, when local understandings of needs do not match donor priorities.

These discourses—interpellated by state governments as well as multilateral organizations—shape the conceptualizations and programmatic objectives of religious humanitarians, who fit their work into these categories in multiple ways. For example, almost every organization I encountered noted its work in training and capacity-building. These are intimately tied to metrics of progress and achievement in ways that both can be counted (numbers of trainings provided and how many people trained are parts of reports to donors) and are evident in the visual images used in NGO marketing techniques. Increasingly, pictures of starving children on NGO brochures have been replaced by smiling aid recipients receiving instruction in schools or immunizations in health clinics, producing crafts, or harvesting crops. Two U.S.-based NGO officials I traveled with in Cameroon took dozens of pictures at each aid-recipient location (in this case, clinics and hospitals),[31] always trying to achieve the perfect shot of happy children, new mothers, or gleaming equipment in one of the sponsored programs, in the hopes that one of their photos would appear in the home office's publicity brochures.[32] Public-private partnerships—which blur the lines between state and nonstate, profit and nonprofit—have also become critical components of NGOs' accountability and success stories. World Vision Kenya, for example, focuses on partnership in its 2005 Report, "Building Collaborative Bridges," and states, "We worked with the government, churches, United Nations Agencies, other NGOs, FBOs, CBOs and communities. We do this for children. Our prayer for every child is to know life in all its fullness." The report notes success in partnering with, among others, the Kenyan Parliamentary Committee for Orphaned and Vulnerable Children on child-welfare programs and Barclays Bank on malaria and HIV/AIDS programs.[33]

Accountability and assessments of the worthiness of programs are not unreasonable requirements. Combined with the competition for funding, however, they create a corresponding vulnerability to trends that can hinder the goals of any humanitarian NGO, perhaps particularly those promoted by faith-based groups. In Nairobi, after hearing interviewee after interviewee describe his or her group's work using the same terminology, I observed to one representative that I was hearing a uniform, globalized NGO jargon that reflected market imperatives. He stopped his recitation of activities and agreed, reflecting that he was usually the person in his organization who protested against the constant pressure to fit the group's programs and goals into categories created by outside donor agencies.

NGOs, including faith-based ones, both replicate and sometimes resist the terminology as well as questionable metrics driving donor-recipient relationships. However, they must also cope with the unintended effects of these discourses for their theologies of care. A major contemporary example is the way faith-based humanitarians cope with diseases such as HIV/AIDS and malaria. Considerable resources continue to be expended on HIV/AIDS assistance and prevention programs, although worries about flat or diminished funding for global AIDS programs have increased under the Obama administration. Malaria eradication, on the other hand, has become a priority for many faith-based and secular groups and NGO networks such as the "Nothing But Nets" campaign. As a result, when I asked one Western Christian development NGO official in New York about the denomination's HIV/AIDS programs, the (cynical) response was "Where have you been? Everyone is interested in malaria now." Campaigns targeting malaria offer Westerners the opportunity of contributing (five dollars to fifteen dollars, depending on the organization) to buy a treated bed net for a recipient in sub-Saharan Africa, thereby "saving a life."

When asked to explain the shift in emphasis, another New York Christian NGO director referred more positively to the logic of success, saying that malaria is "winnable." Treatments for HIV/AIDS entail large start-up costs, as well as continued monthly visits, while treated bed nets appear to be a simple, inexpensive, and relatively available solution to a perceived crisis (although this belief is challenged by many health workers on the ground). Yet several Kenyan religious representatives appeared bemused by the new interest in malaria, one remarking, "It's not as though we haven't been dying of it forever."

Given that market liberalism encourages clear (if questionable) metrics of programmatic development and success, theological differences about sexuality might also influence faith-based NGOs' enthusiasm for programming to eradicate malaria. In addition to the "winnability" of malaria over HIV/AIDS (itself a questionable proposition, given the resistance in some communities to using bed nets, as well as the spread of virus-carrying mosquitoes to new areas through global climate changes), religious traditions are divided among themselves about the ethics of preventing HIV/AIDS, including abstinence versus the use of condoms. Faith-based NGOs all agree on the devastation wrought by AIDS on village structures, and religious organizations routinely set up services for "AIDS orphans," even when they do not agree on theologically acceptable modes of prevention.

A major complaint of women's-rights organizations is that men reject prophylactic devices, endangering themselves as well as women. But religiously based mores can reinforce this phenomenon. The Bush administration's requirements that all funded programs abroad follow the "ABC" hierarchy of prevention and treatment (Abstinence, Be faithful, use Condoms if infected) in all of its HIV/AIDS-supported programs at home and abroad became notorious for discouraging condom promotion among many "secular" health NGOs. Yet the mainline religious denominations also have not resolved tensions regarding the ethics of HIV/AIDS prevention.

In Cameroon, for example, all clinics, as well as public signage in every village I visited, call on men (especially) to be tested for HIV and to obtain treatment if infected. But a clear hierarchy or even silence about preventive options is also common. For example, a Presbyterian hospital posted signs encouraging (a) condom use among married couples and (b) abstinence outside of marriage but (c) condom use in extramarital relations only if one could not refrain from extramarital sex. A Catholic hospital, however, posted signs calling exclusively for abstinence, even among married couples with one infected partner, and the hospitals' German doctors confirmed that they were not allowed to promote condom use. The only place that openly encouraged condom distribution was the classroom (for "training") of a women's clinic in the capital city, where long rectangular shipping boxes had been affixed to the wall and rededicated as dispensers. In Nairobi, an interfaith group including Christian, Hindu, and Muslim representatives said that, operating on principles of consensus, it avoided open debate about the use of prophylactics because of Roman Catholic opposition.

Technocratic assistance models, emanating from liberal market discourses, thus shape religious (as well as secular) NGO priorities in significant ways.

Moreover, humanitarian actors may subsume tensions in their religious sensibilities in order to focus on areas of "success." But do we label the resulting actions, programs, and ethical sensibilities "secular" or, following Casanova's helpful distinctions, view them as part of a process of "secularization"?[34]

The move from "charity" to "development" among many Christian NGOs, for example, indicates at first glance a potential secularizing trend which is complicated by further investigation. The head of a major Christian denomination's humanitarian assistance organization said that the "charity model" was a post-World War II invention, implying that as an ethical framework for providing assistance, it no longer corresponded to material or theological needs. He explained that the charity model has difficulty in fulfilling the Gospel mandate to "heal" the world, instead promoting Band-Aid solutions to suffering. The tripartite work of his organization, in food security, primary health care, and disaster response, in contrast, resulted in a programmatic focus on *long-term development*. This development model, he asserted, was more in line with the Gospel understanding of Christian ministry and healing. Similarly, a study of the Mennonite Central Committee argues, "The MCC is successful in its contribution to development and empowerment in the 20 African countries in which it works because of its philosophical and programmatic focus on accountability, its holistic approach to basic rights, and a 'listen and learn' approach which embraces empowerment and social justice."[35] In these articulations, accountability, progress, and social justice are fused into a more or less unified ethic of care.

One reaction to these explanations is that discourses of liberalization have secularized interpretations of the Christian message. Another, which I believe is more accurate, is to view such faith-oriented claims as partially redefining assumed boundaries between the religious and the secular. In this view, "development as healing" becomes, along with other terms, an arena in which claims and meanings are articulated and contested, leading to the possibility of new types of actions and ethical understandings. I do not claim either an essentially religious or secular basis for these claims and meanings or that resulting claims, actions, and ethics are "better" or "worse" than previous ones.

Such redefinitions and reinterpretations are not a new feature of the constitutive nature of theological, political, economic, and social interactions. In twentieth-century Christianity alone, for example, liberation theologians of the 1970s shifted from liberal to Marxist categories to understand the relationship between politics and "sin." In the process, they redefined the relationship between the immanent and the transcendent in order to argue and act in favor of liberation from oppression "in this world," similar to the way contemporary religious humanitarians employ liberal human-rights categories to argue in favor of "dignity" and "justice" in development.[36]

We can see similar constitutive dynamics at work in discussions by NGO and religious representatives of the intersection of traditional and mainline religious practices.

"Traditional" and "World" Religions in a Secular Age

Many scholars note that Weberian notions of secularization have not come to pass. Weber's thesis regarding the processes of rationalization produced by the mutual conditioning between economic logics and religious values, however, endures. Nevertheless, the continuing dynamic relationship between "world" and "traditional" religions begs additional questions about science, medicine, and the secular.

Third World (or postcolonial) Christianity has for some time been debating the merits of "inculturation," "indigenization," and "syncretism." These terms are applicable to Christianity in the global North as well as the global South and among Anglo-European as well as Asian, African, Latin American, and other indigenous peoples. But questions about the legitimacy of indigenization and the appropriateness of syncretic beliefs have arisen primarily through the reactions of Anglo-European Christians to the practices of their counterparts in Africa, Asia, and Latin America. Rather than understanding their own identities and practices as inevitably hybrid, Anglo-Europeans too often regard other regions as the sites of interaction between "pure" Christianity and "local cultures."

Before arriving in west-central Africa, I had been conditioned by reading a variety of Third World liberation theologians and students of comparative politics to understand that many African Christians had come to a more or less comfortable synthesis of traditional and mainline denominational practices and beliefs, despite the criticisms of their Anglo-European counterparts, and that many African Muslims had done the same.[37] For example, among the "people of the coast" (on the Indian Ocean coast of Kenya), religious NGO activists spoke of the historically hybrid nature of Swahili practices and beliefs, echoing the work of scholars with expertise in the region.[38] In interviews in Cameroon, however, I found the people I met to be more conflicted in their everyday blending of traditional versus mainline beliefs and practices, and they approached their decisions about whether and how to combine rituals without reference to the thinking of theological syncretists.

All but one of the Cameroonians I talked to felt that the relatively peaceful multireligious and multiethnic character of the country (according to statistics, Cameroon is approximately 40 percent Christian, 20 percent to 30 percent Muslim, and 30 percent to 40 percent adherents of "traditional African religions," although these statistics do not capture syncretic identities; Cameroon also has 252 linguistically distinct ethnic groups) was something they were proud of and believed the population as a whole wanted to support, especially because they saw the effects of violence in neighboring Congo to the south and Chad to the northeast, as well as farther west in Sierra Leone and Ivory Coast. Yet this multireligious character was also layered with internal and external tensions.

In interviews with representatives of different groups belonging to an NGO consortium, the observations of two people stood out. One, a woman who worked on issues of women's health, including programs to eradicate female circumcision, said that she had been raised in a mainline Protestant church and that her parents did not allow the immediate family to follow traditional practices in their home. She spoke of this as a "loss," because in larger family and communal gatherings, she felt there were subjects that were avoided in her presence or ideas and topics that she simply did not have the experiential background to understand. The other, a man who was trained as a lawyer but who at the time of our interview directed an NGO consortium working to eradicate hunger, was Roman Catholic but said that he also followed traditional practices (in communal rituals, family celebrations, burial rites, and medicinal treatments). He reflected that his Catholic training made him feel guilty about engaging in traditional practices, but his family and communal traditions were important to him and would make him feel guilty if he stopped participating in them. He said that he had reached an uneasy compromise, which involved "drawing the line" at certain practices, such as bodily scarification. Such practices, he felt, represented a clear violation of Christian precepts regarding the sanctity of the body.

This sentiment of being caught in the middle was repeated many times by others in formal interviews and informal conversations. One woman, a professional living in the capital, Yaoundé, had recently been fêted by her local village, which awarded her the title of elder. She said that this title also came with responsibilities to look after younger women in the village. She was honored to be so named, but she also had to contend with her own sense of conflict and others' disapproval in her mainline Protestant church, where she was an active member.

Some people claimed no contradiction between traditional and religious beliefs. One well-known imam and political figure said that he experienced no conflict; once one embraced Islam, one followed its teachings wholeheartedly, overriding any other beliefs or practices. Yet he had also just been involved in a leadership dispute regarding the chieftaincy of his village (and the government had tried to assassinate him two weeks before our interview, when he had returned to the village to act as power broker in the line of succession). Moreover, it was clear that he was concerned about conflicting interpretations within Islam itself, because he founded an Islamic studies institute in Cameroon to provide an alternative for young Muslim men who would otherwise travel to Egypt or Saudi Arabia, where they might become less tolerant of the pluralist nature of Cameroonian society.

An issue on which most interviewees were united (including Europeans living in Cameroon, as well as Cameroonian medical, religious, and NGO representatives) was in making a strong distinction between traditional healing and witchcraft. One priest said that the difference between witchcraft and healing was that the former dealt in revenge, not life. A Presbyterian hospital in Kumba, which was in the process of founding an AIDS clinic, posted hand-written signs stating, "AIDS is a reality and should not be linked to witchcraft." Medical practitioners and NGO workers confronted problems of people refusing to be tested, blaming early death and seemingly unnatural sickness on being cursed or possessed and, in the worst-case scenario, having such beliefs result in revenge killings.

Conversely, most talked about traditional medicinal practices as potentially helpful; one European priest who had lived in Cameroon for forty years said that when the local hospital staff could not alleviate his kidney problem, they sent for a healer who used Ghanaian traditional methods to cure him. (Another doctor, in contrast, told of a local healer who hired a private hospital room at considerable expense so that the people of his village would not know that he was being treated there.)

Yet, as medical anthropologists have indicated, it is difficult to draw a clean line between "witchcraft" and "traditional healing," and the elevation of the latter is part of a global trend to discipline local religious beliefs and market traditional herbs and medicines. For the purposes of the religious/secular binary, what is interesting are the claims regarding the dividing line between healing and witchcraft being made by the NGO, UN, and medical communities and their intersections with discourses of progress and science. Religious thinkers from Teilhard de Chardin to Albert Schweitzer, in addition to contemporary associations of traditional healers, have made claims regarding this intersection.

Associations of traditional religious healers have organized to gain legitimacy and participate in both local and transnational debates about HIV/AIDS and malaria. For example, PROMETRA, an NGO founded in Dakar, Senegal, that represents healers from twenty-two countries, is "dedicated to the preservation and restoration of African traditional medicine and indigenous science." PROMETRA appeals to both discourses of modern science and African tradition in describing itself as "an institution of scientific and cultural research, medical practice and ... an instrument for African integration and international relations. Our purpose is to preserve African traditional medicine, culture and indigenous science through research, education, advocacy and traditional medical practice."[39] PROMETRA has gained a hearing at the World Health Organization, which has held conferences on the role of traditional medicine in the fight against HIV/AIDS and malaria. One Cameroonian NGO director asserted that practitioners of traditional medicine held important reservoirs of knowledge but needed to be helped to "stabilize their products" regarding storage, education about toxicity, trials and responsiveness to treatment.[40]

Despite these trends, which link back to the influence of market logics on religious practices, local resistances to the disciplining of local traditions and practices remain. The European priest said that he did not believe witchcraft would ever be completely eradicated, another doctor said that many of the Cameroonian Catholic priests he knew had no moral qualms about combining "sorcery" with Christianity, and a village leader assembled the religious and political elites in an important meeting to discuss a recent case of sorcery and take steps to eradicate it. The constant self-questioning that takes place on the part of adherents of "world religions" such as Protestantism, Catholicism, and Islam regarding the appropriateness and legitimacy of traditional practices and beliefs indicates that the boundaries between traditional and world religions, as well as those between religion and secularism writ large, are extremely fluid in many postcolonial societies.

The Dynamic Nature of the Religious and the Secular

This chapter focuses on the ways in which the religious/secular binary is disturbed by the engagement of contemporary religious humanitarians with global discourses of market liberalism and terror and local contexts, practices, and beliefs. The resulting intersections are dynamic, not static, demonstrating both the power of these global discourses and the sites of resistance and reformulation that occur when they are appropriated and potentially transformed at the local level. Trends in these transformations can be observed in new forms of "secularized" NGO identity in several Muslim-majority societies, the reconfiguration of humanitarian ethics from charity to development, and the appropriation and resistance of traditional practices to the globalizing discourses of science and "world religions."

These trends do not settle questions about the religious/secular binary. Specifically, questions of modernization cannot today (nor could they in the past) be discussed in exclusively secular terms. Theologies evolve to cope with political conquest, liberalizing economies, and the junctures between individual and communal rights and practices. Similarly, humanitarian actions done in the name of charity, dignity, or the preservation of communal traditions cannot be deemed exclusively religious; likewise, proselytizing serves to advance market liberalism and participatory democracy, as well as to promote particular religious beliefs and practices. Rather than advancing a new model for social theory to account for an alleged point of separation between the religious and the secular, therefore, this chapter argues that the experiences of religious humanitarians point to new places to look for its continued destabilization.

Notes

1. See Charles Taylor, *A Secular Age* (Cambridge, Mass.: Harvard University Press, 2007); and Peter L. Berger, ed., *The Desecularization of the World: Resurgent Religion and World Politics* (Grand Rapids, Mich.: Eerdmans, 1999).

2. I conducted interviews for a larger project on "Islamic and Inter-faith Religious Ethics in World Crises" in Cameroon (Southwest Province, including Buea, Mamfé, and Manyeman, plus the capital, Yaoundé, and the largest city, Douala) in December 2006 and January 2007; in Kenya (Nairobi, Masai Mara, and Mombasa) in June and July 2007 and August and September 2008; in Accra, Ghana, in July and August 2009; and in the Middle East (Jordan, Bethlehem, West Bank, and Jerusalem) in December 2007. Interviews were conducted in New York from November 2006 to March 2007, in Geneva in July 2008, and in Southern California from 2006 to 2009. Interviews with approximately 140 subjects have been conducted for this project (thus far), each lasting between forty-five minutes and two and a half hours. I thank the Andrew W. Mellon New Directions Fellowship for supporting this research.

3. Audie Klotz and Cecelia Lynch, *Strategies for Research in Constructivist International Relations* (Armonk, N.Y.: M. E. Sharpe, 2007).

4. José Casanova, *Public Religions in the Modern World* (Chicago: University of Chicago Press, 1994), 12–13.

5. Talal Asad, *Formations of the Secular* (Stanford, Calif.: Stanford University Press, 2003), 23.

6. Talal Asad, *Genealogies of the Sacred: Discipline and Reasons of Power in Christianity and Islam* (Baltimore, Md.: Johns Hopkins University Press, 1993).

7. Casanova, *Public Religions*.

8. Armando Salvatore and Mark Levine, eds., *Religion, Social Practice, and Contested Hegemonies: Reconstructing the Public Sphere in Muslim Majority Societies* (NewYork: Palgrave, 2005).

9. Neither of these views, however, sees secularism as an ahistorical ideal type. See, for example, Gil Anidjar, "Secularism," *Critical Inquiry* 33 (Autumn 2006): 52–77; and Saba Mahmood, "Secularism, Hermeneutics, and Empire: The Politics of Islamic Reformation," *Public Culture* 18, no. 2 (2006): 323–347.

10. See S. N. Eisenstadt, ed., *Reflections on Multiple Modernities: European, Chinese and Other Interpretations* (Leiden: Brill Academic, 2002); and Elizabeth Shakman Hurd, *The Politics of Secularism in International Relations* (Princeton, N.J.: Princeton University Press, 2007).

11. R. Scott Appleby, *The Ambivalence of the Sacred: Religion, Violence, and Reconciliation* (New York: Rowman & Littlefield, 2000). Daniel Philpott, "Explaining the Political Ambivalence of Religion," *American Political Science Review* 101, no. 3 (2007): 505–526. Cecelia Lynch, "Dogma, Praxis, and Religious Perspectives on Multiculturalism," *Millennium: Journal of International Studies* 29, no. 3 (2000): 741–759.

12. Taylor, *A Secular Age*.

13. Jonathan VanAntwerpen, "Reconciliation Reconceived: Religion, Secularism, and the Language of Transition," in Will Kymlicka and Bashir Bashir, eds., *The Politics of Reconciliation in Multicultural Societies* (Oxford: Oxford University Press, 2010).

14. Nicholas Onuf, "Humanitarian Intervention: The Early Years," *Florida Journal of International Law* 16, no. 4 (December 2004): 753–787.

15. See "The Emblem Debate," http://www.ifrc.org.

16. Margaret E. Keck and Kathryn Sikkink, *Activists beyond Borders: Advocacy Networks in International Politics* (Ithaca, N.Y.: Cornell University Press, 1998).

17. Mustapha Pasha and David Blaney, "Elusive Paradise: The Promise and Perils of Global Civil Society," *Alternatives* 23, no. 2 (1998): 417–450.Cecelia Lynch, "Social

Movements and the Problem of 'Globalization,'" *Alternatives* 23, no. 2 (1998): 149–173. Cecelia Lynch, "Liberalism and the Contradictions of Global Civil Society," in Antonio Franchaset, ed., *The Ethics of Global Governance* (Boulder, Colo.: Lynne Rienner, 2009).

18. Rosemarie Muganda Onyando, "Are NGOs Essential for Kenya's Development?" (1999), http://www.netnomad.com/NGOSDN.html.

19. Mahmood Mamdani articulates the "good" versus "bad" Muslim distinction for contemporary foreign policy in *Good Muslim, Bad Muslim: America, the Cold War, and the Roots of Terror* (New York: Random House 2004).

20. Mark Juergensmeyer, *Terror in the Mind of God: The Global Rise of Religious Violence*, 3rd ed. Berkeley: University of California Press 2003).

21. S. N. Eisenstadt, "Reflections on Multiple Modernities: European, Chinese and Other Interpretations," in Timothy A. Byrnes and Peter J. Katzenstein, eds., *Religion in an Expanding Europe* (Cambridge: Cambridge University Press, 2006).

22. Janine Clark, *Islam, Charity, and Activism: Middle-Class Networks and Social Welfare in Egypt, Jordan, and Yemen* (Bloomington: Indiana University Press, 2004). Sara Lei Sparre and Marie Juul Petersen, "Islam and Civil Society: Case Studies from Jordan and Egypt," *Danish Institute for International Studies Report* (October 2007): 13.

23. Author's meeting with representatives in Nairobi, June 2007. The Somalia Aid Coordinating Body, facilitated by the UN, arranges meetings of donors, Western NGOs, and Somali NGOs, both individually and with one another.

24. David Campbell, *National Deconstruction: Violence, Identity, and Justice in Bosnia* (Minneapolis: University of Minnesota Press, 1998).

25. See "Sabeel's Statement on the Israeli Invasion of Gaza, June 28, 2006," Sabeel Ecumenical Liberation Theology Center, http://www.sabeel.org.

26. Their appeals at the conference parallel the increasing recourse to international law in the brochures and documentation of Palestinian rights NGOs in the West.

27. James Ferguson, *Global Shadows: Africa in the Neoliberal World* (Durham, N.C.: Duke University Press, 2006).

28. Ole Jacob Sending and Iver Neumann, "Governance to Governmentality: Analyzing NGOs, States, and Power," *International Studies Quarterly* 50, no. 3 (2006): 651–672.

29. Onyando, "Are NGOs Essential?"

30. Graham Burchell, "Liberal Government and Techniques of the Self," in Andrew Barry, Thomas Osborne, and Nikolas Rose, eds., *Foucault and Political Reason*, 29 (London: University College London; quoted in Sending and Neumann, "Governance to Governmentality," 657.

31. These particular NGO representatives worked for a "nonsectarian" international NGO based in the United States, but all of the clinics and hospitals we visited were run by Catholic, Presbyterian, or other faith-based local groups or people adhering to one of these faith traditions.

32. However, they also took pictures of the boxes of expired medicine that had been stuck at the port for months before being released by local customs, the washed sterile gloves hanging out to dry in order to be reused in examinations and surgeries, and the bare bulbs hanging precariously over worn-out operating beds, in order to catalogue local needs and demonstrate them to superiors back in the United States.

33. World Vision Kenya, *Building Collaborative Bridges* (Nairobi: World Vision Kenya, 2005).

34. José Casanova, *Public Religions in the Modern World* (Chicago: University of Chicago Press, 1994); José Casanova, "Rethinking Secularization: A Global Comparative Perspective," *Hedgehog Review* (Spring–Summer 2006): 7–22.

35. Susan Dicklitch and Heather Rice, "The Mennonite Central Committee (MCC) and Faith-Based NGO Aid to Africa," *Development in Practice* 14, no. 5 (August 2004): 660–672.

36. See Cecelia Lynch, "Acting on Belief," *Ethics & International Affairs* 14 (2000): 83–97.

37. Jean-Marc Ela, *African* Cry, trans. Robert R. Barr (Maryknoll, N.Y.: Orbis, 1986). Mercy Amba Oduyoye, *Daughters of Anowa: African Women & Patriarchy* (Maryknoll, N.Y.: Orbis, 1995). Emanuel Martey, *African Theology: Inculturation and Liberation* (Maryknoll, N.Y.: Orbis, 1996).

38. Susan F. Hirsch, *Pronouncing and Persevering: Gender and the Discourses of Disputing in an African Islamic Court* (Chicago: University of Chicago Press, 1998).

39. PROMETRA, http://www.prometra.org.

40. At the time of our interview, however, he had not yet gained Institutional Review Board approval for such projects.

10

Rethinking Fundamentalism in a Secular Age
R. Scott Appleby

I

The term "fundamentalism" continues to be used broadly in the media and by some policy makers and scholars to refer to individuals, movements, and organizations judged to be religiously committed to an envisioned moral order and to an accompanying political or social project, to such a degree that they are actively intolerant of those who do not share their faith and ideology, and are willing to impose their vision and program by force if necessary. Although this popular working definition could be applied to certain nation-states with little or no qualification, the term is generally used to refer to movements of opposition against the state. The label continues to be applied most frequently to Islamic movements and parties, although it is also used to describe Jewish, Hindu, Sikh, and Buddhist actors. Christians are now treated with more nuance; it is less common to conflate fundamentalists and Evangelicals.

In its most egregious misapplication, "fundamentalism" is applied to any movement, party, or individuals who offer theological or religious warrants for their public positions and programs, when those positions or programs are judged by the labeler to deviate significantly from liberal, secular, or "cosmopolitan" norms.

To the extent that the academy could properly be expected to have a discernible impact on public discourse in the United States, Canada, Europe, and nations beyond the West, through the dissemination of careful scholarship that undermines inaccurate and irresponsible reporting and evaluation of complex and multivalent phenomena, then one would have to account the academy largely a failure in the area of public and politicized religion. More distressingly, some of the scholarship on fundamentalism no doubt contributed to the imprecise use of the term, which can have serious consequences for politically active, law-abiding people of faith.

Is "fundamentalism," then, merely a shibboleth, a construct of anxious or predatory opponents of politically engaged religious groups that are deemed conservative or orthodox, antiliberal or "extreme"? In what follows, I offer a conditional "no" in answer to this question. But getting there requires a more refined and nuanced understanding of the term and of the realities to which it gestures. It also requires rethinking the relationship between the secular and the religious in line with the ways that relationship is constantly being negotiated and renegotiated by so-called fundamentalist movements and parties.

In 1988, the American Academy of Arts and Sciences (AAAS) launched a massive project on "global fundamentalisms." Two years earlier, the MacArthur Foundation had awarded the AAAS a sizable grant bearing the following stipulations: the money was to be used to study a phenomenon that would have public implications well into the twenty-first century and require the perspectives of several disciplines of the academy in order to be understood in its various dimensions. The council of the AAAS then debated which "phenomenon" should be examined according to these broad guidelines; suggestions included the global emergence of HIV/AIDS (still dawning on public awareness at that time), new scientific and ethical horizons opened by genetic engineering, and teen pregnancy across cultures. In the end, however, the council decided to devote the resources to an exploration of the "global resurgence of religion," instances of which journalists had been referring to, promiscuously, as "fundamentalism" at least since the Khomeini-led Shi'ite revolution in 1978–79 and the establishment of the Islamic Republic of Iran. The AAAS initiative, which I codirected, was called the Fundamentalism Project (TFP).

The task of this chapter is to reflect critically on the study of "fundamentalism," with specific reference to TFP, with the following question in mind: What might a reconsideration of the project's methods, assumptions, themes, and findings contribute to this book's remapping of secularism? Given that TFP was an extraordinary example of how knowledge is produced, reproduced, and disseminated within a specific and limiting historical, political, and social context, I offer here, by way of introduction, three observations on the project's origins and structure, and on the challenges inherent in pulling it off.[1]

A MIRROR TO THE SECULAR ACADEMY?

Initially, several AAAS council members opposed TFP. The opponents were senior U.S. scientists, some of whom had worked on the Manhattan Project and other important policy-related initiatives of the postwar period. At a memorable meeting of this old guard, shortly after TFP was announced, it became dramatically clear that most, if not all, of these distinguished academic elites were profoundly secular in the most antireligious sense of the term; in the late 1980s, they were distraught at the prominence of any kind of religion in public life, and many were particularly incensed by the teaching of creationism in some public schools. Among scores of similar comments at that meeting, one beautifully crystallized the dominant attitude among the scientists: "If we are giving this much money to the study of *religion,* then the project should help to wipe it off the face of the earth."

My senior colleague in directing TFP, the religious historian (and Lutheran minister) Martin Marty, shared not one iota of this sentiment. When he described the purposes of the project to the waves of historians, anthropologists, sociologists, political scientists, religionists, and regional specialists who contributed to it, Marty would insist that the main purpose of TFP "is to hold up a mirror to the academy and learn what assumptions, prejudices, distortions and incomplete understandings color our perceptions of religion and religions, believers and those cast as 'other.'" He liked to compare the academy's perspective on those called fundamentalists with the ancient cartographers whose maps contained wildly imagined illustrations of uncharted territories, which were inscribed with the warning "Here be Monsters!"

As earnest as Marty's injunction to critical self-reflection was, some authors ignored it. In defining "fundamentalism," they focused on the "antisecularism" of the fundamentalists, who were therefore a bane to the enlightened, liberal academy and the progressive society it existed to serve. One author defined fundamentalists exclusively by what purportedly they were not: not secular, not feminist, not liberal, not democratic, and so on.[2] Despite the fact that we gave explicit instructions to the contributors *not* to reify the category "fundamentalism" by forcing into it the movements or groups they knew best, several did exactly that. (Thus, for example, a particular Christian Evangelical movement in Latin America became "fundamentalist" owing to its politicized opposition to family planning.)

METHODOLOGICAL AND CONCEPTUAL CHALLENGES

Although our assignment was to describe "the world of fundamentalism," we hastened to render "world" and "fundamentalism" in the plural: we would chart the worlds of fundamentalisms. This adjustment, of course, obscured a deeper challenge, namely, how to compare (or make any substantive, defensible generalizations about) movements, groups, and individuals from such disparate historical, geographic, and cultural backgrounds, different host religions, political orientations, and so on, while using one umbrella term.[3] To avoid the clumping and clustering pitfalls of broad comparative study, we considered alternatives to "fundamentalism" (e.g., "radical neo-traditionalism," a term employed by William Shepherd to describe essentially the same phenomenon) and discarded them as (equally) inadequate to the task. If we intended to influence the public discourse about religion, some members of the advisory committee argued, it would be best to stick with the onerous term and attempt to modify its usage. Second, contributors in the early stages of the project were encouraged to set precedent by indicating in each essay the problems with the term and to suggest different language to describe the movement(s) they knew best and about which they were writing. Third, members of that core group, especially the editors, were careful to place the term "fundamentalism" in scare quotes, and to introduce it with the following caveat: "In this project, we use 'fundamentalism' as a broad comparative construct to investigate the possibility that a number of otherwise disparate religious movements and groups share certain 'family resemblances' (Wittgenstein) in their method of responding to a host of challenges facing them in the secular modern world. It should be emphasized that these movements emerge from different religious traditions and historical contexts, differ in religious doctrine, worldview, ideology and structures of religious organization and authority, and are often at odds with one another if and when they come into contact."

THE RECEPTION OF TFP AND THE VAGARIES OF DISSEMINATION

One of the aspects of TFP that raised the stakes for its observers and critics was the fact that the AAAS billed it as "an interdisciplinary public-policy study." Apart from the use the essays may or may not have been put to by public officials, policy makers, educators, and journalists, the very fact of a massive public-policy study of "religious fundamentalism" itself reinforced the perception that religion, and especially "strong religion," was becoming a significant national-security problem. Although reinforcing the notion of a "clash of civilizations" was far from the editors' intention (Huntington's essay appeared during the last publication phase of TFP) and despite the fact that TFP never offered policy recommendations of any kind, it quickly became clear to us that the project would not be able to escape implication in the political and ideological battles raging around the significance of Islamist movements, the New Christian Right, Jewish irredentism, Hindu nationalism, and other manifestations of newly empowered "antisecular, antidemocratic, antiliberal" religion. Of course, this was not the first or last scholarly project that left itself open to being construed and applied in various ways by public officials and policy makers; scholars of political Islam, for example, have plenty of stories to tell on this score. But we maintained a studied neutrality on policy matters, beyond repeatedly (and ineffectively) urging educators and policy makers to study the original sources and develop an empathy for religious sensibilities not their own, and we tried to comfort ourselves in the knowledge that if we could not prevent the project from being overwhelmed by political and ideological critiques of left and right, at least we were being attacked from both sides. That is, while many reviewers claimed that we were being "too soft" on the fundamentalists—"were they in power, they would not be so tolerant of academics," as Rosemary Radford Ruether put it in the *New York Times Book Review*—others insisted that we were out to discredit any form of religious expression that did not conform to our bland liberal variety.

In sum, to be fair to TFP, the editors and core contributors were not naïve or dismissive of the significant methodological and conceptual challenges that accompanied the endeavor from the outset. But our strategies for mitigating these problems may have been inadequate to the task, and the failure fully to anticipate the sharpest ideological and political dimensions of the project probably served to exacerbate the conceptual and methodological difficulties.

II

WHAT THE FUNDAMENTALISM PROJECT ACTUALLY CONCLUDED

It has been the source of no little disappointment to me that, despite all of the hoopla surrounding the Fundamentalism Project, many of the most important interpreters of religion in the academy are not conversant with its findings, including the refined definition of fundamentalism and the explanation of the religious logic and corresponding mode of religiosity that we found manifest in seventeen movements, or clusters of movements, around the world. These results were published in 2003, after a decade of winnowing the field of candidates for inclusion in the family of religious fundamentalisms. In that final statement, we cautioned readers against reintroducing into the family any of the numerous candidates we had rejected, including most forms of Pentecostalism, Muslim missionary movements such as the Tablighi Jamaat, and apolitical Hindu, Buddhist, or Jewish movements.[4]

The lack of familiarity with TFP's mature findings has not prevented scholars from weighing in critically on them. To be fair, the diligent reader of the entire published works of the project would have to read roughly 3700 printed pages before arriving at the cumulative, synthetic, refined, and more defensible final statement contained in the two volumes just cited. That the overall project was judged by many critics solely on the basis of its earlier publications, or publicity about them, is perhaps understandable; the monograph-length essays collected in the first four volumes contain invaluable information and analysis. Many rightly remain the standard treatment of their topic. Still, those essays were also winnowed in the preparation of the final statement.

Accordingly, when I present the findings of TFP, at least in terms of delineating the "family resemblances" that justify the comparative endeavor, I rely largely on that final synthetic statement and on its explanations of the ideological and organizational characteristics and dynamics that identify a movement as belonging to the family of fundamentalisms. Briefly, I now recapitulate these characteristics, with the caveat that no one or two or three of them can be taken in isolation from the others—indeed, many religious, as well as secular, movements share a number of these characteristics without being "fundamentalist." But in the real world of lived religion, fundamentalism has a distinct religious logic unlike any other, and this logic is evident only when one views the following characteristics as feeding off one another, existing in a synergy that produces a unique attitude and approach to the modern, secularizing, globalizing world.

Ideological traits

The movements we call fundamentalist are both *reactive* and *selective,* and these two orientations reinforce and condition each other. Fundamentalisms react primarily to *the marginalization of religion*—that is, to the displacement of "true religion" by nationalist political leaders, scientific and cultural elites (feminists being a particular bête noire), modern bureaucracies and institutions, and competing religious or ethnic groups that find public space under the banner of pluralism.

The marginalization of religion, a disease spread by the West and its hubris, produces many symptoms, against which militant Islamicists, Hindu nationalists, and Christian extremists rail. One is "Westoxication," a phrase coined by an Iranian intellectual to describe the seduction of the devout by the indulgent lifestyle of the West, offered in exchange for one's integrity and soul. Another is the "liberation of women," which, fundamentalists claim, turns the natural order on its head and disrupts God's social plan, leading to divorce, sexual depravity, and crime. Other symptoms of irreligion, in addition to hedonism and paganism, are antinomianism, the disregard for God's law, and its close cousin, relativism, the rejection of moral absolutes.

The modern assault on public religion, furthermore, is not a mere accident of history but the intended fruit of a diabolical conspiracy to uproot authentic religion. Insidiously, fundamentalists warn, the disease infects even those previously within the domain of Islam, the kingdom of Christ, the people of Israel, the Hindu nation: one can no longer trust one's own co-religionist. Thus, the Sunni ideologue Sayyid Qutb warned darkly of the descent of *jahiliyya* (the era of paganism reminiscent of the time before the Prophet); the Baptist pastor Jerry Falwell accused fellow born-again evangelist Billy Graham of being "the most dangerous man in America," owing to Graham's functional endorsement of U.S. religious pluralism (he appeared on platforms with rabbis, priests, and mainstream Protestants); and the Jewish mystic Rabbi Kook, forefather of Gush Emunim, spread the doctrine that secular Zionists had lost touch with their inner Jewish identity and needed to be awakened to their true destiny.

When fundamentalists react to the marginalization of religion, they do so as quintessentially modern people. They are not the Amish, seeking a cultural return to premodern purity, or restorationists, hoping to rebuild the lost kingdom or return to the golden age. Although their rhetoric might pine for the pristine moment of origin or the apotheosis of the Davidic kingdom or Christendom or Islamic civilization, the fundamentalists are looking ahead, not backward. Educated and formed epistemologically under the banner of technoscientific modernity, most "middle managers" of fundamentalist movements are engineers, software experts, medical technicians, soldiers, politicians, teachers, and bureaucrats. They are pragmatists of the soul. Few are astrophysicists or speculative philosophers. Stinger missiles, modern media, airliners, and cyberspace are their milieu. They have little patience and no time for the ambiguities of the vast, multivalent religious tradition.

Given their emergence from the heart of secular modernity, these would-be defenders of traditional religion approach the scriptures and traditions as an architect reads a blueprint or an engineer scans his toolbox: they plumb the sacred sources for the instruments appropriate to the task. By this habit, they reveal themselves to be modern, not traditional. In competition with the Westoxicated moderns, the fundamentalists select, mix and match, recombine, innovate, create, build. They grow impatient and angry with mere traditionalists, who insist on disciplining themselves to the tradition as an organic, mysterious, nonlinear, irreducible, life-giving whole. There is no time for such luxuries, such refinements. As the fundamentalists implore, we are *at war*; our souls, as well as our lives, depend on swift and powerful retaliation. This is *urgent!*

And so the mode of reaction to the marginalization of religion is, ironically, fundamentally modern, instrumental, rational—and manipulative of the religious tradition.

And yet fundamentalists, whether vaguely or explicitly aware of the compromises they are compelled to make, practice *selective retrieval* not only of aspects of secular modernity but also of the host religion. From the religious sensibility, they choose the elements most resistant to relativism, pluralism, and other concomitants of secular modernity that work to reduce the autonomy and hegemony of the religious. Hence fundamentalists embrace *absolutism* and *dualism* as tactics of resistance and as justification for extremism in the service of a sacred cause.

In an attempt to protect the holy book or hallowed tradition from the depredations of historical, literary, and scientific criticism—that is, from criteria of validity and ways of knowing that deny the transcendence of the sacred—fundamentalist leaders claim *inerrancy* and *infallibility* for their religious knowledge. The truth revealed in scriptures and hallowed traditions is neither contingent nor variable but absolute. To underscore the transrational (and thus countermodern) nature of absolute truth, each movement selects from its host religion certain scandalous doctrines (i.e., beliefs not easily reconcilable to scientific rationality, such as the imminent return of the Hidden Imam, the literal virgin birth of Christ, the divinity of the Lord Ram, the coming of the Messiah to restore and rule "the Whole Land of Israel"). These "supernatural dicta" they embellish, reify, and politicize.

The confession of literal belief in these hard-to-swallow "fundamentals" sets the self-described true believers apart from the Westoxicated masses. Moreover, it marks them as members of a sacred remnant, an elect tribe commissioned to defend the sacred against an array of "reprobate," "fallen," and "polluted" coreligionists—and against the forces of evil that have corrupted the religious community. This *dualist* or Manichean worldview valorizes the children of light, in stark contrast with the children of darkness, and reinforces the fundamentalists' conviction that they are specially chosen by God to withstand the forces of irreligion.

Yet a reliance on absolutism and dualism as a mode of selective reaction to the marginalization of religion is not enough. Fundamentalist leaders typically are drawn toward extremism, that is, toward extralegal, often violent measures to realize a meaningful victory over their enemies. But they have a recruiting problem, for their pool of potential disciples is drawn not only from the religiously illiterate and untutored or drifting youth but more centrally from conservative and orthodox believers—people who are familiar with their scriptures, embrace the tradition in its complexity, and recognize that it enjoins compassion and mercy toward others, not intolerance, hatred, and violence. Theoretically, at least, violence and retaliation are not the only strategies for resisting evil. Separatism or passive resistance might suffice to withstand the encroachments of the world. Guerrilla war, terrorism, and the killing of innocents seem a breathtakingly severe and indeed unorthodox reaction.

This is why *millennialism* is the ideological characteristic that stands at the heart of the religious logic of fundamentalism. By the single term "millennialism," TFP means to include the full array of doctrines, myths, and precepts embedded in the history and religious imagination of the major religious traditions of the world. Certainly, Islam, Christianity, and Judaism all anticipate a dramatic moment in time, or beyond time, in which God will bring history to a just (and often bloody) culmination. In certain religious communities, such as Shi'ite Islam or Evangelical Protestant Christianity, this expectation is highly pronounced and developed. (Indeed, the term "millennialism" refers to the prophesied 1000-year reign of Christ, following his return in glory, to defeat the Antichrist.) What is striking, however, is the recent retrieval of "millennial" (or messianic or apocalyptic or eschatological) themes, images, and myths by "fundamentalists" from religious communities with a muted or underdeveloped strain of "end times" thought.[5]

How does this retrieval and embellishment of apocalyptic or millennial themes function within fundamentalist movements that seek recruits from among their orthodox coreligionists? Leaders seeking to form cadres for jihad or crusade or anti-Muslim (or anti-Jewish, etc.) riots must convince the religiously literate fellow believer that violence is justified in religious terms. Luckily for them, most scriptures and traditions contain ambiguities and exceptions, including what might be called "emergency clauses." Thus, the Granth Sahib, the holy book and living guru of the Sikhs, repeatedly enjoins forgiveness, compassion, and love toward enemies. It does, however, also contain an injunction calling believers to arms, if necessary, if the Sikh religion itself is threatened with extinction—a passage put to use by Jarnail Singh Bhindranwale, the Sikh militant who cut a swath of terror through the Punjab in the early 1980s. Such "emergency clauses" can also be found in the Qur'an, the Hebrew Bible, and the New Testament. And what better "emergency" than the advent of the predicted "dark age" or reign of evil that precedes the coming of the Messiah, the return of the Mahdi, the vindication of the righteous at God's hands?

The fundamentalist invocation of "millennialism," in short, strives to convince believers that they are engaged not merely in a mundane struggle for territory or political power or financial gain but in a cosmic war, a battle for the soul and for the future of humanity. In such a context, violence is not only permissible; it is obligatory.

ORGANIZATIONAL TRAITS

The organizational traits of fundamentalist movements reflect and reinforce their ideological dynamics. As in any social group, ideology, organization, and behavior must cohere to create a way of life, or culture. A fundamentalist movement takes original shape as an *enclave,* a community set apart from the larger society and concerned with maintaining boundaries to prevent its members from deserting. Moral persuasion is the glue that keeps the enclave together as a social group. Enhancing the effectiveness of moral suasion are ideological claims such as the doctrine that the enclave members are elect, chosen, set apart from the fallen world (i.e., "dualism") and practical rewards such as social or economic benefits (e.g., deferment from the army for Haredi Jews in Israel, employment of women by the Baptist church as teachers, the granting of loans by Islamic banks, etc.). Relations within the enclave tend to be egalitarian, despite functional differentiation.

As the fundamentalist movement grows, however, the enclave may become a movement, or a *network* of enclaves, and eventually, it may establish permanent *institutional* presence in the larger society (through the founding of schools, libraries, health-care clinics, political parties). As the movement grows from enclave to network to institutional presence, the reactive and exclusivist oppositional stance of "pure" fundamentalism becomes more difficult to sustain; that is, the enclave's boundaries become porous, the organization more complex, the internal pluralism of the movement more difficult to manage without making the compromises that are the heart of politics. In this sense, fundamentalism becomes less stable as a religious mode as it becomes more successful in winning recruits and making alliances.[6]

Unlike relations among the rank and file, *leadership* of the fundamentalist movement or organization is *hierarchical.* It is also *charismatic, authoritarian,* and *patriarchal.* The founder is usually possessed of charisma and spiritual/religious virtuosity, and succession at his death often precipitates a crisis in authority. In any case, leaders atop the pyramid are authoritarian, an organizational tendency that is reinforced by the opposition to relativism and critical attitudes toward religious truth ("absolutism"). In movements that are founded by women, males eventually assume central positions of authority. (Some scholars argue that fundamentalisms are best understood as patriarchal protest movements against feminism.)

The evolution of the enclave into a network (and perhaps a regional or transnational network) requires a more complex organizational structure (e.g., separate wings or divisions for finance, recruiting, ideology, arms) and multiple leaders. Some instincts of the enclave survive the transition to more complicated organizational structures, however, including the emphasis on differentiating the members of the movement from outsiders, including co-religionists. Accordingly, fundamentalism as a religious mode entails the requirement of *distinctive behavioral codes* such as special dress, dietary, and sexual restrictions and obligations. In itself, this means of differentiating believers from nonbelievers is not a departure from traditional, time-honored religious practice. But in keeping with their reactive and militant attitude toward even their own co-religionists, the self-anointed true believers practice an exaggerated and chauvinistic form of the host religion (e.g., larger than average *kippahs* for Gush extremists or supervised dating for Christian students at Bob Jones University).

Because the fundamentalists believe themselves to be engaged in a cosmic war against evil, in other words, only a double dose of "strong religion" will suffice. As the religious logic outlined above indicates, they are modern warriors, and they are happy to select and retrieve organizational features from modern ideological movements that they admire (e.g., fascism) but that failed because these predecessors were insufficiently religious.

III

What have we learned in the decade since the major research of TFP was completed? Because fundamentalist movements are moving targets, ever adapting to changing circumstances and to their own internal pressures and experiences, one fruitful line of analysis in answering this question is to revise the findings based on how certain movements (e.g., the Muslim Brotherhood, the Christian Right, Gush Emunim, the Hindu RSS) have evolved. A related strategy is to consider how a revised appreciation of the dynamics of the secular alters our descriptions and explanations of "fundamentalism."

The interaction and mutual construction of "the religious" and "the secular" are clearer to us than ever before, and this enhanced understanding has consequences for how we comprehend religion. Rather than stipulate "antisecularism" as a marker of fundamentalist groups, for example, it now seems more accurate to depict the fundamentalist mode of religiosity as being *critically engaged with secularism.* Fundamentalisms, like all other modern movements, unfold and evolve, react and select within "the immanent frame" of awareness, perception, and knowledge that characterizes secular humanism. Even as they strive to transform certain attitudes and values associated with secular humanism, while rejecting others, the fundamentalists are inscribed within the discourse of immanence. In this process of creative adaptation to and attempted transformation of exclusive humanism, the true believers also strive self-consciously to sustain and in some cases retrieve through religious discipline the experience and sense of "fullness" that Jewish, Christian, and Muslim groups and individuals identify as an encounter with the living God.

If, for the moment, we retain the term "fundamentalism" and understand fundamentalists in this way, as sharing a concern to refashion the relationship between the secular and the religious that obtains in cosmopolitan societies, how might this revised account bear on our attempt to identify and parse the meanings of secularism in the contemporary world? And how best to incorporate into the revised understanding of fundamentalism the relevant insights from the recent debates on globalization and the intensified direct contact between peoples and cultures that it entails? What assumptions (and culturally conditioned worldviews) brought to the earlier studies of fundamentalism must be refined or jettisoned in light of our studies of secularism in its various forms and dynamics? Finally, in light of the severe conceptual and methodological problems associated with employing a comparative construct such as "fundamentalism," why retain the term (or a cognate) at all?

RETHINKING THE CHARACTERIZATION OF RELIGIOUSLY COMMITTED ACTORS

First, to the extent that scholars exoticized religion in the fundamentalist mode (or, worse, religion in general) by positing dynamics of human behavior and belief unique to "the religious," such characterizations must be refined or withdrawn. The assumption standing behind this "other-ing" of religious believers and practitioners seemed to be that people of deeply held faith, and certainly those possessed of "fundamentalist fervor," inhabit a radically different universe of meaning and morality from secular or "moderately religious" people. An unfortunate implication of this move is that religious people are inherently inclined toward acts beyond the pale of ordinary, civilized human behavior, including indiscriminate violence and other forms of terrorism.

Greater effort must be given to reducing the conceptual distance between deeply religious actors and other players in international politics and on the world stage. In his chapter for this book, Craig Calhoun offers useful suggestions for filling in the spaces along the continuum of orientations toward reality described by Charles Taylor as "immanence" and "transcendence." Human beings obviously have the capacity, as Calhoun notes, for acts of self-transcendence that do not require the practice of religion or belief in God (e.g., self-sacrifice in a cause greater than oneself, "militant" devotion to a higher good, participation in projects dedicated to transforming history beyond one's lifetime, etc.). The point is not that people whose self-understanding and personal and political commitments are shaped by belief in a transcendent reality or being are no different from others as a result of that orientation and the distinctive rituals and religious practices that reinforce and make it plausible to them. The point, rather, is that they are not thereby exempted from the kinds of considerations, calculations, anxieties, and sense of existential autonomy that accompany what Taylor calls the experience of "the buffered self." Those religious actors who might properly be called fundamentalists cannot be said to be in the grip of an enchanted world any more than others who are participating actively in the ongoing construction of modern societies. In fact, the decision of fundamentalists to be bound by strict rules of religious law or by in-group dynamics and obligations is in part a response to dissatisfaction with the empty experience of the disembedded self.[7]

Similarly, it will not do to assume a standard model of the rational, enlightened, educated modern person, against which the fundamentalist can be neatly juxtaposed. In part, given its vintage, too few of the case studies and analytical essays included in TFP situated their accounts of religious—and secular—agency in the context of what has been learned regarding the depth and range of cultural, social, and epistemological diversity, through recent advances in such fields of inquiry as cultural anthropology, comparative sociology, and subaltern studies. Eisenstadt's concept of "multiple modernities" gains added resonance when the range of human self-understandings, values, and social constructions of reality is on full display. Even less persuasive is the "other-ing" of the "religious extremist" in this cognitive setting. In addition, while the best books and essays on fundamentalism, religious nationalism, and political religions more broadly demonstrate familiarity with primary sources and first-person accounts, too little attention was given to the diversity of individual profiles and histories that render absurd any kind of schematic portrait of "the fundamentalist" as an ideal type.

RETHINKING FUNDAMENTALISM AS A MODE OF RELIGIOSITY

Having identified major weaknesses in the scholarly literature on "fundamentalism," not least the comprehensive use of the term, often with pejorative connotations, it is now time to stand my ground, as it were. "Fundamentalism," by whatever name, does signify a late-modern mode of religiosity—a religious public presence—the underlying logic of which, though not the particular political, social, or cultural expressions, is shared by individuals, movements, groups, and political parties that claim adherence to a religious tradition and are dedicated to defending that tradition from marginalization, erosion, privatization, and decline—that is, from the hard edge of secularism in its most antireligious form. In this sense, "fundamentalism" is properly understood as a subset and instance of the more inclusive category "public religion."

The literature on fundamentalism is vast and self-contradictory at points, including within TFP itself. But the project did develop a core notion of fundamentalism as a specific religious logic, summarized above in the sections on ideological and organizational dynamics. Less clear in the core analysis was the awareness that this logic itself is evolving and shifting as fundamentalists negotiate secularity and religious plurality in their own lives and in the societies in which they live and to which they have migrated.[8] Within fluid, evolving, and increasingly transnational movements/organizations such as Hezbollah, the Muslim Brotherhood, Hizb ut Tahrir, the Gush Emunim, the "hard Evangelical" Christian right (including the Christian Reconstructionists), and the Hindu RSS, one is challenged to keep track of the ongoing internal debates (e.g., over the use of violence, the relationship between political and military wings, the timing and targets of propaganda campaigns or public demonstrations, etc.); the diversity of interpretations of texts and traditions (e.g., concerning the religious status of the nation or homeland, or the theoretical as well as functional place of end-times or eschatological expectation in the movement worldview); disagreements regarding practical issues, as well as principles of operation (e.g., how to obtain political goals, what alliances to form and when, how recruiting is to be conducted); and actual changing behaviors (e.g., the development of new religious NGOs affiliated with or supported by the group, the evolution of political parties and their positions on questions such as participatory self-governance, the building of seemingly unlikely coalitions). Such "surprises" sprung by fundamentalisms are underreported but should no longer come as surprises.

As a way of entering the fundamentalist logic, we might formulate the basic question or dilemma confronting these otherwise incomparable groups in terms taken from our discussion of the multiple modes of secularism unfolding in the late-modern world. Like everyone on the planet, religious actors face a globalizing milieu characterized by an array of competing forces, each possessed of its own value systems, each vying for public space, and some for hegemony, through the amassing of resources and political capital. Familiar boundaries and "givens"—geographical, religious, cultural, economic—seem to be eroding or reconfiguring more rapidly than at any time in history. To some, globalization appears to be an economic project first and foremost and a project by and for elites, who are also widely perceived as secularized and committed to material development and little else. The right of nation-states to a monopoly on legal violence seems to go uncontested, long after weapons of mass destruction have been placed in their hands and used irresponsibly or immorally. Within this global context, in which homogenization and flattening of values can be seen as concomitant with secularism in a form virulently hostile to religion, how are people committed to transcendence, to the priority of the spiritual and religiously moral, to ensure continuity with the "traditional" religious past? How best to contest the meanings of core concepts of cosmopolitan discourse, such as "freedom," "development," "human rights," and the like?

Note that the last question crucially presupposes engagement with the cosmopolitan project "from within." The literature on fundamentalisms has certainly grown more sophisticated on this question of locating fundamentalists socially. Several essays in TFP, for example, underscore the "secular modern" profile of the membership core of fundamentalist movements—medical technicians, software designers, biologists, chemists, career politicians, and other mid-level techno-bureaucrats at home in the domain of applied science and, more recently, cyberspace. Sharpening the profile of fundamentalists as "the person next door, your professional colleague," has been a project of some particularly savvy members of the media. Notwithstanding the cartoons of bin Laden in his cave or other depictions of Muslim fundamentalists, in particular, as decidedly uncosmopolitan, it is now less typical to read or hear that the young men (and women) recruited into fundamentalist movements hail from impoverished backgrounds and represent "the poorest of the poor." More widely available are descriptions of "relatively deprived" or socially alienated engineers, computer-software experts, medical technicians, and mid-level bureaucrats. The fundamentalist profile has sharpened to include Christian millionaires in Dallas, Orlando, and Oklahoma City; former IDF soldiers and Jewish mothers settled in the West Bank; middle-class Hindu women who entered the ranks of the VHP in the mid-1990s in order "to move out of their homebound existence, to reclaim public spaces and even to acquire a political identity [that] gives them access to serious intellectual cogitation"; and displaced young Muslim professionals and technocrats, isolated in London or ghettoized in Paris.[9] This more nuanced composite profile underscores the fact that the contest, in the minds of the so-called fundamentalists, is not between the religious and the secular but between different formulas for their interdependence and coexistence in a rapidly modernizing world.

The fundamentalist logic of reaction to the challenges of this milieu through selective appropriation of elements of "traditional religion," on the one hand, and "secular modernity" (driven by techno-scientific, instrumental reason), on the other, does not in itself set these religious activists apart from other modern people attempting to create a workable synthesis of these elements. We come closer to a distinctive fundamentalist logic when we acknowledge the decisive presence of the religious imagination—incorporating a "passion for the infinite," the striving toward "fullness," the preoccupation with matters of "ultimate concern." How to inhabit the buffered self without loosening or dissolving ties of solidarity with the *umma*?

This is not a question faced only by so-called fundamentalists, of course.

Previously, however, the typical manifestations of the fundamentalist approach to prioritizing the religious imaginary were described in largely negative terms, as "absolutism" (both epistemological and political), "dualism" (sharp, buffered boundaries between the elect and the reprobate), and "millennialism" (an end-times expectation that can justify the suspension of "ordinary time" ethics and legitimize extraordinary acts such as the killing of innocents). Given the fluidity of these movements as they interact across geographical, cultural, and denominational boundaries, the question arises about the accuracy of this description. Fundamentally, does the category of fundamentalism itself melt away under the pressures of globalization, at least if it is understood as a militant reaction to the aggression and encroachments of secular modernity?

In sum, fundamentalists, like other religious and secular thinkers, are engaged in negotiating the boundaries between and interpenetration of the religious and the secular. To cast them into the outer darkness, where "Here be Monsters," is to reveal a basic and in some cases willful misconstrual.

RETHINKING THE ROLES OF "STRONG RELIGION" IN POLITICS

The study of fundamentalist political parties, like that of religious politics in general, has been held hostage to wrong-headed assumptions fueled by the secular/religious binary (critiqued in chapters by Elizabeth Shakman Hurd and Cecelia Lynch in this book). As a result, fundamentalist politicians and political parties are routinely underestimated and their ability to adapt to changing circumstances and to develop creative responses overlooked. Indeed, the application of the term "fundamentalist" to religious parties has led analysts to apply rigid stereotypes based on the assumption that fundamentalism and democracy are incompatible; thus, we are told, fundamentalists participate in democratic processes only for the purpose of taking power and then restricting or undermining democracy; fundamentalists are incapable of building or unwilling to build coalitions across religious/secular barriers; women can have no leadership role in fundamentalist power structures or social programs; and so on. Such stereotypes contain an element of truth only to the extent that the term "fundamentalism" is employed as typology, or broad political category, within which a dizzying array of actors could be made to fit. In such efforts, that is, the term is made so encompassing as to be rendered virtually meaningless. Despite heroic attempts by some talented political scientists and sociologists to construct fundamentalism as an overarching political category comprehending a variety of discrete religiopolitical movements and political parties from disparate settings, it makes little empirical sense to defend a category that could include the Taliban, Hamas, the Muslim Brotherhood of Egypt, the Islamic Salvation Front of Algeria, and the Justice and Development Party of Turkey, to name just some of the *Islamic* candidates.[10]

   Would it be more accurate to cluster together and label "fundamentalist" those religious parties that do, in fact, discriminate systematically and in principle against women, reject democracy out of hand as a Western imposition, and pursue a theocratic regime? To do so would be both to narrow and to expand the meaning of the term, as I have developed it above (i.e., as a mode of religious presence that critically engages secularisms, rejecting some forms and modifying or attempting to transform others) in unhelpful ways. The Islamic Republic of Iran may or may not belong in such a category, though its political and religious leaders certainly qualify as "fundamentalist" in my version of the phenomenon. No, the reality seems to be quite different, namely, that religious actors who participate in the fundamentalists' project to remake secularity do so from a variety of political perspectives and platforms ranging across a continuum from "democracy, liberty, and progress" to "theocracy, tyranny, and subservience to illegitimate authority," as Elizabeth Shakman Hurd describes the standard oppositional relation in which secular and religious actors typically are interpreted.

   The truth is that neither a conventional religious perspective nor a conventional secular perspective adequately comprehends the dynamism of "fundamentalist politics." The Shi'ite cases—Iran, the different approaches of leaders such as Moktar Al-Sadr and Grand Ayatollah Ali al-Sistani in Iraq, the evolution of Lebanon's Hezbollah over the last two decades—are illustrative of the internal pluralism and shifting political configurations, alliances, and ideologies of religious politics more generally. The ongoing self-creation of fundamentalist parties and politicians appeared as a theme of some of the more prescient essays in TFP. Acute awareness of the way in which hegemonic discourses operate, and of the attempt of some states to frame as deviant a range of actors, including religiously inspired political parties and movements of opposition or resistance, informed the most provocative essays. This is true, for example, of Abdulaziz Sachedina's indictment of the Western framing of Iranian Shi'ite "fundamentalism" as an awkward imitation of the West, on one hand, and a betrayal of "authentic," "quietist" Shi'ism, on the other. Sachedina responded with eloquent repudiation of any attempts to interpret Shi'ite politics without sustained reference to the distinctive features of collective Shi'ite religious experience. The experiences of persecution, martyrdom, and constant witness to the unity of God within the context of the challenges of syncretism and internal pluralism—all these and more, he argues, constitute the background to the efforts of Iranian leaders to fashion a secular/religious politics that can compete on its own terms with the West.[11]

   Significantly, religious critics of fundamentalism, including some operating within fundamentalist movements or organizations, express a feeling of unease about the risks inherent in pursuing coercive power, in "fighting fire with fire." And yet—the other horn of the dilemma—the avoidance of politics is not feasible, nor is the flight from "the secularizing world" possible. The retreat to the desert, to the unmarked terrain of otherworldly contemplation, is difficult these days, even for the Amish; it is hardly the solution for the engineer and the computer programmer. Nor is it desirable. The current generation of fundamentalists is responding to the marginalization of religion, yes, but the immediate provocation is their abiding sense of being the victims of discrimination: they are entitled to the good things of the developed world, they are prepared to make competent use of them, they are inheritors of the scriptural promise of abundance and prosperity, but they are unfairly held back because of their religion (or perceived religion)—the last acceptable prejudice in an increasingly irreligious, Westernized world.

Whatever their religious persuasion, these rebels of the professional class share the conviction that the Enlightenment model of secularization is woefully inadequate, owing in large part to its marginalization of religion and disrespect for God's law. Their prescribed remedy is a rerouting of medical and scientific expertise, an ethically and spiritually guided redeployment of modernity's material blessings toward the establishment of a morally upright society governed by divine law.[12]

The politicization of religion in competition with what Taylor calls "exclusive humanism" entails the identification and practice of religion as a means of transforming this world, and also saving the religious remnants within it, through exercising political power, if not political hegemony. In the more radical or revolutionary movements, control of the state is sought in the expectation that such control would make possible the enforcement of orthodoxy and the regularization of the young professionals and middle-class women and men who have become fellow travelers, often for mixed reasons (i.e., not only to advance orthodox religion, per se). The fear and envy of the threatening forms of secularism—of the entity lurking outside the increasingly porous walls of the enclave—lure the fundamentalist into trying to harness its awesome power. The encompassing modern nation-state, perceived as bent on ushering religion from the public square, is perhaps the most feared creature in the fundamentalist imaginary. How to protect against *that?*

As many religious actors have realized, however, the fundamentalists' attempt to co-opt the secularists is fraught with risk. The strategy raises anxiety even among its practitioners, who may or may not openly acknowledge their fear that the result will be the dilution of the religious imagination itself. Hence the ratcheting up of aggressive, triumphal God-talk among some of the movements and groups deeply engaged in negotiating with the secular "other." The Israeli sociologist Gideon Aran describes the fundamentalist group he knows best, Gush Emunim, as "a religious phenomenon" but hastens to add: "True, by now [the early 1990s], the movement's politics have virtually assumed a life of their own, complete with a clear national ideology devoid of celestial theological premises." In an attempt to parse this seeming contradiction, he goes on to explain that "rather than religious politics, Gush Emunim represents a political religion."[13]

The leaders of Gush Emunim, Aran notes, were duly wary of the possible consequences of politicizing Judaism: "The harnessing of secular Israelis to political and operational activism was never conceived as more than a phase, and means, on the road to returning Jews to the religious fold." As the process unfolded and the Gush internalized the secular calculations and rhythms of Israeli politics, however, they were forced to justify their program—and their acknowledgment that their membership contained no more than a dozen "penitent Jews"—with a new, esoteric doctrine: the inner sanctity of the politics of redemption (of the Land and People of Israel). Aran describes their "bold interpretation of Judaism which surpasses the religious-secular dichotomy." It entailed the pseudo-mystical assertion that Zionist fundamentalist victories in the political arena and on the battlefield would effect a spiritual awakening among their secular Jewish allies, revealing their "hidden saintliness." Flush with worldly success, the previously secular Zionists, the Gush theologians predicted, "will speedily begin to observe Torah rules."[14]

This example calls to our attention the fact that those called fundamentalists are faced with challenges not unlike those posed to other individuals and communities living within "the immanent frame"—that is, the situation constituted by "the buffered identity of the disciplined individual [moving] in a constructed social space, where instrumental rationality is a key value and time is pervasively secular." How is meaning discovered or constructed within such a milieu? Furiously religious as a matter of choice, the fundamentalists embrace a disciplined commitment to staying religious as they confront this commanding question of the age. But this zeal does not relieve fundamentalists from the burden of negotiating both the hazards and the undeniable advantages of secular modernity. The attractions of the latter, not merely the evils of the former, are well documented in materials they produced. The benefits of "soft" secularity include greater levels of personal security and prosperity, legal protection of rights (including the right to convert—free speech—and to be converted), and a culture of tolerance that provides space for growth of the movement. In the face of the dual promise of secular modernity, the fundamentalists make palpable their commitment to live, over against the grain, as if the transcendent were not only real but vividly alive to their every decision and act. This insistence itself is the substance of their deliberate response to the challenge.

Indeed, it is precisely the concentrated, even defiant resolve to "choose transcendence" despite the lure of exclusive humanism—in Taylor's terms, to spin the immanent frame in the direction of openness to something beyond—that makes the fundamentalist encounter with secularity a particularly promising window on our age. We may find powerfully instructive the fate of their simultaneous insistence on the radical otherness of the transcendent and their decision to try to bend the world to the will of the divine through the application of instrumental rationality within the confines of secular time. Certainly, it is the extreme case that sheds light on what is and is not possible.

Conclusion: What's in a Name?

Adequately contextualized accounts of religious movements will situate militant religious actors within the contemporary milieu of "multiple modernities" that are constantly being contested and negotiated. The heightened differentiation of functions and types of actors within fundamentalist movements, as well as the diversity of types of such movements (diversity of political goals, cultural projects, outreach, target audiences, etc.), is one of the consequences of the extension of the processes of globalization and increased cross-cultural and transnational migration. Pinning down fundamentalisms, like other social movements, is trickier than ever.

Among those religious movements caught up in the processes of globalization, the fundamentalists are those for whom the growing secular milieu is experienced not as fluid and variegated but as a homogenizing juggernaut. The marginalization of religion, the most aggressive fundamentalists suspect, is not an accident of history but the inevitable consequence of the willful abandonment of faith in a transcendent reality that is in control of history and individual destiny. The replacement of that transcendent orientation by an exclusive humanism that believes, wrongly and tragically, that human fulfillment and flourishing can be achieved within an immanent frame and on materialist terms is nothing less than a conspiracy by atheists, who control the financial and political institutions of the world and seek to discredit religion, drive it from the public sphere, and doom it to the slow death of privatization. In this context of understanding, the struggle of the self-anointed true believers to retain the "passion for the infinite," to place themselves under the judgment and governance of the transcendent, and yet also to do whatever is possible to reverse the progress of secularization in its most virulent (i.e., God-denying) form is both poignant and arresting and deserves to be appreciated in its full complexity.[15]

The animus against the term "fundamentalism" in scholarly circles is understandably high. Its pejorative connotations, which obscure the richness of the phenomenon to which it is intended to point, are unmistakable. Indeed, the definition of the phenomenon that I have provided in this chapter, extracted and developed from the core of TFP, jettisons many of the elements of most standard definitions. The phenomenon may therefore deserve a different name.[16] In any case, it is foolish to assume that if the term "fundamentalism" is rejected, another label will not arise to take its place. This is because, like "secularism," "modernism," "liberalism," and other messy, unmanageable kitchen-sink terms that endure in the lexicon, "fundamentalism" points, however imperfectly, to a social reality that people encounter every day.

Whatever label we employ, it must capture the complexity of this mode of modern religiosity, which finds itself trapped in a dilemma. *On the one hand,* the dominant form of secularism in the world, that which originated with the European Enlightenment and identified with the modern West, and especially with the United States "superpower," is perceived as mortally threatening to traditional and still closely held forms of religious belief, practice, and community. Thus, there is a clear logic to the militant, reactive, selective, Manichean, absolutist, "millennialist" responses of the "true believers" from several religious traditions who are currently mobilized in pursuit of political power, including control of the state in some cases.

These religious actors are drawn to power and are defined in large part by their attempt to acquire it. *On the other hand,* these so-called fundamentalists are increasingly integrated into the institutions, practices, and processes of secular modernity, consumers of its wares and, not least, browsers and brico-lage builders in the open marketplace of religious ideas, practices, and sensibil-ities imported via the pluralism that accompanies modernization. The engineers, office managers, municipal bureaucrats, teachers, scientists, medical techni-cians, and middle-class working mothers who form the ranks of fundamen-talist movements have internalized the habits of mind enjoined by secular modernity. Religious virtuosi and charismatic preachers, presumably less taken by the flux of material culture, are supposed to keep the movements honest, that is, to train at least one eye on the heavens, but they must also abide a new class of lay religious technocrats who read sacred scriptures the way an engi-neer reads a blueprint.

Rather than posit a straightforward, to-the-death opposition between the religious and the secular in fundamentalism, then, it is more accurate—that is, truer to the dynamics of religion itself within a secular age—to understand fun-damentalism as a mode of late-modern religiosity informed, decisively, by sec-ularity. Going beyond the extant literature on fundamentalism, one would argue in this vein that the fundamentalist dance with secularity is neither merely a reaction against the secularizing trends of the age nor even an awkward mimesis of the secular enemy.

Instead, the late-modern religious mode known (previously?) as fundamen-talism has increasingly become a default mode for those who fear the loss of the sacred. This religious mode is defined by an intentional appropriation of constitutive elements and dynamics of the secular. The appropriation is some-times awkward, sometimes shrewd, but consistently erosive of premodern, "traditional" religious sensibilities. In this fact lies the poignant irony at the heart of "fundamentalism."

Notes

1. From 1988 to 1995, TFP held fifteen international meetings at which approximately 120 scholars from eighteen nations gave papers or formal responses; published five volumes of essays that amounted to more than 3700 printed pages, and generated dozens of spin-off books and articles; and cooperated in the production of a three-part television documentary aired on PBS and a seven-part radio series broadcast on NPR. See the volumes edited by Martin E. Marty and R. Scott Appleby and published by University of Chicago Press: *Fundamentalisms Observed* (1991), *Fundamentalisms and the State: Remaking Politics, Economies and Militance* (1993), *Fundamentalisms and Society: Remaking the Family, the Sciences and the Media* (1993), *Accounting for Fundamentalisms: The Dynamic Character of Movements* (1994), and *Fundamentalisms Comprehended* (1995).

2. Majid Tehranian, "Fundamentalist Impact in Education and the Media: An Overview," in Martin E. Marty and R. Scott Appleby, eds., *Fundamentalisms and Society: Reclaiming the Sciences, the Family and Education* (Chicago: University of Chicago Press, 1993), 313.

3. The project was criticized for even attempting such comparisons, to which Marty responded by quoting Marc Bloch on the necessity and inevitability of drawing structured comparisons if scholars are to make sense of complex cross-cultural phenomena. See Martin E. Marty, "Fundamentalism as a Social Phenomenon," *Bulletin of the American Academy of Arts and Sciences* 42 (November 1988): 15–29.

4. Gabriel A. Almond, R. Scott Appleby, and Emmanuel Sivan, *Strong Religion: The Rise of Fundamentalisms around the World* (Chicago: University of Chicago Press, 2003).

5. Barbara Freyer Stowasser, "A Time to Reap," *Middle East Studies Association Bulletin* 34, no. 1 (Summer 2000): 1–13.

6. Emmanuel Sivan, "The Enclave Culture," in Almond, Appleby, and Sivan, *Strong Religion*, 1–89.

7. A surprising number of Americans have failed to internalize the awareness that fundamentalists are not uneducated or undereducated "yokels," as H. L. Mencken put it in 1925, or even "anti-intellectual and simplistic," as the president of Georgetown University put it in 1981. Mencken went on to call his Christian adversaries "half-wits," "hillbillies," "anthropoid rabble," and "morons," among other choice compliments. See H. L. Mencken, *Prejudices: Fifth Series*, quoted in James Davidson Hunter, *Culture Wars* (Basic Books, 1991), 142. Even the ardent opponents of creationism and intelligent-design theory have conceded, if only by dint of reviewing their books and painstakingly pointing out the flaws in their evidence and logic, that the fundamentalist thinkers are, indeed, thinkers who are fluent in contemporary scientific discourse and theory, however twisted their divinely guided, biblically inspired logic might be. See H. Allen Orr, "A Religion for Darwinians?" *New York Review of Books* 54, no. 13 (August 16, 2007): 33–35.

8. Earlier attempts to chart the change in fundamentalists' ideologies and organizational structures over time are found in Marty and Appleby, eds., *Accounting for Fundamentalisms*, and the discussions of shifting fundamentalist priorities and the conditions under which decisions are taken by leadership ("structure, chance, choice") in Almond, Appleby, and Sivan, *Strong Religion*.

9. T. Sarkar, "Women's Agency within Authoritarian Communalism: The Rashtrasevika Samiti and Ramjanmabhoomi," in G. Pandey, ed., *Hindus and Others*, quoted in Christophe Jaffrelot, *The Hindu Nationalist Movement in India* (New York: Columbia University Press,

1996), 426–427. A variation on the Muslim technocrat was Mohammed Bouyeri, the twenty-six-year-old, well-educated Moroccan-Dutchman who murdered the filmmaker Theo van Gogh in Amsterdam in 2004 after coming under the influence of Abou Khaled, a Takfir preacher in exile from Syria. Bouyeri joined an Islamist cell known by Dutch authorities as the Hofstad Group, where he became the house intellectual and posted ideological tracts on Web sites. Ian Buruma, *Murder in Amsterdam: Liberal Europe, Islam and the Limits of Tolerance* (New York: Penguin, 2006), 211–212.

10. See, for example, Said Amir Arjomand, "Unity and Diversity in Islamic Fundamentalism," in Marty and Appleby, eds., *Fundamentalisms Comprehended*, 179–198; and similar efforts in Said Amir Arjomand, ed., *The Political Dimensions of Religion* (Stony Brook: State University of New York Press, 1993).

11. Abdulaziz Sachedina, "Shi'ite Activism in Iran, Iraq and Lebanon," in Marty and Appleby, eds., *Fundamentalisms Observed*, 403–456.

12. There is copious evidence of religious and political leaders from various cultural and religious backgrounds who have blamed a host of social crises on the relegation of the sacred to the sidelines. In 1992, for example, the Sudanese lawyer Hasan Turabi, the self-proclaimed leader of the "Islamic Awakening" in the Arab world, told audiences in Washington, D.C., that the high rates of divorce, drug use, sexual promiscuity, white-collar crime, and other signs of the moral decline of the United States, which he said would be followed by a political collapse, were the direct result of the secularization of the once Christian society. Former speaker of the U.S. House of Representatives Newt Gingrich, an unlikely ideological ally of a Sudanese Islamist, hit the lecture circuit not long after September 11, 2001, to reinforce essentially the same message. Gingrich displayed charts and graphs intended to demonstrate his argument that the rise in divorce, teen pregnancy, white-collar crime, and illicit drug use could be traced to 1962–63, when the U.S. Supreme Court outlawed prayer in the public schools. Half a world away, Hindu nationalists were linking the loss of Indian territory and political hegemony to a lapse in devotion to Hindu gods, especially to the Lord Ram. In 1988, the RSS reprinted and distributed widely an article from a publication of the Jana Jagaran, a militant offshoot of the VHP. Entitled "Angry Hindu," the article sacralized the religious nationalists' grievances against Indian secularism and pluralism by giving voice, as it were, to the wrath of Ram: "Yes for too long I have suffered affronts in silence.…My number have dwindled. As a result, my adored motherland has been torn asunder. I have been deprived of my age-old rights over my own hearths and homes. Afghanistan, N.W.F.P., Sindh, Baluchisthan, half of Punjab, half of Bengal and a third of Kashmir—all these have been usurped from me.…My temples have been desecrated, destroyed. Their sacred stones are being trampled under the aggressor's feet. My gods are crying. They are demanding of me for reinstatement in all their original glory.…You get my vote but you pamper those who attack me.…For you, our national life minus every bit of Hindu is secularism. In short, you want me to cease to be myself. Even the Haj pilgrims are subsidised from my money. For so long—for too long—I was lost in a deep coma.…Now I have begun to see, I have begun to hear, I have begun to understand, and I have begun to feel—what tragedies have overtaken me for my centuries-old blunder. Hereafter I will sleep no more." *Organiser*, February 14, 1988, anonymous article published in the form of a pamphlet with the same title: *Angry Hindu! Yes, Why Not!* (New Delhi: Suruchi Prakashan, 1988). Quoted in Christophe Jaffrelot, *The Hindu Nationalist Movement*, 391. In short, the scapegoating of secularism is a familiar and time-tested trope in the fundamentalist's rhetorical arsenal.

13. Gideon Aran, "Jewish Zionist Fundamentalism," in Marty and Appleby, eds., *Fundamentalisms Observed*, 295–296.

14. Ibid., 329.

15. A poignant sense of loss felt as a result of ultra-Orthodox Judaism's "negotiation with secular modernity" in the twentieth century is captured in Haym Soloveitchik's description of the transition from "a culture of mimesis" to "a culture of performance." See Haym Soloveitchik, "Migration, Acculturation and the New Role of Texts in the Haredi World," in Marty and Appleby, eds., *Accounting for Fundamentalisms*, 197–235.

16. Pentecostalism, for example, is a fascinating case of the attempted reshaping of secular modernity, which would normally not be included in discussions of "fundamentalism."

11

Secularism, Religious Change, and
Social Conflict in Asia
Richard Madsen

In his monumental book *A Secular Age,* Charles Taylor distinguishes three meanings of secularism, at least as it refers to the "North Atlantic societies" of western Europe and North America.[1] The first meaning is political. In this sense, secularism refers to political arrangements that make the state neutral with regard to religious belief. The legitimacy of the government is not dependent on religious belief, and "the political society is seen as that of believers (of all stripes) and non-believers alike."[2] The second meaning of secularism can be termed sociological. It refers to a widespread decline of religious belief and practice among ordinary people. The third meaning is cultural. It refers to a change in the conditions of belief, to "a move from a society where belief in God is unchallenged and indeed, unproblematic, to one in which it is understood to be one option among others, and frequently not the easiest to embrace."[3] In the North Atlantic world, all governments are (for all practical purposes) secular in the first sense, western Europe but not the United States is secular in the second sense, and all societies, including the United States, are secular in the third sense. Taylor tells the story of how the three modes of secularism have developed throughout the course of Western history and of how they have mutually influenced one another. He is especially concerned with the third mode, the development of secular conditions of belief.

Can this analytic framework be applied outside of the North Atlantic world, particularly to Asian societies? Taylor himself would not claim to have created a framework for a universal theory of comparative religion. But a framework grounded in a particular cultural and historical experience may nonetheless be useful for cross-cultural comparisons—if it is as profound and thoughtfully constructed as Taylor's. The conditions for its comparative use, however, would be as follows. First, we acknowledge its limitations from the outset. Second, we apply it as a first-draft approximation to understanding the historical transformations of religion in another culture to see if there is at least a rough fit with these processes. Third, we are careful to see how it doesn't fit and then use this discrepancy as a stimulus to expand our horizons. This can set into motion not an objectifying, essentializing gaze upon cultural difference but a fruitful dialogue across cultures.

This is the approach I will try to take in this chapter, as I explore the fit between Taylor's framework and contemporary developments in East and Southeast Asian societies. To keep the analysis focused, I will concentrate mainly on the political and religious transformations taking place in these societies in the aftermath of the Cold War.

Political Secularization

In form—at least that part of the form that is usually displayed toward international observers—most modern East and Southeast Asian governments are secular in the first sense of the term defined by Taylor. They are based on constitutions that do not ground the state's legitimacy on beliefs in realities that transcend this world but are, rather, geared toward providing economic development and political security for their citizens. They grant the basic rights of citizenship to believers and nonbelievers alike. Even the constitution of the People's Republic of China guarantees freedom of religious belief as long as it is kept private—so private that it is not expressed in any venue that is not approved and regulated by the state. East and Southeast Asian governments arrived at their present-day secular constitutions through various and often tortuous paths throughout the course of the twentieth century, but in formal terms, at least, they conform to North Atlantic models of secularity. This is an example of what sociologist John Meyer and his collaborators would call global "institutional isomorphism," a tendency of political, economic, and cultural institutions around the world to assume a uniform style of formal organization (based on Western templates).[4]

But the secular form of Asian political institutions often masks a religious spirit. Japan, for example, has a secular constitution, but many of its government leaders have felt compelled to pray for the spirits of the war dead at the Yasakuni shrine, in the face of strong criticism from China, South Korea, and many other Asian countries, not to mention the United States. The pressure to visit the shrine comes from nationalistic constituencies within Japan, but it is, indeed, a pressure to *worship* at a Shinto shrine, presided over by a priest, which purports not just to memorialize the names of the dead but actually to contain their spirits. (Japan's Asian neighbors are more upset about this than Americans. Could this be because Asians take more seriously the living presence of spirits of the dead?) Through its "Vigilant Center" at the Ministry of Culture, the government of Thailand is supposed to protect the nation's culture and values by, among other things, keeping people from using images of the Buddha for profane purposes. (In any case, the government does not seem very effective in doing this.) The Indonesian government is based on a national ideology of "Pancasila," which proclaims a national unity based on mutual tolerance among believers in an "Almighty Divine." And even the government in China, which is supposedly led by an atheist Communist Party, takes it upon itself to carry out religious functions. It has claimed the right to determine who is the true reincarnation of the Panchen Lama (and will undoubtedly do the same for the next reincarnation of the Dalai Lama). It claims to be able to determine the difference between true religion and "evil cults" and tries to root out even private belief in "evil cults" such as Falun Gong. Moreover, the Chinese government invests enormous amounts of money in spectacular public rituals, such as the opening ceremonies of the Olympics, which are redolent with symbols of Confucianism, Daoism, and Buddhism.

Often, the secular political form is what outsiders see, while the spirit is what insiders apprehend. In the 1950s and 1960s, Western scholars took the formal structure of Asian states as evidence of "modernization," a universal process of (among other things) secularization that was transforming the whole world. Even Communist China was seen as an example of modernization, though one that had perversely gone astray. Inside all of this putative political modernization, however, other meanings were being constructed.[5] Emerging and consolidating states were being seen not merely as providers of worldly goods but as necessary mediators between citizens and cosmic forces that transcended the visible world. States contained sacred power, which could be benevolent but could also turn demonically ferocious, as did the cult of Mao Zedong during the Chinese Cultural Revolution.

Political secularization, in Taylor's sense, therefore, is a reasonably accurate way to describe the formal structure, the external surface, of most East and Southeast Asian states. But it doesn't adequately describe the interior spirit of these states, which must be comprehended through a closer examination of how these states have developed within modern history. Taylor's account of political secularization does, however, help us pose the questions of how the external forms and interior spirit of modern Asian states have interacted with one another and what the practical consequences of this interaction have been.

It would be beyond the scope of this chapter to give a full account of the development of Asian states. But as we consider the development of the social and cultural life within some Asian societies, we can get some sense of how these societies and cultures have been influenced by the interplay between secular form and religious substance within their states.

Social Secularization

The secularity of modern Asian states has by no means led to widespread social secularity, that is, to secularity in the second sense defined by Taylor, a decline of religious belief and practice among ordinary people. Taylor shows how and why many western European societies have become at least partially secular in this second sense, while the United States has remained highly religious, albeit with a predominantly individualistic form of religious practice.

In terms of the numbers of people regularly taking part in religious practices, most Asian societies are more like the United States than western Europe. The degree of religious practice varies from country to country, but almost everywhere, temples, mosques, churches, and shrines are ubiquitous—and full of people, especially during festival seasons. Even in China, where the government actively propagates an atheist ideology and has severely restricted open religious activities, it has been estimated that as much as 85 percent of the population engages from time to time in some form of religious practice.[6] Moreover, throughout Asia, there have been impressive revivals and reformations of Buddhist, Muslim, and Christian religious belief and practice—a veritable religious renaissance. Asia is religiously dynamic.

However, this dynamism is of a different kind from that found in the United States, and it cannot be explained in terms of the narrative Taylor uses to account for patterns of popular religious commitment and social secularism in the North Atlantic world. Asian religious developments are often misread by Western observers (and also by Asian scholars trained in the paradigms of Western social science). When Western scholars have looked for religion in Asian societies, they have often looked for it in the form of private faith. But in most Asian societies, much of religion is neither private nor faith.

It is often not faith, in the sense of a personal belief in doctrines. In China, for example, there have been literally millions of temples built or rebuilt in the countryside during the past three decades.[7] Most people doing this rebuilding would be hard pressed to give a consistent and coherent account of the Daoist or Buddhist philosophies that one might think were behind this revival. Even the rural Catholics whom I studied in China could only give a vague account of the creed to which they were supposed to assent. Most of the people building temples and, for that matter, churches, seem driven by desire to create a place where they can carry out rituals that would give shape to some order in their lives and in their community life. It can be meaningful to carry out such rituals even if one does not believe in the theology that supposedly underlies them. For example, in the Chinese Catholic villages that I studied—which typically consisted entirely of Catholics who had carried on their identity through many generations—there are many "lukewarm" Catholics who don't regularly pray, are skeptical about doctrines, and don't follow many of the moral teachings of the Church. Yet they still consider themselves Catholics and would still want to be buried with Catholic funeral rituals because that is the way to connect them in life and death with their natal communities.[8]

Collective ritual, then, in this context—and in many Asian contexts—comes before personal faith. And for that matter, collective myths—stories about gods

or spirits or blessed events such as apparitions, healings, or miraculous occur-
rences—also come before personal faith. Rituals and myths are public rather
than private. Even when they have to be carried out surreptitiously, out of sight
of suspicious government regulators or condescending urban-based mass
media, they are, in the local context, public. Under such circumstances, they
create alternative public spheres that sometimes complement but other times
contradict the public projects of their governing states.

This is a form of religious practice akin to what Charles Taylor calls
"embedded religion," which was the prevalent form in Europe during the Middle
Ages. The world of embedded religion is "enchanted," filled with good and bad
spirits. Religious practices are used to call upon the good and control the bad, as
much for the sake of the material health and prosperity of oneself and one's
community as for any otherworldly salvation. One's community is under the
protection of local spirits—patron saints in the European Middle Ages and
ancestors and various local protector spirits in many parts of Asia—and
although these local spirits may be imagined to be under the control of a supreme
being, much of actual popular religious practice is aimed at getting one's own
local spirits to take care of one's family and friends in the here and now.[9]

These forms of localized, socially embedded religious practice have by no
means entirely disappeared in the North Atlantic world. But, as Taylor shows,
they have, through a long, complicated historical process extending over 500
years, largely been eclipsed. A key event in this process was the Reformation,
which condemned much of Catholic sacramental ritual as "magic," to be
replaced by personal devotion driven by interior faith. By now, in the United
States, at least, the prevalent forms of religion are individualistic expressions of
a desire for personal authenticity carried out through voluntary association
with other like-minded individuals.

Until relatively recently, scholars in the North Atlantic world have usually
assumed that modernization entails the eclipse of localized, socially embedded
religion (and of the "magical" ritual practices oriented to this worldly success
discussed by Peter van der Veer in this book). Just as the American government
during the Cold War convinced itself and its publics that governments allied
with the United States were part of the "free world," even when these governments were dictatorships, so did American scholars imagine that societies open
to influence from the West were becoming "free societies," composed of instru-
mentally rational individuals who had sloughed off communal traditions, especially religious traditions. (If there was any future for religion in such societies,
it was assumed that it would be in the form of Christianity, brought by Western
missionaries, who were welcomed in by most governments in the free world.)
The real processes of social development in Asia, however, usually took a
different path.

Whether through colonialism or through anticolonial and revolutionary
movements that sought national autonomy, wealth, and power by building

strong, bureaucratically organized governments modeled on those from the West, national political leaders imposed centralized states upon societies that had not undergone the North Atlantic world's path to modernity. In particular, these societies had not radically loosened the ties that bound local corporate communities together—especially the local rituals and myths that generated the enchanted identity of such communities.

Thus, the governments that emerged or consolidated themselves in Asia during the Cold War were imposed on top of societies that were still largely assemblages of corporate groups, rather than the voluntary associations of a (Western-style) civil society. Popular religion was mostly an expression of the identities of corporate groups—extended families and local village communities, mostly, but also in some cases larger-scale ethnic identities, as with the Muslims in the western regions of China. Religious ritual and myth expressed and reinforced particularistic loyalties within ascriptive communities. The construction of local temples, churches, and mosques was connected to a wide range of economic, social, and political activity. Places of worship were also venues for commerce and public entertainment, institutions for ensuring trust, mediating disputes, and providing welfare to those in need. They were also nexuses in regional networks of communities with similar religious practices. Such communities and their networks constituted a kind of public sphere—a framework of connections within which discussions about local affairs could take place, a system of statuses that marked out paths of social mobility and recognition, a site for common celebrations and shared experiences. These diverse bubbles of publicness introduced potential weaknesses into the sturdy foundations on which authoritarian governments wanted to build their version of public order.

To create national unity, maintain social control, and mobilize large and diverse populations, modernizing governments needed (or thought they needed) to get control over religious practices that fostered particularism, regionalism, and ethnic distinction. There were two main strategies. One was to suppress religious practice—destroy temples, ban public religious rituals, eliminate religious leaders (by forcing them to change their professions, by imprisoning them, and sometimes by executing them)—and to replace this with a quasi-religious cult of the state and its leader. This was the strategy of the People's Republic of China and North Korea. An alternative strategy was to co-opt religious leaders and to segregate religious communities. This was the strategy followed by Indonesia under Suharto. There, in the name of "Pancasila," the regime restricted proselytization among the five main religious groups (Muslims, Catholics, Reform Protestants, Hindus, and Buddhists), and co-opted the leaders of each group by making them members of state-sponsored commissions. Some countries adopted a mix of the suppressive and co-optive strategies. This was the case in Taiwan under the Kuomindang, which we will describe in more detail below.

During the Cold War, these various strategies seemed to work, at least on a superficial level. Throughout East and Southeast Asia, local religions seemed to be tamed, to be rendered irrelevant to the big issues of the day. In some cases, as in China, religious practices disappeared from sight. In societies that relied less on sheer repression and more on co-optation, religion contributed some vibrant local color, while remaining comfortably within the grip of the state and seeming to be irrelevant to the politically directed processes that supposedly constituted national modernization. As such, they were mostly invisible to Western social scientists. Anthropologists studied them but mostly in an attempt to document them before (as it was presumed) they inevitably faded away or to develop comprehensive theories about the roots of premodern religious experience. But even anthropologists did not generally assume that such religious activities were especially relevant to current political or economic developments. Meanwhile, political scientists, economists, and even sociologists almost completely ignored them.

However, none of these strategies used by Asian states to tame local religions actually destroyed them. The suppression strategies simply drove the practices underground while in many cases maintaining the communal ties with which these religious practices had been intertwined. The co-optation strategies helped to reproduce and maintain communal religious identities.

The recent emergence of religion as a visible force in Asian social and political life is at least partially connected with the end of the Cold War. After the Cold War, Asian states in the "free world" that could once count on strong support from the United States have found the support diminished and at least partially contingent on adoption of democratic reforms. Such states, including South Korea, Taiwan, the Philippines, and Indonesia, have been losing the capacity to tame local religions through suppression or co-optation. Meanwhile, the Communist regimes of China and Vietnam have had to loosen some of their social controls to permit economic reforms and integration into global markets. Throughout the Asian region, a plethora of religious practices have blossomed forth.

Nonetheless, it is unclear whether the loss of capacity to tame local religions through suppression or co-optation has actually led to a quantitative increase in religious practice. But the weakening of state capacities to control religion has at least made local Asian religious practices more visible, more energetic, and potentially more politically consequential. All of a sudden, the increased visibility of religion breaks down the imaginary communities of modernizing societies that Western intellectuals had created for themselves. Asian religious transformations now command the attention of all sorts of social scientists.

Thus, like America, Asia is "awash in a sea of faith." But the Asian sea of faith is different from the American one. Asian religious practices are less individualistic and more communal, socially embedded, and locally particularistic. This makes it more difficult to imagine how Asian religions could be accommodated into the standard liberal model (all too often unreflectively based on the American experience) for political incorporation: officially consider religious belief as a personal preference of individual citizens, who will then form all sorts of different but overlapping private religious associations in an open religious marketplace; and expect that these private associations will share enough in common that they will tolerate one another but have enough differences that they will not coalesce into any unified opposition to the state. We are becoming more aware of the limitations of this liberal model, even in established Western liberal societies such as the United States. How much more difficult might it be for this liberal model to accommodate the local, particularistic, communal religions that are becoming newly visible in Asia?

Probably too difficult. But does this mean that it will be impossible in most parts of Asia to develop moderate, democratic, stable, but adaptable polities? It is not impossible, but we would have to expect that the paths to such an outcome would be different from the North Atlantic path. The direction of these paths may depend on the precise ways in which local religious cultures are affected by secularism in the third sense defined by Taylor: a move to a society in which religious belief and practice are no longer unchallenged but are seen as one option among many, and not necessarily the easiest to embrace.

Cultural Secularization

Although religion in most Asian societies has been more a matter of communal practice than of individual belief, the meanings of such communal practice have been changing. This is the result of social mobility, social differentiation, and the expansion of cognitive horizons. Social mobility happens mainly when people move from countryside to city, from agricultural to industrial labor or to commerce. Social differentiation refers to the separation of work (which is increasingly dependent on a globalized economy) and education from family and kinship. The expansion of cognitive horizons is the result of the exposure to diverse people and ideas through exposure to modern media and to life in the metropolis. Most Asian societies have experienced all three of these processes, but the processes have unfolded in different ways along different paths. The result is that these processes now intersect so as to form different contexts, which shape the specific transformations of religion in different societies.

When members of rural communities travel to the city, either within their own country or abroad (as with Indonesian or Filipino guest workers in Hong Kong, Taiwan, and South Korea), often as low-paid migrant workers, they do not leave behind the rituals that sustained their community life back home. Often, indeed, migrants travel through chains of relationships—extended family ties, regional associations connected with their local communities—and once in the city, they set up little shrines to the deities of their homes. Often, though, the pressures of industrial work make it difficult for them to reconstitute the full range of community liturgical life in the city. But they remit money back to the countryside partly to support their home community shrines, and they make pilgrimages home for important festivals. While at work in city or town, they encounter many people with different gods, different rituals—including, of course, highly educated cosmopolitans. Moreover, they have to conform to rhythms of work that do not fit their communities' customary patterns, and they try to educate themselves and especially their children in "scientific" education that contradicts folk practices but provides some hope for upward mobility.

Becoming all things to all people, they are skeptical with the skeptics, politely tolerant with those who worship strange gods, all the while never rejecting the ritual practices of their home communities. As they do so, however, the result must be a kind of hybrid consciousness. In Chinese culture, at least, there has been a long tradition in favor of such consciousness. In different aspects of their lives, people could adhere to Confucian, Buddhist, and Daoist teachings without worrying much about their logical inconsistencies. Such are the flexibilities of a nonmonotheistic culture, rather than a culture that assumes that there is a single jealous God who demands that all things conform consistently to his will.

However, another result of the possibility to choose one's own faith from among various options can be increasing demands for purified religion. If one is going to choose one's own faith, rather than simply adapt to the various practices that have been handed down through one's corporate group, one may want a system of practices and beliefs that seem consistent. This may be one reason for the attraction of Christianity (especially Evangelical Protestant Christianity) among rising middle classes in South Korea and to some degree in urban China. It may also be the reason for the embrace of reformed versions of Buddhism and Daoism in Taiwan and of movements toward stricter forms of Islam in Indonesia, Malaysia, and western China. The attempt to "modernize" religious practices by rationalizing them and making them more universal may help to create new forms of religious fervor—and in turn inspire missionary tendencies. Maintaining one's religious conviction cannot depend on hiding within an enclosed community. It requires getting other people to follow it as well. The stage is set for development of large-scale religious movements that can then clash with one another in new ways.

Will this new cultural churning lead to syncretistic, hybrid practices that peacefully knit together various strands of traditional practice? Or will it lead to sectarian struggles among those devoted to purified faiths? Answers to such questions are highly context-dependent. The restructuring of cultural boundaries between the religious and the secular will be influenced by a confluence of factors, such as the rate and pace of social mobility, the extent and pace of social differentiation, and the suddenness of expansion of cultural horizons—as well as the cultural resources provided by various traditions for reconciling diversity.

Let us consider how the cultural boundaries between the religious and the secular have been shaped by three different contexts, chosen because they represent a wide spectrum of political regimes: China, where the state tried to suppress and dominate religions totally; Indonesia, where the state tried to co-opt religions into a corporatist regime; and Taiwan, where the state tried a mixture of suppression and co-optation but finally moved toward a liberal tolerance of religions.

China

At the time the Communists established their government in China, the primary form of social affiliation among the peasantry (who made up at least 80 percent of the population) was the extended-family lineage, whose identity had long been maintained through rituals of ancestor worship, reinforced through popular versions of Buddhism and Daoism. This led to a society plagued by "localism," which presented a major challenge to the project of creating a powerful modern state. Besides rituals and myths that solidified local solidarities, however, there were other forms of religious practice that linked people in large regional and even national networks. One example of this was the Unity Way (*yi guan dao*), which propagated a syncretistic mix of Daoist, Buddhist, and Confucian practices and had branches throughout northern China.[10] Another example was the Christian "Little Flock" established by the charismatic preacher Ni Tuosheng ("Watchman Nee"), which developed an extensive network of an indigenous Pentecostal-style Christianity throughout northern China.[11] Such local solidarities and extensive regional networks presented obstacles to Communist ambitions to build a strong, mobilizing state.

The strategy of the Communist government of the PRC for overcoming these obstacles was to impose a thick net of organization, justified by its version of Marxist-Leninist ideology, upon the whole society. This entailed the harsh suppression of popular religious practice. Local temples were destroyed, "superstitious" customs forbidden, religious practitioners eliminated, and scientific socialism incessantly propagated. Independent regional religious networks such as the Unity Way were methodically attacked. Watchman Nee, of the Little Flock, was imprisoned for the rest of his life. (He died in prison in 1972.) Although freedom of religion was officially guaranteed in the Chinese constitution, the only forms of religious organization permitted were the headquarters of five officially recognized "world religions": Daoism, Buddhism, Islam, Catholicism, and Protestantism. The leadership of these approved religions were incorporated into official patriotic associations, which were tightly controlled by the Communist Party's United Front Department. The leaders were not allowed to promote any grass-roots development of their religions.

In the 1960s, however, China's leaders went beyond suppressing and controlling religion. They attempted to create a "new socialist person," whose life would be given meaning and purpose through total dedication to the Revolution. This was to be accomplished through ritual and myth, culminating in the "worship" (*chongbai*) of Chairman Mao. The new socialist person was supposed to be detached from all particularistic loyalties to family or friends. Indeed, he or she was supposed to be willing to sacrifice his or her own life for the good of an imagined community of equal comrades. To learn how to do this, he or she was supposed to recite continually the "three constantly read articles"—short, mythic stories written by Mao Zedong that told the tale of a humble soldier who had sacrificed his life for revolutionary comrades who hailed from the four corners of China ("Serve the People"); of the Canadian doctor Norman Bethune, who died while serving the Red Army and manifested the spirit of revolutionary internationalism ("In Memory of Norman Bethune"); and the "Foolish Old Man Who Moved the Mountain," who was willing to begin a task that would only be completed many generations in the future.[12]

These stories were true myths. They were not supposed to be critically discussed or analyzed. They were memorized (even by illiterate people) and recited over and over. They were supplemented by other stories of revolutionary heroes who had died serving the People—for example, Lei Feng, a humble PLA soldier killed in an accident, who had written in his diary that he just wanted to be a "small screw in the great locomotive of the Revolution." These messages were embedded in the Chinese People's identity through great political rituals carried out in incessant political campaigns. Some of these were rituals of struggle, in which "class enemies" were brought before screaming mobs and literally expelled from among the People. The People (*renmin*) consisted of all of the people in China with the exception of "class enemies"—and according to the logic of the Cultural Revolution, which began in 1966, one's class status was determined not only by one's socioeconomic origins but also by one's moral attitude. Even senior political leaders with impeccable Communist credentials (such as Liu Shaoqi and Deng Xiaoping) could be labeled "class enemies" because they had taken the "capitalist road." In the end, the final arbiter of who did or did not belong to the People was Mao himself, the "Great Sun Shining in Our Hearts."

Besides the rituals of struggle, there were also what I have called "ceremonies of innocence," in which people told stories about how sweet things were in the present in contrast with the bitterness of the past, sang songs in praise of Mao, and even danced a "loyalty dance" to the chairman. In doing so, they were ritually affirming a common transcendent unity as Chinese People, in spite of all of the things that divided them in this world.[13]

Can we call this "religion"? Heir to the defiance of early Christians facing the cult of Roman emperors, the common Western understanding of religion recoils against this. But the cult of Chairman Mao makes no sense in terms of the positivist categories of standard, secular modernization theory. It begs for some interpretation and explanation in terms of the categories of the sociology of religion, categories that try to make sense of ritual, myth, and transcendence. So, from a comparative-sociological perspective, we can say that the cult of Chairman Mao with his project to create a "new socialist person" was at least as much a religion as was the cult of Emperor Nero. It might even be fruitful to see analogies between the rise and fall of the cult of Chairman Mao and the rise and fall of the cult of Roman emperors. Both were attempts to unify a realm that had been fragmented into a pantheon of many gods. Both attempted to do this through the sacralization of the leader of an imperial state. Both eventually exploded into absurdity because of the hubris, cruelty, and ultimate pettiness and decadence of the rulers who were supposed to embody the holy. There are also similarities in the consequences of the downfall of such imperial cults. In Rome, the downfall of the imperial cult lead to a partial "secularization" of the emperorship. Constantine did not make himself divine, only the patron of Christianity, the new state religion, whose martyrs had died in defiance of emperors' pretenses to divinity. But in many parts of the empire, the Christian faith was embedded in the mundane social fabric of families and villages and imbricated upon local cults and local rituals—eventually provoking calls for purification and reform.

The story of China after Mao follows a roughly similar script. Political scheming and infighting between Mao and other top leaders sent the Cultural Revolution spiraling into chaos. Millions of Maoist devotees had their faith utterly shattered. For all of its effort to create a new socialist person, the Maoist state had only applied a thin veneer of ideology to community consciousness. Rural people, especially, learned to recite the slogans just as they sometimes recited Buddhist *sutras*, as efficacious incantations that need not be understood to bring good fortune *ex opere operato*. Other customary religious rituals were put aside—most Chinese gods aren't jealous gods who demand martyrdom— but not forgotten. Maoism had created a syncretistic, hybrid consciousness.

After Mao died and his coterie of close followers was overthrown, power was seized by Deng Xiaoping, whom Mao had once condemned as an arch-capitalist-roader. Deng launched a "reform and opening" whose goal was defined as the creation of a "small well-being" (*xiao kang*) society, as opposed to the great unity (*da tong*) that been the goal of the Maoist era. The Classic of Rites (part of the Confucian canon) had described "small well-being"—a life of this-worldly comforts achieved through care for family, friends, and neighbors—as a moral devolution.[14] It was what one had when the Great Dao was lost. One might call the Deng Xiaoping reforms a secularization of hope. The new regime would be legitimated on the basis of its ability to provide a comfortable standard of living for all. Deng Xiaoping, the paramount leader, did not claim the awesome power of the holy but just the practical wisdom of a skilled politician and economic manager. The leadership of the Chinese Communist Party was now at least partially secular.

As Deng Xiaoping's reforms got under way in the 1980s, however, there was no replacement cult to unify the nation. Into this vacuum flowed modernized versions of China's old-fashioned polytheism. Now, after Deng Xiaoping's reforms, the various religious forces in that pantheon have begun to reassemble in new ways. As Chinese society becomes much more porous, millions of farmers migrate to cities in search of work, although most still cannot obtain permanent urban residence, cannot gain access to the health and welfare institutions of the cities, and periodically have to return to their rural communities and depend on their families of origin for social and moral support (even as these families depend on the migrant laborers for economic support). The obligations of mutual support are expressed through ritual and myth.

But conditions of belief have changed, and one consequence is an abandonment of religious practice. Even then, the abandonment is often only partial. While sojourning in the city, for example, many migrant workers may have little interest in participating in religious rituals (with the exceptions of those who seek good luck). But when they return home, they may contribute to the construction of an ancestral temple and take part in community festivals.

Another consequence of the new conditions of belief, however, may be an openness to new religious movements, guided by visions that transcend family and locality. There were antecedents of these in so-called sectarian movements, such as the White Lotus movement, in premodern Chinese history. Now, with the help of globalized communications, these take on new forms and new force.

One set of new religious movements entails a search for physical healing and moral reform based on *qigong,* the evocation and channeling of the primordial energy that in traditional Chinese cosmology pervades the universe. The most notorious form of this *qigong* practice was the Falun Gong ("wheel of *dharma* practice"), which developed an elaborate ideology based on Daoist and Buddhist ideas to explain and guide such practices. But there were many other forms, including the *xianggong* ("fragrant practice") and the *zhonggong* ("middle practice"), which were popular in both rural and urban milieus. Such forms of spiritual practice transcended local corporate communities. They spread through ramifying personal networks that linked people throughout China and have even spread globally. As is well known, the Chinese government has found such large-scale religious organizations threatening and has ruthlessly moved to suppress them. Nonetheless, some of the movements have gone global. From havens in exile, the Falun Gong leaders spread their message and gain adherents around the world through the use of modern media. The message becomes increasingly polarizing and even apocalyptic: the Chinese Communist regime is an evil regime that must and inevitably will be destroyed.[15]

Another example of a disembedded religious movement is the rapid spread of Evangelical, mostly Pentecostal, Christianity in China (especially rural

China). Because the government inhibits systematic research into this topic, accurate statistics about the spread of Christianity are hard to come by. But it appears that the number of Christians has grown from less than 1 million to more than 50 million within the past thirty years. And some observers (mostly associated with Evangelical churches themselves) claim that the population of Christians has grown to more than 100 million.[16]

Much of the religious ferment is found in the countryside, which is still the primary home of more than 60 percent of the Chinese population. But new devotions are also taking hold among the urban population. The Falun Gong, after all, mainly attracted middle-aged city dwellers. It has become fashionable for city people to undertake various forms of Buddhist meditation, often in an attempt to overcome the various addictions that urban life brings. Among intellectuals, there is a renewed interest in "cultural Christianity," a search for ultimate meaning through study of Christian theology without necessarily any corresponding institutional affiliation. And around major university campuses, there is a lively array of "house churches," unregistered (and therefore officially illegal) Evangelical Christian fellowships.[17]

Thus, after Mao, Chinese society and culture have been churning with religiosity, much of it a hybrid mix of modern symbols (communicated through modern media such as the Internet and cell phones), polytheistic myths, and socially embedded rituals. This hybrid religious mix mirrors the contemporary Chinese political economy—an inconsistent, ad hoc assemblage of state socialism and globalized market economy, a blend of inconsistent pieces that makes little logical sense but for the time being seems to work to deliver economic growth and political stability.

An authoritarian government tries to impose some stability on the unstable mix of social and cultural forces boiling up beneath it. To maintain such order, it claims the capacity for religious discernment that Chinese emperors once had and popes still have today: the infallible authority to distinguish between true and false religion. Thus, in the fall of 2008, the Chinese Communist Party's Propaganda Department issued a video about the distinction between true and false religion. Religions such as Buddhism, Daoism, Catholicism, Protestantism, and Islam (at least, those parts of them that accepted surveillance and control from the government) were true religions because they promoted social harmony and respected modern science. The Falun Gong was a false religion, because it did neither.[18] It has been reported that some members of China's ruling elites have concluded that the Communist Party overreacted in 1999, when it launched a campaign to crush Falun Gong, but that the party cannot admit that it was wrong because this would destroy its myth of infallibility.

Meanwhile, local religious groups and local officials work out compromises and construct appropriate fictions to make the friction between state and society tolerable. "Underground" Christian communities build big churches in plain sight, and these are usually tolerated (as long as officials receive sufficient bribes), although they are sometimes subject to demolition when the government decides to make a show of toughness. Local temples get renamed as "museums" for preserving "nonmaterial cultural heritage," even as the temples continue to carry out the full range of religious ritual.[19]

Indonesia

The United States turned Indonesia from nonalignment to a stable pro-Western stance after 1965 by firmly backing the anti-Communist dictatorship of General Suharto. Under the Suharto regime, the religious diversity of the vast Indonesian archipelago—88 percent Muslim, but fragmented into a variety of Muslim sects, and significant populations of Christians, Hindus, and Buddhists, as well as practitioners of a wide variety of folk religions—was contained from the top down within an authoritarian political structure based on the national ideology of Pancasila, which kept the various approved religions from encroaching on one another while keeping all of them dependent on government patronage. In some areas of Indonesia, religious attachments are deeply intertwined with ethnic or regional attachments. One's religious identity is ascribed at birth, and religious rituals and practices render sacred one's ties to family or local community. Such ascriptive identities were deepened and solidified by the Suharto regime's policy of keeping each religious group in its place. Eager to maintain political stability in Indonesia, the United States endorsed this top-down effort to achieve "unity in diversity."[20]

Shifting balances of global power have led to a demise of this system of integrating Indonesia's diverse religious communities under a dictatorial regime. From the 1980s on, increased connections of Indonesia's Muslims with global Islamic movements led to movements of reform and revival. One side effect of this was the opportunity to carve out spaces for resistance to the Suharto dictatorship. After the Suharto dictatorship collapsed in 1998 (a victim of popular outrage caused by economic hardship brought about by IMF demands for "structural adjustment" of its economy in the wake of the Asian economic crisis), ethnic and religious tensions began to escalate. In the first five years of the twenty-first century, there was a brutal pogrom directed against Chinese in Java and violent clashes between Christian and Muslim communities in Ambon and Aceh. Since then, however, efforts of both political and religious mediation have maintained peace.

Even as religion reinforces local communal or ethnic identities, however, believers in Indonesia are becoming influenced by global movements of religious renewal, which encourage dissatisfaction with habitual adherence to local custom and inspire believers to seek more systematically reflexive understandings of universal truth. Thus, some Indonesian Muslims are inspired by global Islamist movements, Christians by global missionary movements, and Buddhists by international revival movements.

This creates the potential for even more harsh clashes among groups who are now filled with enthusiasm to undertake universal missions to promote their particular understandings of God. For example, some Christian groups (with help from networks of Christians around the world) are getting new energy by trying to win souls away from Islam, and Muslims (with connections to global Islamic movements) are excited by the possibility of expanding at the expense of Christianity. At the same time, ecumenical countermovements have arisen, such as Dian Interfidei, founded in 1991 by the late Dr. Sumartono, which has built networks of Muslims, Christians, Hindus, Buddhists, and Confucians and holds seminars and workshops that introduce participants to the history, theology, and ethics of the various traditions. The goal of all of this is to create a new kind of religious person, a person Sumartono called a "cross-religious person," who does not abandon a faith tradition for another but becomes an intentional religious citizen of the world.[21]

Such efforts at reconciliation and mediation seek to produce a hybrid form of religiosity, rather than a consistent devotion to one single truth. Such hybridity is perhaps the most viable way to knit together a public moral order in an archipelago with such diversity of communities interlaced with so many levels of economic development.

Taiwan

When it was defeated in the civil war and moved the entire government of the Republic of China (ROC) to Taiwan in 1949, the Nationalist Party (KMT) confronted the challenge of maintaining control over a hostile population. The KMT had taken control of the former Japanese colony after its return to Chinese sovereignty in 1945. Although they initially welcomed their new government, the native Taiwanese population soon became outraged by the KMT's corruption and incompetence. In response to widespread protests against KMT rule that had erupted in February 28, 1947, the government killed and arrested tens of thousands of Taiwan's indigenous elites. This "White Terror" continued throughout the 1950s.

The society that the KMT was trying to control was at the time mostly agrarian, a society of extended families in farming villages. The major source of community life in such villages was the local temple, with its deities and rituals celebrating the particularistic obligations of membership in ascribed communities. Unlike its counterpart, the Chinese Communist Party on mainland China, however, the KMT did not attempt to destroy local religious practices. But it did attempt to weaken them. For example it limited the scope of local festivals "in the name of improving frugality in folk sacrifices." At the same time, it provided various forms of patronage in order to co-opt the leaders of local temples. This produced a fragmented religious landscape that was conducive to the KMT's agenda of control. Local temples could not coalesce in ways that might have challenged the government.[22]

The KMT strongly suppressed any pan-Taiwanese religious movements, such as the Unity Way (*yi guan dao*). It established firm control over all national religious institutions, such as the Buddhist Association of the Republic of China, and denied them permission to establish educational and research associations that would enable such Chinese religions to develop sophisticated interpretations of their doctrines that might appeal to educated elites. The big exception was Christianity. Because some of the ROC's main American supporters during the early phases of the Cold War were former China Christian missionaries and since American ideology considered the United States to be a "nation under God," the ROC could hardly afford to suppress Christianity. It allowed Protestants and Catholics to establish major universities, and it allowed Protestant and Catholic missionaries to be conduits of American foreign aid, especially of food and medicine. Most of the Christian missionaries had been displaced from the Chinese mainland. They spoke Mandarin, the official language of all of China, rather than the Taiwanese prevalent among the native population. In general, they had cooperative relationships with the KMT government and did not threaten its rule.

There were inevitably cracks in this hybrid program of co-optation and suppression. Pan-Taiwan movements such as the Unity Way went underground and continued to grow despite government suppression. Maverick Buddhist leaders established the core of new organizations in out-of-the-way locations beyond the range of the government's surveillance. Christian groups that had sunk deep roots in Taiwan during the Japanese colonial period, such as the Taiwanese Presbyterian church, benefited from the general protection offered to Christian churches, even though they were important sources of native Taiwanese consciousness, including a Taiwanese form of the "theology of liberation." These openings to new forms of religious practice and new vehicles for religious identity would become important as the KMT's authoritarian structures began to crumble.

The crumbling began in the 1970s as the result of both local and global factors. Chiang Kai-shek, Taiwan's dictator, died in 1975. During this time period, Taiwan was beginning the transition from an agrarian to a predominantly urban industrial society. Taiwan's key patron, the United States, was beginning a rapprochement with the PRC and switched its diplomatic relations from the ROC on Taiwan to the PRC on mainland China in 1979. An opposition to the KMT monopoly government began to grow, and it could not be completely suppressed with the heavy-handed tactics of earlier decades. Finally, in 1987, the KMT government of Chiang Ching-kuo—Chiang Kai-shek's son—lifted the martial law that had served as the justification for autocratic rule. The way was opened for multiparty elections and for the development of a lively civil society dominated by voluntary associations of Taiwan's middle classes.

Modernizing religious movements played a vital role in the constitution of this civil society. During the 1970s, under the KMT's radar screen, "socially engaged" Buddhist movements began to develop and propagate a universalistic vision of compassionate religious action to improve this world. With the end of martial law, some of these movements exploded in membership among middle classes eager for new forms of social affiliation. Especially important were Tzu Chi (the "Buddhist Compassionate Relief Association"), Buddha's Light Mountain, and Dharma Drum Mountain. Although there were monastic communities at the core of these associations, they developed large lay organizations and made sophisticated use of modern media to propagate their messages. Although most of them did not take part in partisan politics, they played an important political role in the transition to democracy. They smoothed out some of the rough edges of demanding civil societies and helped to nurture some of the civic virtues that make democracy possible.[23]

These Buddhist organizations are globally expansionist. By the 1990s, they had begun to spread branches throughout the world. They carry out works of charity and education throughout East and Southeast Asia (including, for Tzu Chi, the PRC and North Korea) and, to a lesser but important degree, in Europe and the Americas, even the Middle East and Africa. In most such places, they form branch communities of devout laypeople drawn from local Taiwanese diasporas. Although they preach a religion of universal love and peace, they do so with a Taiwanese accent. They are an important way of representing the best qualities of diplomatically isolated Taiwan to the rest of the world and thus play an important role in the spread of Taiwan's "soft power."

One indication that this globalization of Taiwan religion is at least indirectly connected with the growth of Taiwanese nationalism is the fate of the Christian churches. At the same time that socially engaged, middle-class Buddhist—and also to some degree Daoist—groups had begun explosive growth, most Christian churches had started to decline in membership and vigor, with the notable exception of churches such as the Taiwanese Presbyterian church, which had long been associated with Taiwan nationalism. The Christian churches have perhaps been on the decline precisely because they had earlier gained special privileges through the connection between the KMT government and the United States during the Cold War.[24]

Patterns

Charles Taylor's framework for understanding the advent of a "secular age" in the North Atlantic world offers a useful first draft for understanding the place of religion in Asian modernity. Modern Asian countries have secular states, but despite efforts of some states to destroy all religion, they still have religious societies. New cultural conditions of belief give religion a different valence from what it had in premodern times.

This framework is only a first draft. While presenting a secular face to the West, many Asian states have what could only be described as religious pretentions. This is true of the Chinese state under Mao and to a lesser degree even under Mao's successors. The Indonesian state under Suharto was the guardian of a sacred canopy that was supposed to encompass Indonesia's major religions. Taiwan's state has taken a secular turn with democratization, but it still relies on religion to provide public stability and generate international recognition.

Although many people in these and most other Asian societies continue to practice religion, it is a different kind of religion from that in most Western societies—more a matter of ritual and myth than belief and deeply embedded in the social, economic, and political life of local communities. It is part of the public life of local communities. Religion has not undergone the transition from public practice to private belief that Taylor discerns in the West.

Finally, although in an age of social mobility and global communication, Asian religions are practiced under new cultural conditions of belief, the result is somewhat different from what Taylor describes in the North Atlantic world. There, modern people are presented with a stark choice between understanding existence through an "immanent frame" or a "transcendent frame." In many Asian societies, including China, the immanent and the transcendent are much more mixed up in various hybrid combinations. In accord with widespread traditions of syncretism, many people believe and practice many things at once.

But modern conditions of belief also impel some believers to purified forms of religious practice. This is something like what happened in Europe during the Reformation, as Taylor describes it. When it happens in the unsteady world of Asia today, this is not necessarily a good thing—at least, for those who love peace, predictability, and order.

A purification of practice usually involves an attempt to recover the axial-age roots of local traditions.[25] Buddhists, Daoists, Muslims, and Christians seek purified versions of their practice. This means rejecting the accretions of tradition and of all those practices that embed religion in local communities with particularistic loyalties. Rituals are deemed to be efficacious not *ex opere operato* but on the strength of the interior conviction that they express. Religious practice gets transformed into religious faith—a personal belief in world-transcending ideals that demand universal loyalties.

These purified faiths grow up in parallel with older, community-embedded practices, but they often claim continuity with them. Often, they gain inspiration and energy through connection with global religious movements. At least when they are appropriated by ordinary people, these forms are never purely universalistic. Under conditions of belief where one can never take one's religious practices for granted, religious believers yearn for signs that their beliefs are on the right track. One important sign is that their kind of faith is expanding. There is thus a strong missionary impulse in all of these new universalizing movements.

Fearing that such faiths could inspire independent social movements, most Asian governments used some combination of suppression or co-optation to prevent such universalizing faiths from flourishing and to keep them firmly within bounds. The collapse of such political structures after the Cold War has given a new impetus to such globalizing faiths. They were attractive at least partly because they were once forbidden fruit. With the crumbling of political barriers that once confined universalizing, missionizing religions in place, there is now a global scramble for souls.

Depending on the particular contexts in which they develop, new expansionist religious movements can lead to serious social and political conflict or can provide resources for reconciliation and healing. In China, the scramble for souls leads to relatively more conflict. In general, the movements direct their adherents to otherworldly concerns, rather than to this-worldly political activity. But some of their beliefs give the government cause for concern, especially eschatological beliefs. The Falun Gong believes that a great millennial transformation is coming in which the good will be saved and the evil punished. Many Chinese Pentecostal Christians believe in premillennialism, which holds that the end times are coming soon and that those who have accepted Jesus will be raptured up to heaven, while the world undergoes great tribulations, which will end with the triumphant second coming of Christ. The government also worries about the public-health implications of practices such as faith healing. Thus, it steps up efforts of surveillance and sometimes suppression. But eschatological religious movements organized through ramifying networks cannot easily be suppressed. If the government punishes particular leaders, the act only inspires members who revere martyrdom. If the government cuts off a part of the network, other shoots can quickly grow up elsewhere. The networks cannot easily be co-opted. Members who expect otherworldly salvation do not need anything that the government has to give them. Despite government attempts to stop such beliefs and practices, the networks that foster them are expanding very rapidly.

In Taiwan, though, the socially engaged Buddhist movements I have described here seem to have made a positive contribution toward healing the tensions of a democratizing society. Their ideologies stress generous acceptance of all people, and they motivate their members to build a better world through sustained, gradual effort. By dampening the tensions that have come from Taiwan's many conflict-producing forms of identity politics, the Buddhist movements have helped shore up the shaky foundations of Taiwan's democracy. In this context, the universalization of religious visions has led to confluences of care, rather than conflict.

In Indonesia, on the other hand, the record is mixed. In places such as Aceh, newly energized Islamist movements have clashed with newly energized Christian missionizing movements. (Such clashes, of course, often are intertwined with clashes over the distribution of natural resources—in Aceh's case, petroleum.) Fortunately, these clashes have subsided in recent years with the help of astute efforts at political compromise and reconciliation. In the long run, though, sustainable reconciliation may involve a religious dimension. This is the promise—and the challenge—of groups such as Dian Interfidei that seek through ecumenical dialogue and creative common ritual to create "cross-religious persons."

Internationally, the new scramble for souls can lead to intensified conflict, especially since the universalistic, world-transcending impulses often get submerged quickly into worldly nationalisms, enlarged, ambitious communities created by expanded imaginations. The newly universalizing impulses do not have to lead to conflict, however. As we have seen, much depends on the content of the traditions out of which they arise and the specific context in which they evolve.

Notes

1. Charles Taylor, *A Secular Age* (Cambridge, Mass.: Harvard University Press, 2007), 1–22.

2. Ibid., 1.

3. Ibid., 3. Taylor says that even in countries such as Britain and the Scandinavian countries that have established churches, the state connections with those churches "are so low-key and undemanding as not really to constitute exceptions."

4. John Meyer, J. Boli, G. Thomas, and F. Ramirez, "World Society and the Nation State," *American Journal of Sociology* 103, no. 1 (1997): 144–181.

5. Richard Madsen, *China and the American Dream* (Berkeley: University of California Press, 1994).

6. According to the 2007 Chinese Spiritual Life Survey conducted by Fenggang Yang and the Institute for Religion at Baylor University, in partnership with the Horizon Research Consultancy Group, with a nationally representative sample of more than 7000, only 15 percent of the Chinese population could be classified as "pure atheists." Fenggang Yang, "Explaining the Failure of the Greatest Secularization Experiment in Human History," paper presented at the ISA XVII World Congress of Sociology, Gothenburg, Sweden, 2010.

7. Kenneth Dean, "Local Ritual Traditions of Southeast China: A Challenge to Definitions of Religion and Theories of Ritual," in Fenggang Yang and Graeme Lang, eds., Social Scientific Studies of Religion in China (Leiden: Brill, 2011), 133–162.

8. Richard Madsen, *China's Catholics: Tragedy and Hope in an Emerging Civil Society* (Berkeley: University of California Press, 1998).

9. Taylor, *A Secular Age,* 24–43.

10. David K. Jordan and Daniel L. Overmyer, *The Flying Phoenix: Aspects of Chinese Sectarianism in Taiwan* (Princeton, N.J.: Princeton University Press, 1986).

11. Daniel H. Bays, "The Growth of Independent Christianity in China, 1900–1937," in Daniel H. Bays, ed., *Christianity in China: From the Eighteenth Century to the Present* (Stanford, Calif.: Stanford University Press, 1996), 307–316.

12. Richard Madsen, *Morality and Power in a Chinese Village* (Berkeley: University of California Press, 1984).

13. Ibid.

14. Hanlong Lu, "To Be Relatively Comfortable in an Egalitarian Society," in Deborah S. Davis, ed., *The Consumer Revolution in Urban China* (Berkeley: University of California Press, 2000), 124–141.

15. David Palmer, *Qigong Fever* (New York: Columbia University Press, 2008).

16. Yu Jianrong, "Religious Demography and House Churches 2008," cited in Compass Direct News Service, July 3, 2009. For higher estimates, see David Aikman, *Jesus in Beijing* (Washington, D.C.: 2003).

17. Fenggang Yang, "The Red, Black, and Grey Markets of Religion in China," *Sociological Quarterly* 47 (February 2006): 93–122.

18. See http://www.kaiwind.com.

19. Gao Bingzhong and Ma Qiang, "From Grass-root Association to Civil Society: A Close Look at the Organization of a Temple Fair," in Fenggang Yang and Graeme Lang, eds., op. cit., 195–226.

20. Douglas E. Ramage, *Politics in Indonesia: Democracy, Islam, and the Ideology of Tolerance* (London: Routledge, 1995).

21. Clare B. Fischer, "Democratic Civility: Interfidei and the Work of Social Harmony in Indonesia," University of California Pacific Rim Research Project, 2004.

22. Paul Katz, "Religion and the State in Post-War Taiwan," in Daniel L. Overmeyer, ed., *Religion in China Today* (Cambridge: Cambridge University Press, 2003), 93–97.

23. Richard Madsen, *Democracy's Dharma: Religious Renaissance and Political Development in Taiwan* (Berkeley: University of California Press, 2007).

24. Ibid.

25. The term "axial age" was coined by Karl Jaspers to refer to the period in the first millennium BCE when visions of a universally transcendent reality were created in Israel, Greece, India, and China. Karl Jaspers, *The Origin and Goal of History* (New Haven, Conn.: Yale University Press, 1953).

12

Smash Temples, Burn Books: Comparing Secularist Projects in India and China

Peter van der Veer

Much sociological attention and imagination have gone into, first, the development of the secularization thesis and, more recently, its dismantling. José Casanova has been in the forefront of this dismantling with his important book *Public Religions in the Modern World*.[1] He has argued that the three propositions of the secularization thesis—namely, the decline of religious beliefs, the privatization of religion, and the differentiation of secular spheres and their emancipation from religion—should be looked at separately in a comparative analysis. He comes to the conclusion that comparative historical analysis allows one to get away from the dominant stereotypes about the United States and Europe and to open a space for further sociological inquiry into multiple patterns of fusion and differentiation of the religious and the secular across societies and religions. This means moving away from teleological understandings of modernization. Or perhaps better, it means questioning that telos by recognizing its multiplicity and its contradictions. Casanova's intervention can be understood as building on the Weberian project of comparative and historical sociology but going beyond it by avoiding the reduction of civilizations to essences that can be compared and by avoiding a Hegelian evaluation in terms of "lack" or "deficit" in the world-historical process of modernization and rationalization. Eisenstadt's proposal to speak about multiple modernities similarly creates space for such a post-Weberian project, but it has to be asked what the role of secularity and secularism is in the production of these multiple modernities.[2]

My attempt here to examine secularism in India and China in a comparative historical analysis accepts this post-Weberian perspective, but I want to make a few introductory observations. The first is that the project of European modernity should be understood as part of what I have called "interactional history."[3] That is to say that the project of modernity, with all of its revolutionary ideas of nation, equality, citizenship, democracy, and rights, is developed not only in Atlantic interactions between the United States and Europe but also in interactions with Asian and African societies that are coming within the orbit of imperial expansion. Instead of the oft-assumed *universalism* of the Enlightenment, I would propose to look at the *universalization* of ideas that emerge from a history of interactions. Enlightened notions of rationality and progress are not simply invented in Europe and accepted elsewhere but are both produced and universally spread in the expansion of European power. This entails a close attention to the pathways of imperial universalization. Examining secularism in India and China uncovers some of the peculiarities of this universalization by showing how it is inserted into different historical trajectories in these societies.

The second observation is that with all of the attention to secularization as a historical *process,* there is not enough attention to secularism as a historical *project.* Casanova has in his recent writings rightly drawn attention to the importance in Europe of secularism as an ideological critique of religion, carried out by a number of social movements.[4] Secularism as an ideology offers a teleology of religious decline and can function as a self-fulfilling prophecy. It is important to examine the role of intellectuals in furthering this understanding of history but also their relation to sources of power: state apparatuses and social movements. Secularism is a forceful ideology when carried by political movements that capture both the imagination and the means to mobilize social energies. It is important to attend to the utopian and, indeed, religious elements in secularist projects in order to understand why many of these movements seem to tap into traditional and modern sources of witchcraft, millenarianism, and charisma. Much of this remains outside the framework of discussions of secularization, but the cases of India and China show us how essential this is for understanding the dynamics of religion and the secular.

Third, I would like to point out that the religious and the secular are produced simultaneously and in mutual interaction. As many scholars have been arguing, religion as a universal category is a modern construction with a genealogy in universalist Deism and in sixteenth- and seventeenth-century European expansion.[5] One needs, therefore, to analyze how the categories of "religion," "magic," and "world religion" are universalized. This is also true for the category of the secular that has a genealogy in church-world relations in European history but is transformed in modernity both in Europe and elsewhere.

To analyze Indian and Chinese secularism, one has to start not with the interactions between India and China, which are very few and relatively insignificant in the modern period, but with their interactions with Europe and especially Britain. It is imperialism that forces Indians and Chinese to interpret their traditions in terms of the category of "religion" and its opposition to "the secular." While there are multiple histories involved here, it is the imperial context that produces a remarkably similar trajectory which essentializes Hinduism, Buddhism, Islam, Christianity, Daoism, and even Confucianism into comparable entities, subjects of the new, secular discipline of comparative religion or science of religion, which attempts to emancipate itself from Christian theology. One also has to look carefully at ways in which European notions of science and its opposite, of progress and backwardness, capture the imagination of Indian and Chinese intellectuals and how this relates to the creation of the modern state. I will first deal with secularism in China, then with secularism in India, in order to show what kinds of problems secularist projects attempt to address and what kinds of violence their interventions entail.

Secularism in China

"Smash temples, build schools" (毀庙办学 huimiao, banxue) is a particularly telling slogan that was used in a campaign against temple cults and religious specialists during reforms in late Ching at the end of the nineteenth century. According to the reformists, led by Kang Youwei (1858–1927) and to an extent supported by the emperor, China had to modernize quickly, and this had to be done by promoting education and getting rid of religious superstition. These two elements belonged together, since education should train people in modern, rational thought, while superstition and magical thought should be discouraged. Before the Communist victory in 1949, a number of campaigns, first in late Imperial China and afterward in the Republic, destroyed or "secularized," according to one estimate, half a million existing temples.[6] What the Communists did after 1949 was, to a very great extent, a continuation of these campaigns. While one might have expected that the nationalists in Taiwan, with their Confucian nationalism, would have had a fundamentally different policy toward religion from that of the Communists, the opposite is, in fact, the case. Until the late 1960s, the nationalists kept religious activities under very tight control. All of these campaigns against religion should have produced a secular China, but the contrary is true. In Taiwan, religious activities are all over the place, and with the loosening of the tight controls over religion in the PRC, we see religious activity flourishing everywhere. This paradox can be understood by closely examining the nature of these secularist campaigns.

Secularism as an ideology and as a practice in China is in the first place an anticlericalism. Anticlericalism has deep roots in Chinese history, but at the end of the nineteenth century, it gains the attention both of the popular media and of intellectuals who grapple with modern, Western ideas. Intellectuals, such as Liang Ch'i-ch'ao (1873–1929), Chang Ping-lin (1869–1936), and Ch'en Yin-k'o (1890–1969), separated Buddhism and Taoism from their clerical roots and made them into national moralities that could serve the modernization of China. Buddhist leaders such as Taixu (1890–1947) and Daoist modernists such as Chen Yingning (1890–1969) made great efforts to bring their religions under the rubric of secular nationalism. The popular press also was opposed not to religion as such but to Buddhist and Daoist clerics, who were described not only as ignorant buffoons but also as criminals, drunkards. gluttons, and, foremost, sexually debauched. Temples and monasteries were described in the emergent press in the late Qing period as dungeons for sexual debauchery, places of great pornographic potential. Clerics are portrayed in stories as visiting houses of pleasure. The main theme here is, in fact, that monastic celibacy and techniques of self-improvement are a *disguise* for a lawless, unbridled sexuality.[7] This theme of sexual scandal is certainly crucial in the emergence of the popular press in the nineteenth century everywhere, but the Chinese focus on clerics recalls especially the pornography that was printed in the Netherlands but distributed in revolutionary circles in France in the decades before the French Revolution. Here we see a genealogy of *laïcité* in the underbelly of the Enlightenment that connects religion with sexuality in ways that are never made explicit but that are, in my view, also behind the social energy in anti-Islamic gestures today in France.

Clerics in China were also seen as dangerously violent, since their ascetic disciplines and martial arts that inflicted violence on their own bodies could be turned against others for criminal or rebellious purposes. Obviously, this theme gained prominence in the late nineteenth century during the failed Boxer Rebellion. Clerics were able to connect to secret societies that threatened the state monopoly of violence. They combined fighting techniques with magic that made the believers think they were invincible and thus extremely dangerous. The failure of the Boxer Rebellion, however, showed Chinese intellectuals that there was no future in using magical means to defeat the imperial powers. Again, the theme of *delusion* and *disguise* comes up here with the notion that the illiterate masses are led into meaningless and ultimately fruitless violence by cunning clerics.

Besides a form of anticlericalism, Chinese secularism is a form of scientism and rationalism. From a nineteenth-century enlightened and evolutionary perspective, it pitches scientific rationality against magical superstition. Secularism is thus a battle against the misconceptions of natural processes that keeps the illiterate masses in the dark and in the clutches of feudal rulers and clerics. The term for superstition (迷信 *mixin*) comes from Japanese, as do many other terms that are employed in the discourse of modernity, such as the term "religion" (宗教 *zongjiao*) itself. Using these neologisms makes a distinction between religion, which contributes to the morality of the state and superstition, which is detrimental to modern progress. These views are shared by intellectuals of all persuasions, including the nationalists and the Communists, but also by many reformist religious thinkers. This is both a discursive and an institutional shift as an aspect of the transition from the ancient regime of the Qing empire to the modern Republic. The traditional system of three teachings (*sanjiao*)—Confucian, Buddhist and Daoist—in which Confucian state ritual defined the framework for the other two, was transformed in the Republic by the notion that there were five acceptable world religions: Buddhism, Taoism, Catholicism, Protestantism, and Islam. Confucianism was kept outside of this arrangement, because it was considered to be both national instead of global and in essence secular rather than religious. Confucian intellectuals did try to turn it into a secular civil religion, but this met with little success outside of the nationalist elite. These religions, which are officially recognized today, are being organized along the models of Christianity in nationwide associations that are ultimately controlled by the state. What remains outside of this is what is often called popular belief (民间信仰 *minjian xinyang*), namely, all of those cults that are, in fact, closely connected to Buddhist and Daoist ideas and practices but are not controlled by the traditional Buddhist or Daoist orders or by the modern state-engineered associations. Moreover, many of the Buddhist and Daoist local cults are hard to transform into nationwide associations. Especially Daoism had been deeply intertwined with local cults, or, as is sometimes said, Daoism is "the written tradition of local cults."[8] The opposition between officially approved religion and local forms of superstition gives authorities a great space for controlling and repressing all kinds of religious expressions.

Anticlericalism and scientism together were deeply connected to Western, enlightened ideas about progress, in which magic had to be replaced by scientific rationality and by moral religion as a basis of national identity. Major currents of Western thought, such as social Darwinism, neo-Kantianism, and Marxism, were absorbed in China. Not only did prescriptive thought about society come to stand in the light of rationality, but also descriptive social sciences, such as sociology and anthropology, lost their ability to describe the effects of these ideologies on society, since they could not distance themselves from them. Intellectuals played an important role in the secularist projects of nationalizing and rationalizing religion, and, crucially, they were part and parcel of large-scale state interventions to produce a modern, national identity. While Buddhism and Taoism were to some extent sources for the creation of national religion, Confucianism was itself being considered as already both national and rational. The attempts to transform Confucian traditions into a civil, national religion were extremely interesting as a form of social engineering, but they ultimately failed, largely because Confucian teachings could encompass Daoist and Buddhist teachings but not the social energy that local Daoist and Buddhist cults could mobilize.

I do not want to detail the sordid history of state persecution of clerics and destruction of temples both before and during Communist rule. I only want to draw attention to the fact that under communism, the antisuperstition and anticlerical campaigns were combined with antifeudalism campaigns. The 1950s saw not only the brutal elimination of millenarian movements such as Yiguandao (一贯道) but also the destruction of feudalism and thus the redistribution of temple land and temple property, secularization in its original sense. Mao, as a good Marxist, predicted the decline of religion as part of the creation of a socialist China in the following words: "The gods were erected by peasants. When the right time comes, the peasants themselves will throw away these gods with their own hands."[9] But as matter of fact, Mao and the party did everything to destroy the gods, but the peasants did everything to rescue them.

One of the great puzzles of China today is not that it proves the secularization thesis wrong but that despite a century of secularism, religion has not been destroyed. In fact, we see everywhere in China a more open performance of religious rituals. This raises a number of issues. First of all, if the secular and the religious are produced simultaneously, what has happened to the religious under secularist attack? What is the nature of Chinese religion today? Has it been hiding, and does it now come out of the closet, and what does that mean? Second, how can we explain that secularism has not been able to fulfill its world-historical task? Third, what may be the future of secularism in China under the current conditions of religious expansion?

First, then, what is the nature of Chinese religion and secularity today? On the one hand, we find a general acceptance in China of the idea that religion is not important to the Chinese, that the Chinese have always been rational and secular and with modernization are even more so. This view is not only prevalent among intellectuals but is also more generally held. And on the other hand, there is a widespread interest in religious practices, in visiting shrines during tourist trips, in religious forms of healing. Both in cities and in the countryside, communities are rebuilding their temples and have started awkward negotiations with the authorities to be allowed to perform their ceremonies again. Religious activity seems to be embedded in a fully secular life, in which job insecurities, health, and desire for success and profit create a demand for divine support. With the decline of the iron rice bowl of the state, this demand has only increased. The same intellectuals who deny the importance of religion pray for their families' welfare wherever they can. The chain of memory, to use Hervieu-Leger's term, however, seems to have been broken and needs to be patched up.[10] In general, people who engage in rituals (rather than theology or philosophy) are not very knowledgeable about them, but in China this is quite extreme. This is enhanced by the fact that the clergy has been largely exterminated or so much brought under control of the party that they have lost their liturgical bearings. This situation in itself gives a lot of space for new religious movements in which laypeople play an important role, such as the many *qigong* movements.

Second, how do we explain the failure of a century of systematic destruction of Chinese religious life? One answer lies in the millenarian nature of Maoism itself. The party absorbed quite a lot of the social energy that is available in religious movements. Yiguandao was a huge movement with millions of followers at the moment of the Communist take-over, but it was destroyed quickly after the killing and torturing of its leadership without inciting huge rebellions. One of the reasons was that the Communists, like the Yiguandao, also promised paradise on earth and seemed to have a better go at it. Mass mobilization (群众 运动 *qunzhong yundong*) for the transformation of self and society has a central place both in Chinese religion and in Maoism. Studying and especially reciting Mao's writings again recall religious chanting. The finding and expelling of class enemies and traitors follow quite precisely the trappings of Chinese witch-craft beliefs and exorcism, even in the giving of black hoods as symbols of evil to the accused.[11] The practice of public confession likewise continues religious practice.

Third, what is the future of secularism in China? As I already indicated, sec-ularity is well established in China in daily life, as well as in people's self-understanding. Secularism as repression of religion is also widely accepted by the general public if a movement, such as the Falun Gong, is shown in government propaganda to threaten the social and political order. It is much less tolerated as such when local authorities try to intervene with manifesta-tions of popular religion. In fact, in many cases today, the authorities are pleased with religious activities that draw outside money. Secularism is also cer-tainly still the frame in which clerics have to operate. The Buddhist and Daoist associations are still largely controlled by the state.

Secularism in India

At first sight, it may look as if Chinese and Indian secularisms are totally dif-ferent, since in China secularism is antireligious, while in India secularism is a form of state noninterference in religion. Such a view is not untrue, but it is instructive to compare Chinese and Indian secularisms. Secularism in India has a number of elements in common with Chinese secularism, although the mean-ings of these elements are structurally altered by the nature of the caste system and of interethnic and intercommunal relations. In Hinduism, Brahmans are the most important clerics, but anticlericalism has deep roots in Brahmanical thought. Priests who perform a religious service to the community and are paid for that in gifts are looked down upon by Brahmans who devote themselves to studying the Vedas. This strand of anticlericalism fuels many of the reforms of the large temples in South India, in which powerful middle-class laymen demand that ignorant priests are reeducated to learn Sanskrit and ritual perfor-mances. More generally, the Brahman caste as a whole came under attack in the nineteenth and twentieth centuries with the rise of explicitly secularist move-ments, especially in South and West India. Jyotirao Phule (1827–1890) began a movement in Maharashtra against the alleged exploitation of low castes by Brahmans. E. V. Ramaswamy Naicker (1879–1973), also known as Periyar, founded a social respect movement in Tamil Nadu that became the basis of an anti-Brahman Tamil nationalism. He connected his anticlericalism with a theatrical atheism that was expressed in publicly burning sacred books, such as the Sanskrit Ramayana. The sources of this anticlericalism that evolved in the case of Periyar in atheism were twofold: Christian missionaries had for a long time vilified Brahman priests and their rapacity and ignorance in their project to convert especially tribals and low castes away from Hinduism. This rhetoric is taken over by the anti-Brahman movements. It is combined with racial and linguistic theories, developed by Orientalist scholars such as Friedrich Max Muller, which distinguish the Aryan invaders from the indigenous low castes. Brahmans are then shown to be really different from, say, the (South Indian) Dravidians and are portrayed as exploiting the indigenous peoples. We can already see that Indian anticlericalism is decidedly different from Chinese anti-clericalism because of the connection between caste and religion. It is the Brahman caste that comes under attack, and Brahman priests are taken to be the symbols of that caste. On the other hand, both in China and in India, the main issue is the introduction of modern egalitarianism in a hierarchical society and thus the connection between feudalism and religion.

We also find scientism and rationalism in India as an element of secularism, as we did in the Chinese case. However, already in the nineteenth century, Indian intellectuals did not emphasize the opposition between science and religion but instead emphasized the scientific nature of indigenous traditions. Secularist attacks on traditional religion were rare, although attempts to purify religion from so-called superstition and to show the scientific foundations of religion were taken up by reformers in a number of proto-nationalist and nationalist movements. Rational religion, as a major current in these reform movements, offered a home to intellectuals who wanted to reflect on developments in science from Hindu traditions. A good example is J. C. Bose (1853–1937), a renowned physicist and plant physiologist, whose work on electrical waves and plant consciousness was animated by attempts to understand the unity of nature from the perspective of the Hindu philosophical school of Advaita Vedanta, in which Bengali intellectuals had been trained.[12] The social network formed by such scientists and Hindu reformers such as Swami Vivekananda shows how the development of scientific and religious thought was interwoven. Philosophers such as Henri Bergson and Aurobindo embraced Bose's vitalistic science eagerly. While Chinese intellectuals also found rationality and science in some religious traditions, especially in the field of medicine, there is a much stronger sense than in India that progress can only be made by separating science from magic and by destroying magic.

Secularism in India emerges in the context of a secular colonial state that is professedly neutral toward religious divisions in society. The British in India are deeply concerned with projecting an image of transcendent neutrality. They were at least partially successful in doing this, since Indians today often see *dharma-nirapeksata,* the indigenous term indicating the neutrality of the state as a distinctive character of Indian civilization, rather than a colonial invention. Sometimes, for example, by Gandhi, this neutrality is more positively interpreted as *dharmasamabhava*, the equal flourishing of religion under the state's neutrality. After the Mutiny of 1857, the British were afraid to be seen interfering with the religious activities and sensibilities of their Indian subjects. This implies that the colonial state had to hide its modernizing and secularizing interventions in society under rhetoric of neutrality because it derived its legitimacy not from India but from a democratic process in Britain. This neutrality, however, is interpreted by Indian nationalists as forms of divide-and-rule, especially in the area of Hindu-Muslim relations. The state is thus condemned as pseudo-secular, an argument that is later revived by Hindu nationalists against the postcolonial government. The postcolonial state derives its legitimacy from democratic elections in India and is thus even less able than its predecessor, the colonial state, to hide its interventions in society and religion, such as the Temple Entry Acts and the abolition of untouchability, under the cloak of neutrality.

Since the colonial state is secular in the sense of being neutral toward religion, this gives wide scope for connecting religion with anticolonial nationalism. Anticolonial nationalism in India draws deeply from religious sources, both ideologically and organizationally. In earlier work, I have made a distinction between a moderate, pluralist vision of the Indian nation and a radical vision that wants to promote a singular religion as the core of national identity.[13] The pluralist vision is the ideological foundation of India as a secular state, as distinguished from the radical vision of Muslims separatists that was the foundation of Pakistan as a "homeland for Muslims," as well as from the radical vision of Hindu nationalists who fight for a Hindu India. The moderate vision has always been part of the secular ideology of the Congress Party, a party which ruled India for most of postindependence history.

Congress found itself confronted with two major problems. First of all, Hindu-Muslim antagonism was a major threat to the creation of an Indian nation. This problem became increasingly crucial in the struggle for independence, and secularism was conceived as the answer to it. Second, Indian society was marked by one of the most pervasive systems of inequality in the world, which was religiously sanctioned by Hindu traditions. Again, secularism was conceived as an answer to this. While state interventions were recognized as crucial to the transformation of Indian society into a modern nation, Congress leaders agreed that large-scale violence should be avoided. A major argument in developing Indian secularism was made by Gandhi when he pleaded for nonviolence and tolerance. However, except for a brief period, Gandhi was not officially a member of Congress leadership but a moral exemplar outside of party politics. Gandhi's moral example could be an element in producing secular tolerance, but such an example is not enough for the daily business of regulating social life. After independence, the modern state could not refrain from intervening in society.

Critics of Congress secularism today, such as T. N. Madan and Ashis Nandy, have understood the rise of communalism in India as a backlash against a long-term campaign of an interventionist state to impose secularism on a fundamentally religious society.[14] While their emphasis on state power is correct, their criticism of Nehru's Congress seems fundamentally mistaken. Nehru's position was that the state should not attempt to make India a monocultural society in which the minorities would feel alienated. Pragmatically, Congress adopted the role of neutral arbiter of religious difference, just as colonial administrators had done. Separate civil codes for Hindus and Muslims, which had developed in the colonial period were continued in secular India. Potential sources of violent conflict, such as the disputed site of Babar's Mosque in Ayodhya, had to be controlled and managed, rather than fundamentally solved. In fact, it is this policy to which the BJP, a Hindu nationalist party, today objects. It does not claim that an antireligious secularism has dominated Indian society but that it has been a pseudo-secularism that has given religious minorities special benefits in order to get their votes. So, it argues not that secularists had launched an attack on the religious traditions of Indian society but that it had left minority traditions intact for electoral reasons. The BJP claims to be secular, but it has launched campaigns to destroy mosques that had been built on Hindu sites and rebuilt Hindu temples, arguing that the majority religion on which the nation is built is Hinduism and that the only traditions that had to be dealt with by the secular state were those of the (Muslim and Christian) minorities. Nehru's cautious but sometimes ambivalent policies toward multiculturalism and the ways they came to be challenged in the 1970s and 1990s show the importance of the definition of state secularism.

The limitations of Congress secularism that tries to avoid violence in its interventions in society are clear from the failure to get rid of untouchability and caste hierarchies. Ambedkar, one of the great untouchable leaders of Congress and architect of India's secular constitution, came to the conclusion that the secular, liberal state could not solve the problems of untouchability that were deeply embedded in codes of honor and respect. Early in his career, he demonstrated his stance against Hinduism by burning Hindu law books in public; at the end of his life, he decided to convert to Buddhism in order to escape from the Hindu caste system.[15] In a very original manner, he came to grips with the dualism of redistribution (class) and recognition (caste). His conversion shows that religious conversion can address these issues sometimes better than conversion to secular ideologies such as socialism or liberalism.

Conclusion

Secularisms in India and China are a product of the imperial encounter. Certainly, there are precolonial traditions of anticlericalism and antisuperstition in India and China. These do not disappear, but they are transformed by the imperial encounter. That encounter itself is crucial, and it is fundamentally different in India and China. In India, the colonial state has to perform a certain secular neutrality toward religion because of its colonial nature. It avoids an outright attack on the beliefs and customs of the natives, while masking its fundamental interventions in society by cloaking it them neutrality. In China, reformers within the Qing dynasty and later in the Republic do not have to perform this neutrality while introducing Western notions and enforcing them in society. Chinese reformers can therefore call for the destruction of temples, whereas Indian reformers call for open access to temples for untouchables in temple-entry agitation and burn books to challenge Brahman hegemony. In India, religion becomes the basis of resistance to the colonial state, and it has to be reformed and modernized in order to make it part of the morality of the modern state. The Indian discussion, then, is primarily about reforming Indian traditions, not about destroying them. The Indian reformers who want to destroy Hinduism as a form of oppression are certainly important, but they do not dominate the nationalist movement. In fact, their political position derives precisely from their social marginality as untouchables, as in the case of Ambedkar, or from their regional marginality, as in the case of the Tamil leader Periyar. They may burn sacred texts but certainly not temples.

The secularisms found in India and China are emancipatory projects, and by their very nature, they are violent. The transition to modernity is obviously violent, it does violence to traditional arrangements, and therefore the relation of secularism to violence is crucial. The secular mobilization of social energies in China is incredibly violent, discursively and practically. The Chinese secular utopia is strikingly millenarian and magical and thus reintroduces the traditional elements that it wants to eradicate but in another configuration. The mobilization of social energies in India is also violent, but it is not secularism that produces antireligious violence. On the contrary, Indian secularism tries to stem the violence between religious communities. The secular utopia, as is clearest in Gandhi's campaigns, is thus one of the peaceful coexistence of equal religions within a neutral state. Nonviolence is therefore the center of Gandhi's attempts to create a secular India. It is not only the emancipation from the colonial oppressor that has to be nonviolent but, even more, the emancipation from inequality and communal opposition that has to be nonviolent.

The Chinese and Indian cases show us that secularism is not simply antireligious in these societies, although there are antireligious elements in it, but that it simultaneously attempts to transform religions into moral sources of citizenship and national belonging. The masses have to be reeducated to realize their emancipatory potential, and religions can be used as state apparatuses to perform this reeducation. One does not have to smash temples to build schools; one can also use temples to educate the people. In the regime of secularism, religions are nationalized and modernized. While religion is an important element in the production of these imaginaries, it can never be entirely contained by the secularist frame. It may produce linkages outside of the nation-state as world religions do; it may produce alternative visions of the moral state and thus become dangerous for secularist control, as in millenarian movements that have emerged in China after the demise of Maoism. Precisely because secularism is a project and not a process, it is bound to be incomplete and is bound to produce contradictions that it itself cannot explain.

Notes

1. José Casanova, *Public Religions in the Modern World* (Chicago: University of Chicago Press, 1994).

2. Shmuel Eisenstadt, ed., *Multiple Modernities* (Edison, N.J.: Transaction, 2002).

3. Peter van der Veer, *Imperial Encounters: Nation and Religion in India and Britain* (Princeton, N.J.: Princeton University Press, 2001).

4. José Casanova, "Religion, Secular Identities, and European Integration," *Transit* 27 (2004): 1–15.

5. Talal Asad, *Genealogies of Religion* (Baltimore, Md.: Johns Hopkins University Press, 2004).

6. Vincent Goossaert, "The Beginning of the End for Chinese Religion?" *Journal of Asian Studies* 65, no. 2 (May 2006): 307–336.

7. Vincent Goossaert, ed., "*L'anti-clericalisme en Chine*," Special Issue, *Extreme-Orient/Extreme-Occident* 24 (2002).

8. Kristofer Schipper, *The Daoist Body* (Berkeley: University of California Press, 1993), 6.

9. Cited in Thomas Dubois, *The Sacred Village: Social Change and Religious Life in Rural North China* (Honolulu: University of Hawaii Press, 2005).

10. Daniele Hervieu-Leger, *Religion as a Chain of Memory* (New Brunswick, N.J.: Rutgers University Press, 2000).

11. Barend ter Haar, *Telling Stories: Witchcraft and Scapegoating in Chinese History* (Leiden: Brill, 2006).

12. Gyan Prakash, *Another Reason: Science and the Imagination of Modern India* (Princeton, N.J.: Princeton University Press, 1999).

13. Peter van der Veer, *Religious Nationalism: Hindus and Muslims in India* (Berkeley, University of California Press, 1984).

14. T. N. Madan, *Modern Myths, Locked Minds: Secularism and Fundamentalism in India* (Delhi: Oxford University Press, 1997). Ashis Nandy, "An Anti-Secularist Manifesto," *India International Quarterly* 22, no. 1 (Spring 1995): 35–64.

15. Gauri Viswanathan, *Outside the Fold* (Princeton, N.J.: Princeton University Press, 1999).

13

Freedom of Speech and Religious Limitations
Talal Asad

For many years now, there has been much talk in Europe and America about the threat to free speech, particularly whenever Muslims have raised the issue of blasphemy in response to some public criticism of Islam. A recent crisis was the scandal of the Danish cartoons. A decade and a half after the Salman Rushdie affair, the old religious denunciation of blasphemy had reared its head again among Muslims in Europe and beyond, seeking to undermine hard-won secular freedoms. Or so we were told. There were angry protests and some violence on one side, many affirmations of principle and expressions of revulsion on the other. The affair was discussed largely in the context of the problem of integrating Muslim immigrants into European society and related to the global menace of "radical Islam." Coming after the attack on the World Trade Center and the London bombings, the cartoon scandal was linked to a wider discourse: the West's "war on terror," a conflict that many saw and still see as part of an intrinsic hostility between two civilizations, Islam and Europe—the one religious, the other secular. Because Islam has no notion of freedom of thought, so it was said, it has no conception of free speech.

The attitudes displayed in the cartoon affair by Muslims and non-Muslims were quite remarkable. However, this chapter is neither an apologia for Muslim reactions nor a criticism of those who defended the publication of the cartoons. I want to think about blasphemy claims through some moral, political, and aesthetic problems that have crystallized in the form of the idea of free speech. So I will have less to say about traditions of Islamic thought and behavior than about liberal secularity. And when I do talk about those traditions, it will not be to criticize or defend them but to think through them as a way of reflecting on the modern secular condition we all inhabit.[1]

My starting question is this: If blasphemy indicates a religious limit transgressed, does it really have no place in a free, secular society?

I ask this because modern secular societies *do* have legal constraints on communication. There are laws of copyright, patent, and trademark and laws protecting commercial secrets, all of which prohibit in different ways the free circulation of expressions and ideas. Are property rights in a work of art infringed if it is publicly reproduced in a distorted form by someone other than the original author with the aim of commenting on it? And if they *are* infringed, then how does the sense of violation differ from claims about blasphemy? My point here is not that there is no difference but that there are legal conditions that define what may be communicated freely in capitalist societies and that consequently, the flow of public speech has *a particular shape* by which its freedom is determined.

There are laws that prohibit expression in public and that appear at first sight to have nothing to do with property, for example, indecency laws and laws relating to child pornography, whose circulation is prohibited even in cyberspace. The reader might say that the first set of laws (copyright, etc.) has to do with the workings of a market economy and so with property, whereas the second (pornography) is quite different because it deals with morals. But although infringement of the laws relating to the latter evokes the greatest passion, both sets of constraint are clues to the liberal secular ideal of the human, the proper subject of all rights and freedoms. *Both sets of limits articulate different ways in which property and its protection define the person.* In a secular society, these laws make it possible to demarcate and defend oneself in terms of what one owns, including, above all, one's body. Thus, liberal conceptions of "trespassing" on another's body and of "exploiting" it are matters of central concern to laws regulating sexual propriety. They also relate to slavery, a nonliberal form of property, for modern law holds that one cannot transfer ownership of one's living body to another person or acquire property rights in another's body. Freedom is thus regarded as an inalienable form of property, a capacity that all individual persons possess in a state of nature, rooted in the living body. (Women have only very recently achieved that capacity in liberal societies.) There are, of course, exceptions to this principle of absolute ownership in one's body, some old and some new; for example, suicide—destroying oneself—is not only forbidden but also regarded by most people in liberal countries with horror, even though the person is said to be the sole owner of the body he or she inhabits and animates. This exception to self-ownership is often explained by humanists as a commitment to "the dignity of human life," a principle that is not seen as conflicting with the demands of war.

In theory, the self-owning secular subject has the ability to choose freely what to do, a freedom that can be publicly claimed. The reality, as we have seen, is more complicated. Famously, there are two subject positions—one economic and the other political—whose freedom is invested with value in liberal democratic society, both of which are linked to a conception of the freely choosing self and the limits that protect it. Thus, as a citizen, the subject has the right to criticize political matters *openly and freely* and to vote for whichever political candidate he or she wishes but is obliged to vote *in strictest secrecy*. There is a paradox in the fact that the individual choice of candidates must be hidden to be free, while critical speech to be free must be exercised in public. This difference actually indicates that while the former takes for granted that the citizen is embedded in social attachments and memories, the latter assumes that he or she is an abstract individual with universal rights. This contradiction runs through liberal discourse on democracy.

As an economic individual, the subject is free to work at, spend, and purchase whatever he or she chooses and has the right to protect his or her property legally. Marx was surely right when he pointed out that in modern liberal societies, the freedom of the worker to sell his or her labor is the condition of capitalist power—and, as some might put it today, the freedom to consume is a source of corporate profit. What he failed to point out, however, is that *that* freedom, in turn, may limit the liberty of the citizen.

Social constraint (and, as Freud has made us aware, psychological constraint) lies at the heart of individual choice. It seems probable, therefore, that the intolerable character of blasphemy accusations in this kind of society derives not so much from their attempt to constrain as from the theological language in which the constraint is articulated. Theology invokes dependence on a transcendental power, and secularism has rejected that power by affirming human independence. But *that* freedom from transcendence is secularism's *ideological claim*. In fact, political and economic dependence is massively present in our secular world, transcending the subject or agent's ability to know and to act.

I am not making the banal argument that free speech in a liberal society is necessarily conditional. I want to ask what the particular patterns of liberal restriction can tell us about ideas of the *free* human. The self-owning individual is a famous liberal idea,[2] and although there are limits to what one may do to oneself, there is greater latitude in relation to one's material property. The ownership of property doesn't only establish immunity in relation to all those who don't own it. It also secures one's right to do with it what one wishes—as long as no damage is done to the rights of others. The right to choose how to dispose of what one owns is integral to the liberal subject—and the subject's body, affections, beliefs, and speech are regarded as *personal property* because they constitute the person.

I will return to this point about discourse as personal property below, but first, I want to introduce a concept central to Islamic traditional thought but not to liberal thought, or at least not central in the same way: the idea of *seduction*.

In liberal society, rape, the subjection of another person's body against his or her wish for the purpose of sexual enjoyment is a serious crime, whereas seduction, the mere manipulation of another person's desire, is not. The first is violence; the other is not. In the latter case, no property right is violated. Compare this with ancient Greece, where seduction was a more serious crime than rape because it involved the capture of someone's affection and loyalty away from the man to whom they properly belonged.[3] What this indicates is not only that the woman's viewpoint did not matter legally in the ancient world but also that in liberal society, seduction is not considered a violation—except where minors are concerned. In liberal society, seduction is not merely permitted, but it is positively valued as a sign of individual freedom. Every adult may dispose of his or her body, affections, and speech at will as long as no harm is done to the property of others. That is why the *prohibition* of seduction between adults—that is to say, of the exchange of sexual signals—is regarded as a constraint on natural liberty itself. Such a prohibition is normally regarded as of a piece with the curtailment of free speech.

So, how clear is the liberal distinction between coercion and freedom that underlies the notion of free speech? There is, in fact, a large area between these two opposites in which everyday life is lived. The game of seduction—in which both consent and coercion are ambiguously present—is played in this area. And it is in this area, too, that our everyday understanding of liberty is deployed, making our sense of its restriction—whether caused by internal compulsion or external coercion—less fixed and therefore less predictable.

In liberal democracies, the individual as consumer and as voter is subjected to a variety of allurements through appeals to greed, vanity, envy, revenge, and so on. What in other circumstances would be identified and condemned as moral failings are here essential to the functioning of a particular kind of economy and polity. Innumerable studies have described how television as a medium of communication seeks to shape viewers' choices of commodities and candidates. (Film, which is so central to popular experience, works to seduce the audience even where no political or commercial message is intended.) To seduce is to incite someone to open up his or her self to images, sounds, and words offered by the seducer in order to lead him or her—whether half-complicitly or unwittingly—to an end first conceived by the former.

Let me take up again the question of copyright, which marks out some of the limits to freedom of speech in liberal society, because it brings up the question of how artistic creation is related to law. In a detailed account of the legal disputes over the perpetuity of copyright in late-eighteenth-century England, Mark Rose traced how the idea of incorporeal property (the literary work) emerged through the concept of the author as proprietor. To begin with, those who argued for perpetual copyright did so on the basis that the author had a natural property right to something he had created. When opponents of unlimited copyright insisted that ideas as such couldn't be considered property and that copyright should therefore be treated as a limited personal right exactly like a patent, they were countered by the argument that the property being claimed was neither the physical book, which could be purchased, nor the ideas communicated but something made up of style and sentiment. "What we here observe," Rose writes, "is a twin birth, the simultaneous emergence in the discourse of the law of the proprietary author and the literary work. The two concepts are bound to each other."[4] That is to say, the work of art and its creator define each other.

I will return to the question of aesthetics below. Here I want to emphasize that the law of copyright is not simply a constraint on free communication but a way of defining how, when, and for whom literary communication (one of the most valued forms of freedom in modern liberal society) can be regarded as free, creative, and inalienable. A person's freedom to say whatever he or she wants, how he or she wants, depends in part on a particular notion of property. It implies a particular kind of property-owning subject whose freedom of speech rests on the relationship of what is spoken to truth—that is, to what is truly created and offered to the public. In a splendid study on the beginnings of copyright law in early-modern England, Jody Greene has demonstrated in detail that "owning one's book was synonymous with owning up to it," that having one's authorial rights recognized legally was combined from the beginning with accepting liability for its contents. Copyright was not only an expression of possession but also a condition of control.[5]

Thus, while cultural historians have already written at length on the Romantic vocabulary of freedom and the nation, historians of literature have now begun to trace the Romantic roots of the concept of "the literary work"—and thus of "the work of art"—through the mutual shaping of freedom and constraint.[6] To what extent the general valuation of "freedom of speech" also has those roots remains to be investigated. Such a genealogy would reveal it not as the demand of secular reason but as the aim of a Romantic project in which the drive for freedom produces, paradoxically, a strengthening of power.

Let me now turn from this brief discussion of freedom of speech as a property of the liberal subject to blasphemy as a necessary way of breaking religious restrictions.

The French historian Alain Cabantous once noted that when Jesus claimed for himself a divine nature, this was condemned as blasphemy. That blasphemy led to his death, and the death was followed by resurrection. "In this one respect," Cabantous wrote, "blasphemy *founded* Christianity."[7] We might add here that every new tradition, whether it is called religious or not, is founded in a discursive rupture, which means through a kind of violence. Cabantous doesn't say this, but others have done so. Some have even made the argument that the disruption of blasphemy may be seen as the attempt by a lesser violence to overcome a greater.[8] This may sometimes be so, but I will say only that it does not follow that every blasphemous utterance is therefore a new founding, a new freedom; blasphemy as an act of violence (whether by the weak or by the powerful) may be little more than an *obsession*, in which the act serves as the reinstantiation of an established genre, the restoration of a style *that itself has no foundation and no content*. In other words, blasphemy may simply be violence masquerading as creative rupture.

At any rate, Cabantous could have observed that in the foundation of Christianity, the blasphemy was not perceived as such by *believers*. From a Christian point of view, the *charge* of blasphemy was merely an expression of disbelief. And although that disbelief eventually led to Christ's death, Christians have historically held that the violence done to him was part of a divine plan. Did Christ *know* that his unbelieving listeners would take what he said as blasphemy because his crucifixion was essential to the project of human redemption? He was, after all, both man and God, and that could not, therefore, have been absent. Strictly speaking, of course, what founded Christianity was not blasphemy itself but a new narrative of sacrifice and redemption—a story of martyrdom (witnessing) that would be, for believers, the door to eternal life.

The truth, Jesus told his followers, will set you free. The unredeemed human condition is lack of freedom; free speech—truthful speech—releases the human subject from his or her servitude. The truth must be spoken openly, even if those who do not possess it regard speaking it freely as blasphemy. In this context, a modern New Testament scholar writes: "In spite of the opposition of those who are unbelievers, of those who criticize the apostle [John], the Christian may speak freely because he knows Him who conquers all opposition, because he knows that wonderful communion with God which transcends everything in the world."[9] Of course, the liberal principle of free speech does not depend on the proviso that speech to be free must be literally true, but the Christian idea of truth as the necessary outcome of speaking and listening *freely* helps, I think, to explain why that principle has come to be thought of as "sacred."

Blasphemy has a long history in Christianity—a sinful act that is liable to worldly punishment. In England, it became a crime in common law only in the seventeenth century, at a time when national courts were taking over from ecclesiastical courts and the modern state was taking shape. Common law did not distinguish between heresy (the holding of views contrary to church doctrine) and blasphemy (the utterance of insults against God or his saints), as medieval canon law had done. So, from the seventeenth century on, the crime of blasphemy was entangled with the question of political toleration and the formation of the modern secular state. During the next two centuries, differences of legal opinion arose regarding whether public statements lacking defamatory intent or expressed in moderate language were liable to criminal prosecution. It was felt that scholarly debate and discussion needed protection, even if they appeared to be "irreligious." This led to increasing legal attention being paid to the language (i.e., the style and context) in which "blasphemy" appeared, regardless of how disruptive of established truth it was.

The tendency to emphasize manner of expression—to see blasphemy in terms of form rather than content, of style rather than substance—had some interesting legal consequences: vulgar working-class speech was less protected than the polite speech of the middle and upper classes. A scholar who has studied blasphemy trials in nineteenth-century England calls them "class crimes of language" on account of the class bias that they indicate.[10] That an exceptionally large number of them took place during the period when a national state and class system began to be formed is itself of some significance. For this reason, I am inclined to say that, rather than simply *indicating* class bias, the identification of blasphemy helped to *constitute* class difference in which asymmetrical power was repeatedly inscribed. I want to suggest that we see the charge of blasphemy in these cases not as a discursive device for suppressing free speech but as one indicator of the shape that free speech takes at different times and in different places, reflecting, as it does so, different structures of power, subjectivity, and truth.

What, in contrast, do Islamic ideas of blasphemy tell us about our modern liberal assumptions about free speech? Obviously, not all Muslims think alike, but questions about Islamic ideas of blasphemy are aimed at a moral tradition. And even that tradition contains divergences, tensions, and instabilities that cannot be attributed to an entire "civilizational people." Nevertheless, I will draw on aspects of that tradition in order to explore further some liberal ideas about freedom. One of these is the assumption that the Islamic tradition is rooted in a more restrictive system of ethics, that it does not allow the freedom (especially the freedom of speech) provided and defended by liberal society. Although there is something to this, the simple notion of liberty as something that is either present or absent seems to me unsatisfactory.

But first, let's consider the term "blasphemy." Is there an equivalent in the Islamic tradition? Although the Arabic word *tajdīf* is usually glossed in English as "blasphemy" and is used by Christian Arabs to identify what in European religious history is called "blasphemy," Arabic speakers, in the case of the Danish cartoons, did not (as far as I am aware) employ it. Of course, there are other words that resonate with the English word "blasphemy" (e.g., *kufr*, "apostasy, blasphemy, infidelity"; *ridda*, "apostasy"; *fisq*, "moral depravity"; and *ilhād*, "heresy, apostasy"), but these were not, to my knowledge, used in response to the Danish cartoons. When the World Union of Muslim Scholars made its statement on the cartoons affair, for example, it used the word *isā'ah*, not *tajdīf*. And *isā'ah* has a range of meanings, including "insult, harm, and offense," that are applied in secular contexts.[11] The World Union stated that it had waited so that the efforts exerted by numerous Islamic and Arab organizations, and by several states, to elicit appropriate expressions of remorse from Denmark could be given time to succeed, but this was to no avail. Therefore, "the Union will be obliged to call upon the millions of Muslims in the world to boycott Danish and Norwegian products and activities."[12] Thus, the right to campaign freely against consumer goods confronted the right to criticize beliefs at will: one social weapon faced another, each employing a different aspect of the modern idea of freedom. If physical violence was sometimes used by some of those who advocated a boycott, we should not forget that a commercial boycott is always a kind of violence, especially if it is infused with anger, because it attacks people's livelihood. The European history of boycotts (the refusal to purchase commodities) and strikes (the withholding of labor), with all of their accompanying physical violence, has been a story of the definition of modern rights. And yet in this case, many European commentators described the two quite differently: the one as an expression of freedom, the other as a violent attempt at restricting it and as yet another sign of the conflict between civilizations having opposed values.

More interesting than the defense of free speech as an absolute value in this case was the argument that it was a good thing that pious Muslims felt injured, because being hurt by criticism might provoke people to reexamine their beliefs—something vital both for democratic debate and for enlightened ethics. This point, in contrast with the first, valorizes the *consequence* of free speech rather than the act itself. The criticism of questionable (religious) beliefs is presented as an obligation of free speech, an act carried out in the service of education toward the truth, making truth the door to liberty. Many even in post-Christian Western society agree with the Christian claim that the truth makes one free (John 8: 32).

That this is not an Islamic formulation emerges from a brief examination of the widely discussed trial of Nasr Hamid Abu Zayd, a professor at Cairo University, for apostasy (*ridda*) because he had advocated a radically new interpretation of the revealed text of the Qur'an.[13] Of course, both *truth* and *freedom* are valued in the Islamic tradition, but they are not tied together quite as they are in Christianity. (It may be pointed out in passing that the many cases of apostasy in the contemporary Middle East that have received much publicity in the West are actually relatively recent and closely connected with the formation of the modern nation-state, a modern judiciary, and the rise of modern politics. In this context, one may recall the burst of blasphemy trials in nineteenth-century England to which I referred earlier.) My question, therefore, is whether these trials should be seen solely in terms of the suppression of freedom. What do they tell us about the secular idea of the human subject?

In a book that deals with the Abu Zayd case,[14] the Islamist lawyer Muhammad Salīm al-'Awwa emphasizes that the shari'a guarantees freedom of belief: "Freedom of belief means the right of every human being to embrace whatever ideas and doctrines he wishes, even if they conflict with those of the group in which he lives or to which he belongs, or conflict with what the majority of its members regard as true."[15] He goes on to say that no one may exert pressure to get another to reveal his or her religious beliefs—that is to say, the shari'a prohibits the use of inquisitorial methods. The right to think whatever one wishes does not, however, include the right to express one's religious or moral beliefs publicly with the intention of converting people to a false commitment. Such a limitation may seem strange to modern liberals, for whom the ability to speak publicly about one's beliefs is necessary to freedom. This ability is, after all, one aspect of "the freedom of religion" that is guaranteed by secular liberal democracies. Al-'Awwa is aware of this, and he cites two Qur'anic verses that seem to guarantee freedom of religion: *lā ikrāha fi-ddīn*, "there is no compulsion in religion" (2: 256), and *faman shā'a falyu'min wa man shā'a falyakfur*, "let him who wills have faith, and him who wills reject it" (18: 29). But for the Islamic tradition, what matters is the Muslim subject's social practices—including verbal pronouncements—not that person's internal thoughts, whatever these might be. In contrast, the Christian tradition allows that thoughts *can* commit the sin of blasphemy and should therefore be subject to discipline: thoughts are subject to confession.[16]

According to al-'Awwa, publishing one's thoughts changes their character, makes them into publicly accessible signs. "To publish something," he quotes an old saying, "is to lay oneself open to the public."[17] It is one thing to think whatever one wishes, he argues, and quite a different thing to publish those thoughts, because the latter always has a social objective. So the point at issue here is not a threat to *social* order (as many argued in the affair of the Danish cartoons) but evidence of the publisher's relation to the *moral* order. In a well-known book published in Lebanon in 1970, responding to the accusation of apostasy against the Syrian philosopher Jalal Sadiq al-'Azm for his famous *Naqd al-fikr al-dīnī* (The Critique of Religious Thought) of 1969, Shaykh 'Uthman Safi makes a similar distinction but without reference to Islamic religious authorities. His approach, instead, is to make an explicit distinction between "natural, innate freedom" and freedom as defined and limited by the law. The individual may give free rein to his thought and imagination, accepting or rejecting as he wishes within the limits of what he contemplates. "When these possibilities of freedom that the human being enjoys remain within his soul, the law, especially, cannot interfere with them except when the belief is moved from secrecy to broad daylight [*min as-sirr ila al-jahr*]."[18]

The principal issue in the Abu Zayd case is not the correctness or otherwise of "belief" but the legal and social consequences of a Muslim professor's teaching ideas that were said to be contrary to Islamic doctrine.[19] In the classic shari'a position, the strength of personal conviction is said to be a matter between the individual and God. At any rate, disbelief incurs no legal punishment; even the Qur'an stipulates no worldly punishment for disbelief. In the classical law, punishment for apostasy is justified on the grounds of its political and social consequences, not of entertaining false doctrine itself. Put another way, insofar as the law concerns itself with disbelief, that is as a matter not of its propositional untruth but of the open repudiation of a solemn social relationship. Legally, apostasy (*ridda, kufr*) can therefore be established only on the basis of the functioning of external signs, including public speech or writing, publicly visible behavior, never on the basis of inferred or internal beliefs that have been forcibly or deceptively extracted. There has, incidentally, been considerable disagreement in modern Islamic history over the criteria for determining apostasy, as well as whether and, if so, how it should be punished. Thus, one of the medieval collections of *hadith*, by Bukhari, records a statement by the Prophet Muhammad that apostates must be killed; but another canonical collection, that by Muslim, declares this statement to be inauthentic. The debate has continued in modern times.

The crucial distinction made in liberal thought between *seduction* and *forcible subjection* to which I referred above, in which the former is legally permitted and the latter penalized, is here absent—at least in al-'Awwa's argument. In the Islamic tradition, to seduce someone is to connive at rendering him or her unfaithful, to make him or her break those existing social commitments that embody standards of truth.[20] Even in medieval Christendom, the term *infidelitas* could be used not only in relation to personal departures from authorized doctrine but also, in a secular sense, to breaking a contract. "Unfaithfulness" in this worldly sense now has a quaint ring about it in modern secular society and relates only to sexual seduction. Infidelity is not quite the vice it once was.

In Islamic theology, seduction is a matter of great concern—and not merely in the sexual sense. The Qur'an contains numerous words that can be glossed as "seducing" and "deluding"—among them the verbal roots *fatana*, *rāwada*, *gharra*. *Fatana* (from which comes the familiar noun *fitna*) always has the sense of "temptation and affliction as a testing," of "persecution, treachery, or social strife."[21] Muslim theologians and jurists assumed that seduction in all of its forms was necessarily dangerous not only for the individual (because it indicated a loss of self-control) but for the social order, too (because it could lead to violence and civil discord). They were wrong, of course, because they didn't know about market democracy, a system that thrives on the consumer's loss of self-control and one in which politicians, prompted by the corporations, have learned to seduce their audiences in the context of liberal democracies.

In market democracy, it is possible to control belief—as well as emotions, attitudes, and desires that go with it—in ways other than brainwashing. As long as we recognize that coercion takes many forms, seduction may be counted as one of them, because seduction can be interpreted as the dynamic between internal compulsion and external capture, between desire and power. As many critics have pointed out, the violence of modern capitalism consists precisely in its capture of the desires of consenting subjects.

In contemporary secular democracies, it would seem that while the state must be denied the power to coerce belief, the market may employ that power in its own fashion. Whether this coercion has any relevance for *religious* belief depends on how the self-described believer (and the state to which he or she is subject) defines "authentic religion" and its place in social life. It also depends on whether one wants to protest against it or to excuse it. Market and political seduction in modern secular society are not always irresistible, of course. But suppose that the resistance, to be effective, requires stubborn religious convictions. It is not clear whether democrats will want to delegitimize that resistance in principle because it conflicts with a secular political order or to accept it only on the liberal grounds of "free speech." But whether those grounds define that freedom as *instrumental* (whose value derives from what it can achieve) or as *absolute* (which justifies itself) is not always clear. In other words, one cannot be certain whether the secular right to blaspheme (and the right to criticize or create publicly) rests on pragmatism or on transcendence, as I tried to show in my examination of the reasons given for defending the Danish cartoons.

It is in liberal universities that "freedom of speech" in the form of public critique has come to be asserted as an absolute value. *Professional* critique, however, has less to do with the right of free speech than with the reproduction of intellectual disciplines and the aesthetics and ethics that go with them. Jon Roberts and James Turner, in *The Sacred and Secular University*, have described the emergence of the modern university in the United States, together with its secular culture, starting in the last quarter of the nineteenth century. They recount how the marginalization or exclusion of formal "religion" in the American university was accompanied by an emphasis on research, professionalization, and specialization and how these things, in turn, led to a fragmentation of the traditional map of knowledge, which had until then been articulated in a theological language. It was in this situation that the humanities eventually emerged out of the traditions of moral philosophy and philology and restored coherence to knowledge while according it a distinctive "religious" aura. One consequence was that a less sectarian, less doctrinal idea of religion became part of a liberal culture and therefore part of its understanding of criticism. "This new edition of liberal education had two key elements," they write. "The first was to acquaint students with beauty, especially as manifest in 'poetry' broadly conceived.... A second element thus entered the humanities: a stress on continuities linking the 'poetry' of one era to that of succeeding periods and ultimately our own." Roberts and Turner then describe how there developed a sharper sense of imparting the moral essence of European civilization to students in higher education through the study of great literature and great art. Thus, the idea of European civilization became fused with great aesthetic achievements, both literary and artistic. Literary and art criticism accordingly became the disciplinary means to celebrate those achievements.[22]

During the last few centuries, modern powers have encouraged and used the developing sciences and humanities to normalize and regulate social life—and that has included legitimizing a particular kind of disciplinary criticism. Critique that is integral to the growth of *useful* knowledge is part of a process of power wielded by the imperial state and by transnational corporations. Thus, while the freedom to criticize is represented as being at once a right and a duty of the modern individual, its truth-producing capacity remains subject to disciplinary criteria, and its material conditions of existence (laboratories, buildings, research funds, publishing houses, computers, tenure) are provided and watched over by corporate and state power to ensure that citizens can be *useful*. For reasons that are not difficult to understand, people in the academy are rarely prepared to challenge the controlling limits set by modern transcendent power.

So how does the scandal of the Danish cartoons fit into what I've said so far? The cartoons are, clearly, at once politics and art. For those who denounced them, the cartoons represented a political provocation against Muslim immigrants; for their defenders, the publication of the cartoons constituted at once an act of political freedom and an act of artistic creation. The political claim is clear enough here, but what is the connection of artistic creation to it? The answer may lie in the fact that aesthetics is particularly valued in industrial capitalist society because to the extent that it is useless, it is free from external constraint.

"Most aesthetic concepts are theological ones in disguise," Terry Eagleton writes:

> The Romantics saw works of art as mysteriously autonomous, conjuring themselves up from their own unfathomable depths. They were self-originating, self-determining, carrying their ends and raisons d'être within themselves. As such, art was a secular version of the Almighty. Both God and art belonged to that rare category of objects which existed entirely for their own sake, free of the vulgar taint of utility.... It was no accident that this exalted vision of art grew stronger with the advent of industrial capitalism. The artwork was the enemy of industrial production because it was an example of creativity rather than manufacture. That it was fast becoming just another market commodity made this all the more poignant.... Perhaps the artwork was the one thing left that had a value rather than a price, and didn't exist for the sake of something else.... As the idea of God was gradually ousted, art was on hand to fill his shoes. Like him, it was a repository of absolute value. Like him, too, it was transcendent, universal, unified, all-seeing and all-sympathetic.[23]

Eagleton does not say this, but the sanctity of modern art depends partly on its having been reimagined: from art as the eighteenth-century mirror of nature to art as the twentieth-century creator of reality. It is this, I think, that enables us to understand why the influential literary critic, cited by Eagleton, declared that poetry (broadly conceived) was the path to secular salvation—because all of life has now becomes material for an expanding redemptive project. And although Eagleton does not mention the Danish cartoons or Rushdie's *Satanic Verses*, it is clear that this view of aesthetics gives them a unique justification.

Eagleton's conclusion is that aesthetics never acquired the powerful political role religion once did because whereas devotion to God involved millions, art remained the preoccupation of the very few. This is suggestive, but surely Eagleton takes too much for granted in equating art with elite theories of "the beautiful" that have no political aspiration, because this ignores the enormous investment the modern state has in the enchantment of the nation. And it is not only fascist theatricality or socialist realism that I have in mind here. My thought is that while we may all be enmeshed in a global economy, the killing machines are essentially national. Whether the killing machine faces the threat of "Islamic terrorism" in Palestine, Afghanistan, Iraq, Somalia, or Iran, it seems to require an aesthetics and erotics of war. TV viewers and combat soldiers—as well as the designers of IBMs and other modern weaponry—are encouraged to experience the seductive, horrific beauty of violent destruction. And bear in mind that the killing machine destroys not only the political conditions of free speech but the human subjects of freedom themselves. Understandably, liberal opposition to it is minimal and ineffective.

So here is my question: Does the modern secular aversion to the category of blasphemy derive from a suspicion of political religion? Yet it is specifically *Islam* that is the object of hostility, and even the head of the Catholic church has learned to express it as pointedly as any rigid laicist. How to account for this? Islamophobia is a symptom, not an explanation. All phobias point to an uncontrollable and irrational anxiety on the part of the subject, in this case of European non-Muslims imagining European Muslims as the bearers of a religion, a culture, a race. Islamophobes often refer to the general fear of "Islamic terrorism." But isn't there something odd here? For while terrorists typically work in quiet secrecy, the scandal surrounding blasphemy charges are full of public noise.

And now consider some figures. According to the first Europol report on terrorism published in 2007, of the 498 acts of terrorism that took place in the European Union during 2006, Islamists were responsible for only one. The largest number was carried out by Basque separatists. Yet more than half of those arrested on *suspicion* of terrorism were Muslims. Almost all media in Europe ignored these figures while playing up "the threat of Islam." What accounts for this voluble silence? One commentator to whom I presented these figures observed that they might, in fact, show that it was the justified suspicion of the European police that had forestalled Islamic terrorists. The reader may recognize that attitude as the essence of paranoia, for paranoiacs have a tendency to make accidental concatenations into meaningful signs of a threat (or the forestalling of a threat) toward themselves. So I am inclined to say that Islamophobia is rooted, in part at least, in paranoia, in a pathological sense of danger whose final elimination is never possible.

Paranoia is the condition that some literary historians have, interestingly, identified as integral to modernist aesthetics.[24] It denotes a range of affective states, including horror, loathing, and nausea, generated by uncontrolled migration, by movement not from Europe to non-Europe but from non-Europe to Europe. As such, aesthetics, no less than theology, is a dimension of all modern politics, national and international. Modernism—the aesthetics accompanying modernity—engages with powerful feelings of visceral disgust. And it is in *mimesis* that modernism finds one of the most potent sources of revulsion and of paranoia, revulsion because modernism values only independence of judgment and despises imitation, paranoia because modernism seeks to penetrate disguises that make things (people, actions, words) appear normal and innocent and shows them to be really meaningful and hostile.

Whatever one may think is the reason for European revulsion against Muslim immigrants, I want to end with some questions that seem to be raised by the idea of blasphemy. Why is it that aggression in the name of God shocks secular liberal sensibilities, whereas the art of killing in the name of the secular nation, of democracy, does not? Can this differential response tell us something about the way secular and religious violence and experiences of beauty and horror come together to constitute the model secular subject? Apart from the sense of sanctity attaching to the idea of free speech, what accounts for the undercurrent of powerful emotions of loathing and fear?

Notes

1. An earlier and rather different version of this chapter was published as "Reflections on Blasphemy and Secular Criticism," in Hent de Vries, ed., *Religion: Beyond a Concept* (New York: Fordham University Press, 2008). A similar version has also appeared more recently as "Free Speech, Blasphemy, and Secular Criticism," in Talal Asad, Wendy Brown, Judith Butler, and Saba Mahmood, *Is Critique Secular?* (Berkeley: University of California Press, 2009).

2. The classic study on this question is C. B. Macpherson, *The Political Theory of Possessive Individualism* (Oxford: Oxford University Press, 1962).

3. K. J. Dover, "Classical Greek Attitudes to Sexual Behaviour," in M. Golden and P. Toohey, eds., *Sex and Difference in Ancient Greece and Rome* (Edinburgh: Edinburgh University Press, 2003), 117–118.

4. Mark Rose, "The Author as Proprietor: *Donaldson v. Becket* and the Genealogy of Modern Authorship," *Representations* 23 (1988): 51–85.

5. Jody Greene, *The Trouble with Ownership: Literary Property and Authorial Liability in England, 1660–1730* (Philadelphia: University of Pennsylvania Press, 2005).

6. See Martha Woodmansee, "The Genius and the Copyright: Economic and Legal Conditions of the Emergence of the 'Author,'" *Eighteenth-Century Studies* 17, no. 4 (1984): 425–448.

7. Alain Cabantous, *Blasphemy: Impious Speech in the West from the Seventeenth to the Nineteenth Century* (New York: Columbia University Press, 2002), 5.

8. Hent de Vries has made precisely this argument by drawing on Derrida, as well as Benjamin, in his excellent *Religion and Violence* (Baltimore, Md.: Johns Hopkins University Press, 2002).

9. W. C. Van Unnik, "The Christian's Freedom of Speech in the New Testament," *Bulletin of the John Rylands Library* 44 (1962): 487.

10. See Joss Marsh, *Word Crimes: Blasphemy, Culture, and Literature in Nineteenth-Century England* (Chicago: University of Chicago Press, 1998). Marsh deals with more than 200 blasphemy trials, all of which had a strong class component.

11. In this respect, it overlaps with such words as *shatīma*, *sabb*, and *istihāna*.

12. "*Bayān al-ittihād hawl nashr suwar masī'a li-rrasūl* [Statement of the (World) Union (of Islamic Scholars) about the Publication of Images Insulting to the Prophet], Cairo, January 23, 2006, http://www.iumsonline.net/index.php?option=com_content&view=article&id=417:2009-05-31-11-30-01&catid=6:data&Itemid=83.

13. The book that got Nasr Hamid Abu Zayd declared an apostate (and hence no longer legally married to his wife) was *Mafhūm al-nass: Dirāsah fi 'ulūm al-Qur'ān* [Understanding the (Sacred) Text: A Study of the Sciences of the Qur'an] (Beirut: Al-Markaz al-Thaqafi al-'Arabi, 1990). Two interesting articles on Abu Zayd's methodology should be noted: Charles Hirschkind, "Heresy or Hermeneutics: The Case of Nasr Hamid Abu Zayd," *Stanford Humanities Review* 5, no. 1 (1996); and Saba Mahmood, "Secularism, Hermeneutics, and Empire: The Politics of Islamic Reformation," *Public Culture* 18, no. 2 (2006): 323–347. Mahmood deals with Abu Zayd among other liberal Islamic reformers.

14. A detailed account of the case is given in Kilian Bälz, "Submitting Faith to Judicial Scrutiny through the Family Trial: The 'Abu Zayd Case,'" *Die Welt des Islams*, n.s. 37, no. 2 (1997): 135–155. A more interesting account is provided in chap. 1 ("The Legalization of *Hisba* in the Case of Nasr Abu Zayd") of Hussein Agrama's PhD dissertation, *Law Courts and Fatwa Councils in Modern Egypt: An Ethnography of Islamic Legal Practice*, Johns Hopkins University, Baltimore, Md., 2005. Extended extracts from the judgments in the court of first instance, the court of appeals, and the court of cassation are given (in French translation) in "Jurisprudence Abu Zayd," *Egypte/Monde Arabe* 34 (1998): 169–201. The original Arabic judgments are contained in Muhammad Salim al-'Awwa, *Al-haq fi al-ta'bīr* [The Right to Free Speech] (Cairo: Dar al-Sharuq, 1998).

15. Al-'Awwa, *Al-haq fi al-ta'bīr*, 23. See also Ahmad Rashad Tahun, *Hurriyat al-'aqīda fi-shsharī'a al-islāmiyya* (Cairo: Itrāk lil-Nashr wa-al-Tawzī', 1998), who is more concerned with the political issues—especially with the unity of the *umma*—than al-'Awwa is.

16. "It is to be noted that according to the definition (1) blasphemy is set down as a word, for ordinarily it is expressed in speech, though it may be committed in thought or in act. Being primarily a sin of the tongue, it will be seen to be opposed directly to the religious act of praising God. (2) It is said to be against God, though this may be only mediately, as when the contumelious word is spoken of the saints or of sacred things, because of the relationship they sustain to God and His service." *The Catholic Encyclopedia* 2 (New York: Robert Appleton, 1907), 595.

17. Al-'Awwa, *Al-haq fi al-ta'bīr*, 13.

18. Al-Shaykh 'Uthman Safi, *'Ala Hāmish "Naqd al-fikr ad-dīnī"* [A Footnote to "The Critique of Religious Thought"] (Beirut: Daru-ttali'a Li-ttaba'a Wa-nnashr, 1970), 87.

19. Ibid., 12–13.

20. The Arabic word *imān* is often translated into English as "belief"—as in the frequently used Qur'anic phrase *ayyuhal-mu'minīn*, "O Believers!"—but is better rendered as "faith," as in "I shall be faithful to you." Another word commonly glossed as "belief," *i'tiqād*, derives from the root *'aqada*, "to put together." This root gives the word *'aqd*, "contract," and its many cognates, and thus carries a sense of social relationship. Its primary sense in classical Arabic is the bond that commits the believer to God. This is not unlike the premodern meaning of the word "belief" in English and its equivalents in other European languages. See chap. 6 of Wilfred Cantwell Smith, *Faith and Belief* (Oxford: One World, 1998), for an interesting etymology of the word.

21. A typical sentence: *Wa-l-fitnatu ashaddu min al-qatl* (2: 191), "persecution is worse than killing."

22. When the British art critic Kenneth Clark produced his famous 1969 BBC television series *Civilisation*, John Berger responded critically with his own series three years later, *Ways of Seeing*: "when an image is presented as a work of art, the way people look at it is affected by a whole series of learnt assumptions about art. Assumptions concerning: Beauty, Truth, Genius, Civilization...Taste, etc." And Berger proceeded to pull these assumptions apart.

23. Terry Eagleton, "Coruscating on Thin Ice," *London Review of Books* 24 (January 2008): 19–20.

24. David Trotter, *Paranoid Modernism* (Oxford: Oxford University Press, 2001).

{ INDEX }